D1385466

My Brother's Keeper

My Brother's Keeper
Faith-based units in prisons

**Jonathan Burnside
with Nancy Loucks,
Joanna R. Adler and Gerry Rose**

WILLAN
PUBLISHING

Published by

Willan Publishing
Culmcott House
Mill Street, Uffculme
Cullompton, Devon
EX15 3AT, UK
Tel: +44(0)1884 840337
Fax: +44(0)1884 840251
e-mail: info@willanpublishing.co.uk
website: www.willanpublishing.co.uk

Published simultaneously in the USA and Canada by

Willan Publishing
c/o ISBS, 920 NE 58th Ave, Suite 300
Portland, Oregon 97213-3644, USA
Tel: +001(0)503 287 3093
Fax: +001(0)503 280 8832
e-mail: info@isbs.com
website: www.isbs.com

ISBN 1-84392-061-1 hardback
First published 2005

British Library Cataloguing-in-Publication Data

A catalogue record for this book is available from the British Library

Project management by Deer Park Productions, Tavistock, Devon
Typeset by GCS, Leighton Buzzard, Beds
Printed and bound by T.J. International, Padstow, Cornwall

Contents

Guide to organisations

The following is a guide to the main organisations referred to in this book, listed in order of occurrence.

APAC (see Chapter 1) stands for the Association for the Protection and Assistance of the Convicted. It is a Christian approach to the reform and social integration of prisoners that began in Brazil in the 1970s before expanding to other parts of South America in the 1990s. APAC's model prison (called 'Humaitá') was established at its headquarters in São José dos Campos, near São Paulo, Brazil.

Kairos (see Chapter 2) is a Christian ministry to the incarcerated and their families that began in the United States in 1976. It holds Kairos Weekends and follow-up programmes in prisons. Kairos is currently active in 33 states in the US as well as in five other countries (Australia, Canada, Costa Rica, South Africa and the United Kingdom). Kairos began in the United Kingdom in 1997. Kairos is a separate and different organisation to Kairos-APAC and Kainos.

Kairos-APAC (see Chapter 3) was the name given to the Christian-based unit set up initially at HMP The Verne, England in 1997. Three more units followed at HMPs Swaleside, Highpoint North and Highpoint South, also in England. The Kairos-APAC Trust that oversaw this work was dissolved in 1999.

Kainos (see Chapters 4-6, 9-11) was established in 1999 to continue the work begun by Kairos-APAC. Kainos currently operates in three prisons in England and Wales (HMPs The Verne, Swaleside and Parc).

Horizon Communities (see Chapter 7) began in the United States in 1999 and runs five faith-based communities in four states. These communities may be Christian-based or interfaith or multifaith. Between 1999 and 2004, Horizon Communities was known as Kairos Horizon Communities.

InnerChange Freedom Initiative (see Chapter 8) began in the United States in 1997 and runs four Christian-based units in four states. An IFI unit was established in HMP Dartmoor, England in 2005.

Foreword

by Sir Anthony Bottoms

In the year 2000, I received an unexpected telephone call from the Home Office, asking me to undertake an unusual task.

Four faith-based small units had been established in English prisons in the preceding three years – for adult men at The Verne, Swaleside and Highpoint South, and for adult women at Highpoint North. For reasons relating to its internal finances, the independent Trust that had run these units (the Kairos-APAC Trust) had been dissolved in 1999. Following this, the Prison Service rapidly conducted an internal review of the units. The upshot was that a newly-formed replacement Trust (the Kainos Community Trust) was permitted to continue the work in the small units, subject to one very important proviso. The proviso was that long-term continuation would only be permitted if an independent research evaluation of the working and effectiveness of the units showed that they were functioning well. This research would have to be conducted to a rigorous standard; and Kainos Community would itself have to bear the cost of the evaluation.

Kainos raised the money, and the Home Office organised a research tendering process. To use the appropriate jargon for these occasions, the competition threw up as a 'preferred bidder' Dr Jonathan Burnside, who, with a team of colleagues, had put in a tender as an independent researcher. The Home Office thought that Jonathan's bid had a great deal of strength, but they had two anxieties. First, although extremely well qualified academically, Jonathan had never previously conducted empirical research. Secondly, it was no secret that he was and is a practising Christian, with an active interest in the application of Christian principles to criminological issues (see for example Burnside and Baker 1994; rpt. 2004): so, would he be objective enough to carry out a truly independent appraisal of the units?

Hence the telephone call. Would I be willing, as a senior and experienced criminological researcher, to act as an Independent Adviser to the research? More specifically, I was asked to act partly as a consultant to the research team (to ensure, so far as possible, that their research was as good as it could be), and partly as an independent assessor for the Home Office and Kainos Community, offering my judgement on the quality of the research design, and, eventually, the research report. It was definitely an unusual request, but after consideration I was glad to accept the brief.

In the event, the Home Office need not have worried. Jonathan and his team (all of whom were already known to me, because they have all at some stage been connected to the Cambridge Institute of Criminology) did a superb technical job on the research, and there was never any hint of lack of research objectivity in their approach. The results of their research were, in 2001, published on the Home Office website, and they will be found in a shortened version in chapters 4–6, 9 and 10 of this book.

In the closing stages of my role as Independent Adviser, I found to my surprise that one of my main tasks was to try to convince the Kainos Trustees that the results of the reconviction study (chapter 10 in this book) could be relied upon. The Trustees had expected significant reductions in reconviction, but the research did not find them. I tried to emphasise to the Trustees that in other respects the research results were mainly positive (for example, as regards prisoners' attitudinal change, and in refuting allegations of improper religious pressure); but it was the reconviction results that overwhelmingly moulded the Trustees' reactions. When the results were published, a not dissimilar story unfolded in a wider arena (see chapter 11). Indeed, the story of the initial public reactions to the Kainos evaluation is a telling, and not very edifying, case study on the way in which social science results can be received in the policy and political arenas. As the authors rightly say, many responses were 'strikingly partisan, … [with] clichés for and against Kainos … recycled with little regard to the details of the evaluation'.

I am delighted that, with the publication of this book, the results of the Kainos evaluation will reach a wider audience. It is particularly pleasing, however, that in this publication these results have been placed within a broader context. It is widely known that the British faith-based prison units draw upon prior models in Brazil and the United States. What is much less widely known are the details of how those prototype models developed, and their underpinning theoretical assumptions. In this book, the authors have taken the trouble to explore these issues in depth. In so doing, they have also lucidly illustrated the fact that some of the British units were not drawing on the prior experience as carefully and sensitively as they might have done. That in itself is hardly a novelty – penological history is littered with examples of people failing to understand fully the legacy of previous experiments. But there is surely here a particular lesson for those who may be called upon to pioneer, in a given country, any unusual or potentially controversial prison innovations (secular or faith-based). The lesson is – any innovatory development potentially lays itself open to criticism, so make sure you really have absorbed all the relevant lessons from other countries before you shape your own initiatives.

One final comment. In the twenty-first century world of what some sociologists have called 'late modernity', many observers have been surprised at the continuing ideological importance of religious faith. Given that importance, however, the potential future role of faith, and of faith-based units, in the prison context will properly remain an important issue. In part, what is raised in this regard is a human rights concern – prisoners clearly have a right to practise their faith in prison, but exactly what that right means in practice will potentially be subject to interpretation in any given context (and whether that right includes the right to be located in a faith-based unit is certainly one of those interpretive issues). However, as was illustrated by the prominence of the reconviction issue in the Kainos story, faith-based units will also in practice be under pressure to justify themselves by achieving improved reconviction results for their members. In principle, that is clearly possible, because most faith-based units attempt to encourage normative change in their members, and, as I have argued elsewhere (Bottoms 2002), normative compliance is certainly one of the ways of achieving enhanced obedience to the law. As I pointed out in the same paper, however, for a variety of historical reasons criminology has tended to underrate the importance of morality within its field of study. That is now beginning to change; as it changes, one can begin to see more clearly that there is potentially a rich strand of philosophical and social scientific literature upon which those running faith-based units could fruitfully draw, in the future, in seeking to improve their practice.

I am very pleased to commend this book to all those interested in prison studies.

Authors' preface and acknowledgements

This book is the work of four authors. Joanna Adler was responsible for Chapter 9, Nancy Loucks for Chapter 6, Gerry Rose for Chapter 10 and Jonathan Burnside for the Prologue, Chapters 1–3, 7–8 and 11. Chapters 4 and 5 were co-written by Jonathan Burnside and Nancy Loucks. The book is of course a collaborative effort and each chapter has benefited from the comments of the other co-authors.

This book is an expanded and updated account of an evaluation of Kainos Community conducted by the authors, with Jonathan Burnside as lead researcher, for the Home Office, Kainos Community and HM Prison Service. The original Kainos Programme Evaluation was published online in 2001 and can be accessed via the Home Office Research Development and Statistics archive (www.homeoffice.gov.uk/rds/prisons1.html; accessed 5 April 2005). This evaluation was funded by Kainos Community, which has copyright over the research findings. We are grateful to the Kainos Trustees for granting their permission to reproduce materials from the Kainos Programme Evaluation.

Over the course of our five-year journey with this subject, there are naturally many people we wish to thank. The original evaluation of Kainos Community would not have been possible without the generous assistance of management, staff and prisoners at every level in each of the four Kainos establishments (as they were then). We are grateful to all those who gave their valuable time. Special thanks are due to the Kainos staff in each prison who facilitated our day-to-day arrangements; to Local Inmate Data Service (LIDS) and Custody Office staff for granting access to prisoner data and to those prisoners who acted as translators. We are also grateful to staff who gathered prison specific data on our behalf, especially SO Ian Whittle (Swaleside), PO Geoff Hebbern, SO

Stephen Fleming (The Verne) and Stephanie Hope (Highpoint South), as well as Phyllis Bailey and John Witton for their hospitality. We also wish to record our thanks to the National Manager of Kainos Community, Mike Phillips, particularly during the period following the original evaluation.

The research team is also indebted to the Steering Group who provided invaluable guidance during the course of the evaluation. This consisted of Ian Aldred, Prof. Sir Anthony Bottoms, John Broadley, Michelle Crerar, John Ditchfield, Malcolm Ramsay, Jeannie Willan and Sir Peter Woodhead. In addition, Michelle Crerar, John Ditchfield and Malcolm Ramsay ensured the smooth operation of research requests, whilst the Kainos trustees liaised with Kainos Coordinators. We are also very grateful for the close interest taken by Maureen Colledge, Chris Lewis and Nick Sanderson and for their input and suggestions at key stages of the research. Prof. Sir Anthony Bottoms, as Independent Adviser to the project, was on hand from the outset of the research to its conclusion. His advice and support to all parties involved in the research, not least the research team, was of immense value. We are grateful and delighted that he has also written the Foreword for this book.

A debt of thanks is also owed to Julian Prime, Steve White, and Andrew Kalinsky of the Home Office Offenders Index, who supplied the data on criminal histories needed for the reconviction study, and to Caroline Friendship and Paul Crosland for advice on the analysis of reconviction patterns. We also thank Chris Keys (Highpoint) and Sally Birch (The Verne) for their great willingness and thoroughness in gathering identification data for the Kainos reconviction sample.

We are also grateful to everyone who enabled us to place the original evaluation in a wider historical and international context. Along with all those named in individual chapters we want to thank everyone who contributed archive materials, gave recorded interviews and provided written accounts of their views and recollections. We are grateful to Ike and Mickey Griffin of Horizon Communities and to the Wardens of Marion C.I. and Tomoka C.I., Florida, for granting access to their respective prisons in 2000 and 2003 and to the staff, prisoners and volunteers who made those visits such memorable occasions.

Finally, we are grateful to Brian Willan and the staff of Willan Publishing for accepting this book and steering it cheerfully on its way.

Jonathan Burnside
Nancy Loucks
Joanna R. Adler
Gerry Rose
August 2005

For Kees and Doris
(JPB)

Everyone in prison reads the Bible.
If they never wanted to before
They do now: it is an unwritten law.

To prisoners of war the journalist
Offered to send it and a home made cake.
With loved ones far away you pray and bake.

The swindler starting on his five year sentence
Reads a portion as he always has
Done, every single day, so his wife says.

A TV documentary about
A certain prison showed the earnest chaplain
Getting the first offender to explain

What he would like. 'A Bi –' 'Yes?' He could not
Believe his ears. 'A biro' stammered the con.
'Oh yes, of course. Of course I'll get you one.'

Patricia Beer, *Collected Poems* 1997

Prologue

Beatitudes behind bars: Christianity and imprisonment

The subtitle of this book is 'Faith-based units in prisons'. The broad reference to 'faith-based' rather than 'Christian-based' reflects the fact that a few of the units explored in this book are 'multifaith' or 'interfaith'. However, the vast majority of units explored in this book have an exclusively Christian basis. Even in those units designated by their founders as 'multifaith' or 'interfaith', the overwhelming majority of prisoners describe themselves as Christians. In addition, 'multifaith' and 'interfaith' units are managed by Christian staff and depend for their viability upon a volunteer force that is almost entirely Christian. All of this raises the question: what is it about Christianity that leads to this interest in building faith-based units in prisons?

In answering this question one might seek to explain not only the relevance of Christianity but why believers of other faiths are not involved in faith-based units to the same extent. One might thus need to consider the theology of every relevant faith group, as well as the psychological motivation and sociological context (e.g. extent of resources) of different believers in each country that operates a faith-based unit. A full explanation might also explore the fact that, in the UK at least, there is no formal separation of Church and State. The Prison Service of England and Wales, from senior management down to landing officers, may have found it easier to deal with Christian programmes than those from other backgrounds. Part of the answer, too, may lie in the fact that a majority of prisoners are likely to come from a Christian background (albeit lapsed or nominal), especially in those countries where APAC (see Chapter 1) and Kairos (see Chapter 2) originated. Clearly, it is beyond the scope of this book to offer a full answer to this question.

This Prologue was authored by Jonathan Burnside

Nevertheless, it is possible to identify certain concerns, deeply rooted in the heart of Christian doctrine, that may help us to explain the strong interest in faith-based units displayed by some Christians. Not all Christians believe exactly the same things or behave in exactly the same ways. Christianity covers a range of beliefs and practices. Even in countries that have substantial numbers of Christians, work in prisons is not always popular. For example, the US has a strong Christian movement in prison-based work, but it also has the highest level of support for capital punishment in the Western world. Not all Christians agree that work with prisoners is worthwhile.

Nonetheless, there are certain shared beliefs that have a close resonance with building faith-based units in prisons. They are common precisely because it is possible to derive so many of these beliefs from Christianity's core texts namely the Hebrew Bible and the New Testament. The purpose of this Prologue[1] is briefly to identify some concerns deriving from these beliefs that may help us to understand why developing faith-based units in prisons is high on the agenda for some Christians. Christians may have an interest in building faith-based units in prisons as a result of their concerns for: prisoners as such; human decency; justice; relationships; and spiritual transformation.

1. Concern for prisoners as such

No other founder of a world religion identified with criminals in the way that was done by Jesus of Nazareth, the founder of Christianity. Jesus chose to be classed with criminals and to suffer the fate of a criminal. The New Testament describes how the vocation of the Christian Messiah,[2] when fully played out, was to be identified with lawbreakers in his life and to be counted among them in his death. Revealingly, when St. Luke describes the Crucifixion in his *Gospel* he refers to Jesus and 'the two *other* criminals *also*' who were crucified (Luke 23:32; italics added). The only individual to whom Jesus promised eternal life was a violent robber who was crucified with him. '…Today you will be with me in paradise'[3] (Luke 23:43). A pair of criminals (Jesus and the robber) on a hill outside Jerusalem formed one of the first Christian communities. Jesus warned his followers to be ready to meet a criminal's end (Mark 8:34–35). So thoroughly does Jesus identify with prisoners that Jesus nominates caring for the imprisoned as a criterion of judgement ('I was in prison and you came to me'; Matthew 25:36) and one of the ways in which Christians may encounter his presence (Matthew 25:31–46). Christianity thus has a deep-rooted affinity with prisoners. This is one reason why Christians might wish to be involved in establishing 'communities in prisons'.

2. Concern for human decency

This Christian concern for prisoners as such is part of a more general conviction that human beings are 'awesomely [and] wondrously made' (Psalm 139:14) in 'the image of God' (Genesis 1:27). This belief, also common to Judaism, is further enhanced by the New Testament claim that, in Jesus Christ, God 'appeared in the flesh' (1 Timothy 3:16). This hallowing of our humanity means that Christianity must be critical of policies and institutions that violate the *imago Dei* (image of God) in the human person. Whilst there is debate as to precisely what the *imago Dei* means (Westermann 1994: 147–158) it is frequently taken to include human qualities and capacities, including relationships, choice and responsibility.

Imprisonment is designed to take away relationships, choice and responsibility, at least those that might endanger the public (cf. Pryor 2002: 1). '[Imprisonment] is therefore necessarily de-humanizing. That must sit uneasily with the professed aim of prisons to treat those sent by the courts with humanity' (*ibid.*). Imprisonment may also take away relationships, choices and responsibilities to a greater degree than is necessary to ensure that prisons can be run safely. This raises the broader question of whether the practice of imprisonment is consistent with government claims to protect the public and to deliver justice (*ibid.*). The Christian obligation to see the *imago Dei* in all others, including prisoners, may make it difficult for Christians to accept aspects of modern penal practice as legitimate. This is a further stimulus to reform and to Christian engagement with prison regimes.

3. Concern for justice

The question of whether imprisonment upholds human decency leads into a third Christian concern, namely for justice and just punishment. Modern political debate is dominated by questions about public management, efficiency and accountability. 'Justice' is styled as a 'commodity to be measured and delivered, like healthcare and education' (Stern 2004). From this managerialist perspective, the function is to serve 'customers' in the form of victims and witnesses. Justice becomes synonymous with prosecution and punishment (*ibid.*). Escalating the number of sanctions increases justice. In this context, criminal justice is dominated by 'the familiar instruments of government policy or public management – legislation, circulars, directories, targets, performance indicators, contracts, systems of inspection and audit' (Faulkner 2002: 1). Such an approach tends to exclude 'organic...dynamic and more inspirational' (*ibid.*) beliefs about justice, including those found in the Bible.

The Hebrew prophet Amos speaking c. 760 BC said: '...let justice roll down like waters, and righteousness like an ever-flowing stream' (Amos 5:24). This Biblical image sees justice as both organic and dynamic. Justice is seen as something mighty and surging, like the Jordan River in full flood. Justice is not a static state but an intervening power: it strikes and changes, restores and heals, and brings life to a parched land. Justice is an active power that breaks into situations of evil to bring freedom. Justice involves retribution upon the sources of oppression, but it is not complete without the liberation and restoration of the oppressed. It is a rescuing action by God that puts things right.[4]

The New Testament affirms this picture of justice by describing the Crucifixion of Jesus as the fullest expression of God's justice (Romans 3:25–26). The Cross is understood as the ultimate act of God's justice in the Bible because it deals with oppression and restoration in the broadest possible sense. The New Testament understands the Cross as the place where God wins the victory over evil and everything that holds his good creation in bondage to corruption and decay. The Cross is also understood as the place where Jesus is enthroned as King. Christians believe that on the Cross, Jesus successfully overthrew the ultimate oppressor of humanity (namely, 'the Satan',[5] who is opposed to God's good purposes) and bestows freedom from Satan's tyranny (Romans 8:14–17; Hebrews 2:15–16). The Cross itself cannot be separated from Jesus's resurrection and ascension which together amount to God's 'vindication' of his people and his purposes.[6]

The Last Judgement, described in the book of Revelation, is presented as an act of divine justice that finally brings the victory of Israel's Messiah on the Cross to bear eternally upon the whole of creation. In the Last Judgement there is both eternal retribution and eternal restoration. There is judgement upon evil (the 'lake of fire'; Revelation 19:20–21; 20:10, 14–15) which paves the way for healing, transformation and restored relationships, in the closest possible sense: 'And I saw the holy city, new Jerusalem, coming down out of heaven from God, prepared as a bride adorned for her husband' (Revelation 21:2). Everything that oppresses God's creation is overthrown, and everything that seeks freedom from bondage is fully liberated.

The Bible presents Christians with a challenging picture of justice that invites critical reflection on some of the narrower ideas about justice in modern public services (Burnside 2005; Burnside 2003; Marshall 2001). From a Christian perspective, justice is increased not by building more prisons but by rebuilding more prisoners. For this reason Christians may wish to be involved in faith-based prison regimes which they believe offer the chance of change, healing and restoration.

4. Concern for relationships

The need for a more organic and dynamic approach to justice leads us into a fourth area of concern, namely the importance of relationships and community for human well-being (see generally Burnside and Baker, 2004). Christianity is a 'relational' religion, with relational presuppositions and relational doctrines (Cole 2005). The Christian belief that God is a Trinity of Persons underscores the conviction that reality involves relationships. As Knox (1988) writes: 'The doctrine of the Trinity is the glory of the Christian religion. It tells us that ultimate reality is personal relationship. God is ultimate reality and is the ground of all other reality, and yet God is not a single monad or an impersonal absolute, but God is relationship ... Father, Son and Holy Spirit.... Through the revelation of the Trinity, we learn that the living God ... is a God who has relationship[s] within Himself and that the values of relationships ultimately belong to reality in its most absolute form.' For this reason, close relationships between Christians are not optional but essential to Christian living. As noted in (2) above, imprisonment takes away opportunities for relationships and, even where opportunities for relationships remain, imprisonment tends to inhibit real relating, including vulnerability and self-disclosure. Consequently, Christians may seek faith-based prison units as a means of promoting more 'relational' prison regimes where prisoners' relationships with their children, families, representatives of the community and one other are developed appropriately.

5. Concern for spiritual transformation

The fifth concern is the most important, although it cannot be separated from the others. This is the Christian belief that spiritual transformation is possible through faith in Jesus the Messiah. Christians believe that in the life, death and resurrection from the dead of Jesus of Nazareth, the purposes of God for his chosen people, Israel, and through Israel to the world, reached their climax. Christians believe that in the Crucifixion, Jesus freely identifies himself with the plight of sinful humanity under the reign of death and pays the price for doing so. They believe that on the Cross, God absorbed the sin, rebellion, pain, suffering, shame and guilt of the world. The New Testament claims that those who stake their lives on Jesus's accomplishments will experience deliverance from evil and from the judgement of God: 'For the wages of sin is death, but the free gift of God is eternal life in Christ Jesus our Lord' (Romans 6:23). Wright (2004: 174) explains that '"Eternal life" does not mean simply "existence continuing without end" but "the life of the age to come"', the latter referring to the time when God 'would at last act decisively to judge evil, to rescue Israel and to create a new world of justice and peace' (*ibid*.: 173). This is the 'good news' (or in Greek, the *evangelium*) from which we derive the words 'evangelical' and 'evangelism'.

Christianity is 'mission-oriented' in the sense that it seeks to spread this 'good news'. It derives from Jesus's command to his disciples: '… "All authority in heaven and on earth has been given to me. Go therefore and make disciples of all nations, baptizing them in the name of the Father and of the Son and of the Holy Spirit…"' (Matthew 28:18–19). Christian mission thus has a sense of urgency ('There is salvation in no one else, for there is no other name under heaven given among men by which we must be saved'; Acts 4:12). It is declamatory but it is also characterized by humble service ('speaking the truth in love'; Ephesians 4:15). This is especially important in a prisons context because prisoners are not there of their own volition.[7] 'The basic motive for mission is the desire to glorify God and lovingly to serve men' (Sadgrove and Wright 1977: 85). In this sense, Christian 'mission' overlaps with the 'mission' of the Prison Service to 'serve' the public and to 'serve' prisoners by looking after them with humanity.

Christians believe that the resurrection and ascension of Jesus provides proof that Jesus has made a unique way into the presence of God. Those who follow him belong to a different way of living that is empowered by the gift of God's Spirit: 'Being himself freed from the chains of death, [Jesus] now lives to free others from all that enslaves them' (Wright 1999: 100). 'Being in prison' is seen by Christians as a metaphor for the spiritual state of all human beings and 'release from captivity' as a metaphor for spiritual healing and wholeness (e.g. Luke 4:18). There is thus a natural Christian interest in seeing this metaphor enacted in the spiritual reform of prisoners.

Central to this new life is the knowledge that the individual is forgiven by God for sin (wrongdoing) against him. Having thus been forgiven of an incomparable debt, those who receive God's forgiveness are commanded to release those who owe them anything. This includes forgiveness for those who have sinned against them: 'For if you forgive men their trespasses, your heavenly Father also will forgive you; but if you do not forgive men their trespasses, neither will your Father forgive your trespasses' (Matthew 6:14–15). With this in mind, it is understandable why Christians might be motivated to provide an environment where this spiritual transformation can take place and where Christian prisoners can be encouraged to 'work out' and walk in their healing.

At this level of personal responsibility there is a link between the need for the spiritual reform of the individual and the upsurge of neo-liberal ideology in the Western world (Wacquant 2004) which emphasizes the responsibility of the individual for his or her behaviour.

6. A new social contract?

The above concerns have been a longstanding part of traditional Christian social action. In recent years, in England and Wales, there has been growing recognition of the significant role that churches and faith communities play in social welfare. The think tank Demos claims that 'much of the best innovation in the provision of local health, homelessness, community regeneration and drug-related services is now being shaped by people with strong religious beliefs' (Jupp and Mulga 1997). Government policy now invites greater participation of distinctively religious groups in social welfare arrangements. In particular, government has paid increasing attention to the role of Christians and other faith groups in delivering public services.[8] In this context the Christian faith is viewed, not as something that is imposed from outside, but as a response to a need.

These new opportunities for Christians to engage in public life are in part a response to the more diminished role of the institutional church in regard to formal social provision. Longley (2000: 29) has described how the Church of England traditionally saw that its duty was to support the state which meant that, particularly during the twentieth century, '[the Church] no longer needed to make its own separate investment in health, education, child welfare and so on'. The ideology of the welfare state became 'part of the complex network of church-state relations' (ibid.). Instead of having Anglican hospitals and Anglican prisons, Anglican chaplains went on the payroll of state-run hospitals and prisons, with the Prisons Act 1952 establishing a full-time Church of England chaplain for every prison.

However, increasing secularization has made the 1945 settlement on public services appear increasingly outdated. Religious population figures show that the proportion of prisoners professing to be Christians continues to decline. The number of Christian prisoners fell from 75 per cent of the total population in 1993 to 59.5 per cent in 2000. Prisoners professing no religion were an important minority at around 30 per cent of the total population. This was also the fastest growing group, almost doubling (181 per cent) between 1993 and 2000 (Guessous et al. 2001).

'Large holes are appearing in the canopy provided by the Church of England' (Beckford and Gilliat 1998: 203). In recent years there has been a movement towards a multifaith Prison Service Chaplaincy with the appointment of the Prison Service's first Muslim Adviser in 1999. The diminishing formal role of the institutional church in public institutions such as the Prison Service has meant that Christians have sought to take initiative in new ways.

7. Conclusion

Traditional Christian concerns for prisoners as such, human decency, justice, relationships, and spiritual transformation may lead Christians to become involved in reforming prison conditions. In England and Wales, increasing secularization has led to changes in the relationship between Church and State in terms of welfare provision. The result of this is that whilst there is now a smaller role for institutional Christianity, current government policy favours establishing partnerships with faith-based groups. One result has been the development of faith-based, and largely Christian-based, units in prisons in England and Wales. It is to the outworking of this approach, both in the UK and around the world that we now turn.

Notes

1   We are grateful to the Rev Canon Alan Duce and to Dr Julian Rivers for reading and commenting on a draft of this Prologue.
2   Literally 'the anointed one' or God's 'King'.
3   Wright (2001:284) notes that: '"Paradise" in Jewish thought wasn't necessarily the final resting place, but the place of rest and refreshment before the gift of new life in the resurrection'.
4   For this reason some versions of restorative justice acknowledge Biblical justice as their source of inspiration, e.g. Van Ness and Strong 2002, *passim.*
5   Literally, 'the Accuser'.
6   We owe this observation to Jonathan Chaplin.
7   The word 'prison' is related to the word 'apprise' or 'apprehended': they are persons who are 'seized' by the State and taken away.
8   A series of 'Faithworks Lectures', explicitly affirming the role of faith and Christianity in public life, was delivered by each leader of the main political parties in early 2005; www.faithworks.info, accessed 30 March 2005.

Chapter 1

The prison that started it all

God is the great reality, in the face of which nobody can remain indifferent…
The restored image of the Lord, [the] Friendly Father, in the mind and
heart of the prisoner, is the strong stimulus for recuperation.
(Hugo Veronese, Psychologist, Humaitá Prison, undated
unpublished paper)

Introduction

The first Christian-based unit in any prison in the Western world was
established at HMP The Verne in Dorset, England in February 1997. The
first Christian-based unit in the United States was established at Jester
II Correctional Unit near Houston, Texas in April 1997. Similar units in
England followed The Verne in HMPs Swaleside, Highpoint North and
Highpoint South the next year, as similar programmes began to expand
in the United States (see Chapter 7) and around the world in Australia,
New Zealand and a number of European countries (see Chapter 11).
The inspiration was a single South American organization called APAC
(the Association for the Protection and Assistance of the Convicted).[1]
APAC is a Christian approach to the reform and social integration of
prisoners that began in Brazil in the 1970s before expanding to other
parts of South America in the 1990s. APAC established a model prison at
its headquarters in São José dos Campos, near São Paulo, Brazil. Known

This chapter was authored by Jonathan Burnside

1

simply as 'Humaitá', because of the prison's location on Humaitá Street, it was the subject of numerous international delegations in the late 1980s and early 1990s.

Humaitá was a direct inspiration for the Prison Service in England and Wales in setting up its Christian-based units (see Chapter 3). For a time, the Verne initiative was known simply as 'The APAC Project' before being formally launched as the 'Kairos-APAC Project'. Likewise, the UK charitable trust set up to administer the initiative, under Prison Service authority, was known as the 'Kairos-APAC Trust'. From the beginning, the UK Trustees sought permission from the founders of APAC to use the APAC name. APAC and Humaitá were also the direct inspiration for similar initiatives in the United States. It was the prototype for the Horizon Communities Corporation, established in 1999, which were originally described as 'Faith-Based APAC Model Units' (see Chapter 7) and for the InnerChange Freedom Initiative (IFI) programme begun by Prison Fellowship International in 1997 (see Chapter 8). An overview of the APAC approach, and of the Humaitá regime in particular, is thus an appropriate starting point for our exploration of faith-based units in prisons. It was the prison that started it all.

The founder of APAC, Mário Ottoboni, published two books on the history and development of APAC (Ottoboni 2000 and 2003a). The founder of APAC in Ecuador provided an account of the first attempted replication of APAC outside Brazil (Toral 2000). Another useful source is a series of on-site descriptions of various APAC projects prepared by Prison Fellowship International (Creighton 2001). These sources supplement the stream of documentaries and feasibility studies produced since the late 1980s, many of them advocating some application of APAC in the UK and US (e.g. Anderson 1991a; Burnside and Lee 1997; Creighton 1993; Creighton and Rennie 1995; Lee 1995 and Prison Fellowship International 1991). Space prohibits an exhaustive account of APAC or of Humaitá Prison. Nonetheless, we need some account of its history and development.

This chapter reanalyzes previously published material, drawing on the experience of programmes inspired by the APAC approach. It highlights recurring themes, then develops them in subsequent chapters. Every attempt has been made to respect the historical and cultural setting of APAC and Humaitá. We have tried to present APAC from an 'internal' point of view by drawing on the views of its founders. To this end, the chapter draws on tape-recorded interviews with APAC's founders and makes use of internal APAC documents.

APAC's longevity – it has run in various forms for over 30 years – means that the recurring issues in the UK and US experience have usually appeared first in APAC. The chapter is divided into seven sections. 'The role of Christianity' introduces such themes as whether the teaching should be compulsory or voluntary and how explicitly religious teaching should be meshed with 'secular' programmes and (religious) personnel within the prison. The second section, 'Evolution of APAC', introduces the difficulty faith-based organizations have with earning and keeping the trust of host establishments and the place of 'trial and error' in programme development. The third section, 'Who goes to APAC and why', considers selection criteria, the particular incentives of faith-based units, and informed consent. Next, 'The DNA of APAC' identifies the structure, rules and boundaries of the community and the (often innovatory) means by which they are enforced. 'Goals and programming' then highlights the need for a clear identity and goals related to programming. Section 6, 'Rehabilitative agents', highlights the importance of volunteers and peer-prisoner support to programme delivery. Finally, we offer some brief conclusions we can reasonably derive from this account.[2]

1. The role of Christianity

This section considers the role of Christianity in Humaitá. The first and most important point to note is that APAC has a clear and explicit Christian identity, as do its programmes. In fact, a Christian programme called Cursillo is regarded as a *sine qua non* of APAC (Creighton 2001; Ottoboni 2003: 134). APAC began when Ottoboni and 15 couples went on a Cursillo course and subsequently chose to become involved with the prisoners at Humaitá (see Section 2 below). *Cursillo* is Spanish for a 'little course', in this case a 'short course' in Christianity. It consists of 15 talks and five meditations spread over three days, at the end of which participants are said to embark on their 'Fourth Day' – the rest of their lives. For this reason Cursillo-type programmes (including the Kairos Weekend; see Chapter 2) are referred to as 'Fourth Day programmes'.[3] Cursillo was founded by Eduardo Bonnin Aguilo, who prepared the programme in 1942 in response to the suffering caused by the Spanish Civil War (and later the Second World War). The first Cursillo took place in Palma, Majorca in 1949. It was later seen to have value for those suffering from other forms of woundedness and isolation, including isolation from the Church. Cursillo was recognized by the Roman Catholic Church in 1949 before spreading to the US in 1957 and becoming a copyright movement.[4]

Ottoboni claims that prisoners must be shown 'the importance of religion in the life of the human being' (Creighton and Rennie 1995) because 'it is necessary to have an experience of God in order to love and be loved' (*ibid.*). It is Ottoboni's conviction that one of the most potent ways to achieve this is through the Cursillo programme, which he believes leads the attendee to experience Christ (Lee 1995). A Cursillo weekend is held in APAC once a year. Cursillo is compulsory for APAC prisoners and must be experienced 'at least once'[5] (Ottoboni 2003: 87) during the course of their sentence.[6]

APAC thus has an explicitly Christian identity. Ottoboni (2000: 123) observes:

> It should never be forgotten that the whole of the APAC approach finds its inspiration in the sacrifice on the Cross, in the merciful look of Christ when he turned to [the] repentant [thief] ... and announced his salvation.

In a speech to a Prison Fellowship International World Convocation in 2003, Ottoboni claimed that: 'APAC was born at the foot of the Cross' (Toronto, August 2003). Motivational messages and verses from the Bible are painted in blue along whitewashed hallways (Anderson 1991a), whilst one of the so-called 'Ten Commandments' of APAC proclaims: 'God is the Fount of All'[7]. For Ottoboni (2003: 60), Christianity is a 'fundamental factor' in helping prisoners because it enables prisoners to 'recycle' their values.

APAC's psychologist, Hugo Veronese, takes a similar view. Veronese identifies four images as decisive in structuring personality, namely the father's image, the mother's image, the self-image and God's image. Each image is important because each possesses 'a representative content and an emotional content, which makes it [a] live, dynamic, powerful, determinant of our affective states' (Veronese undated). Veronese maintains that criminal behaviour has its roots in 98 per cent of APAC cases, in 'the family, the image of a father or a mother, or of both, who did not play their role of love' (*ibid.*). For Veronese, spiritual development is central because 'no person can be psychologically healthy if there is deep conflict with one of these images'. Christianity has the power to recycle and resymbolize these primal 'images':

> [D]eviations and human failures issue from the deformation of the self-image... He who judges himself evil, even involuntarily, will go for evil. It is imperative to restore in the prisoner the sense of human dignity and divine affiliation, so that he can turn himself to goodness. God is the great reality, in the face of which nobody can

remain indifferent.... The restored image of the Lord, [the] Friendly Father, in the mind and heart of the prisoner, is the strong stimulus for recuperation (*ibid.*).

Lee (2004) claims that 'the work of the psychologist Hugo Veronese was fundamental to the success of APAC. The impact of new-found security and self-acceptance encountered through the unconditional love experienced in Cursillo and its ability to open the heart was the seed-bed for his work'. Veronese's work in the 'closed' section of the prison (see Section 4 below) is said to concentrate on emotional healing, whilst his work in the semi-open section concentrates on engaging prisoners with their families (*ibid.*). The latter may be styled an example of generativity – the social investment into future generations – in prison. Lee claims that in her experience, '[Veronese's] work in these areas has been seminal in the recovery and resocialization of a serial killer previously restrained in a box one metre by one metre and a dangerously violent paedophile' (*ibid.*), documented in *Love Is Not A Luxury* (1995).

Apart from Cursillo, prisoners' participation in religious activities is voluntary. This includes Mass, worship services, classes and conferences on religion, meditation, in-cell rosary and biblical studies. Consequently APAC advise that religious activities in the second stage (see Section 4 below) should be ecumenical and as interesting as possible.[8] Spiritual pro-grammes are delivered by volunteers who have already established relationships with the prisoners and who understand their circumstances. Ottoboni (2000: 121) claims that: 'Only the lay volunteer, doctor or priest, through their Christian spirit, can manage to reach to the soul of the criminal and rescue him from death.' More prosaically, volunteers are potential engines for change (see Section 6 below).

Regarding informed consent, prisoners must sign a contract setting out the range of their commitments (listed in Ottoboni 2003: 171–173), including a willingness to take part in a Christian-based (and predominantly Catholic) environment. Until 1985, nearly all (98 per cent) of APAC prisoners were Catholics. By 2003, however, 20 per cent of prisoners had a non-Catholic background (e.g. a different Christian denomination, different religion or no religion at all; *ibid.*: 18). Non-Catholic prisoners are eligible if their pastor certifies in writing that they are involved in 'spiritual activities' and verifies their willingness to respect the programme's regulations (Toral 2000: 126). APAC in Ecuador operates a similar recruitment policy. Prisoners are asked whether they profess a religion; 'if this is so, they are invited to learn more about it by studying it. If they lack religious beliefs, they are encouraged to study ethics' (*ibid.*: 10). Informed consent is crucial as some religious elements of the programme are compulsory.

5

Ottoboni highlights the dangers of false claims to religiosity (e.g. 'inmates exaggeratedly proclaiming their own conversion'): 'We have learned that, under the mantle of religion, inmates wear masks, negotiate and conceal what goes on inside them in order to take advantage of religious groups [with the purpose of] … obtaining correctional benefits' (2003: 59–60). Volunteers, for all their strengths, can be exploited when they 'thoughtlessly end up proclaiming the 'sanctity' of these 'converts' to the director of the prison or judicial authorities' (*ibid.*).

Another recurring issue is how explicitly religious teaching should be meshed with 'secular' prison programmes. Ottoboni (*ibid.*) notes that 'another usual mistake … is to think that religion itself is enough to prepare prisoners for their return to society'. Spiritual programmes in the three main regimes are combined with programmes designed to further moral development, pro-social behaviour, community-building, responsibility, creative self-expression, specialist professional skills, work experience and responsibility for their families (see below). Volunteers are not restricted to supplying spiritual programmes but are also involved in facilitating other programmes. Drawing a distinction between 'religious' and 'non-religious' programmes is somewhat artificial since APAC sees all its programmes, regardless of content, as having the same purpose: to create a 'rehabilitative' environment.

2. Evolution of APAC

APAC began on an amateur basis in 1972 when its founder, Mário Ottoboni, and 15 couples who had all been on the Christian Cursillo programme, decided to visit the local police-run public jail in São José dos Campos. They were appalled by the squalor of the prison. One prisoner recalls what conditions were like:

> it stank, there was no cleaning material, it was like a pigsty. Lawyers did not go near the place. There were 150 men in a space for 40. Water was scarce, sometimes none for weeks on end. Nobody got any sun, nobody had a bath. The food, which at that time was brought in from a boarding house, was awful. Food was thrown away. And if you complained, you were taken outside by the police and beaten.
>
> (Ottoboni 2000: 30–31)

They were soon joined by Veronese and ordinand Franz de Castro Holzwarth. Together they formed a group to help the prisoners called

Amando al Prójimo, Amarás a Cristo (loosely translated as 'Loving Your Neighbour, You Will Love Christ') – APAC for short (Ottoboni 2003). At that time, jurisdiction over the prison was vested in Judge Sílvio Marques Neto, who understood the Cursillo movement. By the end of 1973, he gave the volunteers unlimited access to half the prison. The following year a legal body was established to supervize the volunteers. This was also called APAC, but with a slightly different acronym: *Associação de Proteção e Assistência aos Condenados* (Association for the Protection and Assistance to the Convicted). This is a rather important distinction because APAC, unlike Christian-based units in the UK and US to date, may have complete authority over a prison, or part of a prison. Unlike a faith-based unit in England, APAC can function as 'a subsidiary body of justice' (Ottoboni 2003: 54) with the power to make decisions that have judicial implications. The legal APAC set up in 1974 was designed to protect the work of the pastoral APAC set up in 1972.

In 1975 a book by the founders of APAC, *Christ Wept In Jail*, brought national attention to the APAC programme, and in 1976 it was presented to the President of Brazil who ordered a thorough study. This resulted in a change in the Brazilian penal code calling for more humane treatment of prisoners. In 1979, the Humaitá prison was closed due to the overall poor condition and level of police brutality, despite the efforts of APAC. National support for the movement continued to grow, and political pressure mounted to recognize its successes. As a result, Humaitá reopened in 1983, and APAC was allowed to administer the prison without the cooperation of the civil and military police. In 1984 the government invited APAC formally to run the prison as a private facility.[9] Completely renovated, the prison reopened again in March 1984 as the first fully-run APAC prison, and a sentencing judge transferred part of the existing prison population to Humaitá. In 1986 the pastoral APAC was reorganized into a body consisting of a General Assembly, Community Council, Board of Directors, volunteers and prisoners.[10] APAC also began to work with prisoners housed in the Jardim Satélite public jails in São José dos Campos, Paraibuna and São Bento do Sapucaí. In 1988 APAC was chartered to Prison Fellowship International and in 1989, APAC changed its name to Prison Fellowship Brazil.

Ottoboni candidly admits that APAC lacked clear direction at first. There were many failures during these early days, including escapes that brought significant political pressure on APAC to close. The breakthrough came in 1986 when they stumbled on the realization that the solutions to prisoners' problems lay with the prisoners themselves. Problems exposed in therapy sessions were restated to prisoners who would come up with their own solutions (Lee 1995). Only after this 'commitment to ongoing dialogue with the prisoner' (Ottoboni 2000: 9) in 1986, did APAC move into a period of relative calm.

Three points are of special interest about this account of APAC's history and development. First, APAC was 'on trial' for a long period, and its future was never guaranteed. Second, part of the reason why APAC survived when its track record on security was less than successful was because judicial authorities were at a loss to know what else to do with the population of Humaitá. Third, APAC did not spring into existence fully-formed but was the product of a long period of trial and error, during which volunteers and administrators became attuned to the particular needs of those prisoners who chose to participate.

To place APAC in context we need to appreciate the poor regard in which prisoners are held in São Paulo state. APAC was an attempt to humanize prison conditions. The largest jail in São Paulo was the Casa de Detenção (a.k.a. Carandiru) which until its closure in 2002 held 8,000 prisoners in a building built in 1956 to accommodate 3,250 men (*Carandiru* 2003; Varela 1999).[11] As the largest jail in São Paulo, Carandiru was not typical. Indeed other prisons near São Paulo have adopted stage 2 of APAC (see below). However there is evidence of public hostility towards prisoners and to improving prison conditions. This can be briefly illustrated by public attitudes to an infamous riot that broke out on 3 October 1992 in Pavilion 9 of Carandiru. 350 military police were called in to control the rebellion, killing 111 prisoners. It was claimed that police poured gallons of oil into the corridors causing prisoners to slip, whereupon they were attacked by military police dogs (Guerreiro 1992). A contemporary news report provides a graphic picture of events:

> The policemen came in, climbed up the stairs as they shot at prisoners. They would get in cells, ask the inmates to put their hands on their heads, take off their clothes and turn towards the wall and then they would machine gun them without pity … Several said, 'Don't kill us', but were ordered to lie on the floor. The policemen shot at their heads as if they were cattle in the slaughterhouse. After the slaughter there were corpses all over the cells, eaten by dogs and with machinegun bullet holes … After the massacre they ordered prisoners to carry the bodies to the basement, adding that if anyone looked them in the eye they would be shot dead … The walls still have brains stuck to them.
>
> (*Jornal da Tarde* 1992)

A poll conducted by the Brazilian newspaper, *Inform Estado*, involving 362 São Paulo residents, found that 41 per cent applauded the police action. Guerreiro (1992) cited a typical response from this minority: 'If they are criminals, they are beasts who need to be killed, especially if those who judge are members of a violent society such as ours'. Some quarters registered surprise that the approval rating was not higher (*ibid.*).

If such punitive attitudes are at all widespread in São Paulo, one would expect APAC's attempts to humanize prison conditions to meet with some degree of public and political opposition. That is, indeed, what the history shows. Julio Ottoboni's biography of his father claims that APAC offended certain private interests, namely 'corrupt police who exploited prisoners' and describes how 'a wave of criticism and discouragement from an ill-informed society with preconceived ideas endeavoured to shake the work of volunteers and weakened the association' (Ottoboni 1998: 6). In 1981 military police called in Ottoboni and Holzwarth to help control a riot in neighbouring Jacareí prison. The prisoners had specifically asked for their mediation in order to avoid bloodshed. Just as they had negotiated a settlement and were driving out of the prison, a volley of gunfire killed six prisoners and Holzwarth, who received 35 bullet wounds. Ottoboni believed Holzwarth was assassinated.

Julio Ottoboni also highlights the vulnerability of the APAC programme to changes in judicial oversight. The arrival of a new judge in the Jurisdiction of Criminal Executions, to which APAC was connected, resulted in the imposition of new rules that had the effect of deactivating APAC for months at a time; after a change of appointment, APAC returned to normal. At the time of writing, APAC is once again deactivated.

Similar pressure has been brought to bear on initiatives in Ecuador, the first country to attempt to replicate the APAC programme outside Brazil (Toral 2000). Christian-based communities set up within two prisons in Quito and Guayaquil face opposition due to a lack of interest and information about the programme within the prison system. Father Timothy Lehane, Chaplain to a Quito prison and a former Board Member of Prison Fellowship Ecuador (PFE), states that the main opposition came from the Ecuadorian prison system itself. The lack of proper governmental support is also a factor since the government is directly responsible for appointing prison governors. Lehane (2003) remarks: '[APAC] is not working that well at the moment because it has very, very little support from the Government'. The founder of the APAC movement in Ecuador, Jorge Crespo Toral, was a former candidate for the Presidency of Ecuador, and some attribute the survival of the movement to his political skill and influence (*ibid.*). A second source is said to be harsh social attitudes towards prisoners, exacerbated by increasing social poverty and violence. Lehane (*ibid.*) remarks:

I think it's a whole lack of knowledge of society in general – they see the prisoners as evil people who do damage, and unfortunately there's more damage being done at the moment because the poor are getting poorer. And I mean they have to fight for survival.

A third source is said to be the lack of dialogue between ecumenical and non-governmental groups because of the absence of any traditional churches in Ecuador other than the Roman Catholic Church. In addition, some prison guards allegedly undermined the APAC system by refusing to allow APAC prisoners who were legitimately allowed outside the prison back inside. Lehane (*ibid.*) comments:

> these guys [APAC prisoners] often had to fight to get back into the prison once they were let out on free leave .... You come back to ... the guard at the prison gate. He's paid by the state. He sees you're on the APAC system, he doesn't want the APAC system to work so he says, 'Run – escape. I'm not letting you back in again'.

For all these reasons Lehane (*ibid.*) claims that 'the [Ecuadorian] APAC system… is beginning to lose its significance in the prisons'.

In summary, APAC's greatest problem appears to be not the prisoners, but public officials and sectors of public opinion unsympathetic to its work. This reminds us of the vulnerability of APAC-type programmes to changes of personnel, 'prison politics' and popular punitiveness.

Around 12 APAC regimes are operating in Brazil, and possibly a further six in other parts of South America (Ecuador, Argentina and Peru; Creighton 2001). The Brazilian APACs are coordinated by a supervisory body, the Brazilian Fellowship for Assistance to the Convicted (*Fraternidad Brasilena de Asistencia a los Condenados* or FBAC; Ottoboni 2003). However, APAC is not monolithic. Four different kinds of APAC can be identified, depending firstly on whether they offer a 'quasi' or 'full' APAC regime, and secondly, on the degree of control over the prison that judicial and correctional authorities grant to APAC (cf. Ottoboni's five-fold schema: Ottoboni 2003). This is quite important for understanding where the UK and US initiatives fit into the broader scheme of APAC-type initiatives. The four types of APAC reflect different stages of development. They can be helpfully strung out along an evolutionary scale that ranges from the rudimentary 'quasi-APAC' to progressively more sophisticated forms.

(a) 'Quasi-APAC'

The first category is those prison regimes that 'partially observe the

[APAC] methodology without meeting all the demands' (Ottoboni 2003: 138). 'Quasi-APAC' is our preferred term for regimes that are inspired by an APAC approach but fall short in certain respects (some avoidable, others unavoidable). The UK and US initiatives, for example, would probably fall under this heading (see Chapters 3–8), as would regimes that retain some features of APAC but no longer operate a full APAC regime (e.g. the St. Augustine Christian Community in Socabaya Prison, Peru;[12] Creighton 2001).

(b) 'APAC but no control'

The next stage is from a 'partial APAC' to a 'full APAC' regime. A 'full APAC' regime is one that bears a sufficient 'family resemblance' to the model set out in sections 3–6 below to justify the 'APAC' label. Such a regime may be worked out in a whole prison or in part of a prison. It is more advanced than the 'quasi-APAC' model. Its primary limitation is that ultimate responsibility for running the APAC regime is in the hands of correctional agencies. Examples of this include the evolving Humaitá prison between 1972 and 1979. During this period, APAC volunteers provided a full APAC service to prisoners, but their activities were under the complete control of the State Secretariat of Security.

(c) 'APAC with partial control'

The next stage is a full APAC regime which is run in agreement with the general administration but without the involvement of prison staff or anyone other than APAC personnel. This can be styled 'APAC with partial control' because APAC has exclusive management of one or more units within the prison but not the prison itself. The APAC facility in Ecuador, 'Hogar San Pablo' ('Saint Paul's Home') which opened in 1994 at Pavilion C of the former García Moreno Prison in Quito, belongs to this category (Toral 2000). The Government of Ecuador agreed that this pavilion would be given over exclusively to PFE (Prison Fellowship Ecuador). Although prison guards paid by the State would still be stationed at the prison gate and elsewhere in the prison, no prison guards or policemen would be allowed into 'Hogar San Pablo' (Lehane 2003).

(d) 'APAC with full control'

The apex of development is a fully-developed APAC programme delivered in a prison over which APAC has complete control. Exclusive management has been delegated by judicial and correctional authorities to APAC staff, volunteers and prisoners with no assistance from civil or military police or correctional agents. The model Humaitá prison, from

11

1984 onwards, is an example of this type, as is the newly-built Itauna Prison in Minais Gerais, Brazil, since 2000 (Creighton 2001).

Several things become clear when we place this fourfold schema alongside the historical development of APAC and the social and institutional backlash. The first is that the model Humaitá prison was the result of 25 years' slow development by its founders. The second is that Humaitá itself had to progress through a number of transitional stages before it attained a position of maximum autonomy. APAC had no control over Humaitá for the first seven years and only had its first opportunity at full control 11 years after its inception. This reminds us that volunteers have to earn respect and responsibility and that this takes time. Even then, the decision to grant the volunteers exclusive management of the prison owed much to the confluence of sympathetic public officials and the lack of any viable alternative. Whatever the volunteers did would be better than outright closure.

This analysis of APAC's history and development has the effect of discouraging the idea, popular in some circles in the 1990s, that an APAC prison could simply come into existence in the UK *ab initio*. Several feasibility documents expressed the hope that staff from a Christian charity and supported by volunteers and prisoners could simply 'take over' the running of a UK prison, attaining 'APAC with full control' or 'APAC with partial control' in one bound. Yet the history of APAC itself suggested otherwise and pointed to the need to gain experience and build trust by operating successfully, over a long period of time, at a more elementary level.

What now exists in the UK and US, after eight years, is something that looks very much like 'quasi-APAC' – the first evolutionary stage. This is hardly surprising. The growth of crime and insecurity in late modernity in the UK and US has shifted the relationship of criminal justice to its social and political environment. The criminal justice State has assumed an increasingly large role for 'crime control', which inhibits the delegation of authority for criminal justice from the State to civilians (Garland 2001). Progress was no quicker for the original APAC itself.

3. Who goes to APAC and why

We turn from the evolution of APAC to its actual implementation. Here we introduce several important recurring themes: recruitment and selection, informed consent, and the particular incentives of faith-based units.

APAC fishes from a small pool. First, under Brazilian law (Act 6416/77) prisoners are allowed to serve their sentence in the county where they were sentenced or where their families are located. APAC exploits the obvious rehabilitative potential of this provision by requiring that prisoners' families should live within ten miles of the prison, with some exceptions. Second, from this pool of eligible applicants, APAC further selects on the basis of the sincerity of the offender's desire for reform and the willingness of his family to participate in the programme. Thus APAC intentionally recruits those who are most likely to succeed, both in terms of external support and personal motivation. Strong personal motivation can compensate for lack of family support (see the experiences of two prisoners, Edsohn and Mesias, documented in *Love Is Not A Luxury*, Lee 1995). Prisoners apply to APAC through a lengthy application form and an interview with APAC staff. The judge in charge of the offender's case makes the final decision, based on a recommendation from the APAC Directorate. Under the Brazilian criminal justice process, judges have the power to send prisoners to a specific prison within each State and have the power to order the transfer of prisoners from one prison to another (Creighton 1993). Successful applicants are placed on a waiting list. Anderson (1991a) noted that at the time of her visit the list contained 300 names.

Prisoners have multiple incentives for applying to APAC. In 1994, Humaitá prisoners in the closed regime drew up a list of 54 incentives (APAC 1993a). This list is a key document because it indicates how transferees perceive APAC compared to other Brazilian prisons. The presence of these perceived incentives is consistent with the fact that all APAC participants transfer from another prison (Lee 2004). This is hardly surprising given the generally poor quality of the Brazilian prison estate.[13] The 54 incentives are not set out in any particular order. However, a number of broad themes emerge, listed in Table 1 below.

The advantages that prisoners perceived are broadly consistent with those identified in judicial and governmental testimonials. A personal letter sent to Ottoboni by a judge with responsibility for the prisons of São José dos Campos claims:

> The existence of the APAC System serves as an incentive for good behaviour for inmates in public prisons. Evidence of this is the fact that nearly all the prisoners of the County, and outside it, are anxious for a transfer to a prison administrated by APAC, where they receive all kinds of assistance and human treatment (Pinho 1998).

The Head of Jurisdiction of the Jury and Criminal Executions of the County of São José dos Campos provided similar testimonials (De Oliveira 1993; see also Junior 1982 and APAC 1993b and 1993c).

Table 1.1   Perceived advantages of Humaitá compared to other Brazilian prisons. (Numbers in brackets refer to numbering on source document)

Universal Incentives	Escaping the 'prison jungle'	(1) No police; (2) No corruption; (3) No violence; (12) No overcrowding;[14] (13) Open to all prisoners, regardless of type of offence;[15] (49) Absence of hallucinogenic drugs
	Better treatment (for prisoner and prisoner's family)[16]	(8) Free judicial assistance; (9) Medical, dental and psychological assistance; (14) Appropriate food; (21) [Body] searches of [prisoner's] relatives are conducted in a dignified manner; (22) No [body] searches of [prisoner's] relatives after a … period of three months; (23) Relatives' visits take place in a cordial environment; (24) [Good] hygiene[17]; (25) Respect for privacy; (36) Absence of oppressive security (literally 'strong cells'); (38) [Prisoner's] own canteen; (39) Telephone; (40) Barbershop; (41) Isolation beds for carriers of contagious diseases; (42) [Hospital] ward; (43) Chemist; (45) Leisure moments; (47) Freedom of access to President of APAC [i.e. to the Prison Governor][18]
Specific Incentives	More active regime	(16) Recuperative prison work; (30) Cultural events; (35) Events auditorium; (44) Handcraft labour therapy; (48) Literacy and professional courses; (52) Physical education every morning
	Sentence reduction	(11) Promotion by merit; (50) "For each working day, a day is subtracted from the sentence"
	'Spiritual' incentives	(6) Spiritual assistance; (27) Daily prayers; (28) [Respect for] religious beliefs; (29) Talks; (32) Prison 'Journey with Christ' [Cursillo]; (33) Praying workshop; (34) Chapel for individual meditation
	'Community' ethos	(4) Prisoners help one another; (5) Respect for the physical and moral integrity of the prisoner; (10) Assistance from 'godmothers' and 'godfathers'; (15) Communal refectory; (26) Active participation in the community; (37) Spirit of union and solidarity; (54) Visits by community groups on Sundays
	Family benefits	(7) Social assistance for the relatives of the needy prisoner; (19) Family valorization; (20) Talks for prisoners' families; (53) Prisoners remain in the county and close to their family
	Greater prisoner responsibility	(17) Prisoners are responsible for prison administration; (18) Human valorization through undertaking trustworthy positions; (31) Improvement courses; (46) Escort with colleagues; (51) Commission of Technical Classification Exams are conducted in the prison

It is reasonable to hypothesize that the first four groups of incentives would appeal to nearly the entire Brazilian penal population, except the inevitable few who prefer the 'prison jungle' to a less chaotic existence. However, four other groups of incentives follow that have more limited interest. They are 'spiritual' incentives, 'community' incentives, 'family' incentives and invitations to assume more personal responsibility. Naturally, these incentives would only appeal to those who wish to live in such a Christian-centred community environment with plenty of family contact and personal responsibility. They are incentives for some but *dis*incentives for others. These 'disputed' incentives are built into the selection criteria and application process because they are matters that require informed consent.

The incentives listed in the fourth category ('Sentence reduction') require some explanation. Toral (2000: 12) comments that 'change and formation are the great stimuli for the prisoners in the APAC, because the length of time they remain imprisoned depends on them. ... The reduction of the sentence or term can be dramatic, depending on the transformation of the offender into an honest person.' Lee's documentary describes how one prisoner in Humaitá (Mesias Fernandes) had his prison sentence commuted from 114 to 30 years within nine years of being sentenced (*Love Is Not A Luxury*, 1995). Accounts differ on the calibration used in Humaitá. Incentive no. 50 refers to remission of sentence by one day for one day's work (APAC 1993a). It is unclear to what precisely this 'remission of sentence' refers, but it seems to refer to time off the full sentence passed by the sentencing judge (in England and Wales, the Sentence Expiry Date or SED).

This system of 'incentives' regarding sentence progression is similar to the legislation governing release under licence in England and Wales. Under the system of Discretionary Conditional Release (DCR) introduced by the Criminal Justice Act 2001, offenders sentenced on or after 1 October 1992 are automatically eligible for parole after serving half their sentence in custody. Prisoners who are unsuccessful in obtaining parole are released on the Non-Parole Date (NPD) at the two thirds-point of the sentence. The difference is that in APAC it seems that the SED can be reduced, whereas in England and Wales the SED cannot be reduced (unless by appeal). Prisoners serving sentences of less than four years in England and Wales are automatically released on parole at the half-way point of their sentence (the Automatic Release Date or ARD) unless the prisoner has Additional Days Awarded (ADAs) for breaking prison rules.

In one noticeable respect, Humaitá is actually *less* liberal than England and Wales. In the open stage of the regime (see below), Humaitá prisoners

15

live in the community for the remainder of their sentence. They remain under close supervision, sign a book at the prison every night and have fortnightly meetings with Ottoboni. This continues for the entirety of their sentence. They also remain informally accountable for a further six months beyond that. By contrast, successful parolees in England and Wales remain under supervision only until the three-quarter point of their sentence (the Licence Expiry Date), although some sex offenders may be supervized for the entire duration if the trial judge so orders.

In APAC Ecuador, the picture appears to be more radical. Toral claims that section 15 of the Code of Penal Enforcement and Social Rehabilitation allowed prisoners to reduce their incarceration period by as much as five-sixths of the total sentence, depending on their recovery. APAC Ecuador carries out the process for accepting this reduction in line with 'certain criteria' (Toral 2000: 75), with the final decision ratified by the National Council for Social Rehabilitation. If so, such provisions are remarkably generous by any standard. It would not be surprising if that alone constituted a strong incentive to apply to APAC. Lehane (2003) notes further advantages of APAC Ecuador over non-APAC facilities in Ecuador as: cleanliness, organization, absence of overcrowding, 'rooms' rather than 'cells', work, and the opportunity to become involved in prison administration.

4. The DNA of APAC

Discussion of the internal structure of APAC allows us to introduce another recurring theme: the rules and boundaries of the community and the (often innovatory) means by which they are enforced.

APAC is a five-phase programme composed of induction, three increasingly progressive prison regimes (closed, semi-open and open) and a period of accountability in the community. It reflects the belief that 'prisoners can make positive, sustainable changes in their lives when motivated and provided with consistent support, guidance and accountability' (Van Patten *et al.* 1991). Identifying these phases is important.[19]

The first phase is *induction*. On admission the applicant stays in a special cell for a 60-day assessment period during which he undergoes physical, psychological, and mental health assessments from APAC's professional volunteers who include psychologists, doctors, dentists and teachers. This is said to give prisoners time to adapt to the APAC ethos, an adjustment which, on anecdotal evidence, some find difficult. One prisoner, Mesias Fernandes, came to APAC in 1987 having been kept in his former prison in a cell measuring one metre by one metre. 'From the day that I arrived and they took off the handcuffs, I never had to wear them again. I had a difficult life from then on because the transition was hard' (Fernandes 1993). Judges control vacancies in APAC's closed, semi-open and open regimes and hence are able to direct prisoners' progress towards release (APAC undated). At the end of this period the prisoner can either progress in the closed regime or be returned by the relevant judge to his previous prison (Creighton 1993).

The second phase is the *closed regime* (see Figure 1.1). Prisoners are confined to their cells or to other secure areas, although cells are locked only at night (Lee 1995). There are five dormitories, each with a shower and low-bunk spaces for 10 to 12 people. The goals and programme for the closed regime are set out in Section 5 below.

The closed regime has a Prisoners' Council of about 100 men. Prisoners who behave in a manner incompatible with the closed section are called to the 15-member Prisoner Council known as the Council for Sincerity and Security (CSS; *Consejo de Sinceridad y Solidaridad*) to explain their behaviour. If the misbehaviour recurs he is called again, this time with the right to present a defence, and served with a written warning. Normally, after the second offence, he is invited to see Ottoboni, and the prisoner is told that full compliance will be required of him in future. The Prisoner Council is the highest level of inmate control and accountability and the primary means of enforcing the rules and boundaries of the community.

A point system is the most frequently used method of discipline. Prisoners who persist after the second warning are punished on a point system ranging from one to 30. The Secretary of the Prisoners' Council maintains a discipline assessment chart which is a weekly record of each inmate's point status. Each prisoner has a daily score recording minor, medium and serious infringements according to APAC criteria. The Director of the Day (a very experienced volunteer working under Ottoboni) reviews point losses, which forms the basis of APAC's grade for each prisoner at the end of the month. The judge in charge of a prisoner's case decides the length of any regress, which varies from 70 hours to three months. The prisoner may be removed from APAC altogether if he sustains negative behaviour over three months. Such cases appear to be rare, occurring less than once a year. Ottoboni claims that every time a prisoner was removed to another prison, the team would meet to see where it had failed.

The use of Prisoners' Councils to facilitate increased prisoner decision-making and responsibility raises difficult issues that 'quasi-APAC' units in the UK and US prisons try to resolve. What balance should

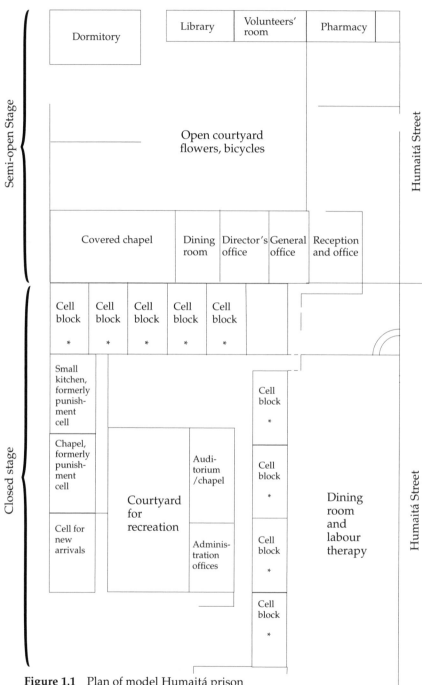

Figure 1.1 Plan of model Humaitá prison

they strike between the need to delegate meaningful responsibility to prisoners and the need to maintain overall control? APAC has tried to strike this balance in the following way. Each cell-block in the closed unit has a representative on the Prisoners' Council. To prevent leadership confrontations, the institution appoints cell representatives. As prisoner maturity develops, prisoners are allowed to choose their representatives themselves. Even here, APAC's directors must ensure that appointments do not aim simply to satisfy prisoners' interests (Ottoboni 2003). As a further safeguard, Ottoboni ratifies Council recommendations. Within these boundaries the Council has real responsibility. It is the Council for the closed section which, in all practical terms, administers the closed section of the prison, taking charge of the pharmacy, secretarial work, security, 'labour therapy' (see Section 5 below) and catering (Lee 1995).

The third, *semi-open* phase is called the *Centro de Reintegracion Social* (CRS; Social Reintegration Centre). Promotion to the semi-open phase allows prisoners free movement throughout the prison. There is a heavy presumption *against* promotion from the closed to the semi-open stage which the prisoner must discharge. Ottoboni (2000: 22–23) claims that this burden of proof '[protects] society and the prisoner himself, who does not re-enter society unprepared'. Van Patten *et al.* (1991) claim that the transition from one stage to the next is carefully protected so unrealistic expectations do not compromise it. The director of the prison and a police representative must approve promotion. They then communicate the decision to the judge in charge of the prisoner's case. It is a key transition, given due solemnity. Again, prisoners give informed consent to the new regime. Prisoners sign a compact to enter the semi-open regime, which sets out the range of their commitments (see Ottoboni 2003).

Prisoners in the semi-open stage live in a 50-bed open dormitory. The Centre has showers, a dining room and an open-air chapel (see Figure 1.1). The semi-open phase also has a Prisoners' Council to represent approximately 50 men (Lee 2004). Prisoners work in the main office and keep the main gates. As they progress they can begin leaving the prison for certain necessary tasks, always accompanied by volunteers or other trusted prisoners (Lee 1995). This allows them 'personally and progressively [to] experience the benefits of freedom' (Toral 2000: 12). It is 'a continuous test of the inmate's decision to continue training without a relapse, since it is at this time that provocations typical of the old environment reappear' (*ibid.*: 13). This is significant because it is one of the criticisms of 'special units' that prisoners do not have any or sufficient practice at relating behaviour learned in the community to the 'real world' (cf. Chapter 4). When prisoners are considered ready, they receive a letter of recommendation to a known employer and may work outside the prison between 7a.m. and 7p.m. They wear black baseball caps to identify them when they are outside (Lee 1995). Bad behaviour or unjustifiable lateness spells a return to the closed section.

The CRS arose by chance. In 1974 an area next to the jail was used to build a half-way house for prisoners. APAC set up its administrative offices there, and prisoners began helping its administration. The 'half-way house' became the basis for the semi-open and open regimes, and the jail became the 'closed' section. This reminds us of the fact that innovatory regimes adapt to local opportunities. For that reason it can be difficult to apply APAC in its entirety in circumstances where similar opportunities are not present.

The *semi-open* regime has legislative support. Articles 91–92 of the Criminal Execution Act govern sentences served in semi-open conditions, although these would normally refer to conditions such as a prison farm or industrial establishment. Non-APAC prisoners in Brazil who qualify for a 'semi-open' regime may serve that part of their sentence under conditions of 'house arrest'. This may be compared with the use of Home Detention Curfews (HDCs) in England and Wales: under the Crime and Disorder Act 1988, prisoners serving between three months and four years may be released early from their sentence, electronically tagged and required to remain in their home between nine and 12 hours a day. Other prisons in Brazil have now adopted the semi-open regime (Lee 2004).

The Centre for Social Rehabilitation has two wings: one designed for the semi-open and the other for the open regime. The fourth phase is the open regime in which prisoners live outside with their families and do not need to spend the night in the CRS. However, they have to sign the attendance roster at the prison punctually at seven o'clock every evening, attend a fortnightly meeting with Ottoboni and appear at all rehabilitation events. In the open regime, the men come in for chapel in the evening and other gatherings (Lee 2004). Their position is analogous to parolees in England and Wales who are granted early release from custody. Prisoners are promoted to the open regime if they have a profession, trade or job offer and have received 'rigorous preparation' (Ottoboni 2003: 59). Again, they give informed consent, and prisoners sign a compact to enter the fourth phase (see Ottoboni 2003).

The fifth and final phase occurs *post-sentence* and is best described as a form of resettlement based on continuing accountability. Prisoners who maintain 'phase four' conduct for six months after being released are regarded as having successfully completed the full APAC programme.

To sum up, the overall purpose of the five-stage system is slow but steady progress towards freedom. Re-entry to society is a gradual, closely-monitored process that involves small steps. Ottoboni remarks that:

sometimes months of activities are necessary....There have been some cases in APAC when over two years were necessary for the *recuperando* to … change his way of thinking … [Not] being in a hurry is a virtue.

(2003: 84)

Despite these precautions there is no denying that the lack of armed guards and the high reliance on prisoner cooperation means that security appears to be extremely compromised from a traditional correctional perspective. Van Ness (2003) rightly observes that, as prisoners progress through the different stages, 'in increasing ways the prisoners stay because they choose to stay and that choice is made not simply when they join, but on an almost daily basis.'

The legitimacy of formal authorities has emerged in recent years as an apparently important factor in promoting pro-social behaviour, not just in prison (Sparks and Bottoms 1995; Woolf and Tumim 1991), but also in relation to other criminal justice authorities (e.g. Paternoster *et al.* 1997; Tyler 1990). Prisons, by their very nature, are thought to have an 'inherent legitimacy deficit' which, if compounded by the absence of certain variable conditions (e.g. fair procedures), can lead to control problems (Sparks and Bottoms 1995). Paternoster *et al.* (1997) identify several elements of procedural justice that promote legitimacy. Adapted to a prison setting they include the following: 'representation' (does the prisoner have the opportunity to play a part in the making of important decisions?); 'correctability' (can the prisoner appeal against low-level decisions where necessary?) and 'ethicality' (do the prison authorities treat prisoners with respect and dignity?). Each is pertinent to APAC and other faith-based units.

APAC's five phases have not always been used in the manner for which they were intended. Between 1979 and 1983 judges assigned prisoners directly to semi-open or open conditions without requiring that they should first graduate from closed conditions. Ottoboni (2003) believed this resulted in a lack of discipline among prisoners and greater reoffending on release. He claims that the prisoner must experience 'the bitterness of prison' and 'every step of the recovery process' in order to appreciate the progressive aspects of the APAC regime (2003: 101).

5. Goals and programming

This section identifies the specific goals of Humaitá and their relationship, if any, to programming. The goal of APAC is straightforward enough: to create an environment that will 'rehabilitate' the prisoner. To understand more fully why a 'rehabilitative environment' is APAC's goal (and not, say, 'rehabilitated prisoners') we must again adopt the 'internal' perspective of its founders. Hugo Veronese, the resident psychologist at Humaitá and one of its founders, justifies the goal of APAC as follows:

> If it is lack of love that creates an ambient [sic] conducive to crime, rehabilitation is only possible through love ... [and] prisons, as we know them, are the surroundings least indicated where to find love. If there is serious will to rehabilitate the criminal, we must face the challenge of changing the prisons.
>
> (Veronese undated)

This revealing explanation tells us that APAC is as interested in reforming the nature of the traditional prison environment as it is in reforming the offender and that implementing APAC will have both individual and organizational implications. This is because APAC sees *individual* renewal and *institutional* change as complementary.

Similarly, the founder of APAC Ecuador claims that 'rehabilitating' prisoners APAC-style means 'turning prisons into communities for individual and collective perfecting' (Toral 2000: 68). Remarkably, the prison is here styled as a *'community-in-perfection'*. The prison is said to be indistinguishable from that of *any* faith-based community, Christian or otherwise. Toral also claims that the goal of APAC is to be a centre for 'encounter for living in friendship, understanding, respect, solidarity, shared work, community action and even joy, recreation and culture' (*ibid.*: 54). This too is interesting because Toral intentionally describes the goal of 'rehabilitation' in terms of certain programmes and social mechanisms (see Section 6 below).

The overall goal of 'rehabilitation' breaks down further to a set of smaller goals that are intentionally developed at each stage of APAC's five-phase regime.

Ottoboni (2003) sees the *closed regime* as the right time for prisoners to discover their own values. Accordingly, following the initial induction stage (Phase 1), the closed regime (Phase 2) has three specific goals: (1) to improve the prisoner's self-image; (2) to nurture 'intrinsic human values' (Ottoboni 2000: 44); and (3) to make some attempt to develop the prisoner's sense of responsibility. Ottoboni (2003) lists ten pages of activities designed to achieve these goals. For ease of analysis, we have categorized these into programmes concerned with six objectives: (1) spiritual development; (2) moral education; (3) building relationships with significant others; (4) community-building; (5) responsibility and service;

and (6) creative self-expression. We shall consider what programmes are involved under each of these headings and how they relate to the three goals of the closed unit.

Programmes of *spiritual development* relate to the goal of the closed unit because they are said to improve the prisoner's self-image and to enable them to discover their own values. These include the three-day 'short course' in Christianity (Cursillo, above). *Moral education* is related to the goal of the closed unit because it is said to help prisoners to discover their own values and to develop a greater sense of responsibility. Compulsory 'human valorization' classes held weekly attempt to instil this. The teaching method is self-reflective. Each prisoner is expected to write a paper on a given topic (e.g. 'Discuss 15 factors that are conducive to a life of crime') and to discuss it with their dormitory group before class. A volunteer teacher then leads the discussion with the entire group. Creighton (1993) reports being 'impressed' with both the written and verbal level of participation and involvement. In sociological terms, such classes may stimulate 'normative compliance' by bringing about changes in the individual's moral sense (Bottoms and Rex 1998; Bottoms 2001 and 2002). Again, volunteers are a social mechanism for sensitizing prisoners to pro-social values. This may also stimulate the kind of 'normative compliance' that arises from 'a changing perspective on the world linked to the value placed on new social attachments' (Bottoms and Rex 1998: 20). Emotional healing is also attempted through weekly small-group sessions with APAC psychologists, including Veronese (see Section 1 above).

Building relationships with significant others is related to the goal of developing prisoner responsibility. These relationships are built through the exchange of correspondence with volunteers and through contact with specially-assigned volunteers (called 'godparents') as well as with prisoners' own families. Sampson and Laub's 1993 reanalysis of Glueck's 1950 study of delinquency found that the strength of adult social bonds has a direct negative effect on adult criminal behaviour. The 'godparenting' initiative is intended to provide prisoners with the opportunity to build such relationships that may in turn provide them with additional support when they experience problems or set-backs either in their sentence or upon release. It is noteworthy that families are mobilized as part of the process of rehabilitation in the closed section in contrast to traditional Western therapeutic communities where there is less family contact and often none at all. To some extent this reflects the high value attached to family life in the Brazilian culture (Creighton 1993). Veronese (undated) claims that:

it is a must to restore the original family ties so that, on his return from prison, the convict can find a healthy surrounding … When the original family persists in rejecting the faulty member the rehabilitation becomes much more problematical.

Emphasis is placed on group programmes, not individual tasks, in order to teach prisoners responsibility and how to behave in a *community* (Toral 2000). Group activities include music, writing, cell-cleaning contests, sports and participation in the Council for Sincerity and Solidarity via cell representatives. Extremes of large dormitories and one or two-man cells are eschewed in favour of ten to 12 man 'collective' cells to maximize group dynamics. Ottoboni claims that in this way the prisoner feels 'he is in a small circle of friends all sharing the same fate: prison. The experience of living together creates a bond of friendship, naturally joining them to the same objective: achieving their freedom' (2000: 53). As far as possible, APAC recommends that 'collective cells' should accommodate prisoners with similar offence histories, alternating at least every four months so that prisoners get to know each other better.

Increased prisoner responsibility and self-image is attempted by encouraging prisoners to serve one another and the regime. Prisoners are made responsible for each other's welfare and begin to learn responsibility by performing simple helping tasks for one another (e.g. cutting hair, cleaning common areas and shared cells). Prisoners are taught that 'the more one gives of himself, the richer he becomes' (Veronese undated), which again recalls the value of generativity in prison contexts (Maruna *et al.* 2004). Over half of the men in the closed section have named positions of responsibility. Every month the men in the closed section of the prison vote as to which of their number has made the most valuable contribution to this section of the prison, and a medal is presented at a special service as a mark of honour (Lee 1995). This is an illustration of what Maruna and LeBel (2002: 167) refer to as a 'strengths-based' paradigm to corrections. This asks '… not what a person's deficits are, but rather what positive contribution the person can make … How can their lives become useful and purposeful?'

Creative self-expression is related to the goals of the closed section because it helps prisoners to think positively about themselves as people who can create things, as well as provide a sense of their uniqueness and individuality. A programme of 'labour therapy' gives prisoners the chance to engage in activities that are capable of 'fostering their creativity and making them reflect on what they are doing' (Ottoboni 2003: 55). This includes activities such as tapestry, oil painting, tile decoration, ceramics, tablecloths, friezes and work with wood, clay and silk screen.

One prisoner commented: 'Through [labour therapy] I discovered that I am important and that my hands can do many useful things for society' (*ibid.*: 56). Labour therapy appears to build 'a sense in the prisoner that they can complete projects, work honestly, and learn patience, respect, perseverance and self-esteem' (*ibid.*: 57). During these periods, prisoners make handcrafted items for their families or for public sale. However, Ottoboni stresses that the work is 'therapeutic and individual in nature and that serial production is never allowed, as this would distort the basic purpose' (Ottoboni 2000: 26). Other programmes include: literacy and numeracy; complementary primary education for juveniles and adult classes in a wide range of subjects, including arts and humanities; nursing; music; religion; typing; debate and technical skills; handcrafts and hairdressing (Anderson 1991a).[20]

The overall goal of the *semi-open stage* is to loosen the prisoner's ties with the prison and intensify his reintegration into his family and society (Ottoboni 2003). Again, this breaks down into more specific objectives: increasing prisoner responsibility within the prison, providing specialized professional training and labour skills and increasing prisoner responsibility for their families.

Thus, increased progress is rewarded with increased responsibility such as escorting prisoners to outside judicial and medical appointments and assisting in administrative work (Veronese undated; Ottoboni 2003). Senior prisoners in the Prisoner's Council discuss which jobs will help a prisoner to develop, shuffling tasks as appropriate (Lee 1995). Second, prisoners are allowed to leave the Social Rehabilitation Centre (following a suitable transition period and with relevant authorization) to take part in professional courses or in-service training in different establishments in the city (e.g. a shoe-repair shop, bakery or tailors). Ottoboni (2000) notes that 87 per cent of APAC prisoners have no defined profession. This training is possible because the Brazilian *Ley de Ejecuciones Penales* (Law on the Execution of Sentences) allows prisoners to leave a prison for periods of time in order to study. Agreements with local companies to offer training are sent to the relevant judge to obtain authorization. The prisoner is also allowed to leave the social rehabilitation centre twice a week for two hours in order to look for a job (Ottoboni 2003). A third goal is increased prisoners' responsibility for their families. In the semi-open stage, families are allowed to visit the men every day. As indicated above, one of the bases of selection is that the prisoner's family should live within a ten-mile radius. Prisoners are now expected to help with their families' problems and to contribute financially, if possible (Lee 1995).

Despite the greater cultural value attached to the family in Brazil compared to the UK and the close physical proximity of prisoners' families, it is not always easy to get families involved. One prisoner, addressing the wives and girlfriends of prisoners attending APAC's first women's Cursillo for prisoners' family members held inside the prison in 1993, noted that only half of those invited to the event took part. He asked: 'How many relatives of prisoners, men and women, do not help when they could easily do so? If our relatives dedicated themselves a little bit more, the APAC of today would be much stronger' (Fernandes 1993). The Cursillo-derived Kairos Outside programme run in the UK and US experienced similar difficulties in involving prisoners' families with their loved ones' rehabilitation (see Chapters 2 and 7).

Finally, the goal of the *open unit* is pro-social living full-time in the community. In the open unit, they serve their sentence in the community. The men are encouraged to be involved in service to the community, whether professional work or victim reparation (Ottoboni 2003).

It is reasonable to suggest that a close relationship between goals and programming increases the intelligibility of the programme to prisoners, as well as its perceived legitimacy (Sparks and Bottoms 1995). One strength of Humaitá is the transparency of a regime in which 'freedom is responsibly won, stage after stage' (Ottoboni 2003: 39). APAC explicitly teaches prisoners about the relationship between goals and programming and does so with the intention of putting the prisoner on an equal footing with the volunteer (*ibid*.: 66). This multiple dissemination strategy requires a clear sense of identity. This raises the issue of how religious-based programmes can develop a clear sense of purpose and articulate this consistently to different groups such as prison staff, prisoners and volunteers.[21]

6. Rehabilitative agents

This section considers the primary rehabilitative agents in APAC: outside volunteers and APAC prisoners themselves. The lack of a national Prison Service in Brazil generates a greater practical need for volunteers and responsible prisoners to be involved in prison administration and programme delivery than in the UK. However, an analysis of internal APAC documents and the writings of its founders indicates that volunteers and peer prisoner support appear to play a crucial symbolic and communicative, as well as practical, role.

APAC has a strong ideological conviction of the unique value of volunteers. This reflects the institutional history of APAC which came into being because of volunteers. Ottoboni (2003: 50) maintains that 'everything must begin with the participation of the community'. Such involvement has legislative support. Article 4 of the Criminal Sentencing Act requires that: 'The state should resort to the cooperation of the community in its activities relating to execution of sentences and security measures'. Item 24 of the Statement of Purpose for the (Brazilian) Criminal Sentencing Act states that 'no programme designed to face problems relating to delinquents and penalties would be complete without the indispensable and continuous help of the community'. Judges are expected to engage with legally constituted voluntary bodies set up to assist prisoner rehabilitation. Ottoboni (2000: 37) quotes a former Secretary for Justice of São Paulo who said that: 'We should not expect the prisoner to be the first to hold out his hand, for obvious reasons. The first step must be taken by society.'

The most mature and experienced of APAC volunteers become 'godparents' (*pardrinos*) who are really volunteer sponsors. Every prisoner is given a godparent on arrival who will support him throughout his sentence and treat him as one of their family. The average length of this process is between five and seven years. The practice was introduced to Humaitá in 1973. This initiative has legislative support under Articles 78–79 of the Criminal Sentencing Act, which deals with sponsorship. Godparents are preferably couples but can be single. They may be older couples, widows or former prisoners. Veronese (undated) offers the following justification for their effectiveness:

> ... when nature is defrauded in something special [i.e. love], the human being hollers, from cradle to grave, to fill this vacuum. The loving presence of a couple (the godparents) ... [are] a bridge to the original family and to the external world.

Godparents accept that 'no-one can take the place of a father or a mother' (Lee 1995, quoting a godparent), but APAC maintains that godparents can help to 'reshape the blurred and negative images of the inmate's father, mother or both' (Ottoboni 2003: 71). Their role is 'supportive parenting, not substitute parenting' (Creighton 2001). For Veronese (undated), what volunteers offer is unique:

> The State, an impersonal entity, can build prisons, nominate agents, assign resources – but cannot give love. It is only we, physical persons ... that can face the challenge of seeding love in the prisons.

In this way, the 'godparents' may be said to offer a form of 'pro-social modelling'. This involves positive role models who act in such a way as to reinforce pro-social or non-criminal behaviour. Bottoms *et al.* (1995) found that the more successful heavy-end intermediate treatment programmes for juveniles were characterized by a strong 'admixture' of anti-criminal messages within the framework of an overtly caring relationship. An Australian study found a strong significant relationship between pro-social modelling and lower rates of recidivism that were sustained over a four-year follow-up period (Trotter 1996). Pro-social modelling differs from non-directive counselling because:

> it provides a clear sense of direction …. That direction is provided within the context of a caring relationship, in which the offender is encouraged or 'pushed' towards pro-social conduct and his or her achievements reinforced through acknowledgement and approval
> (Bottoms and Rex 1998: 18).

If godparents are willing to give the prisoner the attention and care that may have been lacking, and if this is received positively, Veronese (undated) claims this will make him 'unconsciously, establish affectionate ties of filial adoption. When these ties become sufficiently strong, the convict will not return to crime'. The role of the godparent is to build a relationship so valued that the prisoner will not want to re-offend (Lee 1995). As a result, the practical love shown by volunteers is more than merely symbolic: 'it is how … prisoners come to experience love themselves and from that begin to establish bonds with others' (Van Ness 2003).

In sociological terms what is being described is part of a process of 'normative compliance'. As already noted, this can arise in several ways (Bottoms 2001 and 2002), one of which is hypothesized to be 'a changing perspective on the world linked to the value placed on new social attachments' (Bottoms and Rex 1998: 20). To the extent that godparents are seen as responsible for running the prison (which has no uniformed prison staff), normative compliance may also arise from 'a morally-based perception that legal authorities have a right to expect that their demands will be met simply because *they are the demands of legitimate authority*' (*ibid.*: emphasis original).

We noted earlier that not all volunteers are godparents. However, even those who are not godparents serve as role models and mentors (Veronese undated). Because volunteers come from the local community, they are potent symbols of the community to which the offender is seeking reintegration. The symbolic function of volunteers can have several effects upon prisoners. First, volunteers may bring prisoners 'back to life with their presence, awakening hope' (Ottoboni 2003: 123).

This reminds us of the corollary that volunteers' arrival and subsequent withdrawal, for whatever reason, can lead to feelings of abandonment. Continuity in volunteer relationships is thus important (cf. Chapter 2). Second, the godparents' role as 'supportive parents' can help prisoners to restore relationships with their families of origin.

Volunteers can also uniquely embody and communicate pro-social values. They can do this first by embodying a Christian message. For Ottoboni (2003: 111) one of the prime functions of volunteers is that they should communicate APAC's 'core principle', which is 'God [as] the source of everything'. Without this communication, APAC volunteers are merely people with an 'atypical task' (*ibid.*). Second, volunteers can embody a 'spirit of gratuity'. This is central to the APAC approach in which much is freely provided by the volunteers, while the local authority provides only the basic amenities of food, water, electricity and the prison building (Lee 1995). Ottoboni (2000: 122) states: 'In the APAC Method, love has to be free, constant and unconditional.' Because 'the value of free work is beyond measure', remuneration is restricted exclusively to those in certain administrative positions. Paying volunteers damages sincerity and spells 'death' to the project (*ibid.*). This is because payment replaces donation and free service with material interest: 'The convicted person, who is very sensitive, quickly realizes when the person who comes to help him with love holds out his hand without any ulterior motive' (*ibid.*). If this is correct, it implies that the main restriction upon the development and expansion of APAC-type prison units lies in the ability to recruit and retain volunteers who are willing to serve with this 'spirit of gratuity'. Such reliance upon volunteers does not prevent official help from being received, provided that the destination of such resources does not distort APAC's basic objectives.

APAC claims the embodiment of a 'Christian message' and 'spirit of gratuity' have several effects upon APAC prisoners. First, Ottoboni explains that the dialogue and exchange of ideas provided by volunteers promotes prisoner self-awareness. Second, he says volunteers awaken 'spiritual needs' among prisoners who would otherwise feel 'they have more pressing needs than the need of God' (2003: 60). Third, he claims the experience of the volunteer's giving opens the door to real friendship and gratitude, inspiring prisoners to give in return.

New volunteers are recruited from Christian communities, local businesses and industry by existing volunteers via a permanent programme. Volunteer recruitment therefore comes from those who themselves embody the volunteer spirit. Ottoboni sees weaknesses in relying upon paid staff to recruit volunteers ('do as I do, not as I say'). The high value attached to volunteers is reflected in their recruitment and training. 'Exemplary' (*ibid.*: 70) spirituality is the standard expected of APAC volunteers, of whom there were around 75 in Humaitá (Lee 1995). Ottoboni's most recent book, *Transforming Criminals,* sets out four pages of desirable characteristics of APAC volunteers and 11 pages of guidance for their behaviour (Ottoboni 2003a). This reflects the depth of training given: potential volunteers attend a five-month training course which consists of 42 units covering typical prison issues. Ottoboni reasons that since volunteering involves 'contact with people who have multiple problems it is not possible or admissible to allow improvized volunteers' (*ibid*.: 70). This supposedly minimizes the twin dangers of paternalism and amateurism. Volunteers are also required to confront any selfish reasons they may have for participating (e.g. meeting psychological needs) (Van Ness 2003).

Ottoboni maintains that forging affective and effective bonds is impossible simply through visits made during weekends. APAC volunteers are expected to invest a great deal of time to establish a 'permanent presence' (Ottoboni 2003: 111) in the prison. There is thus a connection between the desire for unpaid volunteers and full control of the prison: 'if someone other than volunteers has control of the prison in part or in whole, the prisoners' environments are shaped by those who are present for reasons other than love of the prisoner' (Van Ness 2003). Such persons are thought to 'contaminate' the community (Walker 1999). Van Ness (2003) rightly regards APAC's twin desires for institutional control and unpaid staff as the main barriers to replicating the programme, a theme to which we will return in later chapters. Not only does this present challenges in a Western context, as might be expected, it is a problem in some developing countries as well, as the experience of the APACs in Latin America indicate (at least with regard to operational control) (Van Ness 2003).

Another group of rehabilitative agents is APAC prisoners themselves. Veronese (undated) highlights the significance of peer prisoner support as follows:

> [The] vital point in the system is to awaken in the convict the wish
> to be of service, to be useful, to be the guardian angel of his brother,
> by training his sensibility to perceive the needs and wishes of the
> other and looking for the best way of helping him.

This breaks the 'honour code' (Ottoboni 2003: 53) that usually exists in prisons wherein the strong subdue the weak. It also develops a feeling of solidarity among prisoners and teaches them to live in a community (Ottoboni 2000).

In addition, peer prisoners (whether or not they have 'rehabilitated') have a unique value; at times their experience is what counts most. Ottoboni (*ibid.*) claims that the prisoner who began a sentence two months ago is nearly always worth more than that of a volunteer who has served for many years. This observation does not detract from the value of volunteers to APAC but simply recognizes that volunteers and peer prisoners offer different kinds of strength. It raises the recurring issue of how current and ex-prisoners should be involved in delivering the objectives of faith-based communities.

7. Conclusions

What main conclusions can be drawn from this descriptive account of APAC and Humaitá? We would suggest the following:

- APAC took opportunities as they came along (e.g. the semi-open and open regimes) and expanded slowly, with periods of consolidation.

- APAC operated within the context of a supportive statutory framework (e.g. local prisons, work experience, community involvement and godparenting). APAC worked 'with the grain'.

- APAC benefited from a certain degree of indulgence from sympathizers in authority. Its mistakes were not fatal. APAC costs nothing, and no alternative existed. This more than anything else allowed it to survive.

- Despite these benefits, it was difficult for APAC to earn and keep the trust of host establishments and of penal, judicial and political authorities. It was vulnerable to changes of personnel, 'prison politics' and popular punitiveness, as its present deactivation demonstrates.

- Opposition focused upon its generally liberal character rather than its Christian (and Catholic) identity.

- Particular care is taken over informed consent and to developing a transparent regime in which programmes and organizational structures are closely geared to highly-structured and progressive goals.

- APAC intentionally recruits those who are best placed to succeed on the grounds of their personal motivation and degree of external support and has the benefit of a highly-committed and trained team of volunteers.

- There is a need for realism about what can be achieved even with volunteer strength and full autonomy. The three-year recidivism rate for Humaitá runs at 16 per cent at least. Veronese has remarked that 'If you don't want help, not even God can help' (Lee 1993). Even in APAC, there are limits to the role of religion in rehabilitation.

Notes

1 We are grateful to Penelope Lee who generously gave us access to a rich source of materials from Humaitá Prison during the course of her film documentary project, subsequently published as *Love Is Not a Luxury* (1995). We are also grateful to Luisa Covill for her skill in translating this material from Brazilian Portuguese into English.
2 Reconviction findings for Humaitá are discussed separately in Chapter 10.
3 The particular 'Fourth Day' programme offered by Humaitá is a three-day *Jornada* ('Journey to Christ Workshop', also described as a 'Deliverance through Christ Workshop'). This differs from a regular Cursillo weekend by focusing particularly on the story of the Prodigal Son found in *The Gospel According to Luke*, Chapter 15 Van Ness 2003.
4 The Cursillo model is single-sex weekends (men only until about 1955) and is for Roman Catholics only. Cursillo was gifted to the Episcopal Church in the US who formed the Episcopal Cursillo model. Episcopalians in the diocese of Hudson Valley, New York, wanted an ecumenical version and acquired permission to change the name to *Tres Dias*. Episcopal Cursillo then gifted it to England. Anglican Cursillo is a mixed gender weekend, open to Anglican Church members only. Cursillo was also gifted to the Lutheran Church, who formed Lutheran Cursillo. Their model is single sex weekends for Lutheran church members only. An ecumenical Lutheran version exists called *Dia de Christo*. Cursillo was also gifted to the Methodist Church, who formed Methodist Cursillo, open to Methodist church members and others. An ecumenical Methodist version exists called *Walk to Emmaus*.
5 A repeat experience of Cursillo is unusual. In the Cursillo-derived Kairos Weekend devised for prisoners (see Chapter 2), participating prisoners must not previously have experienced a Kairos Weekend (KPM 1998b).
6 Compulsory participation in a 'short course' in Christianity would be controversial for faith-based units in England; see Chapters 5 and 7.
7 The 'Ten Commandments' of APAC are as follows: '(1) Love as a way of life (2) Dialogue with understanding (3) Discipline with love (4) Work as an essential (5) Brotherhood (fraternity) and respect as goals (6) Responsibility for (one's own) rehabilitation (7) Humility and patience to overcome (8) Understanding to illumine reason (9) The family organized as a support and (10) God as the fount of all'; (Creighton 1993).
8 The question of whether religious programming in a faith-based unit should be compulsory or voluntary, particularly when issues of conscience and sentence planning are involved, is a recurring theme in this book.
9 This differs from a 'privatized' prison because APAC is a non-profit organization.

10 Within APAC itself, the men are referred to not as 'prisoners' but as 'rehabilitees' (*recuperandos*).

11 Occupancy levels (based on official capacity) in Brazilian prisons as a whole is 182.7 per cent (June 2004) (www.kcl.ac.uk/depsta/rel/icps/worldbrief/south_america.html; accessed 5 April 2005).

12 Closed at the time of writing (Van Ness 2003).

13 Violence and poor conditions are rife in Brazilian prisons. In 1991, 31 prisoners died from fire when guards threw a bomb into the Água Santa Prison in Rio after the discovery of an escape plan. In 1989, 18 prisoners died in a cell in São Paulo after 51 of them had been locked in a cell without ventilation (APAC 1993d).

14 In 1992 (roughly contemporaneously with the compilation of these incentives), 124,000 prisoners were in Brazilian prisons built to house a maximum of 51,638 people (APAC 1993d: 14).

15 We placed this in the first category because it is not simply a statement of APAC's selection criteria (as we saw above, APAC is not open to 'all'). The key phrase is 'regardless of type of offence' and reflects the principle that, in APAC, prisoners are not stigmatized according to their offence. Ottoboni claims that the only difference he recognizes between prisoners is 'size and the colour of their hair, or their eyes' (Lee 1995).

16 The second category ('Better treatment') could be subsumed under the first ('Escaping the prison jungle'). However we maintained a distinction on the ground that there is a difference between escaping *from* something (usually negative) *to* something else (usually positive).

17 In 1991 (roughly contemporaneously with these incentives), Anderson (1991b) estimated that as many as half of all Brazilian prisoners had AIDS.

18 This is placed in the 'better treatment' category since access is usually to resolve perceived grievances and is thus potentially related to improved treatment. Ottoboni will see any prisoner with a written request once a week and more if necessary (Lee 1995).

19 The Kairos-APAC project that began in England claimed to implement 'the APAC model' but in fact it only implemented elements from *one* phase of the five-phase regime (Phase 2 the closed section).

20 An estimated 70 per cent of Brazil's prison population is at best semi-literate (Lee 1995).

21 A difficulty for 'quasi-APAC' projects in the UK, for example (see Chapters 4–6).

Chapter 2

From Cursillo to Prison: the story of Kairos

Kairos is the most dominant and dynamic presence in this institution. It pervades the prison environment and affects almost everyone. In short, it is the central core of the ethical, moral and spiritual development within the institution. There have been many men here whose attitudes and behaviour were very destructive. They felt that they were rejected by society and nobody cared about them. I have seen them come to Kairos, and by the third day were openly crying like babies, their hearts melted by the acceptance and love they received from the Kairos team and from a loving, forgiving God. I have observed this over and over again, year after year.

(Eldon Cornett, Chaplaincy Supervisor at Union Correctional Institution, Raiford, Florida, 1977–1999)

Introduction

When HMP The Verne in Dorset, England became the first prison in the Western world to offer a Christian-based unit, it claimed not only to be the first prison to implement an 'APAC'[1] approach outside South America but also the first to introduce a prison ministry called 'Kairos'.[2] Kairos is a ministry to the incarcerated and their families that began in the United States (US) in 1976 (see www.kairosprisonministry.org). Its stated mission is:

This chapter was authored by Jonathan Burnside

34

To bring Christ's love and forgiveness to all incarcerated individuals, their families and those who work with them, and to assist in the transition of becoming a productive citizen.

(KPM Summer Conference 2003)

Kairos is currently active in 33 states and 270 prisons in the US as well as in five other countries (Australia, Canada, Costa Rica, South Africa and the United Kingdom). In 2003, Kairos Prison Ministries (KPM) presented a total of 618 weekend programmes (502 Kairos Weekends,[6] 80 Kairos Outside weekends[7] and 36 Kairos Torch weekends[8]) through a total of 309 ministry sites. In 2003 Kairos volunteers donated an estimated 3,500,000–3,800,000 hours to various Departments of Corrections in the US and abroad. From its inception to 2003, it is estimated that licensed Kairos districts have run well over 5,000 'short courses' in Christianity called 'Kairos Weekends' involving roughly 170,000 male and female prisoners (Thompson 2004). The current rate exceeds 25,000 prisoners per year. As of 2003, KPM is supported by between 20,000 and 25,000 volunteers (KPM Board 2003). Kairos operates wholly under the authority of the Chaplaincy in the host prison and without charge to the prison establishment.[9]

It was for this reason that the four Christian-based units that initially ran in England between 1997 and 1999 were called Kairos-APAC units. Chapters 3–6 explore and evaluate the operation of these units (later called 'Kainos Communities'). Having considered the origins of one aspect of the Kairos-APAC hybrid in Chapter 1 (APAC), we must now turn to consider the history and character of the other aspect, namely, Kairos.[3]

There are several other important reasons for considering Kairos in this book. The first is that, even though Kairos is not in itself a faith-based unit, its stated purpose is to build strong Christian communities inside prisons that will positively affect the prison environment and so benefit the whole population (Kairos UK 1997). At the level of 'building Christian communities in prison', therefore, Kairos has much in common with the goals of faith-based units. It is for exactly this reason that Kairos has been a vital part of the units discussed in this book, including Kairos-APAC (Chapter 3),[4] Kainos Community (Chapters 4–6), Horizon Communities (Chapter 7) and InnerChange Freedom Initiative (Chapter 8). This is despite the fact that in the vast majority of cases, Kairos is presented as a stand-alone ministry in prisons that have no faith-based units. But although Kairos can be understood apart from faith-based units, many of the faith-based units in this book depend upon Kairos for an understanding of their operation. For example, the Kairos Weekend was the most overtly Christian aspect of the Kairos-APAC units and was thus a primary focus for comment (see Chapters 3–6). Evaluating these units means understanding Kairos. This is all the more necessary given that Kairos was not properly understood by many when it was introduced to the UK.[5]

A further reason is the need to distinguish between the different organizations referred to in this book, many of which sound alike. Kairos is a standalone prison ministry that has operated around the world for nearly 30 years; Kairos-APAC was a short-lived group of Christian-based units that operated between 1997 and 1999 in England. Yet they are (and were) easily confused. This confusion was compounded when following the collapse of Kairos-APAC in 1999, the successor organization – heedless of the advantage to be gained from a name that did not start with the letters 'Kai-' – rather perversely chose to call itself 'Kainos'. Appreciating that 'Kairos' is entirely different to 'Kainos' is important.

A final justification for exploring Kairos is because the Kairos Weekend drew the single most positive results of the entire Kainos evaluation (see Chapter 4). Any custodial intervention that achieves so positive a result deserves further investigation, particularly to see what can be learned in terms of its structure, goals and potential engines for change.

This chapter draws on original KPM source materials and on personal correspondence dating to the beginning of Kairos's involvement with the Prison Service England and Wales. It draws on material provided by past Chairs of Kairos UK between 1997 and 2002 and on an interview conducted with Ike Griffin, Executive Director of KPM (1990–2001) (Griffin 2003). Griffin's perspective is particularly valuable because he was closely involved with the introduction of Kairos to the UK and held personal meetings with the Governor of The Verne and with senior Prison Service management.

1. From Cursillo to Kairos

Kairos is an adaptation of the 'short course' in Christianity (Cursillo) as used in APAC (see Chapter 1) but applied to a Western prison context. APAC runs Cursillo in Latin American prisons without the need for adaptation. This is because Cursillo was originally a Catholic programme and until 1985, nearly all (98 per cent) APAC prisoners were Catholic. Even as late as 2003, 80 per cent of APAC prisoners were Catholic (Ottoboni 2003: 18). APAC and Cursillo enjoy a shared social, cultural and denominational background. However when Tom Johnson, a Catholic layman from Miami, led a team of men into Union Correctional Institution

(UCI) in Raiford, Florida, for a three-day Cursillo[10] in Christianity in 1976, he found that running Cursillo in Western prisons without adaptation tended to create rather than resolve problems (Caldwell 2000). Some of the titles of the Cursillo talks were unsatisfactory in a custodial setting: '"Total security", for instance, was not a happy choice for men who were already in a maximum-security prison' (*ibid.*: 173). In addition, US prisoners were frequently 'unchurched' (i.e. with no church background or experience), and those who were professing Christians tended to come from a wide range of denominations. In an attempt to overcome these problems, Johnson and his team began to adapt Cursillo to appeal to those with little Christian awareness and to make it interdenominational (KPM 1996b). Armed with a new version of Cursillo, the group changed its name in 1979 from 'Cursillo in Prison' to 'Kairos', the Greek word for 'opportunity'.[11] Unlike Cursillo, Kairos was a three-day short course in Christianity designed specifically for male and female prisoners in maximum-security prisons.[12]

Although Kairos retains much of the template of the original Cursillo there are a number of differences between Cursillo and Kairos. Cursillo is designed for Christians coming from normal parish life and assumes a certain level of religious education (e.g. knowledge of the Lord's Prayer). Kairos, by contrast, is designed for prisoners who are mostly not church members and indeed may be actively hostile to the church. It also takes account of prisoners' general lack of religious knowledge and excludes, for example, a talk on church 'Sacraments' which in Cursillo is the longest of all. Kairos eliminates a number of other talks presented in Cursillo. For example, a talk entitled 'Obstacles to Grace' or 'Sin' was eliminated because 'we felt that it was rather presumptuous for a group from the active church to go into prison and try to tell them about sin' (Griffin 2003). Kairos also places more emphasis on forgiveness than is found in Cursillo (see Caldwell 2000). The original Cursillo movement recognizes Kairos,[13] and Bonnin attended the 20th anniversary of Kairos in 1996. The upshot is that Kairos now has over 25 years' experience of Fourth Day programmes in prison and is based on a further 30 years of Cursillo experience in Catholic and Protestant churches around the world.

Kairos's roots in the Cursillo renewal movement means that its approach is somewhat different to typical Christian interventions in prison, especially stereotypical 'evangelistic preaching'. Griffin (*ibid.*) characterizes Kairos as an exercise in Christian 'nurture' as opposed to Christian 'proclamation':

> I'm thinking of those who come in to preach and teach and condemn and tell [prisoners] what they need to do in their lives

and perhaps lead them through the 'four steps to salvation' and then disappear and then never return again, hoping that since the inmate has accepted [Jesus] Christ in his or her life that suddenly, magically, everything will be all right. And I'll never forget a chaplain at Darrington Unit in Texas back in the early [19]80s that told our Kairos group that he was really unhappy with many of the ministries that wanted to come in. The reason he had accepted Kairos as a ministry in his prison was that we were a nurturing ministry. He said: 'You won't believe the damage that's done by people of good faith and good heart who come in evangelically with only one goal in mind.' He said: 'They come in, they love them and leave', and he said, 'that's called fornication' and it is simply not helpful to anyone. It makes the person who's engaging in it feel very good, because they have come into prison, they have answered Christ's call in their lives to do something to proclaim the gospel and yet they hurt an individual in doing so because they have sown hope and then there is no help. That is alien to nurturing.

Two parallels with APAC arise directly from this passage. First, Griffin's distinction between 'proclamation' and 'nurture' parallels Ottoboni's following claim:

> [The prisoner] has to feel at a certain moment that God is missing in his life. This is different from the volunteer appearing at the prison with a Bible under his arm or preaching a sermon ... If the volunteer ... begins to reveal a God who is sometimes a bore and a tyrant, or else a God offering easy, immediate or alienating solutions, then he will accomplish nothing positive.
>
> (2000: 115)

Likewise Ottoboni echoes Griffin's warning of the dangers of 'spiritual fornication'. Having observed that volunteers awaken hope in prisoners, Ottoboni continues:

> This is the reason why it is unfair to start an apostolic work with the imprisoned to then abandon them when difficulties appear. If before they were hopeless, they would now feel even worse, having been abandoned by those who said they were the testimony of Jesus Christ.
>
> (2003: 123)

Kairos sees itself as distinct from Prison Fellowship[14] and Prison Alpha[15], which are among the most prominent forms of Christian prison ministry in the UK and US. Kairos differs from Prison Fellowship because, whereas Prison Fellowship normally works with the extant Christian community in prison and their families, Kairos seeks leaders in the prison whether Christian or otherwise (Griffin 1996b). Kairos is different from Prison Alpha in that: 'Alpha … is more evangelical than is Kairos … [Kairos is] designed to nurture and evangelism happens almost by accident rather than by intention' (Griffin 2003). Interestingly, despite being less 'evangelical' than perhaps other Christian prison ministries, Kairos UK was the target of allegations of 'proselytizing' whereas Prison Alpha was presented in the UK press as 'tea and doughnuts' (Bonthrone 2000). Much of the reason for this difference in perception was due to widespread ignorance about Kairos which, we shall note in Section 4(c) below, bans proselytizing.

2. Who Kairos is for

The goal of KPM is to build strong Christian communities in establishments where the prisoner population is sufficiently stable for those communities positively to affect the prison environment. Put in these terms, Kairos is the reverse of APAC. APAC aims to change the prisoner by changing the environment whereas Kairos aims to change the environment by changing the prisoner.

(a) Prisons with stable populations

Kairos is designed for stable (i.e. non-transient) prison populations. This is because it is harder to build strong communities in a transient population and harder for that community to affect the prison environment positively. The ideal setting for Kairos is where it began, that is, in a maximum-security prison. Kairos began at Union Correctional Institution in Raiford, Florida, a maximum-security prison and the only prison in Florida that cannot refuse to admit a prisoner on the grounds of their extreme behaviour. Kairos may also take place in a medium-security prison, but the Kairos Board of Directors must grant special permission for Kairos to go into a minimum-security prison.

Despite this, KPM has experienced widespread demand for the programme even from 'short-term lockups'. Griffin (2003) comments that:

It is paradoxical that the Department of Corrections is almost anxious to have Kairos in a minimum-security prison which is pre-release in order to maybe socialize the inmates and get them used to being with free-world people before their release. But Kairos really does not work well in that setting.

In England, Kairos supported the Kairos-APAC units. This meant that Kairos never operated in the maximum-security prisons in England for which it was designed.[16] The transient populations of two prisons in particular worked against the goals of Kairos. Some prisoners took part in Kairos Weekends with very little time remaining on their sentence and with little possibility of impacting the prison environment.[17]

Between 1999 and 2002 a number of prisons expressed an interest in holding a Kairos Weekend (Kairos UK 1999; Kairos UK 2000a; Kairos UK 2001). Three of these (HMPs Preston, Rochester and Stocken) are either Category C or male local establishments whilst a fourth, HMP Leyhill is a Category D open prison. Only HMP Hull, a Category B establishment, approximated the type of conditions for which Kairos was designed. In 2002 Kairos UK rebranded itself as 'Choices', but no mention was made anywhere in the documentation of the Kairos preference for higher security establishments (Choices UK undated). This again suggests a lack of understanding in England of the types of conditions in which Kairos is designed to function best.

(b) Longer-term prisoners

Consistent with the preference for maximum-security prisons, Kairos is said to work best among longer-term prisoners. Griffin (2003) characterizes Kairos as a 'mid-stream' experience:

> We want ideally to encounter an inmate who has been incarcerated already for a period of time so that they have come to grips with the fact that they are really not in control of their lives. And yet we want to have them experience Kairos well before their release. Quite often it takes a minimum of six months to a year to really realise what they have experienced on a Kairos Weekend – the power, the love that has been poured on them – and to see what effect that has on the others in their community and realize that it has happened to them also. It takes sometimes years for that to happen. It takes a minimum of six months to a year. But sometimes it takes much longer than that for them to ponder what happens there and to realize that 'No it wasn't a dream. It was reality and I experienced it and I felt this way.'

In England the fact that most Kairos participants came from Category C prisons tended to mean that Kairos Weekends did not attract as many longer-term prisoners as would normally be the case.

(c) 'Positive' and 'negative' leaders

The original committee that devised the Kairos programme was convinced that the only way they could effect lasting change on the prison environment was by targeting the Kairos Weekend on prisoners who 'controlled the "turf"' because 'leaders change environments and followers follow where they lead' (Caldwell 2000: 173). That meant targeting 'positive *and* negative leaders, those who dealt drugs in the institution, who ran extortion gangs, who ran rape gangs, or who exercised control of their turf through other means' (*ibid.*). This 'leader selection' policy was formally instituted in 1990. The first Weekend to which the new policy was applied resulted in 42 prisoners who were thought to be so antisocial that the Warden of the prison requested the presence of a SWAT team in the community room (*ibid.*). Griffin (2003) noted that the leaders recruited onto Kairos Weekends 'are quite often negative leaders, they are the destructive people and we want to give the Holy Spirit a chance to work in their lives. [We want] to put them in a setting where they have to be or are left to be quiet and receptive and see what happens.'

Kairos recommends that the Chaplain of the institution identifies six or eight prisoner groups or areas within the institution that have the greatest impact on the largest percentage of the prison population. Under the terms of the Institutional Agreement between KPM and the prison, the Chaplain should make this choice with the help of the whole institution. Good practice is for security staff to make recommendations from which the Chaplain makes the final selection. Only a few participants should be drawn from the Chapel because this is only one environment from which leaders are selected. The idea is to reach prisoners the Chaplaincy does not normally access (KPM 1998b).

The Kairos Weekend is presented to 'leaders' as 'a very positive leadership-building community experience, presented and taught from a distinctly Christian perspective' (*ibid.*: 21). There is nothing deceptive about this presentation. However, it is thought that styling the Weekend as a 'leadership development' seminar makes it attractive to the target group who 'will not want to let others gain a perceived advantage' (*ibid.*: 23). Kairos does not require that participants should be Christian or even Christian-sympathetic. Kairos participants sign a specific consent form that states *inter alia*: 'You do not have to be Christian to attend. There will be much to gain from the programme even if you are not and do not intend to be Christian' (*ibid.*: 21). An Anglicized version of this form was used by Kairos UK. The formal requirements are 'basic faith [i.e. belief in God], openness and a seeking attitude on the part of the participant' (KPM 1998a: 3–3).

In England the Kairos recruiting strategy was compromised by the fact that prisoners could only take part in a Kairos Weekend if they first joined the Christian-based unit. This was an unusual dynamic that had no precedent in the history of KPM. The strategy inevitably excluded negative leaders who might have been willing to take part in a challenging 'leadership-building experience' but who were not interested in becoming part of a Christian unit. It also meant that recruitment was primarily in the hands of the Programme Manager of the unit, which is not normal Kairos policy.

Two points arise directly from this observation. First, given that the only people who could take part in Kairos were those interested in living in a Christian residential community, one would expect Kairos Weekends in the UK to contain a larger proportion of Christians or Christian-sympathetic prisoners than would normally be the case. Our research supported this: prisoners who took part in UK Christian units scored higher on religiosity than those who did not, even before they took part in the Kairos Weekend (see Chapter 9). Second, given the fact that the requirements for living on a Christian unit are different and more rigorous than the requirements for taking part in a Kairos Weekend, one would also expect those selected for Kairos in the UK to be more compliant than 'negative leaders'. Again, our research supported this: the reconviction analysis shows that the Christian units in England had a lower predicted risk of reoffending than the average prisoner population (see Chapter 10). The conclusion is inescapable: in England, Kairos was used for a different purpose than that for which it was originally intended.

This brings us back to another recurring theme, namely whether Christian interventions in prison, in this case the Kairos Weekend, should be voluntary or compulsory. In England (see Chapters 4–6) and initially on Horizon (at Tomoka; see Chapter 7), the Kairos Weekend was compulsory for all those on the unit. This contrasts with the normal practice, which is for attendance at a Kairos Weekend to be strictly voluntary, and created problems. Not all prisoners who wanted to belong to the unit wanted to take part in a Kairos Weekend. US Kairos veteran Jo Chapman, who was an adviser on the first women's Kairos Weekend in the UK at Highpoint North, recalls:

Frankly, I think they just didn't want to be there, and the only reason they were there was because this was part of the expectation to be on this therapeutic unit – was that they *had* to attend Kairos. So they were doing it as something that they needed to do, but most of them didn't, I felt, at least initially, weren't participating so they were not getting the benefit of the experience.

(Chapman 2003)

Their resentment at being made to do so (see Chapters 5 and 7) was even more understandable given that Christianity was generally 'soft-pedalled' on the unit itself, whereas the Kairos Weekend was an explicitly Christian event.

3. Goals and programming

As we have seen, the goal of KPM is to build strong Christian communities in prisons that will positively affect the prison environment. This section explores the mechanisms by which this is thought to happen. There are two main elements to the Kairos programme: the Introductory 'Short Course' in Christianity (known simply as the 'Kairos Weekend') and the Kairos Continuing Ministry programme (a structured follow-up to the Kairos Weekend).

(a) 'Kairos Weekend'

Kairos believes that the most effective way to break through what it sees as 'the almost impenetrable resistance to Christian community in prison' (KPM 1998a: 3–1) is through an intensive 'Short Course' in Christianity or Kairos Weekend. It is consistent with Ottoboni's claim that one of the most potent ways of stimulating growth and change in the prisoner is by means of a Cursillo (or 'short course') in prison (see Chapter 1). Kairos presents these teachings in an intensive three-day event that totals 40 programme hours.

All talks, meditations and events are presented in the sequence and manner specified by the Kairos *Weekend Manual* (KPM 1998b). This runs to 171 pages and covers every aspect of the Weekend. All Kairos districts must conform to the essentials specified in the authorized Kairos *Weekend Manual* to ensure integrity (KPM 1998a). Kairos internal discipline is quite rigorous. A Kairos ministry was rejected by one group of Kairos observers because the Kairos Weekend presented was inconsistent with the Manual (KPM 1997).

This discipline is said to be one of the secrets of Kairos's success. Prison administrators are supposed to know they can count on the programme being presented as directed in the manuals. Griffin (2003) comments:

We want to be able to give the prison authorities a schedule of the entire weekend some weeks before we even start and tell them that if they want to come into the room and check on what's going on we can tell them exactly what will be happening at any time during the three-day event. This gives the administration a great deal of comfort knowing that we are in control of what goes on in the room and we know what we are doing and we have a schedule and we stick to it. That perhaps has more to do with our public relations *vis à vis* the corrections institutions than [the] programme for the inmates but it speaks to the inmates also. They by and large have not been very strong on self-discipline and it speaks volumes to them to see a team of people entering the prison coming from various different denominations, getting along, loving one another, working together and being personally very disciplined in the approach.

Like APAC, the Kairos Weekend is the product of many years of slow development.

The Kairos *Organizational Manual* states that the prime characteristic of the Kairos Weekend is 'an experience of living in a Christian community which includes carefully developed activities and teachings designed toward a personal commitment to Christ, but a conversion experience is not the overt objective' (KPM 1998b: 3–3 and see 4(c) below). A stated Weekend 'essential' is that the volunteers should develop 'a safe Christian environment … as opposed to a coercive or manipulative environment' (KPM 1998a: 3–4). It is said that the easiest community to form in a prison is a negative community and that the most difficult community to form is an inclusive community. Kairos is said to be 'a rare inclusive environment' and that 'most residents will admit they have never seen a group like Kairos' (KPM 1994b).

By creating a 'safe' environment the Kairos Weekend aims to enable prisoners to be vulnerable. As Griffin (2003) explains:

[V]ulnerability is one of those things that is extremely delicate in prison. In the general [prison] population you dare not become vulnerable because the 'hawks' are looking for those that are vulnerable or weak or wounded or hurt and they will prey on them. So the rule of thumb in prisons is to never become vulnerable and never show anything other than your mask and a very stoic mask. The Kairos Weekend is designed to let them know that they have found a safe place. And vulnerability is modelled first by the team members who basically in each one of the talks steps up in front of the group and introduces himself or herself and says that 'I am a sinner' or 'I am a failure' or 'I am less than God created me to be' and becomes vulnerable and tells some of the specifics of why that is so. Then they continue to tell the 'grace' end of the story of how God came to them and helped to heal them and how that has worked out in their lives, how they are able to recognize that.

In recent years there have been three major changes to the Kairos Weekend. First, the Kairos Weekend now intentionally teaches 'listening skills' (KPM 1998b) and, second, includes an optional exercise called 'Lifelines' (*ibid.*) in which volunteers disclose their formative life experiences. Third, Kairos has added a meditation entitled 'The Wall' which 'very dramatically lets people see how their personal behaviours and human experience has led them to isolate themselves from others and how disastrous that has been in their social development and consequently their turn to crime' (Griffin 2003). These changes have been introduced 'to promote more and more sharing and vulnerability which allows for a transaction in love rather than a preaching mission or even a lecture or teaching mission' (*ibid.*). The continuing adaptation of the Cursillo format for prisons means that the latest version of Kairos, and the version applied in English prisons from 1998 onwards, departs further from Cursillo than any other Fourth Day programme. Some Kairos districts in the US have refused to implement these changes because 'the volunteers did not want to become *that* vulnerable' (*ibid.*; emphasis original). Similar concerns were expressed in England: Kairos UK minutes (1999) noted: 'Lifelines is thought to be a dangerous exercise'.

Chapters 3 and 5 consider perceptions of the Kairos Weekend in English prisons. However a former Assistant Chaplain-General makes a general assessment of the operation of Kairos Weekends from a Chaplaincy perspective:

> I served on a Kairos team at The Verne and was greatly impressed with the dedication and commitment of the volunteers, the bonding of people who had not previously known each other, the training given before the Weekend, the prayerfulness of the team, their ability to adjust to different scenarios at a moment's notice, their genuine positive approach – no negative comments, cynicism. It made heavy demands on them in time and finance, and they were happy to have it so. They were sensitive people working at the level of understanding of their hearers. *They did not try to pressurize prisoners.*

I attended most of the Weekends in my capacity as headquarters representative and very impressive they were too – some of the closing services were memorable. There was a lack of space, particularly at Swaleside, in which to deliver the programme … The majority of inmates would speak positively about the Weekend at the closing service. Not all of them were convinced of their need of Jesus as their Lord and Saviour, and they would freely admit that, but most of them were convinced that they needed to change for the better.

(Respondent A 2004; emphasis added)

In England, reports from the Lay Rectors of Kairos Weekends, Kairos National Observers and Minutes of Kairos UK District Council meetings show a high level of cooperation and support from prisons hosting Weekends. In many cases this assistance went beyond that assured in the Institutional Agreement between the prison and Kairos UK. One typical District Council Report claims that prison officers gave up 'valuable time off-duty to support us' and that 'the prison … could not do enough for us' (Kairos UK 1998a).

(b) Kairos Continuing Ministry (follow-up to the Kairos Weekend)

We saw that the three-day Cursillo programme is followed by the 'Fourth Day', meaning the rest of the participant's life. The purpose of the Cursillo weekend is to introduce participants to the experience of Cursillo 'reunion groups'. The expectation is that participants will continue to meet in these small groups and so continue to experience and deepen, in their 'Fourth Day', the fellowship discovered on their Cursillo weekend. For this reason all Cursillo literature clearly states that the Weekend is not an end in itself. It is simply a means of gaining the attention of people who live 'isolated and lonely lives' (Griffin 1996b) and bringing them into an ongoing reunion group 'where the real spiritual work can take place' (*ibid.*). As Griffin (2003) later puts it: 'the Weekend is not the important thing, it is the "share and prayer" group that takes place afterward in the Fourth Day. It is what a person does in their Fourth Day or for the rest of their lives that really matters.'

Kairos, as an adaptation of Cursillo, has exactly the same focus. The Kairos Weekend is not an end in itself but a means of establishing prisoners in 'reunion groups' or 'share and prayer' groups in the prison. The Kairos *Continuing Ministry Manual* states this explicitly: 'Kairos Weekends have but one purpose: the formation of resident leaders in correctional institutions into small share and prayer groups' (KPM 1995a: 1). Kairos literature stresses that the Weekend is *not* the Kairos Prison

Ministry but simply *an introduction* to that ministry (KPM 1998b). This is critical to the overall success of Kairos because they state that 'the Weekend will not produce a permanent effect without post-Weekend activity' (KPM 1998a: 3–3). That said, it is not easy to maintain the sense of community forged during the Weekend in the months that follow, as Griffin (2003) indicates:

> [The] leaders of Kairos have always based their success rate (if you can talk about that) on the number of people that are retained in the 'prayer and share' groups after the Kairos Weekend .... And they found [in 1990] that the retention rate in the 'prayer and share' groups was basically about 50 per cent for the first two or three months and probably 35 per cent to 40 per cent within a year after the weekend itself. That was a huge success as compared to the retention rate of people in 'prayer and share' groups in the free world, Cursillo or *Walk to Emmaus* or *Tres Dias* or whatever the [Fourth Day] experience might be. That particular retention rate at last count was 15 per cent to 17 per cent. So the prison retention rate was twice that of the free world retention rate. But still we saw it as a failure and so various means were examined to try to keep people into 'prayer and share' groups.

This included the changes already noted to the Kairos Weekend designed to promote sharing and vulnerability. The Kairos Continuing Ministry, or post-Weekend follow-up, consists of the Instructional Reunion, 'share and prayer' groups and monthly 'Kairos reunions'.

(i) Instructional Reunion
The Instructional Reunion is described as the 'bridge' between the Kairos Weekend where prisoners receive a broad vision of Christian community to life in a 'share and prayer' group. This is the prisoner's own small 'family' or nuclear Christian community. The Instructional Reunion is designed to be held one week after the Kairos Weekend, although not all who take part in the Kairos Weekend will choose to attend. The purpose of the Instructional Reunion is to affirm 'the very deep inherent need to be known, to be wanted, to be needed and to be loved' (KPM 1995a: 5) and to teach prisoners 'how to meet those needs for one another in the prison environment' (*ibid.*). The day is spent in a practical introduction to the experience of sharing in small groups. It is designed to teach small group dynamics and to encourage vulnerability, along with peer accountability and confidentiality. Several team members from the Kairos Weekend deliver the programme, which helps prisoners to recall and act upon what they learned from that event.

The UK prisons had some initial difficulty implementing the Instructional Reunion (Kairos UK 1998a), although by 2000 these were taking place at each of the four prisons (Kairos UK 2000a) with varying degrees of success.

(ii) 'Share and prayer' groups

'Share and prayer' groups are said to be the 'basic structure' of Kairos (KPM 1995a: 1). They meet for one hour once a week under the direction of the Chaplaincy (KPM 1998a). As Griffin (2003) explains, the idea is to enable prisoners to maintain the quality of relationships and depth of vulnerability experienced on the Weekend (KPM 1995a):

> What happens in a 'share and prayer' group is that, number one, people share their lives and you have a closed community of just a few people. We say three to five is the ideal number and the reason for that is we want people to get to know one another extremely well and to learn over a period of time that they can trust one another and become even more vulnerable and to let those other people know those areas of their lives that are lacking or hurting or wounded or whatever and then allow the rest of the 'share and prayer' group to minister to them … it takes a special strength to be able to become vulnerable to a group and allow them to minister to us. But this is in fact the goal of the 'share and prayer' groups.

The Kairos approach to 'share and prayer' is inspired by a verse in the New Testament which reads: 'confess your sins to one another, and pray for one another, that you may be healed' (James 5: 16). Participants say they are encouraged 'to open our lives to the nurture and support of our brothers and sisters in our Reunion Group in order that we might more completely love them and be loved by them' (KPM 1995a: 22). Each person is invited to speak specifically and honestly about each of the following areas as it relates to their behaviour in the previous week: the moment when the participant most recognized the presence of Christ or their need for Christ; something the participant learned or studied of a spiritual nature; an occasion when the participant helped someone to recognize God's love; and a time when it was difficult to show God's love (KPM 1995a). Participants are then invited to share more general 'joys and concerns' (*ibid.*: 22) that the group can pray about together. Griffin gives an account of this particular small group dynamic:

> The secret of Cursillo is that Jesus comes to us in the person of our reunion group, accepting our wounds, allowing us to heal. Without

this small group, without the Fourth Day, we go on our macho way, relying on ourselves, or the programme, or the system, or any blue-smoke illusion which does not require us to look inside ourselves.
(Griffin 1996b)

Participating in 'share and prayer' groups is a risky venture, particularly in a prison setting, because it 'admits a need for fellowship, for support' (KPM 1995a: 5) in an environment that does not recognize such needs or rather sees their expression as a sign of weakness. It is said that the 'share and prayer' group is 'not an adequate substitute for positive family experience, but it probably is the best and only substitute available to [prisoners]' (*ibid.*). By remodelling close relationships and intimacy in a supportive, but not a substitute manner, there are parallels between the Kairos 'reunion group' and the APAC 'godparents'.

(iii) Monthly reunions
The Kairos monthly reunion is a reunion of all the 'share and prayer' groups in the institution, along with volunteers from the most recent Kairos Weekend. All Kairos graduates are welcome. As part of their commitment to prison participants, each volunteer must take part in 12 'reunions' in the year following the Weekend. A reunion usually lasts between two to three hours, which team members describe as 'a time of continuing affirmation' for prisoners (KPM 1998b: 7). Its purpose is similar to the Kairos Weekend, that is, to provide a 'safe community' in which the individual groups can receive wider support and encouragement (KPM 1995a: 47). Monthly reunions follow the outline provided in the Kairos *Continuing Ministry Manual* (KPM 1998a).

(iv) Kairos 'Two-Day Retreat'
Approximately three months after each Kairos Weekend is the Kairos 'Two-Day Retreat' (*ibid.*). These are designed for all Kairos graduates. It provides some reinforcement of the Weekend, especially the experience of living in community (KPM 1995a). The purpose of the Retreat is to give them 'some intimate experience in the process of becoming vulnerable to another person' (*ibid.*: 59) and an opportunity for further study. The Retreat format is said to be a highly effective way of encouraging prisoners to form small groups following the Kairos Weekend (*ibid.*).[18]

In some ways the Retreat is said to be 'more important to the maturing process' (KPM 1998b: 28) of prisoners than the Kairos Weekend itself. This is because the Kairos Weekend theoretically opens a relationship with God, self and others whilst the Retreat nurtures them and takes those relationships deeper. The Horizon unit at Tomoka, Florida (see

Chapter 7) uses the two-day retreat, in a somewhat modified form, as a community-building event to launch the programme year.

(v) Kairos 'Journey'

The Kairos 'Journey' programme began in 1993 and is a 20-week extension of the Kairos Weekend (KPM 1995a). 'Journey' is a prison adaptation of a church programme called 'Disciples of Christ in Community'. 'Journey' was seen as a way of using 'free-world' people to help prisoners develop the habit of meeting in small 'share and prayer' groups. The heart of the programme is said to be the small group discussions which are the same 'table families' established on the Weekend. It is said that whereas 'the Weekend is an *experience* in Christian love, the Journey is an *experience* in ongoing Christian community living' (*ibid.*: 123, emphasis original) and a deeper exploration of the Christian faith. Griffin (1998) noted that 'the trust level [on the Journey programme] increases with stable groups, but remains rather superficial if the group dynamic changes.'

However, the Journey programme has not been popular in the US, where only about eight or ten prisons use it. The use of the 'Journey' programme may depend on the physical location of the prison. The Kairos *Weekend Manual* notes that 'most Kairos districts do not yet have the trained volunteers support pool to offer it in their institutions' (KPM 1998b: 28). In some states not enough volunteers live sufficiently close to the prison to be able to do the 'Journey' programme every week. That said, the volunteer strength required for the Journey is less than for a Kairos Weekend: only one volunteer is required for each small group. A prisoner trained as a co-facilitator can also carry the group if a volunteer is unable to attend.

4. Elements of Kairos

Key elements of Kairos include its volunteers, its ecumenicalism and its ban on proselytizing, all of which have been misconstrued.

(a) Volunteers

Lee (2004) claims that 'volunteers are the heartbeat of the programme'. KPM Executive Directors estimate that over the past 27 years, Kairos volunteers have filled 150,000 positions. In 2003, 15,000 persons served on Kairos teams and filled 20,000 volunteer positions (Thompson 2003). Each prison with an active Kairos programme requires between 30 and 60 volunteers and an average of 45 local church volunteers to ensure it runs smoothly.

When the UK press discovered that the Prison Service would grant access to KPM, the Assistant General Secretary of the National Association of Probation Officers (NAPO) predicted that 'bizarre and inexperienced volunteers' (Cohen 1996a: 13) would flood the jails (Hardy 1996). This section examines the recruitment, training and ethic of Kairos volunteers.

(i) Recruitment and selection

Kairos volunteers are screened for 'spiritual maturity' according to the following criteria. First, they must be well-founded in the Christian faith, active members of a mainline church (Kairos UK 1997) and recommended by the priest or minister of that church. Second, they must have taken part in an approved free-world Weekend run by an approved Fourth Day movement[19] and actively participate in a free-world 'share and prayer' group. The Executive Director of Kairos must approve any exceptions individually (KPM 1998a). This is partly because team members cannot expect prisoners to participate in something they do not engage with themselves. It also reflects the belief that Kairos is sacrificial and that it is necessary to 'recuperate' in a reunion group between periods of ministry (Kairos UK 1997).

These rather stringent requirements are the means by which Kairos seeks to screen out 'loose cannon' or 'lone ranger' volunteers (Griffin 1996b). Kairos has not always been completely successful in this regard (Bright Griffin 2003a), but as a further safeguard the Kairos Board sends an experienced volunteer observer to report on each Kairos Weekend. Volunteers who are thought to be unsatisfactory for whatever reason are suspended and their names added to a list of those who are not allowed to work on another team because of 'proven instability' (KPM 1998a: 7–3). It seems as though a volunteer 'blacklist' was never formally established in the case of Kairos UK. Kairos UK proposed this in 1999 (Kairos UK 1999) but the mechanics were still being discussed two years later (Kairos UK 2001). That said, certain volunteers were not used again. The *Organizational Manual* notes frankly that:

> Kairos volunteers minister to [i.e. serve] persons who are often unstable, who may be in bondage to drugs, incapable of establishing viable relationships, in rebellion to authority, incapable of following directions and who are sexually promiscuous. These same character failings should automatically disqualify a person from participation on a Kairos team. A Kairos team does not need someone actively suffering from the very character failings that have led those to whom we are ministering to be incarcerated. We do not want to

become the morality police, but we do want to avoid adding to the burden of those we minister to.

(KPM 1998a: 7–3)

It should be said at once that a difficult balance must be struck here between the need to exclude volunteers who are a threat to both prisoners and Kairos and the need, on the other hand, to involve volunteers who have experienced similar vulnerabilities, even though these vulnerabilities may not be very evident. Striking this balance means using, as far as possible, volunteers who have been 'healed enough' to give an honest account of the failures in their lives (*ibid*.: 8-2). As Griffin acknowledges:

> The best volunteers have suffered the same issues that the inmates have suffered; isolation, abuse, chemical dependencies, all sorts of things, isolation from the church, [and from] those that would normally nurture them. These make the best volunteers and yet … they must have healed enough to be able to go in and be helpful to the inmate. If they have not, [and] they're still bleeding from their wounds, they just bleed all over the inmates and don't help the inmates to recognize that healing can come. What you want is an example, a model, of someone who has been there, done that, and God has healed them, so it gives them hope that, yes, it can happen to me. (2003)

These requirements are not perhaps identical to the APAC standard of 'exemplary' spirituality, although Kairos volunteers are not required to assume the same degree of personal responsibility for prisoners as APAC 'godparents' and volunteers (see Chapter 1).

(ii) Volunteer training

Volunteers commit to 40 hours of community building in preparation for every Kairos Weekend. Eight obligatory team meetings take place, usually over a two-month period.[20] Griffin (2003) notes that without the 'inner work' required by team formation 'the ministry can become shallow, showy, mechanical and manipulative.' He explains:

> Kairos … is very intentional about developing a spirit … a bravery and becoming vulnerable. This is something that is not easy for any of us to do. We begin building our barriers early in life and so it's not easy for us to let people see who we really are, rather than our mask. The eight team meetings in Kairos are designed specifically to not only let the team members know how to behave inside a

prison but how to comfortably let someone see who they are. That is done of course so that the gospel message can be delivered with some authenticity.

(ibid.)

Volunteer team training also requires some institution-specific instruction regarding security. Volunteers are a double-edged sword for the institution because their strengths are also their weaknesses. The Governor of a Level 2 (medium-security) prison in Virginia commented: 'The same attribute that [Kairos] volunteers bring that is so valuable, [namely] being open and giving is the same thing that inmates can take advantage of' (KPM 2003, Panel of Wardens and Chaplains). Griffin agrees: 'The volunteer is not worth anything to the prisoners unless they are vulnerable and of course that same vulnerability makes them a security risk' (2003: 13). These remarks parallel Ottoboni's concern that religiously-inspired volunteers are open to abuse by manipulative prisoners (see Chapter 1). Griffin continues:

The volunteers really have to understand that they are going into an environment that is not their very familiar environment and they have to change their mindset just a bit so that they can maintain some arms-length stance between themselves and the inmates. And yet they are called upon to become vulnerable to the inmates and to share their lives with them and to be an inspiration and to love them. There's a fine line ... that's difficult to tread [but], yes, it can be done. The risks are always there but it is absolutely worth every risk.

(ibid.)

There was some disagreement among UK prison staff about how much volunteers should actually know about 'jailcraft'. Some felt that security training could in itself compromise security ('too much knowledge is a dangerous thing'; see Chapter 5). Kairos is a fragile ministry. The misbehaviour of a single volunteer could potentially result in serious damage to the entire ministry (KPM 1998a). Griffin (2003) recalls:

I was once in a prison in Ohio, at Lebanon Correctional. The Warden there was talking about the general quality of religious volunteers that come in. He said he had to be very careful about those that he allowed into the prisons because he said 'Sometimes I think I should have the officers throw a net over them and drag them out. They're sicker than the inmates that they come to serve'. But he went on to say that we [Kairos] could do anything in the prison that we would like to do .... He said 'From what I have seen so far your volunteers are so well trained and they do exactly what you say they will do, and *at this point* you can do anything in this prison you would like to do.' However that may change overnight if the volunteers fail to be reliable.

As with APAC, volunteers have to earn the respect and trust of host establishments. This takes time and is easily lost.

(iii) Volunteer ethic

Cohen (1996b: 18) was sceptical about the introduction of Kairos helpers, characterizing them as 'fervent volunteers who will work for nothing'. This observation correctly notes that Kairos costs nothing for the institution but ignores the considerable cost to the volunteers themselves:

> It's really critical that Kairos always remember the sacrificial aspects of ministry. Where we move into the life of another person sharing Christ and sharing Christ's *agape* [sacrificial] love to meet the needs of that other person without regard to what that cost is to us, it is always a sacrifice and must be a sacrifice and God honours sacrifice. When we begin doing it for any other reason, whether it be paid to do it or moving into that ministry because it feels good to us, or whatever other reason then we begin to lose track of what we are up to and the authenticity disappears
>
> (Griffin 2003).

This commitment to what Kairos describes as the 'authenticity of the volunteer ethic' is very close to APAC's requirement that volunteers embody a 'spirit of gratuity'. It reminds us that not all volunteers are qualified or willing to take part in Kairos. This has serious implications for recruitment and expansion. Neither the Kairos-APAC Trust nor the Prison Service always recognized this. In 1998, Griffin told the Director of Operations (South) that 'it should be evident to anyone that this programme cannot be called up at will' (*ibid.*). Griffin explained that 'even if a correctional facility is ready and willing, the community and the church represent the greater challenge. Kairos is a unique programme and it is presented by a very small fraction of those in the organized church' (*ibid.*). Kairos volunteers only come from Fourth Day communities, and only about 5 per cent of those participating in a Fourth Day movement ever become involved in Kairos (Griffin 1996b; KPM 1998a). Griffin

(1999b) warned: 'It is no easy task to find, qualify and train volunteers in these numbers, knowing their commitment will require more than 200 hours of unpaid service, unreimbursed travel and time away from profitable jobs'.

The UK was no exception, and in fact the position was exacerbated because the UK does not have as extensive a tradition of Cursillo and related programmes as the US.[21] This failure to count the cost in terms of volunteer resources was not exclusive to the Prison Service in England and Wales but is, according to Griffin, common to prisons generally that want the Kairos ministry quickly:

> Strange as it may seem, the greatest threat to Kairos is found in the prison systems we serve. Prisons ask for the ministry with no appreciation of the basic work that is required in and among the local faith communities to support the ministry. They only know that the programme works and they want it, [and] they want it *now*. The Kairos community, driven by desire to respond positively to the requests, have cut corners in the spiritual groundwork our manuals call for in preparation. In some instances, teams have been reduced in size. Team meetings have been reduced in number and run over a shorter period of time, all to the detriment of the ministry.
>
> (2003; emphasis original)

A similar story can be told in relation to Kairos in the UK.[22]

For Griffin, the key thing volunteers bring is extensive pastoral care:

> The Kairos method is to go beyond proclamation of [Jesus] Christ. Kairos volunteers model Christ's love in pastoral care on the Weekend and in the follow-up ministry. I suspect it is the experience of a labour-intensive modelling of Christ's love that makes the message resonate in the hearts of the incarcerated with a purer note than does proclamation alone. They have never experienced the Word in that way before.
>
> (KPM 1998f: 2)

It is not prisoners' *contact* with volunteers but the *character* of that contact which seems to be important. At the 2003 Kairos Conference, a prison Chaplain in a female establishment remarked that: 'Kairos is the best programme we've offered religious-wise. I don't know any other programme that offers the kind of one-on-one and nurturing' (Rossman 2003). At the same event the present Warden of Baskerville C.I., Virginia, when asked what difference Kairos made, cited 'a healing community that passes religious and racial lines' (Williams 2003). As with APAC (see Chapter 1) there is also a sense that volunteers are able to stimulate generativity. One US prison chaplain remarked that prisoners say: 'If they [the volunteers] are able to do that for me, then I'm enabled to do that for other people' (Rossman 2003).

(b) Ecumenical

When it was introduced to UK prisons, Kairos was depicted in the national broadsheets as a 'very right-wing' 'evangelical … religious sect' and as a 'charismatic group' of 'happy-clappies' (Cohen 1996b: 18; Hardy 1996: 11). This is wide of the mark because Kairos is an inter-denominational ecumenical ministry. All of its actions and teachings must be consistent with those of its five sponsoring denominations: Roman Catholic, Episcopalian, Lutheran, Methodist, and Presbyterian (KPM 1998d). The *Organizational Manual* states that a Kairos 'Essential' is that Kairos should 'practice only those things which the denominations have in common but respect those things which are different' (KPM 1998a: 3–2). Consequently, Kairos only presents 'very broad, mainstream theology and practices' (KPM 1994b: 3). Excluded are such practices as 'speaking in tongues', 'deliverances', healing services, Marian theology, 'altar calls',[23] baptisms and the Eucharist. In the US, Kairos is primarily presented by volunteers from the Catholic, Episcopal, Methodist and Lutheran churches (Griffin 1996b).

Interestingly, ecumenicalism is said to be crucial to the symbolic and communicative value of Kairos volunteers:

> The self-sacrifice of our own agendas during a Kairos [event] ensures the peaceful environment where Christ is most readily seen. By entering the prison as a fully united community in Christ, our ecumenisity [sic] is one of our strongest statements to the residents. Most of the religion found in prison is highly divisive. Kairos provides a counterpoint to the cliques and exclusivity found inside.
>
> (KPM 1994b)

The Bishops of the liturgical churches must sign an ecumenical agreement before Kairos can be introduced in a district (KPM 1998a). KPM's commitment to interdenominational ministry was recently reaffirmed in a policy statement that is issued to all participants of Kairos teams (KPM Executive Committee 2004). In the UK Kairos was presented by volunteers from dominant mainstream denominations and included

Anglican, Baptist, Catholic, Methodist, Salvation Army and community churches, although there was a general shortage of Catholic volunteers (Kairos UK 1998b, and Respondent A 2004, a former Assistant Chaplain-General).

(c) Ban on proselytizing

We have already noted that when Kairos was introduced to the UK, Lord Avebury characterized Kairos in the House of Lords as 'a proselytizing organization' (*Hansard* 13 January 1997, Col. WA11) that was in potential breach of s.10(5) of the Prisons Act 1952. The national press carried similar objections from concerned prison chaplains (Cohen 1996b). Even an apologist for Christianity in prisons, Jonathan Aitken, got it wrong claiming that *apart from* the Kairos Weekend 'all other meetings and courses scrupulously avoid religious proselytizing' (2001: 26).

The Kairos *Organizational Manual* lists as a Kairos 'essential' that 'the doctrinal position of each participant is respected' (KPM 1998a: 3–4). It also states that 'those who proselytize team or resident participants [i.e. prisoners] ... should be cautioned and, if they cannot control these inclinations, be separated from the ministry' (*ibid*.: 7–4). Griffin (2003) concedes:

> I would suppose that any Kairos volunteer who's coming from a Christian background and [indeed] all volunteers would experience joy in their heart if someone decided to accept Christ as their Saviour and become Christian. [But] they are specifically instructed to not proselytize on the Weekend. The fine line is that we tell each team member we want them to witness as to what God has meant to their lives and to let people know exactly how they believe. But we also tell them that we want them to make sure that each individual participant knows that however they believe is honoured also and we do not think any less of them if they don't agree with us. We want them to think about the issues of spirituality and religion and we want them to wrestle with their image of God, based on their experience which has brought them to this place [i.e. prison].

An illustration of the 'fine line' is the 'Commitment Service' that takes place on the third day. A loaf of bread is broken and distributed and participants are invited to take a piece as a symbol of 'a commitment, if we wish, of any part of our life and being to God' (KPM 1998b: 305–6). The Kairos UK District Observer's Report for one Weekend noted that on one occasion:

It was not announced that this was not a Eucharist or Communion. Rather it became a type of Communion Service without the cup. It became very evangelistic and hyped. They [the prisoners] were told that they could 'say yes' to Jesus. It was pushy …. It could be that a false sense of everyone becoming a Christian occurs after [the] 'Open Mike' [session, in which participants may address the whole group with an open microphone] … one guy stood up and asked the question: 'Am I here to become a Christian or to enable me to change?'.

(Kairos UK 2000b: 2)

This is a good example of the exception proving the rule. District reports and national observers enable Kairos to police itself. It is also worth noting that each leader on every single Weekend delivers a scripted opening talk from the Kairos Weekend Manual that includes the following paragraph:

Remember, no-one on this team will pressure you to make any kind of decision or commitment. God gave you free will. None of us will ever try to take that away from you. We'll try to answer your questions and share God with you and tell you about His great love. Your response is strictly between you and God. If any of us is making you feel uncomfortable, please speak to your sponsor about it. (KPM 1998b: 169)

It is thus abundantly clear that 'Kairos does not set out to proselytize' ('Constitution'; Kairos UK 1997).

5. Other Kairos programmes

This section briefly outlines two additional aspects of KPM, 'Kairos Outside' and 'Kairos Torch'. This is important because 'Kairos Outside' was implemented in the UK in 1998 and was a factor in determining overall levels of exposure to the 'Kainos' programme in the reconviction study (see Chapter 10). 'Kairos Torch' is important because, as we shall see, KPM recommended it for use in Highpoint North instead of the Kairos Weekend (see Chapter 3). This section draws on a recorded interview with Jo Chapman, Co-ordinator of Women and Youth Ministries in KPM and the founder of 'Kairos Outside' and 'Kairos Torch'.

(a) 'Kairos Outside'

Kairos Outside is a specially-adapted Cursillo-based Weekend for women who have a family member or a loved one in prison. This two-day retreat addresses the issues of having a loved one in prison and builds community among women who are impacted by the incarceration of family members and close friends. Kairos Outside began in Florida in 1993 (KPM 1994a) and has since spread to over 20 states in the US as well as to the UK and Australia (KPM Board 2003), with plans for South Africa and Canada. The only requirement for participants is to have an incarcerated loved one; 'it does not depend on their religion, faith or where they are on their spiritual journey' (KPM 1998a: 3–5). Most team members are former participants who thus have personal understanding of the issues. As with the Kairos Weekend, the intention is not to proselytize:

> It is not a weekend to make them Christian, it is not a weekend to expect anything of them. It is a weekend to tell them that there is a group of Christian women who care about the journey and the pain that they are experiencing.
>
> (Chapman 2003)

We saw that APAC had difficulty attracting prisoners' wives and loved ones to take part in a Fourth Day programme (see Chapter 1). It is thus very noticeable that Kairos Outside faces similar difficulties. Chapman suggests several reasons for this high attrition rate:

> On a Kairos Weekend, when you tell the men and women and youth inside that there's gonna be this Weekend and that there's gonna be food, there's a natural attraction to that! Because it's something different, it's something that they haven't had inside, it's something that they can do, and it's different from what they're doing inside. [With] Kairos Outside – when we call a person and we say: 'You're invited to a Weekend, and the ticket into the Weekend is that you have a loved one who is incarcerated', that has not been a popular ticket in their life, that has not been something that has drawn positive attention. So they're very suspicious, and they worry about us being a cult, they worry about us being … Christian women that will beat them up with the Bible. And so we have to many times just continue to have a lot of communication with these women prior to the Weekend. Still we lose, many times, up to 50 per cent. We can be expecting 40 women for a Weekend and actually only

20 are brave enough to get into their cars or to get into the car of a volunteer, and actually make it to the Weekend.

(ibid.)

Although it is the case that Kairos Outside is a ministry to the non-incarcerated and hence typically takes place outside the prison (hence the name), there have been a few cases of Kairos Outside events taking place *inside* the prison. This has certain advantages according to Chapman:

> Men and women inside have very little that they can give their families ... Kairos Outside can be a wonderful gift that someone can give from the inside to the outside. So when you bring these women inside the prison, they [the prisoners] can become the sponsors, they can become the active gift-givers from [the] inside ...

(ibid.)

It also provides unique and unusual opportunities for public affirmation and bridge-building. Chapman claims that:

> The most marvellous thing that I experienced at the Closing [ceremony] was that a mother is able to look at her son and publicly say to a crowd of people 'This is my son and I love him dearly.' They don't get to do that on the outside, they don't get to talk about their sons and *never* say that they're proud. And wives get to publicly acknowledge their husbands. And sisters. I mean that was the most incredible part for me: to be able to have the family members express love and that they were proud of their loved ones inside. And so I think that that builds the bridge, where they can build on a sense of pride, a sense of love, a sense of 'I notice that your life is changing and I want to be a part of that.' That builds the bridge and I think that heals families.

(ibid.; emphasis original)

(b) 'Kairos Torch'

Experience of the Kairos Weekend in the US has shown that younger prisoners, with perhaps less life experience, may find the programme more difficult than older prisoners. Kairos Torch was accordingly developed as a Kairos Weekend for prisoners aged between 18 and 25 years. As of 2003, there are 28 Kairos Torch ministries in the US, plus one in Australia (KPM Board 2003). This involves young offender institutions and adult prisons where the population includes under-25s.

Kairos Torch focuses upon 'masks'. At the outset blank, physical masks are distributed to prisoners along with art supplies. They are invited to decorate or paint their mask in a way that represents them. This encourages prisoners to examine who they are and what they want to project. Each talk refers to a mask and each speaker appears with a different mask. The programme is very different to Kairos in that it builds on a one-to-one relationship. Ideally one volunteer supports one resident for six months.

Kairos Torch is thought to be an extremely effective ministry (Griffin 2003) although one that presents particular challenges for adult volunteers. 'The experience envelope carried by team members differs so vastly from the experience package carried by the participants that communication is difficult at best. Our images of love, relationship, trust, faith, community, religion, family, authority, wealth, poverty, success and failure have no point of comparison in their experience' (KPM 1998e: 2). For this reason Torch requires even more screening, training and discipline among volunteers than adult Kairos Weekends. In particular, team preparation includes specific direction in projecting an 'adult' Christian image to young people, one that tries to be 'not formal or stodgy, but mature, reliable and loving' (KPM 1998c: 1). The team is mixed gender, and ideally the leaders should be husband and wife. Again, this approach recalls attempts by APAC godparents to resymbolize prisoners' parents in a positive way (see Chapter 1).

In the UK, Kairos Torch was recommended for use in Highpoint North because some of the women struggled with the Kairos Weekend on account of their relative youth and immaturity (Chapman 2003). In addition, Parc YOI expressed an interest in Torch (Kairos UK 2001), but to date no Torch programme has been implemented in the UK. Finding committed volunteers is again a limitation. Volunteers do not have to be members of the Fourth Day, but they still require training. Six months was also thought to be a long time for volunteers to commit to supporting a prisoner on a weekly basis (*ibid.*).

6. Impact

Kairos claims to be widely recognized as one of the most effective programmes available to make positive changes to basic attitudes of the incarcerated (KPM 1998c: 1). Many Kairos graduates return as Kairos volunteers upon release, with others pastoring churches, running re-entry programmes or counselling and mentoring ex-offenders (*ibid.*).

In March 1997, the Department of Corrections (DoC) published the results of reconviction studies conducted in 1995 on 505 Kairos participants who had attended Kairos over a ten year period and 11 Weekends (no. 23–33) at Union C.I. The rate of reoffence for the Kairos group was 15.7 per cent compared to 23.4 per cent for the non-Kairos control group – an overall reduction of 33 per cent compared to the control group. It was noted that if prisoners participated in the Kairos follow-up programme, as opposed to simply attending a Weekend prior to release, the rate of reoffence for the Kairos group was 10 per cent – an overall reduction of 57 per cent compared to the control group (KPM 1998f: 2).

With the exception of a small reconviction study conducted by the Florida Department of Corrections, which is evaluated in Chapter 10, there is little empirical research on Kairos. Accounts are largely anecdotal. Some of these emanate from senior prison management with significant experience of Kairos. Among the weightier qualitative assessments is that of the Chaplaincy Supervisor at Union Correctional Institution where Kairos began. The following observation is based on 20 years' experience of serving on the Chaplaincy staff of UCI:

> The impact that Kairos has had, and continues to have, on this institution is of inestimable value. Kairos is the most dominant and dynamic presence in this institution. It pervades the prison environment and affects almost everyone. In short, it is the central core of the ethical, moral and spiritual development within the institution. There have been many men here whose attitudes and behaviour were very destructive. They felt that they were rejected by society and nobody cared about them. I have seen them come to Kairos, and by the third day were openly crying like babies, their hearts melted by the acceptance and love they received from the Kairos team and from a loving, forgiving God. I have observed this over and over again, year after year, as the Kairos experience has brought about dramatic changes in the lives of inmates. This changed behaviour is of great value to the institution for it reduces confrontations, improves relationships, and makes the prison a safer place for inmates and staff.
>
> (Cornett 1996)

Christine Money, currently Warden of Marion Correctional Institution (MCI) in Marion, Ohio, provides a more recent account. Ten years ago, while Warden of the Ohio Reformatory for Women (ORW), a staff teacher told her about KPM. Several months later Money and her staff agreed to meet Kairos organizers and were impressed with the programme's organization. They were particularly impressed with the extensive training Kairos provided its volunteers (Money 2004). Money claims she 'witnessed dramatic changes in the women who participated in Kairos. I saw angry, bitter and depressed women find hope as a result of the unconditional Christian love shared with them by volunteers. The volunteers showed no judgement only acceptance' (*ibid.*). After five Kairos Weekends at ORW, Money was transferred to MCI in June 1996, a medium-security facility that houses 1,800 male offenders. One year later MCI began hosting Kairos Weekends. By May 2004 15 Weekends had been held. Money (*ibid.*) reports the following effects:

> An institution that formerly was plagued with inmate grievances, racial tension, and gang activity is now an institution with very few inmate grievances and a calm environment with close to 90 per cent of the inmates participating in some rehabilitative programme. There is a large variety of faith-based programmes. Kairos has been the base from which many other programmes have grown. It is in large part the reason that the culture of the institution has changed. I have seen men give up drug use and gang involvement to become positive leaders and mentors to younger offenders. The changes have been miraculous.

7. Conclusions

What main conclusions can be drawn from this descriptive account of Kairos? We would suggest the following:

- The goals of Kairos and the Christian-based unit in a prison intersect inasmuch as both are specifically interested in Christian community-building.

- Despite this intersection, the dynamics of Kairos and the Christian-based unit are different. Kairos draws people together throughout the prison for one weekend only and then scatters them in small prayer and share groups. The Christian-based unit works intensively on a particular wing over a long period of time.

- This means that whilst there may be some overlap of clientele, Kairos and the Christian-based units attract different groups of prisoners.

- The submission of Kairos to the goals of the UK Christian-based units meant that Kairos was never implemented as it was designed to be. It never went into a maximum-security prison, the prison populations were too mobile and 'negative leaders' were seldom targeted.

- Too much was made of the Kairos Weekend and too little of the follow-up programmes.

- Insufficient value was attached in the UK to the importance of volunteers and the importance of the spirit of gratuity.

- The work of Kairos was not properly understood in the UK. Kairos was criticized not because it aimed to improve the quality of prisoners' lives but because of its Christian identity and its use of volunteers. This was in direct contrast to APAC.

- There is little doubt, that had the identity of Kairos been properly grasped from the outset, its passage would have been far less problematic and may have been more productive.

- Kairos should be given the opportunity to operate free of the constraints of serving a Christian-based unit. In this event, however, careful attention should be paid to the location and security classification of potential host prisons.

Notes

1 APAC is a Christian approach to the reform and social integration of prisoners that began in Brazil in the 1970s before expanding to other parts of South America in the 1990s. The operation of APAC and its model prison, known simply as 'Humaitá', is fully described in Chapter 1.
2 We saw in Chapter 1 that the APAC approach regards the inclusion of a Cursillo-type programme (or 'short course in Christianity') as a *sine qua non*. The Verne wished to replicate the APAC approach and therefore needed a Cursillo-type programme. Indeed, early promotional literature from The Verne describes its initiative as 'The Cursillo Project'. Kairos is an adaptation for prison of the Cursillo programme and has an established track record running them in Western prisons. For these reasons the inclusion of Kairos in The Verne programme seemed natural, even though no Kairos Weekend had ever been used to support a faith-based unit and no Kairos Weekend had previously run in the UK.
3 We are grateful to Ike Griffin, Executive Director of Kairos Prison Ministries (KPM) (1990 – 2001) and Mickey Bright Griffin for their generous assistance in preparing this chapter. We are also grateful to John Thompson, Executive Director of KPM (2001 – present) for permission to quote from published KPM materials and from the Minutes of KPM Board Meetings and to past Chairs of Kairos UK (Penelope Lee, Mike Lewis and Andrew Lusby) for

granting access and permission to quote from published and unpublished materials relating to Kairos UK.

4   It was for this reason that Ike Griffin, Executive Director of KPM, gave permission for a Kairos district to be set up (Kairos UK) to administer the programme in the UK under licence. This is because materials such as instructions on how to hold a Kairos Weekend are Kairos copyright. At The Verne's request, Griffin also gave permission for the name 'Kairos' to be included in the name of The Verne project which was now styled the 'Kairos-APAC Project'. It was a generous decision he would later regret (see Chapter 3).

5   At best Kairos was regarded as a vehicle for right-wing American evangelism ('the Prison Service is hearing the Word of the Lord from across the Atlantic'; Cohen 1996b: 18) – five months before the first Kairos Weekend took place in The Verne. In The *Observer* Cohen (1996a: 13) objected to Christians '[going] beyond good works in the Lord Longford tradition' and accused the Government of 'relinquishing control of punishment conducted in our name to a religious minority'. The Assistant General Secretary of the National Association of Probation Officers claimed access was being granted to 'bizarre religious groups' (Hardy 1996: 11). At worst, Kairos was presented as an unorthodox religious sect that could be bracketed with Scientology (*ibid.*), a designated 'cult' that has no religious status with the Charities Commission and is prohibited from UK prisons. In the House of Lords, Lord Avebury made refutable assumptions about Kairos's identity, styling it 'a proselytizing organization' (*Hansard* 13 January 1997 col. WA11), whilst Lord Campbell of Croy referred to Kairos as a "religious sect" (*ibid.*, col. 183).

6   See 3(a)–(b).

7   See 5(a).

8   See 5(b).

9   Kairos and its associated programmes come free to the institution. Contributions from churches, individuals and supporters of the ministry provide for the expenses of the Weekend (Griffin 1996b).

10 After the first Cursillo Weekend in Palma, Majorca in 1949 (see Chapter 1), Cursillo arrived in the US in 1957 and grew nationwide. Cursillo was presented in prison in Florida for the first time in 1976 (Bright Griffin 2003a).

11 See for example *The Book of Galatians* 6:10 and *The Second Letter to the Corinthians* 6:2.

12 Interestingly the founder of Cursillo, Eduardo Bonnin, launched the original Cursillo programme in 1949 with the help of two prisoners on death row in a Spanish prison (KPM 1995b). This made the development of a special Cursillo for prisons nearly 30 years later highly appropriate.

13 All of the liturgical church bishops approved the modification of Cursillo into Kairos (Bright Griffin 2003a).

14 Prison Fellowship, founded in 1976, is a Christian ministry to prisoners, ex-prisoners and their families (www.pfm.org).

15   Prison Alpha, which began in the UK in 1995, describes itself as a practical and contemporary 15-session introduction to the Christian faith that is usually run over ten weeks. It runs in 85 per cent of UK prisons and also in the prisons of 40 countries world-wide (http://alphacourse.org.prisons/).

16   The highest security prison in which Kairos operated was a Category B prison (Swaleside): all the others were Category C.

17   Kairos UK minutes (1999) noted that: 'The [Kairos] Manual recommends that to build strong Christian Communities within a prison we need to have a stable prisoner population. This has not been happening on some Weekends'. They also noted that: 'Prison authorities … insist that the bed space is filled and if not filled quickly they will send just anyone on to the unit. They do their best to follow the criteria laid down in the Kairos Manual but it is not always possible to fulfil it to the letter. They are aware that long-serving prisoners are preferable.' In one case, a prisoner was released the day after their Kairos Weekend. Kairos UK minutes noted problems with the short length of time some prisoners served on the units at Highpoint North and South, which caused some unit staff to question whether the Kairos programme was suitable (Kairos UK 2000a). This was a recurring problem. Penelope Lee (an actress who produced documentaries for the BBC and Channel Four) was on a support team for Kairos 3 at The Verne when an unstable participant was due to be released five days after the Weekend.

18   Although at the time of writing it has never yet been implemented in the UK.

19   See Chapter 1, Section 1, 'The role of Christianity'.

20   In England, training tended to be over one long weekend. This was because to maintain the numbers of volunteers, people had sometimes to travel across the south of England. This was not ideal but it had to be done because of the demand.

21   Initially, there was nothing at all in Dorset to support The Verne. Regarding Swaleside, Canterbury Cursillo was said to have "a big Fourth Day [movement] … but few were found willing to volunteer [for Kairos]" (Kairos UK 1998b). In 1998 Kairos UK lamented that: "In the United States, Kairos was developed within large and active Cursillo movements. We are trying to impose Kairos where the Cursillos are still growing and struggling" (ibid.). Finding "sufficient sacrificial souls willing to submit to the training necessary" (Griffin 1996b) was always going to be a significant limiting factor on the expansion of Kairos-APAC – and one that the Christian-based units and the Prison Service should have taken into greater account (see Chapter 3). Other locations such as Coventry and Liverpool would have been far easier than Dorset.

22   The fourth Weekend at Swaleside had only 15 team members, five fewer than the minimum required for the Weekend to take place safely (Kairos UK 2000b). The fifth Weekend at Highpoint North had to be delivered in 24 and a half hours instead of 40 hours (Kairos UK 2000a). At one point it was

suggested that Kairos take a "Two Day Retreat" into one prison instead of the Kairos Weekend because it would involve fewer volunteers and less time in training (Kairos UK 1999).

23 Formal invitations to make a profession of Christian faith.

Chapter 3

The rise and fall of Kairos-APAC

I've been in the Prison Service over 20 years. I've seen it all and I've seen through it all. But what I've seen on my occasional trips into the wing this weekend I never expected to see in a prison. I saw men open up to one another, talk about their deepest fears, trust and listen, share – even hug one another. I'm not a religious person, but you've shown me something this weekend.

Assistant Governor of The Verne, commenting at the
closing service of the first Kairos Weekend, April 1997

This chapter provides an overview of the unique confluence of events and personalities that led to the development of four faith-based units in the Prison Service England and Wales. These became known as Kairos-APAC units, taking their name from the work of 'APAC' in South America and 'Kairos' in the United States. As we saw in Chapter 1, APAC is a Christian approach to the reform and social integration of prisoners that began in Brazil in the 1970s before expanding to other parts of South America in the 1990s. 'Kairos', as we saw in Chapter 2, is a Christian ministry to prisoners and their families that began in 1976. It aims to build strong Christian communities inside prisons that will positively affect the prison environment and so benefit the whole population. Despite the similarity of names, it is important to bear these differences in mind.

This chapter was authored by Jonathan Burnside

This chapter traces the emergence and development of Kairos-APAC in The Verne, its rapid expansion into three other prisons, its sudden fall from grace and its subsequent rebirth as 'Kainos Community'. The chapter draws on direct personal correspondence from those who were closely involved in these events. From the Prison Service they include former prison Governors, a former Assistant Chaplain-General and a former Principal Officer and, from outside the Service, a former Chair of Kairos UK[1] and the current Chair of Kainos Community.[2] It also makes use of a recorded interview with Ike Griffin, Executive Director of Kairos Prison Ministry (KPM) (1990–2001), who held personal meetings with the Governor of The Verne and senior Prison Service management. The Chair of the former Kairos-APAC Trust declined to contribute, although certain documents were kindly provided. The chapter draws on a variety of public documents relating to Kairos-APAC. It also benefits from personal correspondence received by Ike Griffin and Penelope Lee (former Chair of Kairos UK) between 1997 and 1999 and which offer the viewpoints of contemporary commentators.[3]

Introduction

The first Kairos Weekend took place in The Verne in April 1997, six weeks after the opening of the Kairos-APAC unit on D-Wing of the prison. Attempts had been made to introduce Kairos to the Prison Service some years previously. In 1990, Ian Ferguson, a prison chaplain who had experienced Kairos in the US in 1986, and Max Graham, a Kairos volunteer, planned to introduce Kairos to HMP Strangeways (now HMP Manchester) where Ferguson was part of the Chaplaincy team. Both worked closely with the leadership of KPM. Workshops were planned with John Caldwell, the first Executive Director of Kairos in the US and one of the original team who developed the Kairos programme from Cursillo (see Chapter 2). However, the attempt failed when in April 1990 HMP Strangeways became the site of a 28-day disturbance that destroyed large parts of the prison.

Plans were also afoot in the 1990s to introduce an 'APAC-style' unit to the Scottish Prison Service (SPS). In 1993 Angus Creighton, a Senior Social Worker at HMP Low Moss in Scotland and a Board member of Prison Fellowship International (PFI), visited APAC. Along with the then Governor of HMP Greenock, Ken Rennie, Creighton presented an APAC feasibility study for the SPS Board in April 1995 (Creighton and Rennie 1995). The study recognized that the socio-political climate in Scotland was not conducive to an independent APAC prison (i.e. 'APAC with full control'; see Chapter 1) but suggested the idea be tested in a more controlled environment. Creighton and Rennie favoured a small unit in an existing prison with a low-security regime but with a secure perimeter to facilitate the participation of Category B prisoners. It was proposed that half of a new 60-cell unit in HMP Gateside in Greenock be used because this was a local prison and was supported by Prison Fellowship (PF) volunteers. This proposal had the backing of the Board of PF Scotland. Existing PF volunteers would be able to provide relevant professional services (e.g. social work, education, medical care etc.) in a similar manner to some of APAC's volunteers (*ibid.*). Creighton and Rennie met with the Board shortly thereafter to discuss the possibilities of an 'APAC-style' unit within a long-term prison.

Although nothing came of these proposals as far as SPS was concerned, they are notable in several respects. First, they were characteristic of the high and arguably unrealistic expectations of APAC-enthusiasts at this time (cf. *Baptist Times* 1997). Although the authors' proposal was merely for a 'Quasi-APAC' regime, the lowest rung on the APAC ladder (see Chapter 1), they also envisioned the possibility of a private, charitable, profit-making 'APAC-style' prison within three years (Creighton and Rennie 1995). This extraordinary leap up the evolutionary ladder to 'APAC with full control' had no parallel in the history of APAC itself. It suggested that what was established in Humaitá over 11 years could be achieved in Scotland in one-fifth of the time (although they did of course have the benefit of the Humaitá blueprint). Second, although the proposal claimed to be inspired by APAC, there was little recognition of the value of Cursillo which the founders of APAC identified as central but which the authors then regarded as dispensable (*ibid.*). As we shall see in relation to InnerChange in the US, the history of APAC was useful for getting a 'foot in the door' with prison departments but, once this was established, proponents often wanted to 'do their own thing' (see Chapter 7). Third, in an important sense Creighton and Rennie's proposals did pave the way for an 'APAC-style' prison regime. However, this would not take place in the SPS, as they had hoped, but in the Prison Service England and Wales. The Deputy Chief Executive of the SPS, Alan Walker, left soon after Creighton and Rennie produced their report to become Director of Operations (South) for the Prison Service England and Wales. One of the prisons for which he became the new Director was HMP The Verne.

I. Emergence of 'The Verne Project'

The APAC initiative at The Verne[4] arose from a unique confluence of persons and circumstances. Like Humaitá in Brazil, the initiative grew from Cursillo. In 1995 a 50-minute film about APAC called *Love is Not a Luxury* was shown at the Bishop of Lincoln's Prison Conference. The film maker was Penelope Lee, an actress who had previously produced and directed documentaries for the BBC and Channel Four. In an effort to understand APAC, which the founders claimed was based on Cursillo, she experienced her own Cursillo in 1993. Upon completing the film Lee joined a Kairos team in Florida, met Ike Griffin and showed the film to the US Kairos Board. Early in 1996 she began to set up Tres Dias, an ecumenical version of Cursillo, in the South West of England with the hope that this would provide some volunteers with the necessary background to support the introduction of Kairos in the future (Lee 2004). Lee and several Tres Dias volunteers made a number of visits to prisons and churches to show her film and to talk about APAC, Kairos and Tres Dias. One such screening was to a group of prisoners at The Verne in June 1996, at the Chaplain's request. Afterwards a prisoner complained: 'We're not going to get a prison like that for 50 years.' Lee said: 'Well, why don't you pray about it?' A fortnight later she was invited back by a Principal Officer to advise on how APAC might be applied to the prison (Mathewson 1997).

The immediate reason why The Verne welcomed Lee's film was because of The Verne's particular history of control problems. By the mid-1990s The Verne was the fourth most disruptive prison in England and Wales. In the space of one year The Verne had three 'tornadoes' (i.e. disturbances) that had to be quelled by a special operations unit wearing body armour (Willey 1998).

The most problematic part of the prison was D Wing, a series of Napoleonic armament vaults beneath the walls of The Verne Citadel, a nineteenth century military fortress on Portland. The vaults had been used for storage, but because of pressure on the prison estate they were converted into eight dormitories of nine beds each. The dormitories offered some individual privacy by means of wooden screens around each bed space. However, they were poor in comparison to accommodation in the rest of the prison, which consisted of single cells in one of six modern house blocks (Hebbern 1997). Its use as a reception wing also meant that the wing was 'populated with short termers, often young and with very little to lose' (*ibid.*: 42). Most were prisoners under 25 years old and serving less than three years for offences involving burglary.

This combination of architecture and function meant D Wing prisoners did not develop much sense of 'belonging'. They saw themselves simply as 'passing time' until space became available elsewhere, normally between eight and twelve weeks (Hebbern 1996). The upshot was that 'D Wing was a hot-bed of violence, assaults and fabric damage. Staff endured confrontation and stress not experienced in the rest of the prison. Life was made impossible for inmates who wanted quiet to make the best of their situation' (Hebbern 1997: 42). Nicknamed 'Beirut', 'no officer went to D Wing alone at night' (Respondent A 2004). Unsurprisingly, the Chief Inspector of Prisons condemned D Wing following an inspection report in August 1996 and recommended that the wing should either be shut down or put to alternative use. It was impossible to close 72 spaces, however. In 1996 there was great pressure on Category C prisons such as The Verne not only because of increased levels of overcrowding across the national prison estate but also because fewer prisoners at that time qualified for lower-category prisons (Hebbern 1996).

Following verbal feedback from the Chief Inspector at the end of his visit, the Governor challenged the Principal Officer of D Wing and his staff to provide options for an alternative use for the wing (Respondent G 2004). At this point the Principal Officer on D Wing, Geoff Hebbern, viewed Lee's film, which had been shown in the prison two weeks previously. Hebbern believed that D Wing's problems could be solved 'if we could find 72 men who *wanted* to be on that wing rather than on any other' (Hebbern 1997: 42). Hebbern formed an advisory council of free-world and prisoner participants, including Lee, and together they produced an 'APAC feasibility study' based on elements of APAC's closed section for The Verne (Griffin 1997). About three weeks later, Hebbern invited the Governor to view *Love Is Not A Luxury* and decided to deliver proposals to senior management (Respondent G 2004).

Hebbern's proposal was for a first-phase unit of 24 prisoners in three eight-man dormitories. A Project Team was formed comprising the Governor, Hebbern, a D Wing staff representative, the Chaplain, three prisoners and a member of the local volunteer community (Hebbern 1997). Senior managers gave no negative response, although some were unsure. The Board of Visitors (BOV) and the Prison Officers Association (POA) gave their full support (Respondent G 2004). The Chairman of The Verne's POA, Michael Browne, stated: 'We are all in favour of it, and we see it as an interesting and viable proposition' (*Dorset Echo* 1996: 1). The Area Manager, the Director of Operations (South) and, in due course, the Minister for Prisons, also gave it the go-ahead. 'The general view was that the wing could get no worse and there was nothing to lose' (Respondent G 2004).

This beginning echoes the founding of Humaitá. Humaitá, like D Wing, was declared unusable, but the men had nowhere else to go. As in Brazil, the entire effort at The Verne stemmed from a need for more beds in the prison system and the lack of an alternative. 'Our gut feeling was that many thought it would flounder and die' (*ibid.*). In fact:

The Kairos-APAC Trust did a lot of good work before it was eclipsed by the misdemeanours of its Outside Co-ordinator [Ex-Con B; see Section 6 below]. D Wing became a place of pilgrimage for a considerable number of Chaplains, Governors and other prison professionals, several of whom wanted it for their own establishments. They had learned of the remarkable change in D Wing and were very impressed by its calm and order and by the reception they were given by the men on the wing.

(Lee 2004)

2. Development of Kairos-APAC at The Verne

Kairos-APAC at The Verne developed swiftly, despite fears expressed by some at the time that the Governor and Principal Officer were 'running ahead of themselves'.[5] 'We decided to go ahead step by step rather than spend months planning with no action on the ground' (Respondent G 2004). This was partly because the window of opportunity that the problems of D Wing presented would not stay open forever. In June 1996, not long after the initial screening of the film at The Verne, Lee met Alan Walker who said that he wanted her to 'troubleshoot' for him and to find out what could be done. Lee contacted Ike Griffin, the Executive Director of KPM. Griffin's subsequent visit to England in September 1996 increased support for the project and, following a meeting with Walker, added credibility to the project in the eyes of the Prison Service (Lee 2004).

The first work was to upgrade three dorms for 24 prisoners. The plan was to have the first dorm ready by mid-February and the other two, plus the meeting room, by the end of March. This would be in time for the first Kairos Weekend in April 1996. Walker provided some funding for this work (Respondent G 2004). Other work included fund-raising, the recruitment of a coordinator and establishing a project Trust.

Another task was developing the regime. Lee (1999) claims that originally the basic elements of the regime came together 'on the back of an envelope on our kitchen table' from what she knew of the closed section of Humaitá, with her film to help. These elements included the Cursillo-based Kairos Weekend, the Prisoners' Council, the 'godparents', an evening for small groups and subsequently the Kairos 'Journey' programme instead of Humaitá's 'valorization' classes (see Chapter 1). Other programmes included courses on cognitive thinking, life skills, family matters, communication skills, conflict resolution and Alternatives to Violence (Hebbern 1997). This reflects the history of D Wing, which had also previously been the location of substance abuse projects. Lee (2004) was 'from this point concerned that no interest was shown in the therapeutic work of Hugo Veronese' (described in Chapter 1).[6]

By autumn 1996, the plan was set. Twenty-four men would enter D Wing in March 1997. These would work in the general prison population but have a key to the dorm. Prisoners would run their own Council and set rules of conduct. After six months, these Kairos-APAC prisoners would rotate back into the general prison population and another group would enter. The start of each six-month programme was the Kairos Weekend. The plans were essentially another 'quasi-APAC' package (cf. Creighton and Rennie 1995); *viz.* they partially applied selected aspects of Humaitá whilst management of both the unit and the prison remained with the Prison Service.

The concept of a Project Coordinator grew from the position of Chairman of the Prisoner's Council in APAC; *viz.* an experienced and trusted *recuperando* appointed and responsible to the Governor (see Chapter 1). The Chairman's role was to refer to the Governor all recommendations of the Prisoner's Council regarding the day-to-day running of the closed section (Stage 2). Lee recommended an ex-offender (Ex-Con A) to work (only) on the wing and to chair the Prisoners' Council. Ex-Con A had served a prison sentence for armed robbery before his release four years previously (Jones 1996b; Griffin 1996a). Lee met Ex-Con A when he joined Tres Dias in the same group as the Chaplain of The Verne. He was highly recommended to Tres Dias by a Chaplain of the prison where he completed his sentence (Lee 2004). Ex-Con A was interviewed and accepted by the Governor of The Verne. In October 1996, Ex-Con A showed Alan Walker and Richard Tilt, the then Director-General of the Prison Service, around D Wing. Lee gathered from Ex-Con A and Hebbern that the Director-General was very supportive of the plan, satisfied with security and would speak to the Prisons Minister who at that time had indicated that she was not entirely happy about the programme being overseen by an ex-offender, albeit under Hebbern's jurisdiction. By the end of the year, the Prisons Minister had given her support to The Verne Project (*ibid.*).

Those involved in setting up the project at The Verne widely felt that funding should be sought independently of the Prison Service to secure the project's future. They approached private charitable trusts and within three months had raised sufficient funds to secure the project for three years (Hebbern 1997: 42). The project traded on Kairos's established reputation and heavily referenced the success of both Kairos and APAC (Griffin 1999a).

3. Launch of Kairos-APAC at The Verne

The Prisons Minister, having given The Verne project her approval, allegedly advised those involved not to 'shout about it' (Lee 2004). If so, the advice fell on deaf ears. Kairos-APAC was launched in the autumn of 1996 in a blaze of self-publicity. Some of this publicity, unfortunately, would do lasting damage to its relationship with the Prison Service.

The very first article relating to Kairos-APAC appears to have been in *Inside Time* under the huge, and hugely misleading, front page headline: 'Inmates to take over the prison!' (Jones 1996b). Written on behalf of the Kairos-APAC Trust, this article offers some insight into how Kairos-APAC understood and presented itself at an early stage. It is a rather seminal article because *Inside Time* is a newspaper produced 'by prisoners for prisoners'. Many prisoners and would-be applicants took their understanding of the project from this article, which deliberately highlighted the more dramatic aspects of the Humaitá regime. It claimed that: 'A successful new regime *run by inmates* is to be imported from Brazil … into HMP The Verne' (*ibid.*, italics added). Using the five-fold categories developed in Chapter 1, the implication was that The Verne was introducing the 'APAC with Full Control' model. This was far from the case, but such claims would understandably give rise to concern that the Prison Service was 'losing control' of its prisons (see below).

The article was also wrong to claim that APAC had 'blossomed into similar programmes … in 100-plus penitentiaries in the United States' (*ibid.*) as well as Australia. This was true of Kairos, but it was not true of APAC. There would be much confusion in subsequent years about the identity of Kairos, APAC and Kairos-APAC. This was not helped by ignorance on the part of Kairos-APAC itself about its identity. If the promoters of The Verne project did not know the basic difference between APAC and Kairos, how could anyone else? Kairos-APAC at The Verne opened just weeks ahead of the APAC-inspired InnerChange Freedom Initiative in the US (see Chapter 8).

Kairos-APAC placed great emphasis on how it could achieve lower reconvictions. The article emphasised APAC's claim to have a recidivism rate of 'less than four per cent' (Jones 1996b). Although the Trust could not have known it at the time, Johnson's 2002 study in fact found a reconviction rate of 16 per cent for APAC (Johnson 2002; see Chapter 10). However, the claim was made on behalf of the Trust that: '*Everywhere* the regime has been put in place, or one based on the same principles, the recidivism rate has been dramatically reduced' (Jones 1996b: 1, emphasis added). Such claims spilled into other media with the *Baptist Times* claiming that: '[The] whole system produced rates [note the plural] of reoffending which were the envy of penal systems around the world' (Mathewson 1996). Unfortunately, these grand claims had little empirical support for the simple reason that hardly any empirical research had been carried out on either APAC or Kairos. A single study by the Florida Department of Corrections on 505 Kairos prisoners in 1995 was probably the only example. Yet the implication was clear: The Verne project would produce a 'dramatic' effect upon reconvictions.

With such publicity it was hardly surprising that The Verne experiment caught the attention of national newspapers. A number of articles duly appeared in December 1996 and made unwelcome reading for the Prison Service. The *Sunday Telegraph* ran an article in December 1996 headlined: 'Religious Sect to Take Over Prison Wing' (Hardy 1996: 11). The Assistant General Secretary of the National Association of Probation Officers (NAPO) saw the initiative as evidence that 'The Prison Service is broke' (*ibid.*). The *Observer* ran with 'St Michael sends his Apostles into the prisons' likewise suggesting 'a cost-saving logic behind the choice of churches' (Cohen 1996a: 13). Both picked up on the idea that the Prison Service was surrendering 'control' to 'untried and untested' prisoners and volunteers. This was not true but was nonetheless a view the Trust encouraged. Lee recalls that: 'Apparently there were senior people in the Prisons Department who, though to a degree ... understanding the concept of the prison in Brazil, were alarmed by the extent of its revolution' (Lee 2004). In the light of such publicity it is not hard to see why.

The Director General of the Prison Service, meanwhile, tried to set the record straight. 'Prisoners and religious volunteers would not 'manage the Wing' at The Verne, he said, and all criminals would be asked to do was 'take part in sensible counselling and therapy courses" (Cohen 1996b: 18). His remarks put the question of prisoner autonomy in perspective but did not address broadsheet concerns about religiosity. By laying stress on 'sensible counselling and therapy' the implication was that religion was irrelevant. But the unit was Christian-based, and the programme involved *compulsory* introductions to the Christian faith via the Kairos Weekend and follow-up programmes. These could not be described vaguely as 'counselling and therapy courses'. Once again we see confusion as to the nature and identity of The Verne project, this time from the very top of the Prison Service. Was the programme Christian, or wasn't it?

But if the Director General was content to evade the question of religiosity, others wanted to pursue the matter vigorously. The negative publicity quickly led to questions in the House of Lords. Lee recalls that Hebbern rang to inform her of this and of a call from Lord Longford who said that 'we would be "taken to the cleaners" ' (Lee 2004). Lee provided substantial material to enable an Assistant Chaplain-General to brief the Home Office Minister for a debate the following month as well as for a written answer. Two duty Bishops in the House of Lords also received briefings from a senior clergyman involved with Cursillo (*ibid.*). The controversy resurfaced with the first Kairos Weekend in April 1997. This time a prison Chaplain speaking on behalf of the Chaplain's Union expressed concerns about religiosity: 'The Verne scheme is something we will be suspicious of and asking lots of questions about ... Prisoners are not in a strong position and we don't want to see religion forced onto them' (Grey 1997).

Despite this, there was still much goodwill towards the new project. The local *Dorset Evening Echo* (1996) welcomed the plans, remarking: 'There is no disputing the social advantages of Christian ethics or that self-help and self-determination give people a greater stake in their lives and their community ... [The Verne project] might well be a welcome step in the right direction'. There were similar expressions of support in the House of Lords debate in January 1997 (Lords *Hansard* 15 January 1997).

A former Governor remarks that:

Any sensible strategist would leave Kainos well alone once it had a small footing, thankful for what good it might do, but shy of giving it active support, and wary of anything which might show a strong identification with any particular faith.

(Respondent J 2003)

This is consistent with the experience of another former Governor, who recalls that:

During the early days, there was interest at all levels from the Minister down, once the first [Kairos] Weekend had been success-fully completed. There were always those who kept their distance, perhaps in case it went belly up! Many questions were aimed at the 'religious' aspects of the programme. My response was that the programme was based on Christian ethics which in principle apply to all beliefs. It was not a church-based programme and the Chaplaincy acted as advisers ... The feedback on some parts of the service was cynical and anti, on others curiosity. At the time there was a regime development group working on new programmes. They showed no interest in what we were doing and one received the impression that we should not be operating as it had not come from them. This attitude I find negative and stifles progress and initiative. As there was no HQ funding and the then Director General was in favour there was little they could do. Many anticipated the programme would fold within a few months.

(Respondent G 2004)

4. Early operation of Kairos-APAC at The Verne

A number of crucial issues needed to be addressed in the early stages. These included informed consent, eligibility, recruitment, finding volunteers, establishing the first Kairos Weekend and the general profile of prisoners on the wing.

(a) Informed consent?

To recruit prisoners to the unit, a publicity booklet was published in autumn 1996. This brochure was widely circulated to interested parties inside and outside the prison to describe the emergent unit and explain its purpose (Kairos-APAC 1996). It is a significant document in several respects. First, it reveals how Kairos-APAC advertised itself at a formative stage of development. Second, its use as a recruiting tool makes it rather important from the point of view of informed consent.

Prisoners were told they needed to ask themselves three questions to determine whether they should apply to Kairos-APAC:

(1) Do I believe that there is a power greater than me? (2) Am I ready to learn what respect means and what love is all about? (3) What do I feel about living in close and trusting community with 23 other men?

(Kairos-APAC 1996: 1)[7]

The first question confirmed that the unit was open to prisoners of any religious belief. A key sentence later in the booklet amplifies: 'You do *not* have to be a Christian to participate in the programme, but you do have to understand that the Unit is Christian-based and you do have to have enough humility to understand that there is something out there greater than you. *If a Christ-centred twenty-week course offends you, it is unlikely that The Verne* Kairos *Unit* [as it was then called] *is the right place for you'* (*ibid.*: 7, emphasis original). The second and third questions, however, were rather vague and used the 'fuzzy language' of 'respect', 'love' and 'close and trusting community' – all words, it must be said, that can bear different meanings in prison. In this document we can see the origin of future complaints from staff and prisoners that they did not understand what Kairos-APAC was about and, in prisons outside The Verne, that they did not 'explain themselves very well' (see Chapters 4 and 5).

Rather like the *Inside Time* article, the document emphasizes the success of Kairos and APAC in reducing reoffence rates (Kairos-APAC 1996). Given that this brochure was used for recruitment, it would hardly be surprising if the unit attracted some prisoners whose primary motivation was improving their chances of parole.

The document is also notable for imposing a policy of secrecy regarding the Kairos Weekend: 'It will be a condition asked of all participants that they tell no potential future participants what the weekend course consists of. Suffice to say that very few of the hundreds of thousands who have attended similar courses throughout the world have been left unchanged by it. Be prepared for a life-changing experience!' (*ibid.*: 10). Given that the Weekend was a compulsory point of entry for all participants, it is not hard to see how this deliberate lack of information bred anxiety and distrust. Here too we can see the origin of future complaints from prisoners and staff that Kairos-APAC was 'secretive' (see Chapters 4 and 5). Given the religious basis of the unit, it was only a short step from this to the fear that Kairos-APAC was a cult. Within a short time such rumours had already begun to circulate and would be amplified in the national press within a month. This secrecy was directly contrary to Kairos practice, which specifically allows prisoners to have their fears and questions addressed before the Weekend. The final talk of the Kairos Weekend, as presented in the Kairos Manual, gives the following advice to prisoners who have completed their Kairos Weekend:

> … [W]e should be ready to answer questions [from prisoners who have not been on Kairos] when they are asked … When asked about the weekend, tell them you heard lots of talks, that you sang songs, laughed a lot, told jokes, met some new people. Answer any direct question about anything … Whatever you do, never, never use the word 'secret'. Never say, 'I can't tell you about that"
>
> (KPM 1998b: 318)

The final paragraph of the document warns: '*Do not think you can come to The Verne on the pretext of joining the Unit and then drop out or change your mind.* You will be re-located immediately to another, less attractive institution' (Kairos-APAC 1996: 13 emphasis original). But if prisoners were to be denied the chance to withdraw without penalty they should have had access to more detailed information, particularly regarding the Kairos Weekend.

Prisoners were invited to sign an eight-point compact to join what was then described as 'The APAC Project' (Hebbern 1996). Item 2 states: 'I agree … to work for change in my own life and to be a positive influence within the prison' which embodies the Kairos ideal of impacting the prison environment (see Chapter 2). Item 6 recognizes the ban on the use of drugs, drug-trafficking, alcohol and pornography. The compact did not require prisoners to state their understanding that the programme was Christian and that certain Christian aspects of the programme were mandatory. The absence of this, once again, left Kairos-APAC and later Kainos vulnerable to criticism (see Chapters 5 and 6).

(b) Eligibility and recruitment

Kairos-APAC claimed the programme was voluntary and, although Christian-based, open to prisoners of any religion (Kairos-APAC 1996). The main criterion was a Category C security classification because The Verne was a Category C establishment. The only prisoners excluded were sex offenders who had not successfully completed the Sex Offenders Treatment Programme (SOTP) (Respondent G 2004). The concern was that non-completers would claim that they no longer needed treatment because 'God had forgiven them'. In fact, three of the initial group of 24 men were sex offenders but were allowed to attend because they were already in The Verne. All subsequently agreed to complete SOTP (Hebbern 2003).

(c) Recruiting volunteers

In order for the first Kairos Weekend to go ahead in April 1997 there was an urgent need to assemble a body of trained volunteers. It fell to Lee to find the volunteers – a tough assignment in an area with no Cursillo movement. Griffin was apparently somewhat appalled at the work that had to be done in order to establish a Kairos team in these circumstances and in the time available. Yet what would normally take a couple of years was established in six months (Lee 2004).

The Verne benefited hugely from American generosity and from the active participation of KPM. Griffin personally flew from America in February 1997 to launch the training for the first Kairos Weekend (Kairos #1 at The Verne). In March 1997 Griffin also brought a team of 13 trainers to teach the follow-up Journey programme so that this could immediately follow the first Kairos Weekend. Griffin also attended the first Kairos Weekend itself in April and supported the Kairos Lay Rector, who leads the Weekend. All American support for The Verne came free to the institution.

(d) The First Kairos Weekend

Despite the behind-the-scenes scramble to train volunteers, the first Kairos Weekend (Kairos #1) was deemed a success. Assistant Governor Bill Woodall commented at the closing service:

> I've been in the Prison Service over 20 years. I've seen it all and I've seen through it all. But what I've seen on my occasional trips into the wing this weekend I never expected to see in a prison. I saw men open up to one another, talk about their deepest fears, trust and listen, share – even hug one another. I'm not a religious person, but you've shown me something this weekend.
>
> (Jones 1998)

Despite this, Griffin felt the Weekend was less effective in The Verne than might have been the case in the US: 'I noticed that at The Verne on the first two Weekends I observed (Kairos #1 and #2) the participants were less receptive or less ready to receive the Christian message. They received it with hospitality but with a rather jaundiced eye of, not disbelief, but 'let's wait and see' and didn't seem to want to fall into ready acceptance of what was being taught' (Griffin 2003).[8]

Nevertheless, according to a former Governor, the immediate effect of Kairos-APAC was positive. Behaviour improved (Respondent G 2004). 'D Wing was utterly transformed' (Lee 2004). Kairos-APAC was said to have an effect on all the dorms including those that were not part of Kairos-APAC. In 1995, The Verne was the third most disruptive prison in the country. The level of recorded adjudications in The Verne dropped from 537 in 1996 to 324 in 1998. This was said to be the lowest number ever recorded in its history (Hebbern 1999a).

By 1998, it seemed as though the Kairos-APAC project at The Verne was proving its critics wrong. The highest-level praise came from Sir David Ramsbotham, Chief Inspector of Prisons who claimed that Kairos-APAC had 'transformed' the wing into a relaxed, safe and well-managed unit; reduced tension throughout the jail and restored a sense of 'pride and ownership' among prisoners (The *Independent,* 29th July, 1998; The *Times* 29th July 1998). Ramsbotham concluded:

> No-one should pretend that any one initiative is a panacea … but if the project works for certain prisoners, contributing to their progression towards successful reintegration into the community, with less likelihood that they will reoffend, then it must be applauded.
>
> (The *Independent,* 29th July, 1998)

(e) A 'bolthole for the good'?

Kairos-APAC claimed that it was 'careful not to attract too many regular church-goers and, in the event, less than a quarter have been active Christians' (Hebbern 1999a). But although 'the staff and management of the project made a decision not to be choosy – to just 'take them as they come' (Hebbern 1997: 43) – this does not exclude the possibility that prisoners who chose to join shared certain characteristics.

It is very notable that, in its early years, Kairos-APAC reported a distinct lack of trouble on the wing in *Vernacular*, the newsletter of the Kairos-APAC Trust. It said that 'out of 104 men who have been on the project at The Verne just six were taken off before completing the course' (*Vernacular* 1998a: 1). Kairos-APAC was quick to point out that in 1996, 189 out of 537 recorded adjudications were for D Wing prisoners whilst in 1998 only 13 out of 324 adjudications were for Kairos-APAC residents. Moreover, whilst the D Wing staff observation book for 1996 recorded almost 500 negative incidents (including fires, assaults, abuse to staff, drug-related incidents and damage to the wing), only 48 incidents were recorded for 1998, all of which were said to be of 'lesser gravity' (Hebbern 1999a). Finally, Hebbern (1999b: 3) noted that 'we have only had to move one man from the unit for bullying'.

These figures might be explained on the basis that Kairos-APAC was having astonishing success in changing 'negative' leaders into 'positive' leaders and this was, naturally, the interpretation promoted by Kairos-APAC. Kairos-APAC claimed to 'specialize' in dealing with 'negative leaders' (e.g. the Project Co-ordinator's claim that: 'Every prison wants to get rid of its troublemakers. But we [Kairos-APAC] can channel that'; Willey 1998: 700). But the figures might equally be explained on the ground that Kairos-APAC tended to recruit more compliant and pro-social prisoners than the general prison population. This was indeed consistent with the findings of the reconviction study (see Chapter 10). Kairos-APAC's early claims to success in fact suggested that, right from the start, Kairos-APAC was 'a bolt-hole for the good'.

Kairos-APAC's tendency to concentrate its energies on more compliant and pro-social prisoners would make it more difficult to demonstrate a significant impact on reconviction rates (see Chapter 10); yet the Trust was still resolutely 'talking up' dramatic success with reconvictions. In 1998 Kairos-APAC claimed that '100 per cent of the men released from The Verne Project so far have remained crime-free' (*Vernacular* 1998a: 1) although in fact this claim related to only 11 men, some of whom had been released a mere matter of months. Finally, the Trust noted that: 'In over a year now just four men have left to return to normal prison location after finishing the course – and two of those later came back!' (*ibid.*). The implication was that Kairos-APAC was such a desirable place to live that prisoners could not bear to leave. In some ways this was of course an achievement given that previously prisoners could not wait to leave D Wing. But it might also have suggested that prisoners were having difficulty relating to an environment outside the 'special unit'. If so, it did not augur well for their ability to sustain any positive behavioural change upon release.

5. Expansion: too much, too fast, too soon?

Expansion began within The Verne itself. Another four eight-man dormitories in D Wing were refurbished in July 1997, expanding the unit from 24 to nearly 60 prisoners (*Vernacular* 1997: 1). This was due in part to the beneficial effect of Kairos-APAC on non-Kairos-APAC dorms in D Wing and also to an increase in the number of volunteers (Respondent G 2004).

In the early stages of Kairos-APAC 'everything was directed at The Verne. We had no thoughts of expanding' (*ibid.*). But Alan Walker Director of Operations (South) had other ideas. A Kairos report notes that Griffin met with Alan Walker and 'learned that … [Walker] wants to see The Verne prototype successfully launched and will encourage its rapid expansion thereafter' (KPM 1996a). Yet such rapid development was in contrast to the slower, painstaking development of APAC itself. Lee had a meeting with the Governor of The Verne in October 1996 and subsequently wrote to Griffin expressing her concerns: 'The Governor of The Verne was ebullient, having just spoken to Alan Walker. He talked of a Verne Trust to include high-powered patrons with the possibility of EC money through Alan Walker's contacts and a view to what evolved at The Verne moving out in due course into other establishments. I am concerned by … [the] inclination to think big at this stage' (Lee 1996). 'This expansionist drive was, I believe, premature because I thought that The Verne needed more work' (Lee 2004). Lee felt that 'The Verne should have been made as bullet-proof as possible before it went elsewhere' (*ibid.*).

But The Verne had broken the ice with the Prison Service, and expansion to other prisons was now on the cards. Expansion was encouraged partly by the Prison Service and partly by Kairos-APAC. Respondent A (a former Assistant Chaplain-General; 2004) recalls that Alan Walker sent the Chaplain of Swaleside 'to do some project work and ... provided money for research'. He also appointed someone to his staff to forward the work of the Governor's Steering Group. This was set up in 1997 and included Chaplains, the Chair of the Kairos-APAC Trust and PO Hebbern (Respondent G 2004). There was a desire to 'prove' that Kairos-APAC could 'work' in as many different settings as possible, including a Category B establishment, a women's prison, a Young Offender Institution (YOI) and so on. Respondent G (a former Governor; 2004) recalls: 'By this time Swaleside [a Category B prison] and Highpoint [North, a women's prison] had stated they wished to set up units and asked for our assistance both in setting up and funding .... Discussions included the possibility of moving into a YOI'. To judge from some of the material produced at this time it seemed as though Kairos-APAC was encouraging expansion in all directions. In the spring of 1998, *Vernacular* readers were advised: 'If you visit a prison without a Kairos-APAC unit, sound it out to see if it is a suitable case for future study' (*Vernacular* 1998a: 1).

(a) Swaleside

HMP Swaleside is a Category B prison built in the 1980s in a remote location on the Isle of Sheppey. In June 1997 Lee wrote to Griffin, noting that: '[The Chaplain at Swaleside] and [Swaleside Governor No. 2] went to visit the Verne and the Governor was wholly hooked by what he saw. [The Chaplain at Swaleside] ... rang me not long after. I suggested Kairos on its own for a start. He said he had wanted to do it this way but the Governor wanted the whole thing (i.e. to take on a wing as at The Verne).' Respondent A (2004) confirms this: 'The Governor of Swaleside and the Chaplain were of one mind that they wanted the programme in Swaleside. The Governor was willing to provide resources to set it up'.

A Kairos-APAC unit was established in Swaleside in 1997 and ran for a short while without a Kairos Weekend. However, Swaleside wanted to introduce Kairos as a catalyst for community living. Unfortunately the Isle of Sheppey in the Thames Estuary was remote from a large volunteer base. The only town of any size, Sheerness, was on the other side of the island. This placed a great strain on Kairos volunteers who had to travel substantial distances to take part in the Kairos Weekend and who were not able to support the follow-up programme and monthly Reunions.

(b) Highpoint North and South

Walker was also keen for Kairos-APAC to enter a women's prison, but there were not many to choose from in the area for which he was responsible. In the summer of 1996, Walker suggested to Lee that plans should be developed for Holloway (Lee 1996). This changed to Highpoint

North, a women's prison in Suffolk, because the Chaplain of Highpoint was 'enthusiastic about the programme and managed to persuade his Governor' (Respondent A 2004). But the Chaplain at Highpoint only wanted to consider a faith-based unit for women (Lee 1998).

Expansion to Highpoint North and the adjacent men's prison, Highpoint South, occurred simultaneously because at that time the Governing Governor happened to be the same for both. Ex-Con B was another ex-offender employed to work for the Kairos-APAC Trust. He engaged three Project Workers including a Co-ordinator for a proposed men's unit. Opening dates and numbers of prisoners involved were agreed without reference to Kairos UK and despite Kairos concerns at the lack of available volunteers.

In December 1997 Lee wrote to the Chair of the Kairos-APAC Trust saying that it was again an unprecedentedly tall order to ask for two Kairos teams in Highpoint [North and South] within three months. At a Kairos UK Trust meeting in December 1997 it became clear that about 100 volunteers had to be found to cover the plans for Kairos at Highpoint during 1998, which was a very considerable commitment (Lee 2004). By January 1998 it was clear that large numbers of volunteers were not forthcoming. The Lay Director of Bury St Edmunds Cursillo had thoroughly canvassed the local community, and only three men had come forward (Lee 1998). This was consistent with Griffin's experience that only two per cent of practising Christians are willing to help with a prison population if they live conveniently near to a prison (see Chapter 7).

In March 1998 Lee wrote to Griffin noting: 'the cart is way before the horse!' Kairos UK could, of course, have chosen not to support the Highpoint plan. The Co-ordinator for Highpoint South and the Chaplain for Highpoint North and South informed the Highpoint Kairos Advisory Council that the Prison Service decision for a men's unit in Highpoint South with Kairos in January 1999 would have to be abandoned if Kairos UK could not deliver. Writing to Griffin in July 1998, Lee noted that Kairos UK 'has in effect had a pistol put to its head.'

(c) Brixton

HMP Brixton in south London wanted Kairos-APAC by the summer of 1999. The Chaplain at Brixton had been on Tres Dias and wanted something to develop there. The Governor, senior staff and the local MP were all interested (Lee 1997). The Governor spent two days at The Verne in Dorset in 1998 and said that he 'returned to London *knowing* that I wanted what I saw in Dorset at my prison' (*Vernacular* 1998b: 1).

There were certain advantages to establishing Kairos-APAC in Brixton. There was a local Cursillo and a broad range of local churches. It was also one of few prisons that was local to the vast majority of prisoners: up to 90 per cent came from just three London boroughs. The initiative was highly ambitious. It was planned to involve five distinct units: a 42-man substance misuse programme; 42 men on a series of courses relating to life skills, communication skills, group and one-to-one counselling, and offence-related courses; 42 men on a full Kairos-APAC similar to The Verne; 30 men on the category D (open prison) unit with evening courses and godparenting; and a community and family support team of two staff working in prisoners' home boroughs. Hebbern saw the open prison unit as 'a unique opportunity' to develop the semi-open phase of the APAC model in which prisoners work in the locality by day and return to the prison by night (*ibid.*).

The resources required were considerable. The Kairos-APAC Trust needed to recruit and train enough volunteers for godparenting for 168 men as well as to raise funds to pay for a staff of 11 (*ibid.*). According to Respondent A (2004) Alan Walker agreed to the appointment of a full-time coordinator for Brixton and was going to fund it.

The Governor's Steering Committee also considered entering a YOI. At this point, however, the Committee was informed that 'there could be no further expansion … It is my personal view that this came from the Prisons Board' (Respondent G). If so, it was a sign that at last the Prison Service was applying the brakes.

(d) International

The Kairos-APAC Trust was not only seeking to expand its operations domestically but also internationally. The motive for this did not come from the Prison Service in England and Wales, which had no interest in promoting initiatives beyond its jurisdiction. In August 1998, Ex-Con B was appointed Chief Executive of the Kairos-APAC Trust. The Chair of the Kairos-APAC Trust told Kairos UK representatives that 'Kairos-APAC is going high profile and is going international' (Lee 1998). This was a reference to plans to establish an APAC unit at Mountjoy Prison, Dublin, prompted by an RTE programme on The Verne. Ex-Con B claimed that, since the large majority of Mountjoy prisoners came from a handful of postal districts in and around Dublin, there would be 'a chance to impact not only on the inmates but also on their communities in a dramatic way' (*Vernacular* 1998b: 3). Lee (1998) wrote to Griffin saying that she was not comfortable with these ambitions, 'especially when the volunteers are currently so sparse.' In March 1998 Lee wrote to Walker, pointing out that Highpoint and Swaleside were not the easiest locations for volunteers, particularly for men (Lee 2004). Volunteer resources were pushed to breaking point.

The problem was that few, if any, of those driving this expansion had any experience of what was required. As of July 1998 the Kairos-APAC Trust existed along with a Standing Committee of four Governors and their Chaplains working for Alan Walker. None had served on a Kairos Weekend so had no knowledge of the problems and conditions of building Kairos teams. Nor had the Committee any experience of the problems and pressures of volunteer commitment and recruitment (Lee 1998). This was a grave weakness because 'the whole operation depends initially on knowledge and assessment of the volunteer situation locally – as well as the availability and quality of those prepared to take the necessary steps to train and produce a qualified team' (Lee 2004).

Some supposed that if an insufficient number of trained Kairos volunteers existed to run a programme, other volunteers could be found. But this overlooked the fact that Fourth Day programmes operated under licence and could only be run by those who were trained (see Chapter 2). The only alternative was to devise a completely different programme. But this would not have the benefit of Kairos's experience in prisons. Writing to Griffin, Lee (1998) observed: 'The members of these committees cannot, I suppose, be blamed for not understanding something they have never experienced, nor for trying to push something they have seen to be so successful.' With sufficient warning it should have been possible to build communities of volunteers. But this takes time, and both Kairos-APAC and the Prison Service were in too much of a hurry. 'The Governors' Committee had great expectations but not much practical knowledge' (*ibid.*).

6. The Fall of Kairos-APAC

Having over-expanded from the beginning, Kairos-APAC was now seriously over-stretched. The trigger for its sudden collapse was loss of confidence in its new Chief Executive, namely Ex-Con B. In January 1999, The *Independent* broke the news in a front-page headline that Ex-Con B had a 25-year history of fraud. This included at least 70 previous convictions and prison terms in the UK, Canada and the United States (Burrell 1999a and 1999b). Two days later the Chair of the Kairos-APAC Trust appeared on BBC Radio 4's *Sunday* programme. He claimed that both he and the Prison Service knew about Ex-Con B's background and that Ex-Con B's employment was justified because he was 'a brilliant fundraiser' (Lee 1999).

The Kairos-APAC Trust subsequently sought to distance itself from Ex-Con B. In March 1999, The *Independent* broke the news that Ex-Con B had been sacked by the Trust 'amid allegations of financial irregularities and administrative failings' (Burrell 1999a) including 'failing to report funding deficits, appointing staff without authority, failing to forward correspondence from the Charity Commission and 'glossing over' financial details'. Ex-Con B was arrested in May 1999 and charged with procuring the execution of a valuable security by deception. He was convicted the following year (Burrell 2000a and 2000b).

Media pressure forced the Kairos-APAC Trust into dissolution on 22nd March 1999. Writing to Griffin at the end of that month, Lee (1999) claimed that 'half the Prisons Board would like to close the book on what they know as Kairos-APAC.' A former Governor agrees: 'In 1999 there was a move to try to close down the whole organization. People tried to use the failure of the Kairos-APAC Trust and the adverse publicity surrounding [Ex-Con B] to manufacture that failure' (Respondent G 2004). A former Assistant Chaplain-General shares this view:

> The media was in constant touch with the Prison Service [about Ex-Con B] and Martin Narey [then Director-General of the Prison Service] was not convinced that this was good for the Service. It was obvious that the management would like to have seen the end of the programme when Kairos-APAC folded up. I suspected that those in the corridors of power did not like the idea of Christians having a positive effect on reoffending at no cost to the Prison Service, whereas those injecting considerable amounts of tax-payers' money into a variety of programmes were not seeing the same results.
>
> (Respondent A 2004)

The Prisons Minister, Lord Williams of Mostyn, mounted what The *Independent* later described as 'a damage-limitation exercise', claiming that Ex-Con B had no access to finances (Burrell 2000a). But concern about the Kairos-APAC Trust continued amid other allegations of mismanagement. The 1999 Annual Report of the Board of Visitors at Brixton said the Trust had submitted invoices for £51,000; yet 'not one single prisoner had been processed' in nine months. It claimed £27,360 had been paid, although government accounting procedures had not been followed (Burrell 2000a). The Charity Commissioners launched a formal inquiry into the Kairos-APAC Trust at the same time as the Prison Service announced that it would 'review the Trust's work thoroughly' (Bamber 1999). The *Sunday Telegraph* called the review 'a major embarrassment to prison chiefs who had enthusiastically backed the rapid expansion of the scheme' (*ibid.*). Existing Kairos-APAC units were allowed to continue under close supervision, but the Brixton development planned for February 1999 was scrapped, and future cooperation with the Prison Service was suspended.

Changes in the Prison Service Board had also left Kairos-APAC vulnerable:

> When Richard Tilt was Director General, Kairos and Kairos-APAC were well received, mainly through Alan Walker when he was Assistant Director General. I once sent an impressive written testimony from a prisoner who had been on Kairos-APAC at The Verne to Richard Tilt, and he made positive comments about it in his address to the Prison Chaplains Conference. Attitudes changed once Martin Narey was Director General. Martin Narey did attend the first closing service at Highpoint Women's Prison and was heard to ask afterwards if the programme could be adapted without the Christian input.
>
> (Respondent A 2004)

Walker left the Prison Service England and Wales early in 1999. A few months later Respondent G (2004) was removed from his position as Governor with no reason given and then formally instructed to have no further dealings directly or indirectly with the Kairos-APAC Trust or its successor.

A new Trust, with new Trustees, was formed to continue the work. They decided to call themselves Kainos Community, from the Greek word for 'renewal'. The name fitted the idea of a new trust 'rising from the ashes', but such a name would cause further confusion for Kairos.

The Acting Director of Regimes of the Prison Service England and Wales launched a review of Kairos-APAC's operations, which reported in May 1999. Following this review the Prison Service decided that the newly-formed Kainos Community could continue the work of Kairos-APAC pending an independent evaluation of its effectiveness. The results of this evaluation are summarized in Chapters 4–6, 9 and 10.

7. Lessons to learn

When Kainos received the go-ahead to continue the work of Kairos-APAC, a spokesman for the Prison Service said: 'We firmly believe that Kainos has learned the lessons from its predecessor' (Burrell 2000a). Now that faith-based units are emerging and expanding in different parts of the world (see Chapters 7, 8 and 11), what lessons can be learned from the rise and fall of Kairos-APAC?

Five main lessons are as follows:

(a) The role of ex-offenders

First, Ex-Cons A and B were insufficiently monitored when appointed to the roles of Project Coordinator and External Coordinator (later Chief Executive). Hebbern (2004: 1) maintains that there was nothing wrong in principle with employing Ex-Con B, despite the problems he later caused: 'As part of its resettlement policy the Prison Service is always encouraging employers to give ex-prisoners a chance. Sometimes it works and sometimes it doesn't. To never take the risk would mean that we have no faith in our own product. Whether he should have been given so much responsibility is another issue.' Lee agrees:

> Many *recuperandos* in APAC became highly responsible and trustworthy but this resulted from their passage through the entire programme, the support of their godparents throughout their sentences and working relationships close to the highly experienced volunteers in the prison ... [and] a strong relationship with [Governor] Mario Ottoboni ... I *never* imagined that he [Ex-Con A] and [Ex-Con B] could possibly be allowed to develop the whole project with as far as I could see very little monitoring.
>
> (2004; emphasis original)

A former Governor, however, disagrees:

> The question of the risks of employing ex-offenders is a red herring. All employers are encouraged to employ ex-offenders and not to do so ourselves could have been seen as a failure. There is always a risk and the odds are often not great but at times trust and faith in the individual come into the equation. One succeeded, one failed, but not before he had done an exceptional amount of good work.
>
> (Respondent G 2004)

The question remains whether it was sensible to have placed such a high degree of financial trust in an ex-prisoner with such an extensive history of weakness in precisely that area and who had not demonstrated probity over a credible period of time.

(b) Lack of understanding

Second, it is critical that Trustees responsible for administering a unit that uses Kairos should understand what Kairos does. That may mean spending a Weekend experiencing what the volunteers and prisoners experience. Yet it appears that few members of Kairos-APAC had attended a Kairos Weekend: 'We had suggested that [it] be one of the criteria for inclusion in the Trust as a governing body. And they felt it was simply not necessary. They saw their job as purely a fund-raising activity and it wasn't important that they really understand the ministry' (Griffin 2003). Respondent G (2004), for example, saw attendance at a Weekend as unnecessary provided he had access to programme materials: 'I did not attend a Fourth Day Weekend and believed I should stay removed and objective in my oversight. This same approach I applied to all courses delivered in the prison.' Alan Walker was invited to attend a Kairos in the US in order to provide anonymity, but although Walker considered it seriously, he never found the opportunity (Griffin 2003).

An early Kairos-APAC Trustee who resigned in protest over the appointment of Ex-Con B to the post of External Coordinator commented: 'I felt that it was obvious, even then, that the whole project was entered into with insufficient depth of study and understanding of the basic operational methods of Kairos' (Moore 2004: 1).

(c) The role of volunteers

Third, there was little understanding or communication with Kairos UK and with those who represented the volunteer effort. On the one hand there was a 'grass-roots' understanding that volunteers were important. The Principal Officer of D-wing at The Verne remarked: 'Whatever else we do we have found that regular opportunities to meet 'ordinary people' has a profound effect in changing attitudes and behaviour' (Hebbern 1999b). Despite this, the Kairos-APAC External co-ordinator promoted the projects on a wider basis than Kairos could support. It was apparently easier for Kairos-APAC to raise money and hire staff for these projects than it was for Kairos to raise the volunteer support that was inherently required to support each project (Griffin 1999b).

This was hardly surprising. There was a significant cost to volunteering. Kairos volunteers had to take part in a recognized Fourth Day programme. Then they had to commit to rigorous team training and to the three-day Weekend itself, which actually takes four days. They also had to commit to regular reunions with prisoners for at least one year. This commitment doubles for those doing post-Weekend follow-up such as the Kairos Journey programme. The number of persons qualified and committed to these requirements is limited. If one adds to this the request from The Verne *and* Swaleside *and* Highpoint North *and* Highpoint South for a six-monthly programme, and thus *two* Weekends a year *plus* additional follow-up programmes, the number of volunteers required is considerable.

One early Trustee of the Kairos-APAC Trust commented: 'It seems that while giving was the heart of the matter for those on D Wing at The Verne and the volunteers, a problem can arise for the administrators in undervaluing that which is given so freely' (Moore 2004: 1). This is not surprising. Ottoboni, the founder of APAC, claims that when attempts are made to replicate APAC 'many times the elements being disregarded are those of the greatest importance' (2003: 76–77).

> Griffin (2003) explained this, but to no avail: 'I told Alan Walker that it should be evident to anyone that this programme cannot be called up at will. Even if a correctional facility is ready and willing, the community and the church represent the greater challenge. Kairos is a unique programme and it is presented by a very small fraction of those in the organized church. I continued that they need to begin ploughing the ground to cultivate and grow potential volunteer support within any local community about two years ahead of demand for the programme.' This never happened. Instead both the Kairos-APAC Trust and the Prison Service tried to force support by opening units in places where they had little chance of delivery (Griffin 1999b).
>
> Respondent A (2004) agrees: 'There were a number of factors that needed to be in place before Kairos-APAC could be introduced to an establishment. The enthusiasm should have been with the Chaplaincy Team rather than the Chaplain, i.e. all the Christian leaders should have been of one mind about the programme being in their establishment. Their enthusiasm had to be the overriding factor because they were accountable for what took place. The Governor and senior management needed to be of a similar mind because of the staffing and security implications of the programme and the need for space in the prison. The programme soaks up a large number of volunteers and there needed to be an assurance that such volunteers were available to sustain the programme.'

(d) The need for distance between Kairos and the faith-based unit

Fourth, there should have been some distance between Kairos and the faith-based unit. Griffin gave authority for the Trust to use the name Kairos provided they attached something else to distinguish it from the

Kairos ministry. Thus the 'The Verne Kairos APAC Trust' was born, later shortened simply to Kairos-APAC. The problem was that it gave the impression that Kairos had been 'swallowed up' by Kairos-APAC when in fact Kairos-APAC did not legally represent Kairos. In 1998 Lee wrote to Griffin: 'I am not at all happy about Kairos being co-opted into the Trust … It is bound to give the impression to the world at large that the authority of Kairos is vested in their hands and not in Kairos itself.'

This failure to recognize the distinct nature of the entities involved meant that the Ex-Con B scandal badly damaged Kairos. Although the scandal was exclusively a matter for Kairos-APAC, Kairos was tarred for a time with the same brush.

The decision to call the Trust Kairos-APAC also created tensions with the Prison Service Chaplaincy. We saw in Chapter 1 that Kairos operates at the invitation of and under the authority of the prison Chaplaincy. Kairos participants are expected to play an active part in Chapel life, and reunion groups occur under the auspices of the Chaplains. However, Kairos was used in the prison as a tool of Kairos-APAC, entirely independent of the Chaplaincy. There was no expectation that Kairos-APAC prisoners should be involved in Chapel life, and some Kairos-APAC prisoners gave the impression that they saw themselves as an 'alternative' church group within the prison. This was bound to create problems between Kairos, Kairos-APAC and the Chaplaincy (cf. Chapter 6).

(e) The role of the Prison Service

Finally, the Kairos-APAC Trust erred by trying to succeed over a broad area too rapidly. But senior management within the Prison Service encouraged this (see section 5 above). Griffin (2003) comments:

> If one were to assess blame for the failure of … [Kairos-APAC] in Great Britain, you would have to put that really squarely on the shoulders of the Prison Service … They absolutely dictated that it be replicated in other places where it was impossible to replicate because the volunteers weren't there …. It was a disaster to try to go into three additional prisons within the first year. It was crazy to even think about it. Of course Kairos told [Ex-Con B] it was not possible, and the leadership of Kairos in England told [Ex-Con B] it was not possible but [Ex-Con B] wanted to curry favour with the administration and wanted to please them and so he agreed to what was impossible to do and to deliver.

After its initial success at The Verne, the Prison Service appeared to see it as a tool that could be used in places where it was most convenient for the Prison Service rather than in places where it was most convenient for the ministry and where it would therefore stand the greatest chance of success.

Griffin (*ibid.*) summarizes:

> We need to be clear about what happened in England .... When the Prison Service decided they wanted it to go to other prisons, it was not Kairos that wanted it to go to other prisons, it was the Prison Service that said: 'We will have it over here and there and here'... but they had never really attended a Kairos Weekend. They had very little to go on other than the fact that this programme is successful and they saw it in action and they liked the results, having no idea of how we got to the results ... They wanted to reinvent the wheel according to their vision and that may or [may] not be successful. You just don't know.

In the end, the development of Christian-based units in England was flawed because of a mismatch between the need for long-range planning to build the communities necessary to support the work and short-term timetabling by the Prison Service.

8. Conclusions

What main conclusions can be drawn from this overview of the rise and fall of Kairos-APAC? We conclude as follows:

- Kairos-APAC made an immediate impact on The Verne aided, like Humaitá, by a history of control problems and the lack of an alternative.

- Kairos-APAC started off 'on the wrong foot' with the Prison Service and the Press by launching itself in a blaze of counter-productive publicity.

- Kairos-APAC was not always clear about its identity and who it was for and did not pay sufficient attention to informed consent.

- Kairos-APAC was 'oversold'; success was claimed or promised when the evidence was ambiguous or non-existent.

- There was too much expansion outside The Verne, too soon.

- The charitable Trust wanted to 'prove' that Kairos-APAC could 'work' in as many different settings as possible, yet little thought was given to replicating the programme in those areas where it stood the greatest chance of success.

- Ex-offenders employed in positions of responsibility in the unit or its charitable Trust should be monitored to improve accountability to outside observers.

- There was little understanding or communication with Kairos UK and with those who represented and coordinated the volunteer effort.

- There should have been distance between Kairos and the faith-based unit.

- The Prison Service appeared to see Kairos-APAC as a tool that could be used in places where it was most convenient for the Prison Service rather than in places where it would be most successful.

Notes

1 The work of Kairos UK is described in Chapter 2.
2 At the time of writing (April 2005) Kainos Community runs faith-based units in the wings of three prisons; HMP The Verne and HMP Swaleside, both in England, and HMP Parc, in Wales.
3 We are grateful to each of the sources mentioned, especially to Penelope Lee and Ike Griffin for making their correspondence available.
4 HMP The Verne, Portland is a Category C (medium) security training prison. In 1996 it housed 552 adult male prisoners, most of whom were in the latter half of sentences ranging from six to twelve years or were serving sentences of five years or less. Forty were serving life sentences, and 30% were foreign nationals. Few prisoners were regarded as high risk. In 1996 about a third of prisoners were from South Wales, so it was correctly anticipated that the opening of a new Category C prison at Bridgend, in Wales, towards the end of 1997 would bring about change of role for The Verne (Hebbern 1996).
5 Creighton (2003) recalls being part of a workshop group at an APAC day conference in December 1996 along with 'various HM Prison Service officials, including Governors, one of whom was the Governor of The Verne and also ... the Principal Officer at the prison. Both of them were cautioned by the rest of us about 'running ahead of themselves', until further research had been undertaken ...'. A report of proceedings (including the various workshops) was subsequently published (Prison Fellowship England and Wales 1997).
6 Lee (2004) 'urged the Chairman of the 'Kairos-APC' Trust and later suggested to the Chaplain of Highpoint who had experience as a psychotherapist that they visit Humaitá and explore Hugo Veronese's work, as [she] believed it to be fundamental to the major successes of APAC. But this never happened. Hugo Veronese died in December 2002 but his many students who worked [for] him in the prison understand his work'. Although D-Wing improved greatly, this failure to integrate Veronese's approach was for Lee a significant

limitation. 'The Verne saw the miracle happening under their hands and did not want to know there could be more' (*ibid.*).

7 It is worth pointing out that neither of the parent projects, APAC or Kairos, ask these particular questions. It seems that Kairos-APAC did not understand the parent projects on this issue.

8 Jo Chapman reported to Griffin that this was also her experience in leading the first women's Kairos Weekend in England at Highpoint North (Griffin 2003).

Chapter 4

Kainos Community: views from the inside

I've been in prison six and a half years, and it's different to anything I've experienced in prison or anywhere else.

Life-sentenced prisoner at HMP Swaleside (348)

The following three chapters draw on the evaluation of Kainos Community referred to in Section 6 of Chapter 3. This evaluation took place between August 2000 and July 2001.

This chapter looks at how prisoners both on and off the Kainos Communities viewed Kainos in all four prisons. Questions include: What sort of things did people hear about Kainos before they joined? How were people recruited onto Kainos and how were they selected? Who does Kainos appeal to, who actually goes on it, and why? Who really runs it? What were the advantages and disadvantages of being in a Kainos Community? Did people get special treatment on Kainos? Does it improve prisoners' chances of parole? Did Kainos have any specific effect on them, or on other people, or on other parts of the prison? What were their specific stories and experiences about life on Kainos?

This chapter draws on the findings of nearly 50 in-depth interviews with prisoners as well as group discussions and observations of Community activities at a time when Kainos was running in all four prisons. Numbers in brackets refer to the number assigned to the interviewee as part of the original research interview schedule of Burnside *et al.* 2001. Given the diversity of the populations at the four prisons and the consequent adaptations made to the Kainos programme,

This chapter was co-authored by Jonathan Burnside and Nancy Loucks.

the chapter reports the findings as they pertained to each Kainos Community rather than to Kainos Communities as a whole. In saying this, many of the issues arguably have relevance for faith-based units in any prison setting.

1. Background

(a) Daily life in Kainos Communities

Participation in a Kainos Community is technically voluntary. Prisoners usually learn about Kainos during an orientation session upon arrival at a prison, either from a member of the Kainos staff, from prisoners in the Community, or both. Male and female prisoners may apply to be part of a Kainos programme from any prison, assuming they fit the Prison Service's criteria for placement in the prisons where Kainos Communities are based. They must complete an application and interview and agree to abide by the rules of the Community. These rules are generally that they must attend compulsory meetings and programmes including a Kairos Weekend, that they must not use or traffic drugs, that they take personal responsibility and make an effort to change, and that they continue to abide by the Prison Service's rules, regulations, and sentence planning. Prisoners are not required to be a part of any organized religion, either before they apply or during their time on the unit.

The basic structure of Kainos was largely similar in all four prisons. Each Community held weekly meetings, required for everyone in the unit whether participating in the Kainos Programme or not (though at HMP Swaleside, the highest security prison of the four, these meetings were only for those who were currently involved in the Kainos Programme). The Community President or Chair, a prisoner elected by others on the unit, was responsible for running these meetings. Meetings were used for general Community business and for ironing out conflicts on the unit. For example, we observed announcements of fund-raising for charities (e.g. through sponsored runs), allocation of cleaning duties, discussions with staff about privileges such as use of televisions, concerns (e.g. missing property), and distribution of certificates for completion of courses. The general practice was for meetings to start and finish with a prayer from one of the prisoners. Smaller group meetings, usually by location (e.g. within a single dorm at The Verne) also took place at least weekly and could be called more frequently on request. Civilian staff employed by Kainos facilitated these meetings, which were said to be 'a key element of the cognitive therapy delivery', and the prisoners ran additional small group meetings themselves. Individual counselling was available on each unit, in addition to that available in the rest of the prison, through a trained counsellor on the Kainos staff.

'Godparenting' evenings took place at least weekly, in which volunteers from outside the prison came into the units, usually for informal conversation and befriending. Attendance at godparenting evenings was technically mandatory, but the extent to which this was enforced varied between prisons. Each Community also had some sort of follow-up programme to the Kairos Weekend, though the actual content and duration of these programmes varied considerably between establishments.

Kainos Communities often had talks or activities available on a voluntary basis in addition to the core programme. The Kainos Community on the 'Base' landing at Swaleside, for example, had a daily 'Thought for the Day' in which a member of the Chaplaincy or a Kainos employee would say a few words. Prisoners on all four units often held Bible studies or prayer groups, but these were strictly voluntary and were not organized through the Kainos staff. Attendance at religious services in the prison was also entirely voluntary.

Another variation between the units was the structure of prisoner leadership within the units. At Highpoint North, for example, ten women were appointed as Elders, although this figure was not fixed. The women themselves nominated the Elders and, provided prison and Kainos staff had no objection, the new Elders were appointed following an interview with serving Elders. At The Verne, the number of Elders was somewhat larger (20 at the time of the research) but again this was not limited to any particular figure. No formal election was held: a list of the prisoners' nominees went to the Kainos staff and serving Elders for final selection. The unit at Swaleside, on the other hand, had no system of Elders *per se*, though 12 prisoners who participated in the previous Kairos Weekend remained on the Base landing with the new group, rather than moving on to other landings in the wing with the rest of their colleagues.

(b) The Kairos Weekend and the Kainos Programme

One common element of Kainos Communities at the time of the research was the Kairos Weekend, a required part of participation in a Kainos unit (see Chapter 2). The Weekend lasts from a Thursday night to the following Sunday night, with no participation in the regular prison regime during that time, including visits (with odd exceptions). Kairos Weekends are run by a separate organization called Kairos UK and are staffed largely by volunteers from outside the prison. As outlined in Chapter 2, the Weekends are fully scripted and originate with Kairos

Prison Ministry International (KPM) in the United States, although some adjustments are made to adapt it to a UK audience.[1]

During Kairos Weekends, volunteers bring in large numbers of cakes, meant to demonstrate to the participants the support and goodwill of Kairos and the wider church community. Prisoners and staff both frequently mentioned this aspect of the Weekend and, for some, this was the most memorable part. Visitors are not generally allowed to bring food into a prison, but at the time of the research, prison managers allowed this as concession to the programme. Not surprisingly, non-Kairos prisoners who had the opportunity to share some of the cakes described them as one of the benefits to the prison from the Kairos Weekend.

People who volunteer for Kainos say they are told very little about the Weekend before they participate, except that it is a required part of the programme. One effect of this 'mystique' was to build excitement about the Weekend and to encourage prisoners to trust staff and other prisoners who have been through the Weekend. However, another effect was to create a sense of anxiety and tension: for example, one prisoner mentioned having nightmares about it before he attended. Kainos staff reasoned that since each person's experience of the Weekend is different, it is better for prisoners to come to the Weekend with 'fresh eyes'. The drawback is that this perceived secrecy exposes the Kairos Weekend, and Kainos Communities by implication, to accusations of being 'cultish'. Many prisoners commented in hindsight that they were glad they were not told more about what happens during the Weekend before they attended, despite their initial fears. Some believed, however, that they could have been told a bit more about the Weekend to allay their fears without ruining the experience. One prisoner said she would not have taken part in the Weekend if she had known what was involved:

> If we had been told what the itinerary was going to be we could have mentally and emotionally prepared for it. I like to know what's going on. The secretiveness of it was unnecessary really.
>
> (225)

Not only was the secretiveness unnecessary, it was also directly contrary to established Kairos practice which, as we have seen, specifically allows prisoners to have fears and questions addressed before the Weekend (see Chapters 2 and 3). This was another aspect of the problem that Kairos faced when operating in the service of Kainos. Not all Kainos staff were familiar with the Kairos Weekend, and this allowed some false impressions of the Kairos Weekend to spread. The secrecy also tended to undermine informed consent, which was a problem for Kainos in some cases (see Chapter 6).

(c) Local difficulties and variation

Kainos Communities are not uniform in each establishment. Each Kainos team has a certain amount of leeway to adapt the programme for the population they serve and for the circumstances of the individual prison. To an extent this is essential. For example, both Highpoint North and Highpoint South house very short-term prisoners who are unlikely to be there to complete programmes of several months' duration. The length of the programme is not so much the obstacle here as the fact that the programme is designed to follow on from a Kairos Weekend, which only takes place every six months. Restricting the programme only to those prisoners who would be in the prison long enough to complete the Weekend and full programme proved to limit the population too severely.

This meant that, during the research, prisoners could be part of the Kainos Community at Highpoint North and Highpoint South without ever participating in a Kairos Weekend, even though the Weekend is arguably the centrepiece of the Kainos programme. Rapid turnover of the population was destabilizing to the Community and made a rigidly structured programme impractical to operate. Prisoners at The Verne tended to be serving longer sentences. They were therefore in a better position to complete the (full) 18-week Journey programme which is a possible follow-up programme to the Kairos Weekend. This was notably longer than the ten to twelve week programme offered at Highpoint North and South. Here, however, the content rather than the structure was at issue. The Kainos staff at The Verne had recently replaced the Journey programme with a Life Issues course, which they felt met their needs of the population there more adequately. Based on positive responses from prisoners to relationships begun on the Kairos Weekend, it is possible that follow-up programmes may have more impact if the relationships begun on the Kairos Weekend with volunteers were to continue. Indeed, research into religious conversion, identity change, and desistance from crime (Curran 2002: 71) has shown that the *quality* of conventional attachments are more relevant to enduring changes in identity than the mere existence of these attachments.[2]

Swaleside houses yet another, longer-term population. The issue there, then, was not turnover of the population, but rather what to do with people who remained on the Kainos wing after they completed the programme. Only one of the three landings was actively involved in the Kainos programme; the others were either full of people who had completed the programme or those who were waiting to start it. At the time of the research, attempts were being made to increase the number of Kairos volunteers and 'godparents' in Swaleside. With an increase in local volunteers, it would be possible to include further options for follow-up programmes.

Another concern was that the programmes offered through Kainos often had similar titles and covered similar material (e.g. anger management, offending behaviour) to those required for sentence planning.[3] However, they were not Prison Service accredited courses. This caused confusion for some prisoners who thought they were fulfilling their sentence plans by taking part in Kainos courses when in fact they were not. The placement of Kainos programmes into a prisoner's sentence plan raises important questions regarding human rights as well. This is because Kainos is technically a voluntary programme and should therefore be free from any hint of coercion to participate or penalty should a prisoner choose to withdraw. This issue is discussed more thoroughly in Chapter 6.

In sum, the programme length, content, and status of programmes in Kainos communities varied according to the prison. All included a Kairos Weekend, but not all prisoners were in the prisons long enough to attend it. Follow-up programmes varied in both length and content, as did numbers of required meetings and optional talks and programmes.

The next section looks in more depth at the experiences of prisoners who took part in Kainos Communities and were still based there.

2. Inside Kainos: The views of Kainos prisoners

Interviews with Kainos-based prisoners for this section examined what they knew about Kainos before they arrived on the unit, experiences of the programme, and relations with others who were also part of Kainos.

(a) Prior knowledge

A common theme from all the interviews was that many people, including prison staff when they were posted to the units, knew very little about Kainos Communities. One comment from prisoners on the Kainos wing at Swaleside was that the Kainos compact should be more explicit about the content of the programme. Lack of information about the programme fostered suspicion, rumours, and criticism from prisoners, staff, managers, and beyond. This was particularly evident in interviews from people who had little experience of Kainos (see section 3, below).

Even so, these prisoners chose to go to a Kainos unit. Reasons for this varied. Some said they wanted to practise their religion and to be in a community setting. One said she was 'at a point in [her] life when [she] wanted this' (611). Alternatively they commented that 'It's a way out of the rat race ... This takes you away from all that' (634).

Research into religious conversion in prison (Curran 2002) noted additional benefits to prisoners who convert that seem to apply to prisoners – religious or otherwise – in Kainos Communities as well. Curran notes, for example, that prisoners 'were accepted, and valued as part of a group in a manner that many had never experienced before' and that religious belief 'provided ways of coping with life in prison', gave them a 'sense of purpose', and helped them 'overcome some of their fears about life after imprisonment' (*ibid.*: 302). In sum, Curran comments that:

> adopting Christianity appeared to constitute both an effective means of *coping* with the trauma of imprisonment and *making sense* of the past ... Christianity also provided prisoners with a conventional non-criminal identity with which they could anticipate a meaningful future.
>
> (*ibid.*: 22; emphasis in original)

Adopting religion, or arguably participating in a religiously-based community such as Kainos, is 'an effective means of distancing oneself from the past and the offences that one had committed' (*ibid.*: 35; also Clear *et al.*, 1992; Maruna 2001).

Despite the limited information about what actually happens on a Kainos unit, then, prisoners may be willing to take the chance and join anyway if they want something other than the more traditional prison life.

(b) The Kairos Weekend

In no situation was the lack of prior knowledge more striking than in the case of the Kairos Weekend. As noted above, however, building this 'mystique' seemed to be deliberate practice although it was not established Kairos practice (see Chapters 2 and 3).

Despite (or some may argue because of) the lack of prior knowledge or preparation, responses from prisoners to the Kairos Weekend were overwhelmingly (87 per cent) positive. Indeed, over a third described it in extremely positive terms. These responses were given several months after the Kairos Weekend itself and are therefore unlikely to be the result of a 'post-Weekend high'. Only a minority (9 per cent) was negative or critical, noted above, though admittedly people who were more positive were more likely to remain in the Community than those who were more critical. No other element of the Kainos programme drew such a strong response. It would appear from this that the Kairos Weekend is a critical element in Kainos Community. The Weekend seems to play an important part in bringing prisoners together: 'People you wouldn't have spoken to before because you might have an argument with them; after the Weekend, everyone was friends' (412).

A crucial factor in the success of the Weekend was said to be the participation of the volunteers who come in from outside. This was a common theme in all four prisons, with prisoners often commenting on their significance:

> It's different getting the love from people you don't know. It's unconditional, there's nothing attached to it, at the end of the day.
> (223 Highpoint North)

> What really put love in my heart is so many people write to me a letter who I really don't know and they write all these good things and praying for me. These people don't see me but they love me. The same thing they have done for me, I'm going to do to others.
> (395 Highpoint South)

> They [the volunteers] give you different vibes ... They teach me a lot to communicate with people so when I get outside I can communicate with others.
> (279 The Verne)

> I've been in prison six and a half years [a lifer] and it's different to anything I've experienced in prison or anywhere else. *In what way?* Fifteen Christians coming in from outside to spend three days with prisoners and they put so much effort into it and it's voluntary for them. *Why is the voluntary aspect important to you?* If somebody is putting so much into something then I will repay in kind.
> (348 Swaleside)

Not everyone spoke positively about the participation of volunteers from outside the prison, but most prisoners were clearly touched by the volunteers' attentions and efforts (see also Curran 2002).

The participation of people from outside prisons can be crucial in terms of engaging prisoners' interest and effort. Research into generativity – the social investment into future generations – in prisons states that:

The most critical goal would be to make the high walls, razor wire, and bars to the prison more permeable, allowing normative social forces 'in' through the high security. For instance, when groups of Quakers or other volunteers visit prisons to befriend convicts, not only are they modeling generativity in the prison society, but they also provide a rare niche where prison residents can feel safe to show a softer or more caring side of themselves.

(Maruna *et al.* 2004: 147)

The input of volunteers may have longer-term benefits as well: research into desistance from crime has suggested that sustained desistance is more likely where a prisoner has strong ties to a community and available social supports beyond prison (Bottoms 2001, 2002; Curran 2002). Connection with a religious community outside has the additional advantage of developing a pro-social identity for people who may never have had this before (Curran 2002). Curran explains that the need to belong to a social group is a fundamental requirement for a stable identity. The use of volunteers from outside the prison is a powerful tool:

Belonging to a new conventional community promises to a new member, the development of new relationships, a sense of purpose, meaning, and the lure of others that care.

(*ibid.*: 76)

She goes on to say that 'The arrival of personal letters or visitors can have a 'humanizing effect" (*ibid.*: 121) in an environment where people are stripped of identity, starting with their name being replaced by a number. Social support through the use of volunteers and *agape* letters sent to prisoners taking part in the Kairos Weekend from volunteers worldwide (see Chapter 2) 'provide individuals with much needed feelings of closeness, caring, a sense of belonging and acceptance' (*ibid.*: 134).

Other prisoners said the testimonies of ex-offenders had a big impact on them during the Kairos Weekend. One commented that the Christian aspects of the Weekend largely 'went over [his] head' but that he listened particularly to ex-offenders' testimonies and 'began asking questions after that' (634).

(c) The Kainos programme

Prisoners who completed the Kainos programme were also asked what they thought of this. Whilst a majority (54 per cent) were positive, there was markedly less enthusiasm than there was for the Kairos Weekend.

Only 6 per cent were extremely positive, whilst a fifth were either negative or extremely negative (although those who stayed were generally more positive than those who dropped out). Although a number of prisoners referred to different aspects of the programme with enthusiasm, notably the symbolic victim-offender reconciliation programme 'Sycamore Tree', one of the most valued aspects of the follow-up programme was the 'godparenting' evenings. These again involved volunteers coming in from outside the prison to 'befriend' prisoners. In the vast majority of cases, prisoners said this provided variety, friendship, and a link to the outside world. Crucially, volunteers were seen as offering a different kind of relationship to the dynamic prisoners had with the Kainos-employed staff: 'The people who came in went out of their way to come in, *it wasn't like they were being paid*' (401, italics added).

This bears out the critical importance Ottoboni and Griffin attached to the 'authenticity of the volunteer ethic' (see Chapters 1 and 2). Again, this was not always recognized. In a complete misunderstanding of the dynamics of the Kairos Weekend, the Kairos-APAC Trust offered to pay Kairos volunteers for their contribution. The motive was a misguided and 'very desperate' attempt to raise volunteers and to expand the programme more rapidly (Griffin 2003). The Executive Director of KPM refused to allow this, whereupon the Trust suggested that they might at least pay transportation costs, food and other expendables (*ibid.*). Griffin, however, insisted that the volunteer base needed to raise their own money, pay for their own transportation and enter the ministry sacrificially.

Prisoners generally seemed to like the outside participation:

I liked the fact that Bible teaching was coming from people from outside.
How important is the participation of outside volunteers in Kainos for you?
It's extremely important.
Why?
Because you get a more varied view, the more people who give talks.

(259)

The relative lack of enthusiasm from prisoners for the Kainos programme compared to the Kairos Weekend suggests that Kainos's follow-up programmes are not as effective as they could be in building on the seemingly positive experience of the Kairos Weekend. Several commented on how the sense of community experienced during the Weekend simply fell away in the weeks that followed:

[During the Kairos Weekend] I noticed a change in all of the prisoners on the wing. People wanted to help each other all of a sudden.
Did that last?
No it didn't.

(392)

Doing posters [for] the Weekend was fun but it wasn't the same atmosphere as a Weekend. People drifted away from it quite quickly.

(341)

There was a sense of community during the Kairos Weekend but it died off ... You need the volunteers to keep it all going, they take a great part of it.

(331)

As we saw in Chapter 2, the Kairos Weekend is never intended to be an end in itself but is simply a means of establishing prisoners in 'reunion groups' or 'share and prayer' groups in the prison. We saw that the Kairos *Continuing Ministry Manual* explicitly states that 'Kairos Weekends have but one purpose: the formation of resident leaders in correctional institutions into small share and prayer groups' (KPM 1995a: 1). We also saw that the Kairos Weekend is *not* the Kairos Prison Ministry but simply *an introduction* to that ministry (KPM 1998b: 27) and that 'the Weekend will not produce a permanent effect without post-Weekend activity' (KPM 1998a: 3–3).

However, it seems as though Kairos-APAC and Kainos failed to recognize the importance of the Kairos continuing ministry to sustain a sense of community. Lee (2004) recalls that 'it was felt increasingly by the Kairos-APAC staff that with the Kairos participants living in community and involved in other programmes together, the small groups were not necessary'.[4] The fact that some prisoners in Kairos-APAC were released in as little as three weeks after their Kairos Weekend compounded this (Lee 2004).[5] Griffin had warned that this might happen. In a letter to the first Chair of Kairos UK in 1996, Griffin warned that to focus solely on the Kairos Weekend rather than the follow-up programme 'always portends trouble' (Griffin 1996b). This failure by Kairos-APAC and Kainos meant that, once again, Kairos was never fully implemented in the way in which it was intended.

Prisoners seem to value some continuity between the Kairos Weekend and the follow-up programme:

Not having volunteers delivering the programme is a mistake. Definitely. Without these people there from the Weekend means you lose a sense of continuity.

(281)

This bears out the policy of Kairos Prison Ministry which is that follow-up programmes such as the Instructional Reunion, monthly reunions, the Kairos 'two-day retreat' and the Kairos Journey programme must be delivered by team members from the Kairos Weekend to help prisoners recall and act upon what they learned from that event (see Chapter 2). In England, however, these essential Kairos programmes were implemented only rarely (e.g. the Instructional Reunion), inappropriately (e.g. the Journey programme) or not at all (e.g. monthly reunions and the Kairos 'two-day retreat'). Once again, Kairos was not implemented in England in the way in which it was designed.

Not only the presentation but the structure of the follow-up programme seemed to be in need of a re-think. A discussion with one prisoner who was critical of the follow-up programme exemplifies this:

> *'What things do you think they could do after the Weekend to make you more of a community?*
> Some of the courses need to be better presented.
> *What was the problem?*
> A lot of them were lecture-type courses and I would have preferred more role-playing. Some of the courses need to be a little bit lighter so people can build trust in a fun and positive way.

(337)

The follow-up programme seemed to need to be adapted more fully to the learning styles of most offenders (e.g. oral presentation for prisoners who have difficulties with written work and assistance for foreign nationals with a poor grasp of English). Also surprising was why several Kainos Communities were allowed to be located in areas with low volunteer numbers, given the importance of volunteers to both the Kairos Weekend and follow-up programme and despite warnings to (then) Kairos-APAC regarding the difficulties in recruiting volunteers for some prisons (see Chapter 3). As Griffin remarks:

> If the volunteers have to travel more than 30 or 40 minutes to the prison it becomes very difficult to go back for 20 weeks one day a week. For a Kairos Weekend, which is four days intensive, you can travel from one country to another for that event and you can quite

often go back once a month for a reunion and travel some distance. But to go back weekly is something else and so if the prison is isolated from the major population base from which the volunteers are drawn then you're really dead in the water before you start.

(2003: 18)

A few prisoners mentioned another possible impact of the Kairos Weekend on the prison, namely the possible effects on prisoners who are psychologically more vulnerable. This is a valid concern, as a high proportion of prisoners have extensive histories of victimization and trauma (female prisoners in particular; see for example Loucks 1998). The Kairos Weekend is an intensive time of self-reflection and questioning. While most people are fully able to cope with this, and while those interviewed said they did not find it difficult themselves, there are a few who may find it much more difficult. If such cases arise, it is worth asking to what extent Kairos volunteers and Kairos Community are able to deal with this. It underlines the dangers of introducing a Kairos Weekend without the necessary Kairos follow-up programmes, especially the 'nurturing' environment that is said to be provided by the weekly 'reunion groups' (see Chapter 2).

In view of the possible increased vulnerability of prisoners following the Kairos Weekends, or even generally during a prisoner's time in Kainos, appropriate support is essential. Kainos is meant to support itself: people who are more vulnerable are supposed to be able to rely on support from others in the Community. However, this may not be enough for people who are dealing with more complex issues. With this in mind, we were particularly impressed with facilities at The Verne. By accident or design, the Listener Liaison Officer and the prison's crisis suite were based on the Kainos unit, and many Prison Listeners (prisoners specially trained by the Samaritans to offer peer support) were participants in the Kainos programme. This meant that prisoners had access to support on a 24-hour basis, seven days a week. Such immediate access to support provides an example of good practice for any programme such as the Kairos Weekend which uses cognitive-behavioural therapeutic techniques.

Some research has suggested that the religious element in itself may offer support for prisoners to cope. Curran (2002) found that prisoners' levels of religiosity corresponded directly with their levels of adjustment in prison, while other research too has shown links between religious belief and coping abilities in prison (Day and Laufer 1983; Koenig 1995; Perettie and McIntyre 1984). Not all prisoners on Kainos will have religious beliefs that increase their ability to cope, however, so participants may well be justified in their concerns for the well-being of more vulnerable prisoners.

109

(d) Relations with others

The interviews asked prisoners about any changes in prisoners' relations with their families, other prisoners, and with staff during their time on Kainos. Some Kainos programmes include a Family Day - an opportunity for families to come into the prison for a full day visit, often with food and activities provided by the prison. In those prisons which had them, Family Days were viewed as a positive step in building or maintaining family relations. While some prisoners said that relations with their families had remained the same while they were on Kainos (usually because relations were already good), the general perception was that families had noted changes in prisoners' attitudes and behaviour for the better. As a very experienced and notoriously 'difficult' prisoner at The Verne commented about his family: 'They sense a peace in me now' (634).

Changes in relations between prisoners were more obvious: almost without fail, prisoners who had been on Kainos said they had become more understanding and tolerant of others, and that their behaviour on the wing reflected this: 'I know that I've changed – I can see it for myself' (619). The same prisoner – a Muslim at Highpoint South – said that one's attitude changes, as well as the way one speaks to people, and that the type of humour and language used is 'no longer at someone's expense.' Other prisoners noted that topics of conversation differed from that on other wings, focusing more on personal issues such as family relations and less on their offending. A prisoner on a non-Kainos wing believed this was a distinct advantage: 'I'd go [to Kainos] tomorrow. It's different talk there. I want conversations not talking about their crimes and all that talking about criminal activity, criminal activity' (565). A Kainos prisoner described it as an opportunity to open up, which was not possible on another wing. Prisoners were no longer under pressure from others: 'There's no need to be "tough" ' (616).

Curran explained why participation in a spiritually-based programme may have such an impact:

> In becoming religious, some prisoners felt compelled to opt out of the inmate social system since the prescriptions of religion often ran contrary to the dominant characteristics of prison culture.
>
> (2002: 32)

In such situations, 'positive morality' is accepted and shared by a given social group (Bottoms 2002). This 'positive peer pressure' was evident in Kainos units as well: rather than the negative expectations of behaviour arguably present in many mainstream prison landings, the expectation on Kainos units was for certain standards of behaviour and mutual respect. Chapter 6 explores more fully whether Christianity or indeed religion is a necessary part of this.

Relations between prisoners and prison staff improved as well, and fewer disciplinary problems were evident (see Chapter 5). Curran (2002) noted in her research that prison staff found that prisoners who were sincere in their commitment, in this case to religious conversion, were more amenable to prison rules. A prisoner at The Verne said he 'used to hate [prison staff] before, but now you get the chance to see them as a human being, just doing their job – they give respect, so they *get* respect' (633, emphasis original). For many prisoners this improvement was specifically for prison staff based on the Kainos units, however. One prisoner said '[there is an] invisible line drawn between the staff here [on Kainos] and the staff up front [elsewhere] … not the procedural straightjacket', but instead they discuss things and can sort things out themselves (627).

The most notable exception to the reports of improved relations was a prisoner on the Kainos unit at Swaleside who said he now trusted staff less. It turned out, however, that this prisoner had just been denied a reduction in his security category, which he felt the prison staff had 'promised' him - an issue related to the politics of administrative decisions in prison rather than to Kainos. Both prisoners and staff attributed most of these changes to the experience on Kainos, with some exceptions. One woman said she had changed because she had stopped using drugs, not through choice, but because they were not readily available on the wing. Equally, another said she had stopped using drugs through the support she had on the unit, so she attributed the change to Kainos. Some were more direct in attributing credit for any change: a Muslim at another prison said directly, 'My change in life, I owe it to Kainos' (633).

(Curran 2002) notes that identity change is an integral part both of religious conversion and of desistance from anti-social activities over time. Indeed, she notes that prisoners are more receptive to religion when their 'self-identity is questioned, placed under strain or threatened with annihilation' (*ibid.*: 48). A prisoner at The Verne said he found it easier to overcome 'bad thoughts' – that the Christian aspect of the Kainos Community 'gives me a way out instead of carrying it around with me' (634). But is a Christian-based programme a prerequisite for such positive responses? Again, this question is explored more fully in Chapter 6.

(e) Is Kainos truly a 'community'?

Similar to the question of relations, the issue of whether Kainos is truly a 'community' emerged clearly during the research. An example of this came up as we observed the regular Community meetings, in this case in a discussion about missing property. At The Verne, batteries from a hall clock had been taken, which one of the prisoners had bought for the clock himself. This problem was highlighted at a Community meeting, and the batteries later reappeared in the clock. Whatmore's (1987) account suggests that community meetings were central to the success of the Barlinnie Special Unit. They provided a safety valve for aggressive feelings, enabling grievances to be discussed quickly and perhaps (as in the example just given) resolved.

Prisoners at Swaleside also discussed the theft of property, but in this case items were being taken from cells, and the men suspected a particular individual on the unit. A prison officer present at the meeting suggested that the men lock their cell doors for the time being. This in itself caused a great deal of distress and was a frequent topic during the group discussions for the research, with the men saying that one of the benefits of being on a Kainos unit is that you shouldn't have to lock your cell door. The loss of trust meant a loss of community.

(f) Differences between prisoners

Of interest was the difference in responses between people in prison for the first time and those who had served previous custodial sentences. While the small numbers of interviews preclude formal statistical evaluation, the trend was that the more critical participants in the Kainos Communities tended to be first-time prisoners, while the most positive responses came from people with more custodial experience. While the reasons for the differences in attitude are not certain, the contrast between regimes on Kainos Communities and those elsewhere in the prison estate may well invoke a more positive response (in favour of Kainos) from those with a stronger basis for comparison.

Even more striking contrasts were evident between prisoners who were taking part in the Kainos Communities and those elsewhere in the prison. It is to this latter group of prisoners we now turn.

3. Looking On: The views of Non-Kainos prisoners

Interviews for this section – 27 non-Kainos prisoners in total – included a mixture of those who had never 'set foot on' Kainos, those who had been on Kainos but had never joined the Community, and others who had joined but had been 'thrown off' or who chose to leave the Community. Interviewees were selected to represent a range of theological positions including atheism, agnosticism, Buddhism, various

Christian denominations, Islam, Paganism, Sikhism and Theism[6] (for a full breakdown see Appendix 3, Burnside *et al.* 2001). This section describes the findings from this diverse group.

(a) What is Kainos, and what is it for?

Most knew that Kainos was a 'religious' wing, although there was some confusion about what this meant. Prisoners variously thought that Kainos Community was multifaith, a religion in itself, and 'a group therapy thing' (533). Only half knew it had a Christian basis. Most gleaned their information from multiple sources, including being moved onto the Kainos wings, fellow prisoners, the Chaplaincy, civilian prison staff, prison rumours, and external media. Less than half of non-Kainos prisoners recalled hearing about Kainos during their induction session upon entry to prison.

Prisoners heard mixed reports about Kainos. A majority heard negative things claiming it to be too religious ('it's the God-squad' (541)), too Christian ('just a lot of Bible classes' (566)), or 'a [soft] touch' (555). There was widespread suspicion of Kainos prisoners who were 'playing the system' (561): 'Prisoners see it as a scam, as a bit of a fraud' (559). Kainos was seen as either too 'soft' ('a 'goody-goody' outfit' (559)) or too 'harsh' ('They seem to pound [religion] into people at their most vulnerable' (541)). One prisoner on Highpoint South described Kainos as a 'bit of a shambles' (559) while ex-Kainos prisoners who had chosen to leave Kainos in Swaleside and The Verne criticized what they perceived as the lack of appropriately experienced staff and the lack of a clear programme structure. An ex-Kainos prisoner made a similar comment:

> [Kainos] was not constructive in the sense that it was not actually building something for me. When you do a course it is supposed to shape you into something. But during the [five months] I was there, I felt the people weren't qualified to shape or understand my responses and even if they did understand, they didn't really know how to cope with it and respond back to me. I think Kainos needs to appreciate that every individual is unique and they can't expect a priest or PO to teach anything that's got to do with psychology.
> (539)

Another ex-Kainos prisoner who had been at Grendon for three years saw Kainos and Grendon as complementary:

> [I] met a couple of lads on Kainos I knew at Grendon who failed there and left because they couldn't handle it ... People have left

Grendon for Kainos and been a success at Kainos. Some people are
not for Grendon but they are for Kainos. Likewise there are people
on Kainos who would be better at Grendon. Kainos doesn't have
the time to deal with certain problems.

(586)

This prisoner claimed that Kainos was 'not as deep' as Grendon. 'You've
got a Christian side but you also need a therapeutic side. Whether that
is Christian or not is up to the unit' (*ibid.*).

A large minority, however, claimed to have heard positive things,
including lower levels of noise and violence and 'very supportive' (553)
prisoners and staff:

If you are sick or need a cup of tea, there's someone to assist you,
and if you're feeling down there's someone for you to talk to.

(571)

It's like they are at home; it's a home away from home.

(572)

One approvingly told the story of how a leading Kainos prisoner was
caught

... stealing from someone's locker last year .... He was forgiven and
allowed to stay on the wing .... Elsewhere in this prison he'd have
been given, say, another seven days [in addition to his sentence as
punishment].

(559)

One ex-Kainos prisoner at Swaleside said:

It was like you were in a family, a sense of belonging. In prison
you feel alone and on the community you're doing things together.
You're laughing, you're joking ... it's not like you're in prison.

(540)

Similar comments came from The Verne: 'Everyone respects each
other there, it's like a family' (572). Several were impressed to
learn of its 'more relaxed atmosphere with staff' (553) and that
prisoners could negotiate with prison staff for things they wanted:
'If they want hot water all through the night they can get it because

it's discussed among themselves and agreed with prison officers' (579). The most negative comments came from Highpoint North: 'If Kainos was closed down it would make my Christmas' (555). Some prisoners had alarmingly basic questions about the programme. These related to selection ('Do you have to change your religion?' (577)), accreditation, and the very nature of the unit. One asked:

> I'd like to know what [Kainos's] basic foundation is .... What is it meant to achieve and how do they go about doing it?
>
> (539)

Importantly this question came not from a novice but from an intelligent ex-Kainos prisoner who had been on the Kainos unit for five months.

Some prisoners felt Kainos staff and prison staff had misled them about the religious identity of the unit and the programme content:

> I think Kainos should be more open about what it expects from you. Because if you ask a lot of lads on Kainos it was never explained to them what was expected of them. Some of it is told to you at the beginning [regarding] behaviour, respect etc. but not about the Christian weekend and the [follow-up programme] afterwards. They've got to be open about what's going on.
>
> (586)

This may reflect some confusion among staff about Kainos's identity. Several ex-Kainos prisoners commented about a perceived disjuncture between what they were told about the unit in advance and what life was actually like. One prisoner who spent six months on Kainos before being asked to leave claimed:

> What you're told initially isn't what you're told later on. They should be more open about the Christian side of it.
>
> (586)

Another claimed that, after having been given assurances by the co-ordinator that his being a Muslim was 'no problem ... it was a different ball-game when you were actually on it' (539). It seems to have been the case that the Christian or religious aspects of Kainos were either highlighted or downplayed to encourage individual applications. This may have been a particular temptation given the need for Kainos to operate at full capacity.

(b) The Kairos Weekend

The majority of prisoners saw the Kairos Weekend as a 'religious weekend' characterized by singing ('they have the tambourines buzzing' (575)), praying, outside volunteers, and 'lots of cakes' (555). The cakes in particular seemed to cause resentment amongst prisoners who were not part of the programme. This may seem trivial, but even small gestures which seem innocuous outside of prison can take on great significance within the confines of custody (e.g. if one group seems favoured over another; see for example Woolf and Tumim 1991). The Kairos Weekend was otherwise accepted without any apparent rancour by male prisoners, with one prisoner describing it rather neutrally as 'an initiation ceremony into being part of that community.' By contrast the Kairos Weekend was resented by some female prisoners as 'a right wind-up' (551) and 'another little show' (555). This may in part be explained by the fact that, unlike the other establishments, non-Kainos prisoners share the same houseblock as Kainos prisoners and during the Weekend take on the role of excluded onlookers.

One male prisoner who left Kainos because he failed a drugs test described the Weekend as: 'Overwhelming. The warmth and the love of the people was just totally unexpected' (540). A Catholic, this prisoner initially 'thought Our Lady wasn't getting as much recognition ... as she would within the Catholic tradition ... but as the course went on you realize that they are accommodating for all denominations' (540). Another prisoner left Kainos because he refused to take part in the Weekend:

> It's a hidden thing, the Kairos Weekend, you're not allowed to know about it. [The Kainos co-ordinators] said you weren't to know about the Kairos Weekend. It made me feel worried ... I just felt it was going to be this big pushy Weekend that was going to be rammed down my throat. I was worried about how I might react and I didn't want to stand up and get angry and spoil it for everybody.
>
> (586)

(c) Who is Kainos for?

Most prisoners knew they needed to apply in writing if they wanted to join Kainos, although a minority of prisoners 'hadn't a clue'. One prisoner thought it was by invitation only: 'They've got their own little circle. You've got to be asked in to get in with them' (551). Another thought that selection was on the basis of 'having gone to [the] prison chapel and 'witnessed' to having been 'born again'' (561). The majority said they had not been encouraged to join Kainos, although a minority said they had been encouraged by friends, prison officers, Kainos staff or Kainos prisoners. At Swaleside the recruiting Kainos prisoner encouraged prisoners to join Kainos on the ground that they would 'get a C-Cat' [lower-security classification] (541) although Kainos staff stopped this as soon as they became aware of it.

The vast majority said they had not been discouraged from joining Kainos: 'Nobody said I shouldn't join because I'm a Buddhist' (560). However, a minority said that some staff and prisoners had discouraged them. A Swaleside prisoner said he was discouraged from joining by an officer on the induction wing who described it as 'a fraggle [mentally disturbed] place for not-so-right people' (539). One Muslim who described himself as a Christian 'in his heart' said he was afraid to join Kainos in both Swaleside and The Verne for fear of the reaction of other Muslims: 'Someone might try to kill me ... if they find out a Muslim changed religion' (576). Of those who expressed an opinion about whether Kainos's recruitment and selection procedures should change, most said that there was nothing they would like to see altered: 'I don't feel it excludes me just because I'm a Buddhist' (560). One suggested 'it should be for proper Christians who are into it' (550), reflecting a general concern that Kainos was abused by 'phoneys': 'For every genuine person you've got there, four aren't' (578).[7]

A small majority of non-Kainos prisoners said they would not consider transferring to Kainos Community, citing lack of interest in religion or outright antipathy:

> I'm not going over to a God-bashing Moonie cult who's pushing religion down your throat because you're in prison and can't get out. Over my dead body.
>
> (555)

However a large minority were willing to transfer. Several expressed interest in a 'change of scene' and the chance to learn more about religion. One remarked:

> I'd go tomorrow. It's different talk there. I want conversations not talking about their crimes and all that ... I just want good conversation ... I want a bit of inspiration.
>
> (565)

When asked whether joining Kainos presented any difficulties for them, half of prisoners said either that they lacked sufficient knowledge or that joining Kainos presented no difficulties. The other half identified a range of difficulties. These included, *inter alia*, 'the religious aspect' (553), peer pressure ('you get stick from fellow prisoners who are against religion and who see you as a 'holy Joe'' (559)), loss of visits during the Kairos Weekend, loss of privileges if already on an enhanced wing, dislike of living in community, and of 'phoneys' on the wing. One prisoner expressed a fear of being thrown off the wing or of being nicked 'for petty things' (533) – an ironic contrast to the staff perception that Kainos prisoners are rarely 'nicked' (see Chapter 5). There was also fear of pressure ('There was a lot of pressure put on you to be this religious person from civilian Kainos staff' (586)) and of losing prison-specific coping skills:

> A lot of these prisoners … have been in prison before and they know a certain way of doing your sentence. A lot of people say: 'I wouldn't go over there and end up soft'.
> (539)

There was also a fear of religion being 'forced' upon them and a fear of the unknown presented by the Kairos Weekend.

The majority of prisoners thought Kainos was *intended* for a number of mixed and somewhat opposing groups. These included the religious and the non-religious, the disruptive and the quiet, the vulnerable and the robust and the sociable and the non-sociable. This diversity reflects a lack of understanding of at whom Kainos is aimed. A large minority thought that Kainos was for anyone and everyone. When asked who Kainos *appealed* to in the prison, as opposed to who it is *meant* for, prisoners added several further groups. This implied that certain prisoners were attracted to Kainos even though they were not part of its intended profile. These groups included long-term prisoners, those looking for an 'easy life', fewer 'cell-thieves' (533) and, in the case of The Verne, where Kainos was housed in dormitory conditions, those interested in homosexual activity.

The overwhelming majority of non-Kainos prisoners believed Kainos took anyone who applied. A few thought Kainos preferred 'people who are more laid-back who they think isn't in for trouble' (540). One prisoner thought disruptive prisoners were actively excluded:

> 'Bad girls stay on the wings, good girls go to Kainos. If you're a bad person and if you've been on segregation block you don't get on Kainos.
>
> (550)

One prisoner thought Kainos tried to keep a balance between the different groups: 'They're very aware of people who could benefit, whether that's well-behaved or not so well-behaved' (553). Another prisoner thought Kainos participants inhibited the unit from taking more serious offenders:

> A chap on [a non-Kainos] wing asked to go over onto the dorms but [Kainos] prisoners were scared of him. He was asked to wait 12 months. There were lads who were going to leave [Kainos] if he came over. He'd been a violent prisoner, he'd killed in prison.
>
> (586)

(d) Who runs Kainos – and who supports it?

Not a single prisoner interviewed saw Kainos as a joint operation run between uniformed staff, civilian staff, and the Chaplaincy, although several prisoners did see it as a combination of two of these groups. Perceptions of who ran Kainos were mixed and unclear. Some prisoners exaggerated the degree of prisoner input, seeing Kainos as 'run by prisoners'. One prisoner in Highpoint North thought the Chaplain ran it, which was rather ironic given the Chaplain's view that he was excluded from Kainos at that time (see Chapter 5). On the subject of relations between Kainos and the Chaplaincy, more than twice as many prisoners who expressed an opinion thought Kainos and the Chaplaincy were two groups as thought they were one group. Nearly all who expressed an opinion characterized relationships between Kainos and the Chaplaincy as either good or very good, with many noting that the Chaplaincy actively supported Kainos. One prisoner on Highpoint South perceptively noted the potential for 'some animosity ... [and] rivalry' (560), but while this was true for some time at this establishment, relations between Kainos and the Chaplaincy at Highpoint South improved during the course of the research following the appointment of new Kainos staff.

Nearly all prisoners who expressed an opinion thought that Kainos prison staff supported the work on the wing, although a small proportion qualified this by saying only 'some of them do' or else that they had 'no option'. The strongest affirmative responses came from prisoners at The Verne. Even so, when asked whether they thought non-Kainos prison staff supported Kainos, nearly half said they had insufficient knowledge. Prisoners who expressed an opinion were divided, and a few thought non-Kainos staff were indifferent. One prisoner at The Verne commented:

> I think some of them are [supportive] but they wouldn't say it
> openly.
> *Why not?*
> Prison macho. Staff are as bad at it as inmates. A lot of staff here
> are old school, [they] don't believe in reform.
>
> (586)

According to another: 'At [Kairos] Weekends and Family Days they get proper food and [non-Kainos] staff think this shouldn't be happening [because] they've done this and they've done that' (560). One prisoner claimed there were tensions between non-Kainos and Kainos prison staff: '[Non-Kainos] prison staff call [Kainos] prison staff 'pussies' because they are more prone to pamper [prisoners], coo and ahh and be overly sympathetic' (539). The prisoner cited incidents when Kainos prison staff had difficulty imposing their authority on non-Kainos prisoners when required to cover for colleagues elsewhere in the prison.

The overwhelming majority of prisoners saw Kainos as a place of peer support. One ex-Kainos prisoner at The Verne remarked:

> No-one comes and knocks on my door [on a non-Kainos wing].
> On [Kainos] people would ask you how you were and things like
> that.
>
> (586)

A few prisoners at Swaleside and The Verne qualified their remarks by saying that Kainos prisoners supported each other because they had to: 'that sort of regime over there can't survive without support' (578). Nearly all positive comments came from male prisoners, with several women on Highpoint North preferring to characterize Kainos prisoners as 'cliquey' (550) and 'very clanny' (555) rather than supportive. This again underlined the sense of exclusion of non-participating 'lodgers' on the Kainos housing block.

(e) What are the 'perks' – and the snags?

Prisoners were asked why they thought other prisoners *in general* would want to join Kainos. It was clear that prisoner perceptions of the incentives and privileges on Kainos Communities varied by institution. At Swaleside, the majority commented that Kainos was a way of escaping drugs, troublemakers and 'normal' prison life. Kainos was a 'safe place' in contrast to, say, A-wing, which one A-wing resident described as 'a wild place' (542). By contrast, no prisoner at Highpoint North saw any benefits in terms of safety. Here incentives included material privileges such as greater access to television, more time unlocked, meals in the houseblock rather than the dining hall and a generally more relaxed atmosphere with staff. Unlike Highpoint North, no prisoner on Highpoint South saw any material benefits in Kainos. This was probably because the quality of accommodation on the Kainos unit in this prison was widely recognized to be among the lowest in the prison. Instead, incentives were seen in terms of receiving help, support, strengthening spirituality and, again, a more relaxed atmosphere. It was even accepted that 'potentially, people might move from S5 [the Enhanced unit] to Kainos if they felt they needed help. You don't get much help on S5' (560). Finally, prisoners at The Verne saw incentives to join Kainos largely in terms of opportunities to change, to live together in community, to receive support and to obtain increased contact with their family and the outside world.

Prisoners were also asked why *they* might want to join Kainos, as opposed to prisoners *in general*. Two-thirds of prisoners could think of at least one personal advantage. These ranged from the spiritual and the social to more mundane advantages such as better information about prison events and nicer decoration (Highpoint North). Several thought they might get a good probation report and transfer to a better prison.

Prisoners produced a range of reasons as to why prisoners in general would *not* want to be on Kainos. Common reasons included dislike of religious people ('Prisoners want to mix with normal people' (559)); 'phoneys' ('[P]risoners say, 'I'm a Christian, I'm reformed' and nine-tenths of the time they're paying lip service and I wasn't prepared to do that' (541)); not knowing enough about Kainos ('There's urban myths about Kainos - there's lots of talk about 'Teletubby' group hugs and things' (561)) and prisoners being content with where they are. Other reasons included peer pressure: 'Being on Kainos puts pressure on friendships in other houses ... You've distanced yourself by deciding to do something for yourself' (553). This was especially risky if Kainos itself was seen as an unknown quantity.

Several felt that community living and thinking about others would deter the antisocial and the selfish whilst one thought the 'tagline' of 'challenge to change' was threatening:

A lot of people aren't used to other people believing in them. They're not familiar with people setting goals for them, they're afraid of letting people down, so they'd rather not be put in that position in the first place.

(553)

In similar vein another remarked:

You learn things about yourself that you don't like and can't do anything about. [Prisoners] come off [Kainos] to protect themselves. It can also be mentally too taxing.

(560)

Some drawbacks were prison-specific. One prisoner at Highpoint South cited 'lack of communication with other prisoners' (566) which reflected the concern voiced by another prisoner that Kainos in Highpoint South is like 'a prison in a prison' (560). In Swaleside disincentives included a drop in wages (Kainos prisoners at Swaleside do not go out to work whilst on the course), whilst in The Verne they included lack of privacy in the dorms and a fear of being tarred with Kainos's 'reputation' (586) for homosexual activity. One prisoner thought the lack of accreditation for participation on Kainos would deter those seeking parole.

Prisoners were also asked whether there were any disadvantages *to them personally* in moving onto Kainos. Most prisoners could think of some disadvantages, although a few claimed they could not think of any. Issues included the loss of perks available elsewhere in the prison (e.g. less access to television) as well as the loss of friends, visits and some free time. One prisoner (interestingly a chapel orderly) thought Kainos would put pressure on him to become a Christian: 'I do think they expect you to become a Christian' (541). The same prisoner felt tense towards certain Kainos-employed staff:

I'm always very nervous that someone like [Kainos counsellor] or a couple of the SOs [Senior Officers] might have input into my getting a C-Cat [lower prison classification] and such like. The impression I get is if you don't express any remorse for your crime in the past, [if] you don't say you've found God …. I'd be very nervous about getting reports from those people.

(541)

Once again, some issues were prison specific (dormitory accommodation, not being able to play loud music and allegations of rampant homosexual behaviour in The Verne) and fear of adapting to a 'soft, happy environment' (539) which one prisoner in Swaleside felt could result in a dangerous complacency upon transfer to a regular location.

(f) Favouritism – and parole

Critics of Kainos have claimed that Kainos prisoners received special treatment (see section 3(f), Chapter 5). Among non-Kainos prisoners this concern varied by institution. We have already noted that several prisoners on Highpoint North resented the 'perks' of the Kairos Weekend (that is, more association time, access to outside volunteers and the shared meals). Yet one prisoner on Highpoint North, for example, thought that the time prisoners gave up for this 'balanced out' the extra association. At Swaleside, there was a perception that Kainos prisoners received special treatment, not *during* the programme but after completion. Non-Kainos prisoners claimed that Kainos prisoners got the 'best' jobs in the prison, lower security categorization, and good reports for parole. Prisoners at Highpoint South acknowledged that the Kairos Weekend involved special treatment for Kainos prisoners but, on the whole, Kainos was no different from any other special unit such as the Enhanced (privileged) unit. At The Verne, the general assumption was that Kainos prisoners did not receive special treatment. The belief that Kainos prisoners did *not* receive special treatment was most common in those prisons (Highpoint South and The Verne) where Kainos was generally acknowledged to be located in some of the worst accommodation. Indeed, one prison governor noted that poor accommodation was 'a good defence' (589) against the accusation that Kainos attracts unduly favourable treatment.

The vast majority of non-Kainos prisoners thought Kainos was unique in their prison: 'It's the attitudes on Kainos that counts and you don't find them anywhere else in prison' (553). A few noted similarities with the drug-free units on Highpoint South and Swaleside, which offered a mix of therapy and community living. It was acknowledged that certain elements of Kainos Community could be found elsewhere in the prison, including Family Days, behaviour programmes, prayer meetings, the Alpha course, Chapel, and 'drug-free' wings. Most prisoners said they did not know how visiting arrangements on Kainos compared with elsewhere in the prison, although one prisoner commented that these might be worse on Kainos because visits had to fit around the programme. A large minority had no opinion about the quality of facilities on Kainos compared to the rest of the prison, but of those who expressed an opinion, nearly all thought that it was equivalent. Several prisoners at Highpoint South thought conditions on the Kainos unit were inferior and 'not up to the mark re: cleanliness' (559).

The vast majority of non-Kainos prisoners thought being on Kainos would improve prisoners' chances of parole, although their reasons varied. In general terms, Kainos was thought to help because it showed the prisoner was 'making an effort' (559) and gave the parole board 'something extra' to consider. To this extent, Kainos was 'on a par with other behaviour courses' (553). One prisoner at The Verne thought Kainos helped because Kainos staff were more willing to 'check your case and ... keep pushing' (582). One prisoner thought Kainos helped, despite itself:

> I would say to a prisoner, if you want to get parole or get [a] transfer, do Kainos. But if you want something to actually change, you do R and R [the cognitive-behavioural programme, Reasoning and Rehabilitation].
>
> (539)

One cause for concern is that some unwilling prisoners may feel pressure to take part in Kainos simply because they believe it will please the Parole Board. One non-Kainos prisoner at The Verne, who had also been a non-Kainos prisoner at Swaleside, commented: 'People say, 'If you don't do it, it will look bad on your parole.' That's what they say in Swaleside' (576). Another related issue is the allegation that prisoners who wish to leave Kainos are dissuaded from doing so because it will 'look bad' on their record. One non-Kainos prisoner at Swaleside commented:

> A lot of people go on Kainos who haven't volunteered for it but just because they were recommended to do it. It goes on their sentence plan and they can't come off here because if they do, then it's detrimental to their progress.
>
> (539)

This non-Kainos prisoner had been on the Community and chose to leave the programme:

> They said to me: '[X] if you leave this course it's very, very bad for you. Don't go'. I felt I was being oppressed or blackmailed. I was told that if I came off [Kainos] it would be as a Basic [low privilege level] prisoner.
>
> (*ibid.*)

The prisoner was subsequently moved off Kainos to the induction wing and onto the Basic regime level. He successfully challenged the demotion on the ground that Kainos was a voluntary programme and was returned to Standard status.

Prisoners were also asked whether they thought being on Kainos Community might improve their own personal chance of parole. A number were not eligible for parole, or had already been refused parole. Most said they did not know or that it would make no difference in their case: 'E-wing [the drug-free unit] has done more to improve my chances of parole than B-wing [Swaleside Kainos] because it helped me to address my drug problem and do a lot of one-to-one counselling which they didn't do on B-wing' (540). This contrasts with the position at The Verne, where the Kainos-employed counsellor is a trained drugs counsellor and conducts one-to-one drugs counselling. Only two prisoners said they thought participation in Kainos would help their parole. As to why they did not take the opportunity, one remarked: 'I'd rather not have parole than go over there. It would make one day seem like two' (578).

(g) Impact on prisoners and prisons

Twice as many prisoners thought Kainos helps prisoners not to reoffend as thought it made no difference. One prisoner thought the on-going contact between some Kainos prisoners and Kainos staff was a spur to going straight: 'If they came back here, they'd feel they'd let themselves down and they let the Kainos staff down, so being on Kainos has been an extra motivation' (553). However, much was thought to depend on the prisoner. One non-Kainos prisoner at The Verne commented:

> I saw a lot of fakes – they're all pretending to be religious. They say one thing to [the Kainos Co-ordinator] and another to me. As soon as the gates open they'll find another god, a brown one called heroin.
>
> (105)

A number denied Kainos made any difference, claiming 'it's not a course for offending behaviour, just an alternative Christian-based lifestyle' (539).

Similarly, nearly twice as many prisoners thought Kainos had an impact on the atmosphere of the prison as thought it had no impact. Nearly all saw this as a positive effect:

> At The Verne, the effect of Kainos has been *compassion*. I knew everyone in the prison whilst working in the canteen. The Kainos people were compassionate and that definitely struck me at the time. At The Verne, I'd always heard great things about Kainos.
>
> (560, emphasis original)

At Swaleside it was said that Kainos:

> ... created something that's totally different from the rest of the prison – there's no doubt about that. They've managed to make it feel like they're not in prison.
>
> (539)

Kainos gave prisoners hope: 'I realised that if you could have Kainos in prison then prison can't be all that bad' (540). At Highpoint North, prisoners said that:

> Kainos made people aware of other options. There's more than one way to treat people. Staff aren't convinced yet but management are … [If Kainos closed, prisoners] would lose the choice of living in an environment where it's Christian based and less violent.
>
> (533)

Kainos countered the idea that 'if you trust inmates, my God, the whole system will break down' (553). In Highpoint South prisoners thought that the physical estate and lack of mixing made it difficult for Kainos to make an impact: 'I'm 20 feet away from it and I can't get near it' (560). Only one prisoner (at Highpoint North) thought that Kainos's impact had been negative and had caused animosity and resentment.

Three times as many non-Kainos prisoners said they would recommend Kainos to other prisoners as said they would not recommend it. However, a number qualified their answer by saying it depended on whether the prisoner wanted to change or liked peace and isolation. Some of the recommendations were rather back-handed compliments ('There's a chap who's brain damaged – he would benefit a great deal' (560)), suggesting they would recommend Kainos for weaker or more vulnerable prisoners. A few prisoners in different prisons said they would recommend Kainos to older prisoners or to people in prison for the first time. Prisoners whom they would *not* recommend Kainos to included those serving short sentences, the non-religious, drug dealers, drug addicts (Highpoint South only), 'phoneys' who would exploit Kainos and 'the 15 per cent [of prisoners] who don't give a damn about anybody including themselves' (553).

Prisoners made several suggestions for improving Kainos, even though for most, their contact was minimal or non-existent. A Swaleside prisoner suggested that 'people should be able to come over and see what it's like first' (540), perhaps as a way of countering the 'fear of the unknown' and the 'fear of being trapped'. An interfaith approach was also mooted: 'Kainos Community should be an opportunity to bring all … religions together' (560).

Another prisoner who had been on Kainos for some months before being asked to leave suggested that more use could be made of prisoners themselves to solve their own problems: 'The skill [just] sits on the wing' (586).

As for prisoners who participated in Kainos, some non-Kainos prisoners expressed concern about whether Kainos-employed staff were able to address some of the issues prisoners are likely to present. One prisoner who had been on Kainos for five months before being asked to leave highlighted the need for a psychologist:

> Kainos … is psychologically based but without psychologists … Some people come out with stories of sexual abuse. How are Kainos in a position to deal with that response?
>
> (539)

The same prisoner felt Kainos should encourage prisoners to relate to the world outside the Community:

> What Kainos doesn't realise is that their artificial world doesn't exist out there … They pave a path for [prisoners] every step of the way…. What happens when there's no one around to pave the path? … You're adapted to that soft happy environment that makes people think you're a good person. That's fine for that environment, but that's the only place where it can work. It's not a structure for the real world.
>
> (539)

4. Conclusions and recommendations

What main conclusions arise from these voices from the inside? We would suggest the following:

- Prisoners seemed to have a general idea of what Kainos Communities were, but this was often shrouded in rumour and misunderstanding.

- Each Kainos Community contained the same basic elements, namely community living, regular contact with people outside the prison, and the Kairos Weekend. However, the content of programmes varied locally and strongly depended on the individual personalities involved in running the programme and their relations with key people in the rest of the prison.

- Relations between prisoners and between prisoners and staff in the Kainos units were reported as almost universally positive. This, and other elements of the Kainos regime such as active prisoner committees and the full time support of non-uniformed civilian staff, is likely to have a beneficial effect on the wings above and beyond any effect of the content of Kainos programmes. Important issues for prisons in terms of the impact of Kainos Communities are the potential vulnerability of prisoners during the programme and the most appropriate place for Kainos in sentence planning.

A number of thoughts and suggestions regarding the structure and operation of Kainos Communities logically follow on from the experiences prisoners presented to us during the research:

- Kainos teams could usefully be made aware of the follow-up programmes used in similar communities internationally and that an attempt should be made to develop more effective ways of building on the Kairos Weekend, or its equivalent.

- The findings also suggest that any future expansion of Kainos should place the strength of local volunteer numbers among its top criteria. With an increase in local volunteers, it would be possible to include further options for follow-up programmes such as a Kairos Two-Day Retreat. The retreat would normally happen every three months after the Kairos Weekend. Such a timescale would be particularly appropriate for Swaleside where the men remain on Kainos for some time after the Kairos Weekend with no further participation in the programme.

- Another possibility is introducing the Kairos 'Instructional Reunion' programme which presents the concept of 'small groups' to prisoners. Other possibilities are programmes currently used in similar communities internationally (see examples in Chapter 7).

- Finally, ensuring that all prisoners and staff understand what Kainos Communities do and who they are for is a basic tenet of informed choice that seems to be lacking. Any programme that offers something different in prisons is at risk or rumour and misunderstanding; countering this appears to require proactive, ongoing efforts from all involved.

Notes

1 Kairos UK is an autonomous organization and is independent of Kairos Prison Ministry (see Chapter 2). Kairos UK has some freedom to adapt its materials; however, it is reluctant to do so given the experience that is said to have gone into the current format.
2 We are grateful to Kathryn Curran for allowing us to quote from her unpublished doctoral dissertation.
3 This is a means of setting goals and scheduling programmes for longer-term prisoners in the UK.

4 Kairos UK minutes noted that 'At The Verne, Kainos do not want anything throughout the week but are keen to continue the Weekend Instructional Reunion' (Kairos UK, 2000a).

5 Lee sponsored one prisoner on a Kairos Weekend at Highpoint North, recalling: 'She was 47, homeless with no family and grew up in care. She had been on (and off) heroin for years. She had just five weeks on the unit before her release. She grasped the meaning of the Weekend, holding back at first, but increasingly absorbed and increasingly radiant. I thought: 'What can her future be?' This is what happened to her. On her release she was given a train ticket to Northampton where a place had been arranged for her in a drug rehab. She had to change at King's Cross [station] where she stole some clothes, bought some heroin and went straight to Holloway [prison]' (Lee 2004).

6 Theism is a general but unspecified belief in God.

7 See also Curran (2002: 31) regarding the 'fronter' inmate who 'employs religion for his own manipulative purposes' and has since evolved into a popular view of religious inmates.

Chapter 5

Kainos Community:
views from the top

Kainos Community is something that you either love it or you hate it.
Kainos-supportive prison officer at Highpoint North (557)

This chapter looks at how staff both on and off the Kainos Communities
and prison management in all four prisons perceived Kainos. What impact
did they believe it had on their prison? Did Kainos compromise prison
security? What difficulties did it present for prisoners and staff both
on and off the Community? Was it used to house 'failed' or vulnerable
prisoners? Did they think it would change people's behaviour? Did they
think Kainos was unique? Did it help to involve the community around
the prison? What were their views about using outside volunteers? Were
Area Managers and Prison Service Headquarters supportive?

The information presented in this chapter is taken from in-depth
interviews with prison staff who worked on or off the Kainos units, Kainos-
employed staff, members of the prison Chaplaincy teams, and prison
managers. Again, the chapter reports the findings as they pertained to
each Kainos Community rather than to Kainos Communities as a whole,
though many of the issues arguably have relevance for religiously-based
units in any prison setting.

I. Background

Kainos Communities are located on normal prison wings (or parts of

This chapter was co-authored by Jonathan Burnside and Nancy Loucks

wings) with the normal ratio of prison staff to prisoners. They are subject to the same prison rules and for the most part to the same privileges and regimes. Staff from the Kainos Trust are non-uniformed employees of the Kainos charity who work with prisoners alongside prison staff and in cooperation with the prison management team. At least three Kainos staff should be in post in each prison, namely the Coordinator, the Deputy Coordinator, and the Counsellor. At the time of the research (2000–2001), none of the Kainos Communities had all three of these posts filled, though Kainos units in two prisons had administrative assistants as a third member of staff.

This section explains the context of the establishment of Kainos Communities in the four prisons as well as their impact in more quantifiable terms.

(a) Context

The context of the research played an important role in the responses. At Highpoint North, a Coordinator for the Kainos unit had not been in post for several months, and the newly appointed Coordinator arrived while the research was underway. In the meantime, the Deputy Coordinator had been filling both her own role and that of Coordinator. At Highpoint South, the Coordinator had very recently resigned in fairly acrimonious circumstances. The Deputy Coordinator had been promoted to the Coordinator's post and was in the process of renovating the project. Therefore, while the Kainos Community at Highpoint South had technically been in place for two years, our impression was very much that things were starting from scratch.

In the meantime, relations with the Chaplaincy at Highpoint (shared between North and South) had been notably strained, primarily due to poor relations between the Chaplain and the recently departed Coordinator at Highpoint South. At The Verne, a new Chaplain had very recently been appointed following the retirement of the previous Chaplain, who had been actively involved in Kainos and instrumental in the introduction of Kairos-APAC to The Verne. At Swaleside, both the Church of England Chaplain and the Roman Catholic priest were shortly to leave their posts.

Also likely to be of importance was the context in which the Kainos Communities were introduced into the various prisons. At The Verne, D-wing (the Kainos unit) had previously been notorious for its regular disruptions, vandalism, and violence (see Chapter 3). It was referred to as 'Beirut' and was virtually a 'no-go' area for staff. It housed prisoners primarily at the beginning of short-term sentences who were often far from home.[1] The physical set-up of the wing – nineteenth century military casements, converted into dormitories - made it unpopular with prisoners and difficult to manage. However, it was these dormitories that provided the spur to introducing Kairos-APAC because of their similarity to conditions in the Brazilian APAC prison (see Chapter 3).

The Principal Officer on the wing suggested introducing a Kainos unit (then Kairos- APAC), the first of its kind in the UK. As few other solutions were apparent, the Governor agreed. This meant that:

- Kairos-APAC was seen as a solution to a long-term problem.

- The programme, alongside other changes in the prison (namely the removal of prisoners from elsewhere in the UK, the increased proportion of foreign nationals, and the introduction of a more open regime) had a visibly positive effect.

- It was innovative, and prison staff developed it themselves with Kairos (see Chapter 2) and the 'closed section' element of APAC (see Chapter 1).

- It had the full support of prison staff and managers - perhaps most importantly from very senior members of staff, who had the respect of others.

The Verne had the added bonus of its key figures (Principal Officer, Chaplain and original Coordinator) participating in a Fourth Day Weekend (similar to a Kairos Weekend; see Chapter 2). Several continued together in a 'reunion group' outside the prison before they introduced Kairos-APAC to the prison. The perception is that this paid long-term dividends in building mutual trust and understanding.

The other prisons, in contrast, had less obvious reasons and often limited support for introducing Kainos Communities. Even where governors supported their introduction, not all of the management team agreed, nor did they always have the support of Area Managers.[2] Staff were not always given the choice of whether to work on wings that housed Kainos Communities, and some (notably at Highpoint South) were openly hostile to the regime. All four Kainos Communities were the subject of suspicion and criticism from sources both in and out of the prisons, and the Prison Service visibly distanced itself from their operation, management, and funding (though not initially; see Chapter 3). The lack of consistent, visible support filtered down to staff. As one officer at Highpoint North commented, 'management doesn't help Kainos one little bit' (622). The real and perceived lack of support made the stability of the units extremely vulnerable even to small changes in the make-up of its own staff, prison staff, and prison management teams.

As with differences in population between prisons, changes in the leadership of Kainos Communities and the dynamics of relations between key players (namely the Chaplaincy, prison staff, prison managers, and Kainos staff) all have a bearing on the way (and whether) Kainos Communities work in a prison. Participation by prison staff in delivering these programmes also varied both within and between prisons.

(b) Accountability

The variation in the Kainos programmes and the way each prison responds to them raised the question of responsibility for the programmes. Prison staff working in the Kainos Communities were clear that the day-to-day running of Kainos Communities was down to the Coordinator and to the other Kainos-employed staff. This was done in cooperation with the prison staff on the wing, but prison staff had little input into the content or structure of Kainos programmes. The Kainos-employed staff, in turn, are answerable to the (prison-employed) Senior Officer or Principal Officer on the wing, the prison Chaplaincy, the prison governor, and to the Trustees of the Kainos Trust.

In practical terms, prison managers often made little direct input into the Kainos programme beyond its relations to the working of the prison as a whole. Of more dispute was the appropriate link between the Kainos Community and the prison Chaplaincy. While all the Chaplains agreed that they did not have time for input to the day-to-day running of Kainos, they disagreed about whether the Chaplaincy should in fact have overall responsibility for the units.

Where relations between Kainos Communities and the Chaplaincy were good, such as at The Verne, levels of input and control did not appear to be an issue. Much however seemed to depend upon the individual personalities and religious style of the people involved. At Highpoint, for example, personality clashes between the prison Chaplain and the previous Coordinator, both of whom appeared to fight for overall control of the unit, appeared to leave both groups feeling threatened and isolated. Once new Coordinators at both Highpoint North and South had settled in, the impression was of a complete reversal in relations between the Kainos teams and the Chaplaincy. Roles seemed to be clearer, and newly invigorated, cooperative relations appeared to be both in place and improving (an impression supported in interviews with prison managers). Interestingly, emphasis on individuals rather than on the programme was also noticeable amongst prison staff, who tended to refer to specific members of Kainos staff as the basis for success or failure rather than to the Kainos programme as a whole.

The Kainos Trustees had the most direct responsibility for line management of the Kainos teams, and each prison had its own appointed Trustee. This system had a number of problems in practice. First, with separate Trustees for each prison, Kainos Communities showed a lack of coordination between prisons and a lack of overall direction. This was evident in the differences between programmes at the prisons, as discussed in Chapter 4, and in differences between the literature available about the Kainos programmes (virtually non-existent at Highpoint at the start of our research, for example, but thorough and widely available at The Verne). It was also noticeable from the fact that models for many of the problems which Coordinators faced, including the Kairos Weekend and the nature and scope of the follow-up programmes, were available elsewhere (e.g. through the experience of similar communities internationally, especially Horizon Communities; see Chapter 7), but these had not been brought to the attention of the Kainos teams.

Also of concern was the lack of continuity between Coordinators even within a prison. For example, we found that no written information on the programme was available to the Kainos team at Highpoint South following the departure of the previous Coordinator, despite the fact that the then Kainos Coordinators and Trustees had met in 1999 to set a 'blueprint' for how the Communities should work. Such issues left some staff feeling unsupported by the Trustees. The fact that liaison Trustees work part-time on a voluntary basis with no National Coordinator is likely to be at least partially responsible for this.

(c) Atmosphere

Almost all the staff (and prisoners) on the Kainos Communities were of the opinion that Kainos Communities were generally calmer, quieter places. This contrast was particularly striking in wings which were not made up entirely of Kainos Community prisoners, such as Highpoint North, and when the Community was first introduced at The Verne. The general impression was that prisoners supported each other more, that staff and prisoners had better relations, and that prison staff and Kainos staff for the most part worked together as a team. Relatively few prison staff (or prisoners), however, with the exception of those at The Verne, believed that Kainos made a wider impact on the rest of the prison. On the other hand, some felt it was a calming influence to a degree, as people who had been part of Kainos moved on to other parts of the prison and to other establishments.

(d) Disciplinary reports

The general impression was that Kainos Communities generated fewer disciplinary reports. While this was not possible to assess during the research at Highpoint, figures at The Verne and Swaleside suggest this may in fact be the case.[3] Disciplinary hearings in The Verne as a whole decreased substantially from 1996–1999, from 675 to 306. This is likely to be related to the change in the use of the prison (from short term prisoners to foreign nationals) as well as an overall relaxation of the regime. During this time, however, the proportion of disciplinary reports on D-wing, which houses the Kainos Community, dropped disproportionately to those in the rest of the prison. Despite this disproportionate drop, C-wing actually had even fewer. C-wing is composed of so-called 'super'-Enhanced and Enhanced wings, which means prisoners are on the wing because they have behaved well elsewhere.

Perhaps more striking is the fact that only nine prisoners from the Kainos wing at Swaleside were charged with a breach of prison discipline (once each) in a 12-month period (July 2000–June 2001). Three of these prisoners were not part of the Kainos programme, and a fourth did not complete it.

Comparison of disciplinary reports between Kainos Communities and the rest of the prison can be somewhat misleading. One premise of life on Kainos is that the Community must sort out its own problems if at all possible. This means that, while prison officers are perfectly entitled to place prisoners on report, just as they can on any other wing, they are more likely to 'hand things back to the Community' to sort out themselves, depending on the nature and seriousness of the incident. If the Kainos Community is working as it is meant to, it will by definition have fewer reports because (a) problems are more likely to be resolved before they reach this level of crisis, and (b) prison staff are less inclined to resort to reports unless no other means of resolution is available. Other research suggests the religious element may have some bearing on improvements in behaviour. Curran (2002), for example, noted that prison staff found that prisoners who were sincere in their commitment, in this case to religious conversion, were more amenable to prison rules.

As mentioned in the previous chapter, Bottoms (2002: 27) describes compliance with rules in terms of 'positive morality', which he states is necessary both in the formation of rules and in the maintenance of social order. He also outlines three requirements for 'normative compliance' – a socially based, voluntary form of compliance with social norms. These include acceptance of or belief in a social norm; attachment leading to compliance; and perceived legitimacy (ibid.: 30–31). It is perhaps this *acceptance* of particular norms on Kainos Communities – a requirement for prisoners who wish to remain there – which may in turn evolve into the pattern of normative compliance Bottoms describes and consequently reduce indiscipline on Kainos units.

(e) Alarm bells

Comparison of numbers of alarm bells in Kainos wings as opposed to others was not possible in all prisons. First, The Verne has no alarm bells. Second, Highpoint North has both Kainos and non-Kainos prisoners on the same wing, so the number of alarm bells would not reflect accurately the difference between Kainos and non-Kainos wings. Third, the data at Highpoint South was collected in such a way as to make adequate analysis impractical in the time allowed for the research. During the course of this research, an alarm bell went off in the Kainos unit at Swaleside while one of the researchers was there. Interestingly, the officers' first response was to run out of the wing to reach the alarm: clearly they were not accustomed to responding to alarms on their own wing. Further, the alarm turned out to have been set off by a workman who was making repairs on the wing, and backed into the alarm bell by accident while shifting a ladder. Both staff and prisoners communicated these facts to us afterwards. The statistics available from Swaleside emphasized the point: only four alarm bells and one fire alarm went off on the Kainos wing from July 2000–June 2001. Three of the four alarm bells turned out to be false alarms, two of which involved workmen setting off an alarm by accident.

(f) Drug tests

Most of the respondents on Kainos Communities believed the units were not in fact drug free. However, the majority qualified this statement by saying that Kainos Communities were more drug-free than other wings, and some, notably at The Verne, went as far as to say that the unit was in fact drug-free.

Reliable data was not possible to collect at Highpoint, as the results of drug tests did not always state the prisoner's location. Statistics collected on the Kainos wing at Swaleside from July 2000–June 2001 suggest that drug use may well be less of a problem there. Of 3,892 Voluntary Drug Tests (VDTs) on the Kainos unit, only 11 were positive for drugs (0.3 per cent). This compares with 1,774 VDTs on A-wing (a mainstream wing of the prison), of which 155 were positive or prisoners failed to supply a urine sample (8.7 per cent). Of 103 Mandatory Drug Tests (MDTs) on Kainos, two (1.9 per cent) were positive. This compares with 149 MDTs on A-wing, of which 58 were positive or 'fail to supply' (39 per cent), and 141 on C-wing (another mainstream wing), of which 59 were positive or 'fail to supply' (42 per cent).

(g) Features of Kainos programmes

Even the more cynical officers and managers at the prisons with Kainos Communities commented that Kainos Communities 'work' [*sic.*], though they say they do not understand why. While the reasons are not easy to untangle, several important factors seem to contribute to the working of Kainos Communities.

Based on our observations of Kainos Communities, several important differences stand out between these units and more traditional prison wings. The first is prisoners' perception of a non-judgemental approach, which is central to the success of community living. The emphasis within the unit is that everyone is of value and everyone is 'in the same boat'; people did not appear to be 'rated' by their offence as they felt was the case in a normal prison wing. The Kairos Weekend and godparenting evenings are designed to emphasize this by placing prisoners on equal terms with volunteers from outside the prison.

Related to this is the use of non-prison language and terminology. Meals were referred to as meals rather than 'feeding', as prison staff call it elsewhere in the prison. Prisoners were referred to, at least by Kainos staff, as 'residents' and were usually addressed by their first names – as were the Kainos staff. Cells were 'rooms'. Almost no one swore. Prisoners and many prison staff said 'please' and 'thank you', regardless of whom they were addressing.

The list goes on: Kainos-employed staff wore no uniforms. Differently from other non-uniformed staff in prisons such as psychologists and probation staff, however, Kainos staff were based on the wing full-time and had some responsibility over it. Prisoners had open access to Kainos staff on a drop-in basis, in confidence if desired. Genuine mutual support appeared to exist between prisoners as well, and disputes were resolved informally if at all possible. Prisoners left their cell doors unlocked and mixed freely with all other prisoners on the wing. When prisoners made a request of Kainos staff or prison staff, they seemed confident that it would be done and did not repeat their requests.

Other innovations were in place which have been rejected or not fully implemented elsewhere in the Prison Service in England and Wales. Active prisoner committees were the most notable of these. This system is not unknown to the Prison Service (e.g. at HMP Grendon, a therapeutically-based prison, and other committees at The Verne such as the Inmate Race Relations Committee) and is used in other prisons in the UK (Solomon and Edgar 2003) as well as in Sweden and Canada. However, to date this system is something the Prison Service of England and Wales has not formally endorsed as standard practice. Such committees give prisoners both a voice and a sense of responsibility, both of which are central to perceptions of justice and fairness in prisons (see for example Woolf and Tumim 1991; Loucks 1994). Arguably, the informal resolution of disputes 'in house' works towards the same aim. In Kainos Communities, both of these systems (regular meetings and resolution of issues which arise) are done in cooperation with Kainos employees and prison staff, who participate to a greater or lesser degree depending on the context. The sense of personal responsibility and emphasis on moral choice in Kainos Communities is an element absent from most conventional prison regimes (Pryor 2001; Maruna and LeBel 2002; Curran 2002).

Similar in its emphasis of trust and personal responsibility is the fact that prisoners on Kainos Communities have relatively free movement within the units. All of them had access to all other parts of the unit, and all of them could come and go from the Kainos office(s) as they wished. They also had a very active regime: as part of the Kainos programme, much time normally allocated for free association was spent in meetings, talks, game nights, godparenting evenings, and so on.

Not to be overlooked is the fact that Kainos staff were available on the wing *in addition* to the normal quota of prison staff. This meant that more people were available for prisoners to talk to, and in particular non-uniformed people unassociated with the Prison Service. Other research has found this separation to be an important element in the success of programmes for prisoners: Mobley and Terry (2002: 5) argue that 'Agencies designed for purposes of social control should be kept apart from those developed for social support' or otherwise risk sending 'mixed messages' by combining treatment with coercive supervision. The 'godparenting' was another important element of support unassociated with the Prison Service, as discussed in Chapter 4, and many prisoners seemed deeply touched by the fact that people from outside spent a great deal of time and effort speaking with them. In her research into religious conversion in prisons, Curran (2002: 301) found that prisoners used such people as 'role models for personal change.' One prison manager described it this way:

> I'm not a psychologist or a psychiatrist but if you go back, lots of prisoners of course have come from difficult families and homes and possibly no one has ever taken an interest in them or given them attention. They are put into an environment such as Kainos and somebody actually then is interested in them.
>
> (537)

All of these characteristics – the language, the civilian staff, active participation in the regime, the emphasis on relations – contribute to a feeling of being valued and supported. The question is whether a religious element, Christian or otherwise, must be an integral part of this package. Chapter 6 examines this along with other such issues in the wider context of human rights and equal opportunities.

Bearing the wide range of contextual issues in mind, the next sections look in more depth at how staff and managers in the prisons viewed Kainos Communities.

2. Perceptions from staff inside the Kainos Communities

Interviews for this section – 27 in total – included prison staff posted regularly in the Kainos units, chaplains employed by the Prison Service who had regular contact with the Kainos Communities, and Kainos-employed staff who worked on the units.

(a) What is Kainos – and what is it for?

Staff of all kinds described Kainos primarily as communities in a prison (sometimes described as Christian-based or multifaith) which gave prisoners the opportunity to change their behaviour for the better: '[It] creates an environment that enables someone to challenge the way they have been and encourage them to be different' (629). A member of the Kainos staff described the units as a 'community of [people] in prison trying to pull together to understand trust and God's love, in extreme circumstances' (648).

Some confusion existed regarding the relationship between Kairos and Kainos. Most prison staff interviewed on Kainos Communities realized the two were separate organizations. However, some thought they were one and the same, and others were unsure. Many still referred to Kainos Communities as Kairos, even though Kairos UK was a wholly separate organization to Kairos-APAC and the name changed from Kairos-APAC to Kainos the previous year. Some of the confusion may have related to the fact that Kairos Weekends were still an integral part of the Kainos programme at most prisons.

(b) The Kairos Weekend and Kainos follow-up programme

Kairos Weekends are run by a separate organization called Kairos UK and are staffed largely by volunteers from outside the prison. The Weekends are fully scripted and originate with Kairos USA. This in itself was the subject of comment: although some adjustments are made to adapt it to a UK audience, some staff and chaplains still described the style as too 'American'.

Kairos Weekends have an impact on host prisons in a number of ways. First, they are designed to bond members of the Kainos Community together – to 'create' community through shared experience. In this sense they have a positive impact on residents of Kainos Communities and are arguably an essential part of the Kainos programme. As one chaplain commented: 'How on earth would you ever replace the Weekend?' (636). The impact on the rest of the prison, at least during the Weekend, may be less positive. Kairos Weekends are very staff-intensive because of the large number of volunteers who come into the prison from outside. Prison staff often volunteered their time, working extended hours outside their normal rota to enable the Weekends to run smoothly. Staff shortages generally in the prisons, however, mean that activities for other prisoners may end up being curtailed. The numbers of staff thought necessary to staff the Weekend could mean that the rest of the prison would run a more restricted regime or be locked down.

The Kairos Weekend raised a number of issues for prison staff regarding prison security. This was more frequently a complaint from staff not directly involved in the Kainos units, but prison staff from both camps mentioned it as an issue. The large number of people from outside who come into the prison for a number of days was itself a source of concern, not to mention the food and materials they brought with them. Oddly this concern was less common at Swaleside – the highest security prison – than at the lower security prisons. At all prisons, volunteers for the Kairos Weekend and for the follow-up programmes receive security training and refresher courses as well as written clarification of these rules. An officer at The Verne commented that staff would be happier if they knew what briefing the volunteers receive.

The religious content of the Weekend was the source of much comment. An officer on one Kainos wing said that the prison 'can get some real weirdos and a lot of busybodies' (624) as volunteers for the Weekend. Even an employee of Kainos acknowledged that one 'can see why people have called it cultish' (614) and that if it were run by another religious group, he could see people converting to that religion by the end of the Weekend. Opinion was divided about the benefits of the Weekend, however: while one officer said he had 'heard it's too evangelical' (617), another described its effects on the prisoners who participate as 'amazing', 'phenomenal' a 'shock', and 'a real buzz overall' (620).

A few prison officers, like prisoners in the previous chapter, mentioned another aspect of the Kairos Weekend, namely the possible effects on prisoners who are psychologically more vulnerable and the extent to which Kainos staff and, more particularly, volunteers are able to deal with this. Anecdotally, both staff and prisoners gave examples of people on the wings who tended to self-injure, but who reduced or stopped this due to the perceived safer, more supportive environment. Second, the staff on Kainos Communities (usually) include trained counsellors who are available full time on a one-to-one, confidential basis and on a drop-in basis. Third, support is supposed to be available throughout the Kairos Weekend from, *inter alia*, prison chaplains, volunteers and Spiritual Directors assigned to the Weekend if prisoners have difficulty coping. With these facts in mind, some prison staff and prisoners were concerned that this additional help was not always available when prisoners were most vulnerable (e.g. at night or on weekends), and that Kainos counsellors and staff may not always have the appropriate training for the specialist needs of a prison population or for the group work they conduct on the unit. These concerns were a minority view, as noted in Chapter 4, but merit further assessment.

As mentioned in the previous chapter, rapid turnover of the population in some prisons was destabilizing to the Community and made a rigidly structured programme impractical to operate. Others commented upon the difficulties in developing Kainos further. One Kainos employee noted Kainos had lost the 'high drama' it had in its early days of being *so* different to other programmes (637). Equally, staff noticed 'a decline in the buzz' of subsequent Kairos Weekends (610). Such concerns emphasize the need for good quality programmes to follow on from the Kairos Weekend and to be flexible enough for the needs of the prisoners who take part. However, follow-up programmes after the Kairos Weekend did not always exist for shorter-term prisoners, who one officer said tend to 'get 'left' on the unit' without the intended follow-up work (623). Sudden interruption of a therapeutic programme due to release or transfer, often at vulnerable points, was not uncommon: 'The whole idea of therapy is working towards a planned ending, but this happens with very few of these men' (648). One officer commented that shorter-term prisoners tended to be more focused on their release than on the content of programmes available. More flexibility, such as through a rolling or modular programme, was being explored as a possibly more practical approach, although here too, a clear goal is essential.

(c) Who is Kainos for?

Staff gave a wide variety of reasons as to why prisoners may wish to move to a Kainos wing. They believed some may want what they perceive to be a quiet life or to 'have a break from the system' (638), or they may genuinely want to change. Some officers were more sceptical, saying that Kainos attracts 'people who want toast at 2a.m.!' (635). Some also believed 'the God thing' (638) may put some prisoners off, such as if they view it as overtly religious ('Happy Clappy'/'Jogging with Jesus' (636)). Prisoners were generally not excluded from Kainos units unless they failed to meet security requirements. For example, people whose offence included hostage-taking were excluded because of the close association with volunteers from outside the prison during the programme. The number of sexual offenders also tended to be limited. People who were heavily medicated or seriously mentally ill ('an out-and-out lunatic' (624)) tended to be excluded, as were those who failed to follow the principles of the community, as these prisoners were thought to disrupt the community. On the other hand, Kainos units were thought to take both cooperative and uncooperative prisoners, as 'every inmate is both' (635).

Staff interested in work on a Kainos unit are themselves likely to play an important role in the success of the regime there. Reasons prison staff gave for wanting to work on a Kainos unit were for the challenge, for the opportunity to do something different including participating more actively in prisoner programmes, and because of the quality of relations with prisoners. As one prison chaplain commented: 'It engenders a kind of relationship which is – not *unique* in prison ... but which is not the norm'. One officer said he would rather work on the Kainos wing and 'see people's attitudes and behaviour change towards a more positive thing.' He went on to comment that '[working on a Kainos wing] is *different*; [you] can train a monkey to lock and unlock doors, [but this] challenges you' (646; emphasis in original).

Reasons for staff not wanting to work on Kainos Communities included discomfort with the religious aspect ('religious nut cases' (603); 'God Squad', (637, 648) 'Holy Joes' (628)), but also that more 'traditional' staff did not want closer relations with prisoners, preferring a stricter, more predictable regime. This latter group would not, for example, be comfortable with the concept of letting the Community resolve its own disputes – something which one prisoner described as a 'form of professional emasculation' (611) for some prison staff. One officer explained that 'you have to be flexible to accommodate an extra regime within a regime' (610).

(d) Relations with others

Staff on Kainos wings noted differences in relations between prisoners on the Kainos Communities. For example, staff commented that prisoners were more likely to defuse problems themselves rather than depending upon staff to step in. A particularly striking example of this, mentioned by several staff and prisoners, was an incident in which someone had been stealing items from prisoners' cells in Highpoint South. The thefts were brought up at the weekly Community meeting, and a member of Kainos staff asked who was doing it. Two men stood up and confessed, the thefts stopped, and the men were accepted back into the Community. This brought its own challenges, however, as a former Governor comments:

> The Officers were ambivalent. It was something to have a quiet wing, and something better that, when they asked who had stolen something, the offender declared himself immediately. But it did leave them with two problems. What should they do with an honest man? And should they join forces with the Kainos staff who appeared to have brought about this change, but who seemed remote, though their own office was just next door [?].
>
> (Respondent J 2003)

Managers also noted a difference:

> That's the most surprising thing. I haven't seen support prisoner-to-prisoner like we've got in [the Kainos wing]. Over the last 29 years, I haven't seen that anywhere.
>
> (584)

The majority of Kainos-employed staff thought Kainos prisoners seemed to support each other compared to those in other parts of the prison. One Muslim Senior Officer remarked that Muslim prisoners at Swaleside are 'more supportive of each other because of the Christian indoctrination that goes on … . There is a fear among the Muslims, about the vulnerable Muslim on Kainos, because of all the Christianity that goes on, they might lose their Muslim faith' (536). Others were less sceptical, saying Kainos units showed 'people really making an effort to try to rub along together' (647).

We also asked staff about any changes in prisoners' relations with their families, other prisoners, and with staff during their time on Kainos Communities. Staff information about prisoners' relations with their families was largely anecdotal, though some were able to recount feedback from families and to show letters they had received from former residents. Again the Family Day, in those prisons which had them, was also viewed as a positive step in building or maintaining family relations.

Equally, relations between Kainos prisoners and staff (both prison staff and Kainos staff) were seen as almost uniformly positive. Staff gave positive feedback about good relations and the development of mutual respect in the unit and noted changes in the behaviour of individual prisoners towards them during their time in the Kainos programme. Some mentioned surprise from new or temporary staff when prisoners thanked them or said 'please' when making a request. One officer explained that 'Once these men change, the way they talk to staff changes, and the way they respond changes' (629).

Prisoners and Kainos staff (and sometimes prison staff) at all four prisons usually addressed each other by their first names. When asked about who was part of the Kainos Community in their prison, both prisoners and staff replied prisoners, Kainos staff, and (certain) prison staff. The degree to which prison staff were seen as part of the Community varied between prisons. At The Verne, both prisoners and prison staff viewed staff as part of the Community. At Highpoint North and South, both groups said that *some* staff were part of it.

The overall perspective of increased trust and interaction between prisoners and prison staff as a positive result of Kainos programmes conflicts with the aims of the Learmont (1995) and Woodcock (1994) Reports following escapes from two high security prisons in England, HMPs Parkhurst and Whitemoor. These reports advocated a more distant approach between prisoners and staff to reduce the risk of staff 'conditioning' and thereby preserve prison security. Security was a common concern from staff who worked outside the Kainos units, discussed below, but even Kainos employees acknowledged this: 'We are security's biggest headache' (647). However, the aim of improved relations coincides fully with the spirit of the Woolf and Tumim Report (1991) following the series of prison riots in England in 1990. Woolf and Tumim emphasized the need for increased trust and closer relations as a means of preventing and resolving conflicts and increasing perceptions of justice and fairness. It is therefore of interest that prison managers and staff tended to view improved relations as a benefit of the Kainos regime.

One exception came from an officer who commented that the tendency of Kainos Communities to handle problems 'in house' made them less reliant on prison staff, until the problems became much larger. In the officer's view, the increased proportion of non-Kainos prisoners on the Kainos wing at Highpoint North actually improved relations because it increased the dependence of prisoners on prison staff.

(e) A lasting impact?

Staff were less certain about whether any changes made during prisoners' participation in the Kainos programme would last: 'you're talking about a very damaged group' (648), but equally 'anything *positive* is likely to make a difference' (637; emphasis original). Many were able to provide anecdotal evidence of people who had stayed away from offending after release and of those who were planning to continue similar work outside (e.g. one prisoner wanted to take the Kainos programme back with him to Nigeria). Both prisoners and staff had received letters from previous residents following their release, and these were often read out at Community meetings. A member of the Chaplaincy was particularly optimistic:

> Kainos is not an academic subject that you can learn for the sake of learning, but is a whole lifetime experience in itself ... *not* like some of the courses which you get a certificate for and never do anything with .... The kind of responsibility and respect it engenders is something that will never leave them. (emphasis original)
>
> (654)

Some expressed concern that no formal follow-up support existed for prisoners who left Kainos, either upon release or in other prisons, which could make the maintenance of any change particularly difficult. Again, one made the point that lasting change is extremely difficult in such a damaged and often drug-dependent group. Another commented that 'something *must* stick, even if it's just the experience of it' (604; emphasis original). Some prisoners were able to maintain informal links with Kainos and Kairos volunteers outside and to be introduced into local churches, and some limited follow-up upon release was being developed. Bottoms (2001: 104) has described such attachments as an important element in desistance from further offending:

> Deterrence works best for those persons who have strong ties of attachment to individuals, or to social groups or institutions, in a context where those individuals, groups or institutions clearly disapprove normatively of the behaviour at which the deterrent sanction is aimed.

Curran (2002: 302) explained that positive relationships outside prison helped prisoners 'overcome some of their fears about life after imprisonment' and gave them an 'assurance that their future lives would be positive'. Even life-sentenced prisoners, she found, 'were able to project themselves successfully into the future' (*ibid.*: 303).

Change in prisoners beyond anecdotal accounts is extremely difficult to measure in this type of programme. One cannot guarantee the authenticity of change even for prisoners who appear to have 'reformed' during a programme like Kainos (Curran 2002). The general consensus, however, was that 'something' was different about Kainos. As one officer said, 'It's just a positive way to work' (646). Maruna and LeBel (2002: 168); also Maruna, LeBel and Lanier (2004) describe something similar in their 'strengths model' of dealing with offenders: '[The] strengths paradigm calls for opportunities for ex-prisoners to make amends, demonstrate their value and potential, and experience success in support and leadership roles.' All of these elements are present in the structure and operation of Kainos Communities.

Other research explains why elements of Kainos Communities may be of more lasting benefit. Bottoms (2002: 39–40) noted that: 'Exposure to a different culture from that in which one was initially socialized may cause moral beliefs to change .... [Attachment] to pro-social bonds can be of potentially great importance in preventing recidivism.' Shover (1996: 127) explains that such attachments 'provide both a reason to change and social capital for doing so.' A prison chaplain closely involved with Kainos in his prison commented:

> I think it would be a grave mistake if they [the Prison Service] don't support it, because if you talk to staff here, they don't know why, but [they see that] people have changed, and that's the fact that stands.
>
> (654)

3. Perceptions from staff outside the Kainos Communities

Interviews for this section – 23 in total – included prison staff from other parts of the prisons that had Kainos Communities: some were geographically proximate to Kainos whilst others were further removed. Interviewees were chosen to represent as broad a range of perspectives as possible and included prison officers, Senior Officers and Principal Officers. Some were drawn from Operations, Security and Race Relations (for a full breakdown see Burnside *et al.* 2001).

(a) What is Kainos – and what is it for?

As with prisoners, most staff who worked outside the Kainos units were aware that Kainos was a 'religious' wing, of whom about half were aware of its Christian basis. The most informed response characterized Kainos as 'a community-based project building on relationships with other prisoners, primarily led on Christian ethics' (534). Staff at Highpoint North had only the haziest knowledge of what Kainos was ('something to do with religion' (556)) and blamed Kainos for their lack of knowledge:

> Kainos Community is vague. They haven't publicized themselves ... in such a way that the rest of the prison know what it is.
>
> (552)

A few were aware of the parent programmes in Brazil and the US but a number confessed that they did not know what Kainos did. Only two identified it as a 'therapeutic type of community' (562). Poor staff knowledge was not of itself surprising, with one prison officer in Highpoint South citing similar ignorance with regard to the prison's Voluntary Testing Unit (a drug testing unit in most establishments and an accredited part of the Prison Service structure). However, officers believed the lack of openness and transparency hindered Kainos:

> I feel that I'm not able to give advice to inmates ... and I can't recommend anyone because I don't know what it's about. It's shrouded in mystery, to be honest. I tried to find out ... but people don't really know.
>
> (557)

Prison staff claimed to have heard little about Kainos at Swaleside as well: 'it's not really mentioned' (543). Most said they heard about Kainos as a result of working in the prison, whilst a few learned about it from external sources.

Staff heard mixed reports about Kainos. At Highpoint North, one member of staff said: 'I've never had any terrible comments from inmates about how bad it is, but only a handful have come off and said how good it is' (552). Staff were sceptical of prisoner motives at a number of prisons: 'I don't think the prisoners down there are genuine' (535). Some were also cynical of governors' motives: 'I think Kainos exists because it gives the governor brownie points' (567). Staff described rank-and-file hostility to the Kainos regime. One member claimed:

> Staff [at Highpoint North] resent it being there full stop ... It's because they are treated differently and it's not working ... If I went to [the] Governor and said, 'Can I have an open day and bring in food etc.', it wouldn't be entertained.
>
> (556)

147

The more relaxed regime and belief that 'Inmates are molly-coddled' (557) was also a cause of concern.

At The Verne, opinions were 'half and half' (591). Some staff felt Kainos 'makes a mockery of the prison system and prison routine' (573). One prison officer confessed:

> [It's] not like anything I've experienced before. I'm used to prison as a place of control. Kainos seems to be very free and easy ... It seems to be almost completely independent of the Prison Service.
>
> (580)

A further bone of contention was the authority vested in civilian Kainos coordinators. Several commented on '[the] feeling that Kainos workers don't understand prison issues' (562), that they were 'naïve' (567) and subverted operational procedures. Such comments revealed a lack of trust but should be set against the tendency of prison staff to be suspicious of civilian non-uniformed staff generally, not just Kainos employees.

At the same time, negative perceptions could be reversed:

> I had some concerns about prisoners having their own meetings and having input to the Kainos project because it went against the grain of standard Prison Service procedures. Now I understand how the system works and there is staff input and it is really staff controlled and run, I'm more than happy with it.
>
> (583)

Whilst traditional prison staff may continue to view Kainos with suspicion, others are willing to be persuaded. Some could see potential:

> If it's run properly it can give people the confidence to embrace a side of them that they or other people haven't recognized .... They can get to like that and be quite comfortable with it. There's a lot of 'front' in prison – no one is really themselves. There is the opportunity on Kainos to be more yourself.
>
> (562)

Still other members of staff were enthusiastic about Kainos: 'It's a very positive environment for prisoners - they feel very settled' (583). Another commented:

On [a non-Kainos wing] it's 'dog eat dog', if you've got a smile on your face it's a weakness. On Kainos they're rewarded for being part of a community.

(554)

Some of this enthusiasm was due to anecdotal knowledge of individual change. Staff perceived that Kainos appeared to do some prisoners 'a lot of good' (563).

(b) The Kairos Weekend

Although we did not specifically ask staff for their views about the Kairos Weekend, several at Swaleside and The Verne spontaneously expressed concern about the security aspects of the Weekend and other features of Kainos. At Swaleside, one officer responsible for security claimed that during the Weekend 'a lot of security issues are overridden ... It's trays and trays of goods brought in. We can't effectively search all that' (535). 'Godparents' too were seen as a 'weak link' in prison security because 'people from outside can be easily manipulated' (535), especially when they develop a relationship with one particular prisoner. Nor were godparents in one establishment properly searched due to the small number of evening staff. One officer thought that Weekends and godparents sent out the wrong signal: 'If I saw 20 or 30 people coming through smiling and waving, all piling through, then I'd get complacent and maybe treat security less seriously' (581).

However, a security officer at The Verne said that whilst he 'initially had misgivings about the godparenting aspect totally... that was in my ignorance' (583). Whilst it was acknowledged that there was always a risk in introducing visitors, Kainos volunteers were seen as no greater a liability than any other visitors. Staff in one prison claimed that inappropriate liaisons had occurred on site between godparents and prisoners, then added that the same sort of situations had also occurred elsewhere in the prison. Security briefings were given to all the godparents, and Kainos visitors were searched in the same way as non-Kainos visitors. A security officer surmised: 'Non-Kainos staff aren't ... as aware as they should be that exactly the same procedures are in place for Kainos as well as non-Kainos visitors' (583).

(c) Who is Kainos for?

Most staff were either aware that Kainos recruited by means of application and interview or could make an informed guess that this was the case.

A minority said they had no idea. Of those who expressed an opinion, views were divided as to whether recruitment was satisfactory. Some commented that it 'appears to be working, although mistakes will always be made during interview' (563). Several commented that it was 'more of a bums on bench [beds] policy than a recruitment [policy]' (573). One commented that the Kainos coordinator has 'too much power in selecting prisoners' (536). Only a few staff said they understood the basis on which prisoners were selected, with one pointing out that prisoners 'have to be aware that it's Christian-based' (562). The vast majority of staff said that they had no idea of the basis on which prisoners are selected for Kainos. When asked whether they had made any enquiries, one replied 'No, because I've not been invited to Kainos in any capacity. I feel I'm totally outside the Kainos' (536). Nearly all staff who expressed an opinion said they did not think that Kainos recruitment and selection procedures should change. One officer at Highpoint North said more stringent requirements were necessary to exclude disruptive prisoners: 'There are too many people on it who are disruptive' (554). Such a comment is particularly interesting in view of the aim of Kainos Communities and similar programmes deliberately to include 'negative leaders'.

Most staff thought Kainos existed to serve a number of groups including first time and vulnerable prisoners, religious prisoners, and those who wanted to change:

> [You want] someone who's sensible, not disruptive to members, to groups, loosely based on religion, someone's got something to contribute to the community. Some unruly girls go on it ... and aren't suitable.
>
> (554)

A minority thought Kainos was for anyone. One prison officer thought Kainos was intended not just for the 'whole welfare' of the prison but 'outside the prison as well' (552).

Staff thought Kainos would appeal to a number of mixed and somewhat opposing groups, including the religious and the non-religious, the disruptive and the quiet, the vulnerable and the robust as well as the sociable and the non-sociable. In particular, they thought it would appeal to vulnerable and weaker prisoners: 'I would imagine a lot of poor copers would make a bee-line there' (568). One prison officer at Highpoint North disagreed with this practice, however:

> I don't encourage vulnerable prisoners to go on Kainos Community. If you've got a vulnerable prisoner they're better on a normal unit

where, if you've got a problem, it comes to attention and something is done about them. You don't put them on Kainos.

(552)

The implication from this comment was that Kainos generally was not competent to deal with vulnerable prisoners.

Staff thought Kainos appealed to prisoners for whom it was not designed. These included foreign nationals, drug dealers, and those seeking either an 'easy life', parole or (in Highpoint North and The Verne) homosexual activity ('Queeros' (630)). Kainos apparently attracted these groups because it was a 'cosy little area' (581) that allowed prisoners to 'hide and get away with things' (563). Illusions were sometimes shattered, however:

You get people who say to themselves: 'I want to have a nice, easy run' and then they openly admit after the Kairos Weekend that it wasn't an easy run, it was challenging and stimulating and so forth.

(590)

Nearly all staff thought Kainos was selective about which prisoners they accepted onto the unit. More than half of these thought Kainos was biased towards 'well-balanced' (552) and non-disruptive prisoners: '[Kainos] only take compliant and reasonable prisoners' (544). Only two members of staff interviewed thought Kainos took 'anybody' including prisoners who are 'out of control' (554). One, an officer at Highpoint South, claimed 'there was a perception a while ago that Kainos would *not* take the worst inmates from [a] basic regime, but this was changed largely by wing staff and not by Kainos themselves' (562, emphasis added).

We asked staff specifically whether they thought Kainos took an equal proportion of cooperative and uncooperative prisoners from other wings. Of those who expressed an opinion, most thought Kainos took 'whatever they're given' (552) and did not try to get 'the cream of the crop'. One prison officer supported this by noting that 17 out of 25 Kainos prisoners failed a recent drug test. In Swaleside the best prisoners were thought to be located on non-Kainos units. A minority, however, thought Kainos erred on the side of 'the good guys' (591) because 'you wouldn't achieve anything if you had a majority of nonconformists' (534). One member of staff at Highpoint North remarked:

I wouldn't expect them to take dregs of the earth who are going to be a problem ... The people who went on it originally were

151

completely unsuitable and they had to be thrown off. Perhaps if there's disruption, there's not the staff or the time to be able to deal with it.

(552)

Another staff member at Highpoint North said she recommended 'well-behaved people' to go to Kainos (554). A further staff member at Highpoint North claimed: 'We handle more unruly prisoners on N2 [a non-Kainos wing] than on Kainos' (556). At Swaleside a member of staff said: 'people I know from here who've gone to [Kainos] are decent prisoners and not a control problem' (545). At Highpoint South one staff member claimed: 'They take on people who don't need so much supervision. They try to take on people who won't fail so they'll look better initially' (563). Finally, at The Verne staff claimed that Kainos select 'generally more mature prisoners' (591).

A slight majority of staff expressing an opinion thought management used Kainos to 'try out' prisoners who had failed elsewhere, notably people who self-harm: 'there's some rubbish on [Kainos]' (567). Notably, no member of staff from Highpoint North, the women's prison, shared this view. Several staff members at Swaleside and The Verne thought managers used Kainos to 'try out' prisoners who were a disciplinary problem. No one interviewed at Highpoint North and Highpoint South thought this. Staff in three prisons did not, for the most part, think Kainos was used to 'try out' prisoners who needed protection from others: 'Kainos is not a protection course, it's a behavioural course' (554). The exception was The Verne, where some staff felt this had happened, citing the presence on the Kainos unit of police officers, sex offenders, self-harmers, and a male-to-female transsexual (590).

(d) Who runs Kainos – and who supports it?

Not one member of prison staff outside the Kainos units correctly identified Kainos as a joint operation run between uniformed staff, civilian staff, and the Chaplaincy, although nearly half saw it as a combination of civilian and uniformed staff. Slightly more thought it was run by the Kainos-employed coordinators ('members of the public' (543)) as thought it was run by prisoners. The remainder thought it was run by the Prison Service, local management, or the Chaplaincy. On the subject of relations between Kainos and the Chaplaincy, the vast majority of staff saw Kainos and the Chaplaincy as two separate groups and felt the Chaplain should not have overall responsibility for Kainos.

Opinions were mixed as to whether Kainos helped prisoners and staff to work together. Some claimed that it did help, others that it did not

('Staff I've met don't seem to respect Kainos' (556)) or that relationships were no better than elsewhere in the prison. Some of the more traditional prison staff were concerned that 'staff get too close to prisoners [on Kainos]' (573) and either failed to exercise proper discipline or that Kainos-employed staff prevented them from doing so.

(e) What are the 'perks' – and the snags?

Staff gave a variety of reasons as to why prisoners might choose to be on Kainos. The most popular reasons included less contact with staff ('[they] can get up to all sorts' (580)); perks ('[it's] a fast track to getting goodies' (563)); a 'cushy number' (569); and a perceived means of obtaining recategorization, parole, or home leave. Staff were sceptical of prisoners' motives, with only a handful suggesting that prisoners went on Kainos to 'better themselves', 'live in community' or because they had strong religious beliefs. Whilst sceptical, staff could empathize with these motives: 'If I was in prison, I'd apply to [Kainos]' (591).

Staff also listed a similar range of reasons as to why prisoners might choose *not* to be on Kainos. The most popular reasons included religion and peer pressure:

The biggest issue is the 'Christophobia' – the fear that they're going to be religiously brainwashed and they have to embrace Christianity wholeheartedly to be a success'.

(562)

Another remarked:

It's all sissy and it's not the thing that tasty cons do ... Christianity generally has got an almost effeminate [image], 'choirboys and vicars in frocks'. There's not a lot about the church that is masculine.

(591; see also Curran 2002)

A large proportion of prison staff thought that other prison staff might want to work on Kainos because they believed in rehabilitation and wanted to make a difference in individual lives. But they also thought some staff would be attracted for the same reasons as prisoners, *viz.* the wish for a safer, more relaxed and less confrontational environment: 'There are some people working over there who'd rather have an easy life than digging [prisoners] out' (573). Thus Kainos might attract 'lazy staff ... who want to sit back and relax in the job' (535). One officer thought Kainos was not demanding enough: 'If there's something wrong they won't confront inmates' and that 'it's too relaxed, it's not disciplined enough' (573), whilst another claimed: 'I've seen some very good staff go downhill on [Kainos]' (535). One officer claimed that 'Establishing discipline and procedures are more important than being [the] confidante of a con' (569). In contrast, a few thought Kainos could be a good career move. This group thought that 'traditional' Prison Service staff might see working on Kainos as 'too much hard work' (563). It was generally agreed that 'dinosaurs' (554), 'control freaks' and 'shut-door screw[s]' (563) would not be interested in working on Kainos because they would not see it as 'proper Prison [Service] work' (552):

> Some officers think prison is just 'bang up'... They're 'rufty-tufty' screws and [they] don't want to get involved in something namby-pamby'.
>
> (554)

A further deterrent was the ambiguous role prison staff were expected to play on Kainos. One officer described the problem:

> You're either going to be a social worker and try to help or you're going to maintain discipline ... [Y]ou have to say 'Are officers going to be disciplined or are they going to be counsellors?' and if a counsellor, you have to be taken out of the discipline role. They do a lot of cuddling and comforting over there.
>
> (569)

Related to this was the manner in which staff perceived Kainos as undercutting the traditional role of the prison officer. At Highpoint North one staff member explained:

> To a certain extent staff don't make decisions ... For some staff it can be a frustrating experience that goes against their training. Discipline [prison] staff say their hands are tied if there's a discipline problem.
>
> (557)

The same member of staff spoke of the discomfort of being challenged by Kainos prisoners on matters (e.g. patrol) that would not have been disputed on a regular location. Likewise, on Highpoint South 'a prison officer would search the room and then [the Kainos coordinator] would take that prison officer to one side and say 'You are not supposed to do that here' (562). Similar comments were made by staff at The Verne: 'If you work on [Kainos] you've got to say 'yes' and you can't say 'no' or 'boo' to a prisoner in case they get upset' (580). Elaborating further this staff member said:

> The few times I have been on [Kainos] during the day I think, 'How do they get away with this?' Perhaps it's because I'm not used to it. [Kainos] is almost 'no-go'… [There's] a feel of loss of control over my actions because my actions might undermine what they're trying to do.
>
> (580)

Some staff also viewed the religious aspect as a deterrent.

Slightly more staff said they personally would rather not work on Kainos than said it would appeal to them. Deterrent factors were again religion ('It's religious … and it's something that perhaps the Service isn't used to' (567)) and working with civilians:

> We have so many civilians in the jail we don't know whether there's a place for us anymore … [Civilians] undermine the general security of the prison which is my working environment.
>
> (567)

One staff member who personally supported Kainos said:

> [Staff are] divided into two camps. There are those who thinks it's great and those who think it's not so great.
>
> (591)

Similar comments were heard at Highpoint North from another Kainos supporter: 'Kainos Community is something that you either love it or you hate it' (557).

(f) Favouritism – and parole

Views were mixed as to whether Kainos attracted unduly favourable treatment compared with the rest of the prison. Some staff noted that Kainos attracted particular resources (e.g. the Kairos Weekend, godparenting etc.), but '[if prisoners] are putting effort into the course then why shouldn't they be rewarded?' (563). Some noted that the concentration of resources was limited to start-up and that, at Highpoint South and The Verne at least, other parts of the prison were better-resourced. The same would now also apply to Highpoint North following the opening of a 'therapeutic community' wing in 2001.

155

The vast majority of staff thought being on Kainos would help prisoners with their parole, although a few qualified that by saying prisoners had to prove they had changed their behaviour whilst on Kainos. In that sense, Kainos was no different to 'a behavioural programme or any course that inmates participate [in]' (557). One prison officer pointed out that 'a lot of the stuff they do is beneficial to them *when* they get out rather than helping them to get out' (563, emphasis original). Again, it appears that some prisoners felt they have to take part in Kainos to improve their chances of parole. One prison officer at The Verne said: 'I know lifers who say, "I don't want to go over there [to Kainos] but I've got to get my parole" ' (573).

(g) Impact on prisoners – and prisons

A majority of staff thought Kainos would have some influence on (some) prisoners in the future. At Highpoint South one staff member remarked: 'Even the worst can let their guard drop and behave differently' (562). Staff at Swaleside also made positive comments:

> I've seen the benefits it's had to non-conformist prisoners behaviour-wise .... People come from [Kainos] onto [a non-Kainos] wing having done the programme as changed characters. [It's] a mixture of those who [you] think will change and those you think it won't have an impact on.
>
> (534)

There was also optimism at The Verne:

> Seeing people afterwards, it does change their lives. They say that they've been through other courses, but Kainos is the one that really registered with them and helped them to blossom out.
>
> (590)

> We've had people come with quite horrendous institutional records, and they've been transformed.
>
> (583)

> [The] majority of them who go down there [to Kainos] it seems to improve their behaviour. It works.
>
> (574)

This optimism was heavily qualified, however, with staff noting that much depended on prisoner commitment and the nature of the *post-*

Kainos environment (e.g. the likelihood of reverting to bad behaviour on a 'normal' wing). A quarter of staff preferred not to speculate about future impact, and the remainder were sceptical.

A large proportion of non-Kainos staff thought that Kainos had made an impact on the atmosphere of the prison. At The Verne, Kairos-APAC (the forerunner to Kainos) was credited with having played a large part in calming the whole of the prison since it was based on the wing where trouble usually started:

> Kainos ... transformed [the] dorm into a quite peaceful and manageable environment for prisoners and staff. There's no comparison.
>
> (581)

> It's certainly worthwhile. I worked on D-Wing pre-Kainos and it was an absolute nightmare.
>
> (585)

A former prison chaplain recalled that when the new Governor arrived at The Verne, following the Ex-Con B debacle (see Chapter 3), he was told that because of the financial problems of Kairos-APAC the prison would have to pay for the Coordinators for three months:

> [The Governor] said to me: 'I can't possibly afford to pay Coordinators three months, what do they think this is?'. At the end of the three months I saw him and he said: 'If I was asked to pay for another three months, I'm so impressed, I would happily pay for another three months'.
>
> (590)

Several staff pointed out, however, that the effect of Kairos-APAC was hard to disentangle from other innovations introduced at the same time that also had a positive effect. These included the increased number of lifers and foreign nationals, increased security, and an improvement in the quality of prison food, including a change to a self-select menu. Staff thought the 'calming' influence of Kainos at The Verne was in some cases of less contemporary significance due to 'all the other positive things going on' (581).

Kairos-APAC at Swaleside was also thought to have had a positive effect by giving the prison an alternative way of dealing with non-conformist or problem behaviour. One respondent claimed:

[to offer] prisoners hope and that's quite sound. It gives them something – another option, something to look at, work for and keeps them occupied.

(543)

Again, the positive impact of Kainos was hard to assess because B-wing (the Kainos unit at Swaleside) was the focus of concentrated effort from management from the mid-1990s to turn it around from being 'a very troublesome wing to being a very compliant wing' (544). The result is that B-wing may *already* have had a calming and positive influence on the prison before the introduction of Kainos and, whilst Kainos enhanced this reputation, the history of B-wing makes it difficult to separate the benefits of Kainos from the benefits of a stable wing:

B-wing's good reputation has stuck with them no matter what project is involved. It's not just a Kainos identity, it's a B-wing identity.

(544)

The same senior officer thought that:

Kainos would have had more positive impact if it had been started on A or C-wing [traditionally 'rougher' wings that have no particular identity] … It was the easy option to start it on B-wing

(544)

At Highpoint South staff claimed that the divisive physical structure of Highpoint South militated against *any* programme having an impact on the wider prison:

Highpoint South can be quite divisive. So it's not a comment on Kainos so much as the way the prison is run. Kainos might have the potential to have a big impact but you wouldn't know because of each part of prison being quite separate.

(562)

That said, another claimed that Kainos originally calmed certain parts of the prison 'as do many other projects' (567) by breaking up the prisoner population:

If you're a religious man in prison you get ridiculed from time to time. When you take that element away and put them into Kainos then the others don't have anything to bite at so they just settle down.

(567)

Kainos was also said to lighten the prison atmosphere by enabling 'a more dispersed mix of disruptive prisoners' (568). However, one respondent blamed the acrimonious departure of the Kainos coordinator during the period of research for dissipating any 'calming' influence. By 2001, however, in both Highpoint South and Highpoint North Kainos was 'just another wing' (554).

Several members of staff believed Kainos had a negative influence on their prison. A staff interviewee at Highpoint North said Kainos had a baleful effect because it created 'resentment among staff and inmates ....They don't think it works ... even if they believe in the concept' (556). At Swaleside, one Muslim member of staff claimed Kainos had a negative effect on the prison because it created discontent among Muslim prisoners. Even its positive effect upon The Verne was questioned with one prison officer claiming Kainos undermined security:

If I found something on them [prisoners], [such as] cutting implements, servery utensils, I'd put them on report whereas on [Kainos] they would turn a blind eye. I feel it affects the whole of the prison – it compromises security. It has a demoralizing effect on the rest of the prison.

(573)

The majority of staff said they would recommend Kainos to prisoners, although they qualified this by reference to the sort of prisoners whom they thought would benefit (addicts, foreign nationals, first-timers and religious, sociable or vulnerable prisoners). Some staff said they would not recommend Kainos to particular prisoners, especially 'manipulators' who might try to abuse the Community. A third of staff interviewed said they did not know enough about Kainos to be able to advise. As for recommending Kainos to other staff, of those staff who expressed an opinion, about half said they would recommend Kainos, while the other half said they would not, though again much depended on staff skills. Suitable staff included those who were 'sensible', broadminded, liked a more relaxed environment and were committed to rehabilitation. Unsuitable staff were described as those who were authoritarian and those who lacked 'people skills'.

A proportion of staff at each prison could not suggest ways in which Kainos could be improved because they lacked sufficient knowledge of its current operation. Kainos at Highpoint North could be improved, some staff believed, by making it a separate unit which only housed Kainos participants. This might have addressed the resentment prisoners felt who shared the same houseblock as Kainos but who were not part of the Community. One suggested Kainos should be a two-stage process to reduce the 'culture shock': 'It's too much for them to go from bad girl *boom* into community' (554). This may also provide needed incentive.

At Highpoint South, staff recommended better liaison between uniformed and civilian Kainos workers as well as better communication between Kainos civilian staff and the rest of the prison:

> They expect us to get close to them and be helpful but they [Kainos] don't seem to be prison-orientated in many cases. It's got to be a full team event.
>
> (567)

Other comments were that Kainos needed prison staff who wanted to be involved in the unit and who believed in its purpose. At Swaleside staff thought that Kainos should be advertised more widely in the prison to attract more longer-term prisoners as opposed to prisoners on induction. Better information was also proposed for staff. Several suggested that Kainos should take on board other religious views apart from Christianity. Rather radically, one interviewee proposed that Kainos should be relocated to a different wing where it could make more impact. Staff made little substantive comment regarding improvements at The Verne beyond the need for more transparency, better information and refurbished dormitories.

4. Perceptions of prison management

Six prison managers were interviewed for this section – two from each of the prisons (bearing in mind that senior managers at Highpoint at that time were responsible for both North and South).

(a) What is Kainos – and what is it for?

In contrast with non-Kainos staff, most senior managers were well informed and were able to describe the origins and distinctive features of Kainos (including its Christian aspect) in some detail. Managers generally took a positive view of Kainos and saw it as a place where prisoners were shown trust, enabled to live in community and encouraged to change their behaviour. The following comment was typical:

The average prisoner tends to think of himself first and other people second ... and I'm pretty confident that one of the big issues of living in the way that we hope the prisoners do in [Kainos] is that they think: it's not me first, I'm part of this community, I'm part of a greater community when I'm living outside of the jail.

(589)

One manager suggested that Kainos may work more readily with female prisoners:

I think women tend to mix more easily than men do, and they also tend to get more involved with things, and when they do ... they put their heart and soul into it, shall we say, they give it 90 per cent or 100 per cent whereas men would probably only give it 50 per cent or 60 per cent. So whether that's from a gender base, that it works differently, I don't know. Having said that, I'm not sure that there's any actual difference in outcomes.

(589)

(b) The Kairos Weekend

Again in contrast with non-Kainos staff, managers valued the Kairos Weekend as a means of promoting local community involvement, reducing prisoner isolation and exposing prisoners to positive influences. Some were wary of the more explicit Christian focus of the Weekend, which in one governor's view was not consistent with the approach of Kainos Communities themselves:

We make Kainos a very loose Christian therapeutic community, and Kairos and the Weekend is a very Christian-based, godly weekend which could actually exclude non-Christians.
So it's a conflict, if you like, between implicit, 'Prison Service' Christianity and explicit Christianity?
Absolutely right, yes, indeed, yes.
So do you feel there is a need for distance between Kainos Community and the Kairos Weekend?
I think so. I do, yes.

(548)

Other governors agreed: '[The Kairos Weekend] is so plainly a Christian weekend' (549).

One manager noted that volunteers offered prisoners a different kind of relationship:

[Prisoners] quite clearly see the volunteers as somebody who are not prison staff, and the fact that somebody like that can speak to them and own up to them helps ultimately to them wanting to change themselves.

(589)

Another who had been based in the prison since its first Kairos Weekend commented:

If you look at the wider issues, the effect on the prison generally, the whole prison settles for the weekend for some reason. It has an impact on the whole prison ... For some reason, my cynical side would expect [that], with the staff so busy, the rest of the prison population, would capitalize on that and cause trouble elsewhere. It doesn't happen.

(537)

Staff concern about security and the Weekend was not thought to be valid. One noted, 'There is nothing as far as I am aware that security-wise affects the prison detrimentally' (621). Another said that the Kairos Weekend did not present any greater problem than, say, a carol service. Like any scheme that involved outside contact there were risks, but these were thought to be controlled and the dividends worthwhile. One manager, who was a former head of security, commented:

Security is a balance thing. If you want total security, you don't actually end up doing anything. You don't let anybody into the jail or anybody out.

(584)

Others commented about the impact of the Weekend on the prisoners. One expressed concern about the anti-climax for a prisoner after the 'high' of the Weekend: 'you can get this huge high at a Kairos Weekend, which [afterwards] could leave people hanging' (549). A few managers, as with prisoners and officers, mentioned the possible effects of the Kairos Weekend on prisoners who are psychologically more vulnerable and the extent to which Kainos staff and more particularly volunteers are able to deal with this. This is equally the case for other issues unfamiliar to lay people coming into prisons. One prison governor commented:

Kainos workers have spoken of the strange feeling of dealing with people who are very serious offenders, often far beyond their own experience, but who are, nevertheless, able to discuss that with them, and that's raised a big training question in my mind, as with a lot of contracted people like drug action teams and so on and so forth. They may know about drugs, Kainos may know about the importance of religion for them, but they are being asked to tackle people who have massive offending-related problems that they may not actually be equipped to deal with, which is why there has to be a partnership with the professional prison staff, and why Kainos has to be part of offending behaviour, addressing that.

(549)

Debriefing of Kainos staff and volunteers was also relevant here: 'I don't know who the [Kainos] counsellor offloads to but, well-meaning amateurs are not always aware of all these dynamics, are they?' (537). In saying this, nearly all managers thought Kainos presented no difficulties as it stood at that time, although Highpoint management indicated that their answers would have been different had the interviews been conducted six months previously.

(c) Who is Kainos for?

Prison management hoped that Kainos was for everyone, although several cited difficult and non-conformist prisoners or those who wanted to explore their spirituality. A former prison Governor with experience of Kainos comments:

> As a Governor I knew how important it could be if I could use Kainos to begin to manage the risks of rejection and ridicule, and to learn about our spiritual side – of which prisons do little, and often appear to care less.
>
> (Respondent J 2003)

Managers generally thought Kainos appealed to a mixture of difficult prisoners and those seeking help and support. Managers generally denied that Kainos was used as a place to 'try out' prisoners who had failed elsewhere or who were a disciplinary problem, although several conceded that it happened occasionally: 'it's part of breaking the cycle at times' (537). One manager thought Kainos had taken too many difficult prisoners in the past. Some denied it was a place to 'try out' prisoners who need protection, although several recognized that this did occur: 'if I have a prisoner who is difficult to place within the prison and if he's a suitable candidate for Kainos, then I would say that that is the prisoner's best chance of actually surviving on [an] ordinary location here' (584).

Interestingly, one manager said that if an unsuitable prisoner applied to Kainos from another jail, he would be given further consideration.

Like other people working in the prison, managers were concerned about the use of Kainos Communities with shorter-sentenced prisoners: 'It needs a stable population. It needs to be a training-type prison [prison for people serving medium to long terms in custody]' (537). Equally, governors noted the need to prepare prisoners to leave Kainos communities – a 'weaning off' (549) – as is appropriate upon completion of any prison programme.

(d) Who runs Kainos – and who supports it?

Prison managers believed Kainos was run by a combination of the Senior Officer on the wing, Kainos Coordinators, and Chaplaincy, with the Kainos Coordinators being responsible on a day-to-day basis. When this worked well, as a former prison Governor remarks: 'The combination of good Kainos people and good prison staff was unbeatable' (Respondent J 2003). One Governor warned that if any in-fighting took place between the wing Senior Officer, Kainos Coordinators, and Chaplaincy then Kainos would not continue, though another said this was one of the main difficulties Kainos had in the prison:

> The main [difficulties were] the lack of a management steer, the lack of a management board, [and] the ... infighting between Chaplaincy and Kainos in particular; we now feel that we have now got the balance right.
>
> (548)

Most managers agreed the Chaplain should not have overall responsibility, although several commented that the Chaplain should be satisfied as to the spiritual content of the Kainos programme, including the Kairos Weekend. Several commented that their only difficulties came from higher levels within the Prison Service or from outside the Prison Service altogether. A former Governor, reflecting on his experience with Kainos, recalls:

> I was worried about Kainos. It seemed to exist in spite of management. The prison staff worked in a separate compartment, albeit with a good grace. There were rumblings from HQ and awkward MPs constantly picked at it. They suggested that only nice prisoners were allowed in. They suggested that only Christians were allowed in. They suggested that, if the research showed that it didn't cure offenders, it would be closed [cf. Chapter 11]. I was soon

to learn that Kainos needed someone who could tell the truth, at least the truth that I saw, which was the opposite of what was being said. I met men who had no faith or another faith, who nevertheless found decency, forgiveness and – yes – love as natural tenets in a prison community, supported by uniformed staff and unashamed of its values.

(Respondent J 2003)

As with prisoners and staff on the Kainos units, managers noted changes in relationships between prisoners and staff there. A prison manager described the effect this way:

Lots of staff will hide behind discipline and authority, and it is a hiding [place]. Kainos, or that type of community, demands staff to drop those barriers, so they actually get the strengths of their staff coming out; you actually get the more human side of their staff coming out, and that is reciprocated by the prisoners, and it's probably that prisoners no longer see staff as such a threatening face of authority. So they then react and you see the better side of prisoners. *So it brings out the best in everybody?* That's right. You start to deal with prisoners and staff as people.

(537)

Another commented:

When we turned round and instituted Kainos, we started to get far, far better relationships, far, far better behaviour from prisoners .... [There] is no doubt about it: relationships between staff and prisoners are the best that I've seen in my five years [here]. There is no doubt about that.

(584)

Relationships between prisoners who participated in Kainos also appeared to improve. One prison manager felt positive relationships between prisoners was the strongest feature of Kainos:

I haven't seen that [prisoner-to-prisoner support] operate anywhere else. In terms of community and in terms of support, particularly when things aren't going very smoothly, the prisoners will do their very, very best to manage their own difficulty and go beyond the point that I would expect them to. They've gone beyond that level in many, many cases.

(584)

Of less certainty was the level of support for Kainos from Prison Service Headquarters. One governor noted: 'I don't see evidence of a consensus, either among [government] ministers or in Headquarters, about the value of such a programme', which he believed made 'any programme like this vulnerable' (549). Of course, such programmes are vulnerable anyway, as a former Governor recalls:

> There was plenty of evidence that its very existence depended on the whim of the Governor. As with most voluntary groups working in prisons they can die as fast as they can grow. No matter how painstaking the work done to build up local support over many years, no matter how strong the promises made by a governor as to their glowing future, no matter the good people feel they experience (often dismissed as the 'feel good' factor), such efforts can disappear overnight. A new Governor, or even simply the advancing time in post of the present governor, can lead to a change of heart and commitment among staff and prisoners. Kainos died in both prisons shortly after I left, [see Chapter 11] though in both there was as great a sense of shared ownership as there had ever been.
>
> (Respondent J 2003)

The lack of support from Headquarters notwithstanding, the same Governor explained why the programme had his backing:

> I like fresh air, though it can be rather heady in a really closed prison. Kainos had lots of potential for this. I was determined that I would do what I could to be a fan, and help the prison and Kainos staff and prisoners to blow fresh air into the prison.

(e) What are the 'perks' – and the snags?

Several prison managers thought prisoners would want to be on Kainos because they wanted to address their offending behaviour or because they thought it was an 'easy way' to do their sentence. One, however, was clear to point out that any perceived physical advantages of life on a Kainos unit were a fallacy:

> If being on Kairos [sic.] meant that you were on the best accommodation on the prison and [had] a large double bed and a colour telly and a duvet and you didn't have to go to work and you had visits every week and you had home leave every weekend, if you got all that by being on Kairos and I chose not to go on Kairos

because I was a Buddhist, then I might feel aggrieved. But if I was a Buddhist and looking at what's available on D-Wing, I'm hardly going to turn round and say, 'Hey, it's not fair, they've got this, that, and the other', because they haven't got anything that nobody else hasn't got.

(589)

But a former prison Governor emphasizes that Kainos did offer something unique to prisoners:

As far as I knew, (and know), Kainos was the only residential community offering prisoners the opportunity to explore their spirituality (as against 'practise their religion') – a much neglected side of the person in prison as far as I was concerned. If we could bring the prison and the Kainos culture alongside, we were onto a winner. Each would learn from the other, and the prisoners would have the chance to learn about their spiritual side without the usual prison pressure to think that goodness, Godliness and non-offending were the same thing, or shared the same set of goals.

(Respondent J 2003)

As far as staff were concerned, prison managers tended to think that Kainos would not appeal to disciplinarians. Working on Kainos units does appear to require an adjustment for prison staff: 'Officers have commented on the strangeness of dealing with prisoners who admit they have done wrong' (549) (see Chapter 4).

(f) Favouritism – and parole

In general, prison managers did not think Kainos prisoners were treated differently in prison disciplinary hearings. However, one Governor thought Kainos prisoners would present themselves better on an adjudication because they were more accustomed to dealing with their own shortcomings without being defensive. Indeed, 'there have been occasions when [Kainos prisoners] have said they did something wrong before the staff even know it's happened' (549). Nearly all prison governors who dealt with disciplinary cases personally said they did not tend to look any more or less favourably on Kainos prisoners, although one conceded:

I think I look on them more favourably. If it's not a serious offence I am more favourable to Kainos overall.
Why is that?

167

I know it's not an easy option, and I know it's probably more difficult over there and more demands over there than on this side.

(584)

Prison governors did not think participating in Kainos *per se* benefited prisoners in terms of parole. However, they believed it could be of indirect benefit insofar as prisoners could demonstrate a change of behaviour. In this respect, Kainos was no different to any other programme on a prisoner's sentence plan.

(g) Impact on prisoners – and prisons

Prison managers who expressed an opinion thought Kainos would have an influence on prisoners in future, or hoped that it would. One commented:

I think that it's almost impossible to go through the Kainos programme without feeling a more complete person, and I say that with quite a lot of thought because I think that some spiritual experiences in prison actually diminish people.

(549)

Managers in several prisons were of the view that Kainos had made a very positive contribution, whilst those elsewhere thought Kainos had shown alternative ways of running prison wings and had led to more better-behaved prisoners at the 'top end' of the establishment. One noted:

Certainly as a Governor I'm very happy that there is that influence around .... I've been surprised by the reactions of some visitors to the jail. I've had some senior managers who I've known for a long time in the Prison Service who, when I've sat them down [on Kainos] with a couple of prisoners and they've got chatting, have been gobsmacked by the way the prisoner was talking and their approach to their environment. They know that they wouldn't have had that conversation with them 12 months ago at Prison X or Prison Y or at [name of current prison] if they didn't have Kairos (*sic*), so ... certainly there is something around the jail.

(589)

Prison managers agreed they would recommend Kainos to other governors: 'it might just work for them' (584). They also agreed they would commission Kainos if they had to make that choice again, although one commented that Kainos ought to change its name in the interest of clarity. Another emphasized the value of the additional resources Kainos brought: 'if it's free, I'd want to take it' (589). This governor explained that the value of Kainos units stretched beyond any impact (or not) on reoffending:

> If [Kainos] contributes to lower recidivism, then from a national standpoint that's a real advantage. But if we can actually show genuinely that there is a contribution at an establishment level and/or contribution to reconviction rates, then the programme's proved its worth. If research doesn't show any impact on recidivism, you've still got the advantage of what it presents to the establishment on a day-to-day basis. So, locally there'd still be a reason for running the programme. If the research showed that it delivered nothing at all and that our anecdotal thoughts about the day-to-day bit – then you've got a question of whether to do it .... But certainly at the moment, if a fellow Governor asked me whether it was wise to think about having a Kainos Community in his prison I would say, well come and look at mine, and I think he'd say yes.

Prison managers suggested a mixture of reforms including shared sentence planning targets in all host prisons, common training for and about Kainos, introducing accredited courses to the follow-up programme, only admitting prisoners who volunteer, and ensuring that Kainos Community and the host prison work in a proper partnership 'so that it doesn't become an alien activity in prison' (549). One Governor thought it would be desirable if Prison Service HQ were to make slightly more of a commitment to Kainos Community.

One former prison Governor felt Kainos's desire to treat prisoners with humanity, decency and respect, and so turn 'prisoners' into 'people', challenged the usual trend for prisons to turn 'people' into 'prisoners':

> As always I have a problem with treating people as human beings in prison. It has something to do with treating people with humanity while depriving them of it. My job was to turn people into prisoners. Period. Whether they eventually became people again was up to them. The evidence showed that nearly all did grow out of prisoning as they did out of offending. We had few old prisoners, and the few we had were more nuisance than menace. Something worked, and no doubt God had something to do with that, but it seemed more likely to be 'anno' than any other intervention of Domini.

> (Respondent J 2003)

169

5. Conclusions

What main conclusions can we draw from this descriptive account? We suggest the following:

- Measures such as disciplinary reports, alarm bells, and drug tests seemed positive, but much of this information was patchy or unavailable.

- Relations between prisoners and staff (prison staff and Kainos staff) on the wings were reported as almost universally positive. This, and other elements of the Kainos regime such as active prisoner committees and the full time support of non-uniformed civilian staff, is likely to have a beneficial effect on the wings, above and beyond any effect of the content of Kainos programmes.

- Much of the success of a faith-based unit depends on the individual personalities involved and their relations with prison staff and managers. Staff for faith-based units need to be carefully recruited and must receive thorough, ongoing training.

- Formal follow-up support for prisoners who leave Kainos, either upon release or upon transfer to other prisons, is an important area for development.

- Faith-based unit Trustees and staff need to be absolutely clear about their philosophy and ensure that others understand their purpose and aims as well.

- Kainos Trustees, staff, and Communities need to work in a more coordinated fashion, with more certainty and support from within their organization and more coherence and transparency for those outside it. More uniformity of record keeping by Kainos staff would lead to improvements in any future studies of the effects of participation in Kainos Community, as well as contributing to general accountability.

Notes

1 Despite its location on the island of Portland on the south coast of England, the prison was used as an overspill establishment for prisoners from Wales, several hundred miles away from their families.
2 Senior Prison Service managers responsible for overseeing several prisons in the same geographical area.
3 At Highpoint North, the impression of some staff was that numbers of disciplinary infractions and outcomes of hearings were the same for prisoners on and off the Kainos unit.

Chapter 6

Kainos Community and religious freedom

As soon as people hear the word 'Christian', they close up.
Prison officer, HMP Swaleside (646)

Human rights and equal opportunities have been particularly prominent issues in discussions about Kainos Communities. Concern about whether Christian prisoners are somehow favoured, that non-Christian prisoners may not feel welcome to participate, that ethnic minorities are either discriminated against or favoured, are all questions which various critics and observers of Kainos have raised (e.g. Smartt 2000; Ruthven 2000; Wood 2000; Wyner 2003). This chapter aims to address these questions, none of which are straightforward or easy to untangle.

The information in this chapter was based on interviews with prisoners and staff targeted for a cross-section of cultural backgrounds and religious beliefs. Given the diversity of the prison populations involved and the consequent adaptations made to the Kainos programme, it reports findings as they pertained to each Kainos Community rather than to Kainos Communities as a whole. Some of the wider themes, however, arguably apply to religious communities in any institutional context. The chapter looks at these common themes and highlights particular issues that have sparked concern about the role of religious organizations in prisons.

This chapter was authored by Nancy Loucks

1. Who volunteers for Kainos?

Kainos Communities seemed to attract three main types of prisoners. The first type was those who genuinely wanted to change their behaviour and saw Kainos as an opportunity (if not a last resort) to do this. The second type was the more religious prisoners (usually, but not exclusively, Christian) who wanted to be in a faith-centred environment. Often this meant that it attracted more ethnic minorities, such as prisoners from the Caribbean and African countries and many from Spanish-speaking countries. Some prisoners, and often staff, found this off-putting. In HMP Highpoint South, for example, the prison staff took it upon themselves to maintain a balance of ethnic minorities with white British prisoners.

The third type were those who volunteered because they believed it would be an 'easy option' – that a Christian community would be 'soft' and therefore more relaxed and quieter. In this sense some saw it as an ideal opportunity to sell drugs or otherwise take advantage of other prisoners. Conversely, it was also perceived as an opportunity 'to get away from the nonsense in the other [wings]' (611). In one group discussion, prisoners said that people came to the wing for peace and quiet, but that not everyone who comes is a peaceful, quiet person – rather, they *become* so due to the environment. While real motives may not be discovered during application and interview for Kainos, any inappropriate behaviour was likely to be detected once in the Community, at which point the prisoners would be removed. A number of prisoners interviewed, however, said they originally came on the wing for an 'easy life', but subsequently decided to stay, even when they realized that life on the wing was more challenging than they had anticipated.

The decision to live on a Kainos wing because it was 'quiet' was particularly noticeable amongst prisoners at HMP Swaleside, the highest security prison in the research. At Swaleside, prisoners had a choice of two mainstream wings (which they referred to as 'the jungle'), a drug rehabilitation wing, a lifers' wing, or Kainos. Some prisoners commented that, for them, Kainos was therefore the best option, even though they did not necessarily have any interest in the programme itself. This meant that some prisoners on the Kainos unit at Swaleside faced what they considered to be a difficult dilemma: the choice between participating in a programme they did not want to do, or to leave Kainos and move on to a normal location, which they also did not want. In other words, they wanted the benefits of living in a quieter, safer community environment without the condition of fulfilling the Kainos compact (which, ironically, was designed to promote such an environment). An atheist prisoner on a non-Kainos wing at Swaleside said that friends had told him 'the wing is good, but to stay on the wing you've got to suffer' (541). This view was not as prominent at the other prisons.

In addition to prisoners who were attracted to the unit, a fourth type of prisoner was on Kainos, namely prisoners who did not volunteer at all, despite Kainos's voluntary basis. These were people who were placed on Kainos wings upon reception due to lack of spaces elsewhere in the prison, or those who were deemed 'vulnerable' in some way and were therefore placed on a Kainos wing by prison staff, whose choices usually took priority over the choices of Kainos staff. In a sense this latter group 'volunteered' because their options were fairly limited elsewhere. Several members of staff, particularly at Highpoint North and South, referred to Kainos Communities as a 'dumping ground' for people who could not cope elsewhere. For prisoners who were placed on Kainos at reception without volunteering for the programme, many eventually chose to stay on the wing and signed the Kainos compact. Those who chose not to stay were not expected to participate in the community's activities and were moved elsewhere once space was available.

This last group of prisoners – those who did not necessarily volunteer – has a particular bearing on the stability of Kainos Communities. In each prison, the need to put 'bums on beds' took priority over the Kainos Community's criteria for selection. Application and interview procedures were not as rigorous as many staff would wish precisely because of the pressure to fill spaces, as well as pressure on staff time. Further, the prison staff had priority for the use of the space: if, for example, they felt that a particular prisoner needed to be on the wing because he or she would not be tolerated elsewhere in the prison, prison staff could put the prisoner on Kainos even if the Kainos staff had more appropriate volunteers for the space. In the same way, prisoners being received into the prison took priority for space over voluntary applicants for Kainos. Importantly from a human rights perspective, this pressure on space also meant that prisoners who wanted to leave Kainos could not always do so when they wished.

While Kainos staff and the prison staff who worked on the wings believed that more vulnerable prisoners did in fact fare better on Kainos than elsewhere (some commented that they were 'flattered' that the prison felt they could help in this regard), the fact that Kainos was not always being used for the prisoners it was designed to benefit undermined its role and perceived validity as a programme for rehabilitation. Only occasionally did the programme appear to attract the 'negative leaders' it was technically designed to reform. In fact, it often developed a reputation for being a 'nonces' wing (a wing for sex offenders) or a wing for homosexuals.[1] There was also universal agreement amongst prisoners and staff that Kainos was not an appropriate place for prisoners upon their arrival into prison custody. These 'lodgers' had not volunteered to be there, nor had they agreed to abide by any compact, therefore they risked disrupting the stability of the Community.

A frequent desire of Kainos and prison staff was for more thorough selection, to ensure that people who came to Kainos Communities were there for the 'right' reasons – namely that they genuinely wanted to change and knew what was expected of them – rather than to put 'bums on beds' or to take advantage of what they perceived to be a more relaxed regime. This was not believed to be possible in practice, both due to pressure on space in the prison and due to the limited amount of staff time.

Most prisoners who were part of Kainos Communities had received both encouragement and discouragement in their decision to apply. Some applied because they had friends on the wing or who were applying. Others received encouragement from Chaplaincy staff at various prisons, or from prison staff who thought the prisoner would benefit. Virtually all had heard rumours about 'Bible-bashing', the 'God Squad', and so on – a 'stigmatized social category of their own in prison' (Curran 2002). Some admitted to calling Kainos prisoners such names themselves in the past, but for a variety of reasons chose to apply anyway. Staff often described these as the more 'sensible' people because no 'street cred' or 'kudos' is attached to living on a Kainos unit; rather the reverse. For both prisoners and staff, the religious basis of the programme was by far the biggest reason why they might not want to be part of a Kainos wing.

Very few prisoners chose to keep their decision to live on a Kainos wing hidden from their families. The vast majority not only told people close to them about it, but believed these people supported their decision, even if some were sceptical at first. This was the same for prisoners of all religions and ethnic backgrounds. The only exceptions to this were two Muslim prisoners on the Kainos unit at Swaleside, and one Christian prisoner on Kainos at Highpoint North. One of the Muslims said that it had never occurred to him to tell his family about Kainos, but that he 'wouldn't dare!' (640), while the other said his family would not support his participation in a (non-Muslim) religious programme. The Christian at Highpoint North said that she had told her family about Kainos, but that they had broken ties with her generally because she was in prison.

2. Is anyone excluded from Kainos?

The general consensus from prisoners, staff, and managers was that no one was actively excluded from participating in a Kainos Community unless they chose to exclude themselves, or if prison staff excluded them for security reasons. Prisoners and staff who were not Christians or not comfortable with Christianity may choose not to be part of Kainos, but they are welcome to do so if they wish. An element of self-exclusion was evident in a number of interviews. For example, a Buddhist interviewed on a non-Kainos wing believed he would be too much in the minority on Kainos:

It's the religious factor of Kainos that kind of puts me off. If you put 30 members of staff in a room and one inmate, how would that inmate feel? ... [but I] don't feel it excludes me just because I'm a Buddhist.

(560)

Another prisoner gave the same view:

Being a Christian-based community and me a Pagan, I'd feel like a spare wheel. I don't think that being a Pagan prevents me from going on Kainos Community, but there would be awkwardness.

(561)

Equally, staff who do not agree with the ethos of Kainos Communities (the generally more relaxed regime, closer relations with prisoners, and an element of self-government) may not feel comfortable working there. Staff did not always have a choice in the matter, but most prisoners did.

A few people disagreed with the belief that participation in Kainos was truly a matter of choice. One of the chaplains, as well as a prison manager, believed that many staff and governors *feel* excluded from Kainos, and another said directly that the Imam at Swaleside was deliberately excluded from the wing. In this case, the speaker believed the Imam's reasons for wanting more input into the Community were justified, but that his approach was confrontational and destabilizing (perceived, in other words, as more challenging of the Christian perspective than supportive of Muslim prisoners). The emphasis here was again on the importance of individual personalities in achieving the right balance between Kainos and others (a view a prison manager at Swaleside reiterated).

The Imam himself stated that he felt excluded, that he had to ask permission to go onto the Base unit on the Kainos Wing (the landing for prisoners on the current course), and that he had never been invited to anything involving Kainos, including the closing ceremony of the Kairos Weekend, despite the fact that a general invitation to the closing ceremony is open to all staff at the prison. The researchers' impression in this case was that Kainos staff were concerned that the Imam was deliberately disruptive to the Community rather than supportive of Muslim prisoners; this 'exclusion' did not apply to Imams in the other prisons, for example, where the researchers saw them on the Kainos wings. The Imam at Swaleside also believed that the views of Muslims were discounted or discouraged, and that in his view Kainos showed 'little tolerance to the Islamic faith'. He disagreed with the practice that non-prisoner participants in Kainos (i.e. godparents and volunteers) had to be Christian if the Community, in his view, professed to be multi-faith.[2]

At the time of the interviews, almost all prisoners and staff believed the units did in fact operate as 'communities'. Some commented that this tended to vary, depending largely on the combination of prisoners, but that generally they managed to function as communities. With this came a feeling of mutual support between prisoners, between staff and prisoners, and between prison staff and Kainos staff. The stronger communities tended to be those with less transient populations and at least some longer-standing members of Kainos still in residence.

Opinions from staff about Kainos and its success as a community seemed to depend greatly on the officers' confidence in the individual members of the Kainos staff. Officers who had been in post on the Kainos wings longer often drew comparisons between past and present Kainos Coordinators and commented that things may be different (or had been different) with someone else in post. This was most obvious at Highpoint South, where relations between staff and the previous Coordinator had been strained.

3. Are Kainos Communities favoured?

The question of whether people in Kainos Communities receive any preferential treatment is particularly important in any discussion of equal opportunities. Like many of the issues we found, however, the answer is not straightforward.

Some differences in treatment were evident in some of the Kainos Communities. At Highpoint North (the women's prison), the Kainos house has its own dining area separate from the main dining hall (a particular benefit for prisoners at risk of bullying from people outside the Community), and the women can often get second helpings at meals. The women in the same housing block who are not part of the Kainos programme eat in their cells. The women on Kainos also have access to the television, common room, and hot water during the day, which is not an option to people outside the Kainos Community. At Highpoint South (a medium security men's prison), the men who were not working during the day had been unlocked for an extra hour, though this practice was not in operation during the research. Family Days (extended visits with family members) took place every six months for people in three of the four Kainos Communities. Counselling is also immediately accessible on the unit, often on a drop-in basis.

Many prisoners and staff argued that, while these characteristics of Kainos Communities may cause resentment from other prisoners, they were not in fact privileges in practice. More time unlocked during the day at Highpoint North, for example, was meant to compensate for the extra time spent in meetings in the evenings, which the rest of the prison spent in free association. Other prisoners were also entitled to Family Days, such as life-sentenced prisoners. A prison manager commented that some variation between wings is 'just natural in any organization' (589), and that each wing will have its benefits and drawbacks.

Kainos Communities often had drawbacks as well as advantages. Both staff and prisoners at Highpoint South criticized the unit for having some of the worst physical facilities in the prison. Prisoners there also believed that participation on Kainos could slow down their progress to the Enhanced (privileged) wing: pressure to fill beds in the Kainos unit meant that prisoners who have achieved Enhanced status may not move to the Enhanced unit as quickly. Equally, dormitory accommodation at HMP The Verne (a medium security prison) was generally unpopular, especially since people in the rest of the prison now had in-cell television. As one chaplain commented: 'The cynic would say, Well, they're after something…but there's nothing to gain down there.' Staff in particular mentioned a further drawback of perceived lack of support from management and Headquarters and abuse from other prison staff. One manager also commented that he saw '[little] evidence of consensus at Headquarters' about the programme (549). Lack of official recognition of Kainos as a 'proper' (accredited) programme often made staff feel isolated and that they had to fight for respect and resources.

Of interest was the number of prisoners who said they would want to be on a Kainos unit, even if it meant not moving to a less restrictive or an open (minimum security) prison. For example, a prisoner at Highpoint

North had been in an open prison and chose to move to the Kainos unit, and a prisoner at Swaleside had been categorized as Category C (low-medium security) for several months but chose to stay at Swaleside, a higher security Category B prison, for the Kainos programme. This means that some prisoners were willing to face considerable *disincentives* to remain on Kainos Communities because of the positive personal benefits they had experienced there.

Another accusation is that prisoners on Kainos Communities achieve Enhanced status more quickly. Indeed, 92 per cent of the Kainos residents at Swaleside at the time of the research were at the 'Enhanced' regime level, and 85 per cent were at Enhanced level over the course of a year (July 2000 to June 2001). This compares with 50 per cent at Enhanced level on one of the mainstream wings over the same period. However, both prisoners and staff commented that few prisoners are 'Enhanced' when they arrive on the unit, and that the quiet atmosphere and 'positive peer pressure' makes it easier for them to conform and to develop better relations with staff. A few prisoners (both Kainos and non-Kainos) believed that prisoners from the Kainos wing – specifically those who complied with the Kainos programme – tended to get the best jobs in the prison. Such a pattern is possible due to the Enhanced status and generally good behaviour of prisoners on the wing. Indeed prison staff at another prison commented that prisoners who did well on the Kainos unit tended to be trusted more and therefore to be placed in more privileged jobs. Whether this was the result of any kind of 'favouritisim' is impossible to ascertain.

Prisoners and staff at all four prisons were mixed in their views about whether participation in Kainos had any bearing on parole decisions. Prisoners may think participation in such activities 'looks good', but taking part is not in itself evidence of rehabilitation (Maruna *et al.* 2004; Curran 2002). The preponderance of prisoners and staff from Kainos Communities believed that Kainos appeared to have little or no bearing on these decisions, though prisoners who were not part of Kainos tended to be more suspicious. Further, prison staff working in the Kainos Communities did not believe Kainos prisoners were favoured at prison disciplinary adjudications, and that if anything they were treated *more* severely because 'they should know better'. Many staff suggested that prisoners from Kainos Communities were however less likely to be reported for indiscipline in the first place, both due to behaviour, and due to the ethos of working out problems 'in house' where possible.

In practice the biggest advantage of the Kainos Communities was its 'community' ethos. This aspect tended to attract people to the units and to keep them there once they arrived. Few people named places elsewhere in the prisons which provided something similar, with the exceptions of somewhat community-based wings for drug treatment and life-sentenced prisoners at Swaleside, the drug-free units at Highpoint South and The Verne,[3] and the therapeutic community for drug rehabilitation being built at Highpoint North. The most common defence of any perceived advantages of Kainos Communities was that any prisoner is welcome to be part of it. This forces a choice between the perceived drawbacks of living in a Christian-based community and the perceived advantages of the regime there. The question is to what extent Christian principles were part of the community ethos of Kainos Communities, and whether they were an essential part.

4. Faith Community or Christian Community?

Despite the Christian basis of the Kainos programme, Kainos Communities clearly attracted people from a wide range of beliefs. Rather than being a *Christian Community*, the emphasis of Kainos programmes was technically on being a Community based on Christian principles, as paraphrased in their Vision Statement:

> Kainos Community is an ecumenical Christian organization which seeks to help as many prisoners as possible develop healthy relationships through the combination of community life and Christian values by example.
>
> (Kainos Community 2001)

Theoretically this places no obligation on the members of the community to adhere to Christian *beliefs* – merely to Christian *principles*, primarily 'Love Thy Neighbour'. One prisoner described it as 'not the Jesus Loves, Jesus Saves type of Christianity, but the Do Not Steal from Your Neighbour type', with an emphasis on 'the ripple effect' – to think beyond themselves and about the impact their actions have on other people (608).

Research on generativity – the concern for and commitment to promoting the next generation through activities such as parenting, teaching, mentoring, and otherwise working to benefit others (McAdams and de St. Aubin 1998) – has been linked in recent years to desistance from crime. Maruna *et al.* explain that: 'Generative commitments seem to fill a particular void in the lives of former offenders, providing a sense of purpose and meaning, allowing them to redeem themselves from their past mistakes, and legitimizing the person's claim to having changed' (2004: 133). In this sense, Kainos Communities adopt a generative approach.

The question then is whether (arguably) generative programmes such as Kainos must be run by a Christian organization. Prisoners in the United States, for example, have been involved in the respite care of fellow prisoners dying of AIDS and other illnesses. This is a generative activity, but it does not have a Christian or even a spiritual basis. A warden at one prison noted considerable changes in the prisoners in these settings:

> The philosophy changes in the setting itself. The inmates change. It changes how we look at them.
>
> (Kolker 2000: H2)

Maruna (2001) argues that a sense of higher moral purpose that accompanies generative commitments may be necessary to sustain a prisoner's desistance from offending. But does this 'higher purpose' need to be Christian?

This specific question was addressed in some detail during group discussions amongst Kainos prisoners at The Verne and Swaleside. A non-Christian prisoner at The Verne argued that the Christian element was in fact necessary because 'you can see where people are coming from' – that prisoners will have less suspicion of their motives because they know what those motives are and the ethos behind them. In this respect, prisoners at Swaleside were clear that Prison Service employees should not run such a Community. An interview with a prisoner at The Verne summarizes this perspective:

> *Do you think that you could replace the Kairos Weekend with some other shared experience, for example based on model railways, and still have a community?* I don't think you could because of the whole nature of the religious fervour and belief which the people who facilitate it [the Kairos Weekend, i.e. the Kairos volunteers] hold. I think they need to be Christians to have that level of dedication. And also for the people in my position to believe in their sincerity. Although I'd describe myself as an agnostic, the Christian element of the Weekend is important because it inspires a level of trust.
>
> (281)

The group discussions continued, saying that a different religious organization could not do the work of Kainos as effectively, at least in those prisons. The argument here was that the prisons are located in England: the majority of prisoners will at least have a basic grasp of what Christianity is about, but will have little knowledge of other religions, and too much time would be taken up explaining basic principles. Arguably

Christianity therefore provides prisoners 'with a conventional non-criminal identity with which they could anticipate a meaningful future' (Curran 2002: 22). Equally, both Christian and non-Christian prisoners at both The Verne and Swaleside commented that a multi-faith programme could be too confusing. Another suggestion was that each religion could have its own equivalent community. The problem here was that this was thought to defeat the purpose of a community, creating division and segregation instead of diversity and mutual understanding.

Support of the Christian basis was not universal. As a Muslim prisoner at Swaleside noted:

> I think Kainos is a very good thing, but it should not be based on any religion at all because it gives conflict. The Christian input for some people puts them right off. They should try to build the community thing without Christianity. People wanted more input from other religions.
>
> (354)

As a former prison Governor with experience of Kainos notes:

> That [the Communities] were run by Christians was, if anything, a disadvantage – at least in terms of political neutrality. Inside as outside, Christianity can be an acquired taste.
>
> (Respondent J 2003)

The group discussions and individual interviews showed that people from a variety of perspectives were divided about whether the Christian basis was a necessary part of the Kainos programme. The general (though again not universal) consensus was that a religious basis of some sort was beneficial. One very experienced and notoriously 'difficult' prisoner at The Verne commented that he '[didn't] know what else you would do on this wing without the Christian ethos' (634) because he had not seen anything else work. A Muslim at The Verne believed Kainos needed to be run through a religious organization (not necessarily Christian) in order to 'reflect love, respect, [and] communication', which he believed were the essential elements of the programme, while a member of Kainos staff said that the Christian perspective added the element of forgiveness. A woman at Highpoint North said that Kainos Communities offered something more, in that 'no amount of psychotherapy can fill the *spiritual* void' (611).

A member of staff at The Verne – an agnostic – believed that the impact of Kainos on prisoners was not due simply to its Christian basis.

However he went on to say that 'it wouldn't be the same without it – the Christian element is the *binding* element, like the water in making a pastry' (635). An officer at Swaleside believed a similar programme could work without the religious aspect, but that 'the Christian side sets an example, sets values to live to, [and has] more of a purpose' (638).

Interestingly even the most critical of prisoners said the Christian basis would not be a problem if it were clear in its intentions (such as in Alpha courses[4]), rather than the 'hypocrisy' and 'favouritisim' he perceived it to be at present: 'I'm not against Kainos because I'm a Muslim. I'm against Kainos because the programme isn't making people true Christians' (644). In other words, he seemed to believe that if Kainos were clear about its aims, which in his view were evangelical, he would accept it more readily than if it were (again in his view) less open about this purpose and simply 'favoured' people who claimed a Christian belief. In his view, 'people who are *real* Christians tend to leave' (emphasis original).

Because of the potential for confusion, Kainos Communities need to be absolutely certain that their aims and purpose are clear both within their organization and to those outside it. A member of Kainos staff commented that it would be better for the organization 'to be secular than to be hypocritical' (614) – that its tendency to describe itself as two things at the same time (Christian but not Christian) risked confusion and suspicion from elsewhere.

In practical terms, a number of staff noted that the Kairos Weekend and the Kainos programme depend completely on the 'large army of [Christian] volunteers' (629) from outside the prison. This contact and support from people outside the prison played a vital role in the impact of both the Weekend and the Community: 'volunteers coming in, giving their own time and effort to do this…has a profound effect on people – really touching, [and] they learn they're not alone' (prison officer, 646). All Kairos volunteers have been through an equivalent weekend themselves. Whether the number of volunteers necessary to run an equivalent programme would be available for another religion or for a secular community is an important practical consideration. This does not in itself, however, justify the absence of equivalent non-Christian programmes in prison.

Almost all the prisoners interviewed and the majority of staff believed the Christian basis of the Kainos Community had an impact on prisoners. Responses were generally that prisoners had become calmer, more polite, and more tolerant of others, and that they were more inclined to talk through conflicts. None of the prisoners interviewed on the Kainos Communities said they had converted to Christianity while on Kainos, though many started practising their religion (often for the first time) or strengthened their faith in their own religion, Christian or otherwise. Changes in behaviour are perhaps unsurprising in view of the finding that exposure to a different culture from one's own may cause moral beliefs to change. As Bottoms (2002: 39) explains:

Attachments to individuals and to social groups and institutions may, in different social circumstances, sometimes flourish and sometimes wane, with consequences for behavioural compliance.

Only two prisoners said this impact had been negative, in that they perceived the behaviour on the wings to be hypocritical.

Fewer staff believed Kainos Communities had an impact on staff or on themselves personally, but comments were still largely positive. An officer at The Verne, for example, commented that the Christian basis of the unit:

… brings a positive healing spirit into the wing [which] brings out the best in people rather than the worst…Once these men change, the way they talk to staff changes, and the way they respond changes.

(629)

A member of the Kainos staff at another prison described the 'best' part of Kainos as 'The humbling experience of watching [people] change…or try to change, against extreme odds' (614). An officer at Highpoint South commented on the opportunity to do something actively positive with prisoners: 'If there *is* any job satisfaction in the Prison Service, this is as close as it gets' (620; emphasis original).

Interestingly, one prison manager described the ethos of Kainos as fitting in well with the Prison Service Mission Statement (namely to look after prisoners with humanity and help them lead law-abiding and useful lives in custody and after release), especially in that it works as a shared experience between prison staff and prisoners. Another manager shared this view, saying that:

We [the Prison Service] haven't actually identified what we mean by humanity, [but] I think that the Kainos programme is a fairly good example of what we might mean by humanity…I think the Prison Service hasn't looked at the Human Rights Act in that way, but I think it could, and I think it should, and I think that Kainos helps it to.

(549)

The verdict about the necessity of a Christian basis for Kainos Communities remains open to debate. The same prison manager supported the idea of equivalent religious communities elsewhere, as long as they maintained a principle of inclusion:

> I think the Prison Service ought to invite any religious organization that's willing to work with us on community-based principles of their particular faith. I think that would strengthen Kainos, oddly enough, not weaken it, if there was a Muslim community in Pentonville, or Brixton. But with the same underlying thing: that nobody is excluded, and if you want to see a religious-based community in action, here is one.

The important point from a human rights perspective is that prisoners of any belief should be free to exercise any religious beliefs (or lack thereof) while on Kainos Communities or any equivalent religiously-based wing. The next section looks at the extent to which this was possible in practice on Kainos Communities.

5. Freedom of religion?

Article 9 of the European Convention on Human Rights, incorporated into the Human Rights Act 1998 in the UK, guarantees the right to freedom of thought, conscience, and religion. The vast majority of prisoners interviewed on Kainos Communities said they felt free to discuss their beliefs and doubts, to ask questions, and to practise their religion, and that their beliefs were respected, both on the Kainos Community and during the Kairos Weekend. Prisoners of other faiths said they were free to participate in prayers, songs, and so on to whatever degree they wished, with no pressure from others. A prison manager commented that Kainos did not seem to pose problems for prisoners of non-Christian beliefs:

> I can show you testimonies from Sikhs and Muslims [letters photocopied]. We've had the odd Muslim stirring up trouble, but I think the fact he was a Muslim is irrelevant.

(537)

A few prisoners and staff commented that the views put forward during the Kairos Weekend occasionally leaned more towards statements of fact rather than opinion, but generally responses to both the Weekend and the Community were very positive.

There were of course exceptions to this. The first exception came from an agnostic prisoner at Highpoint North. While she felt her views were respected, she said she did not feel she had the opportunity to debate what was being said during the Kairos Weekend to the extent she wished. She did however stop participating in the Weekend after the first full day; whether she would have had more opportunity for discussion later in the Weekend is unknown.

Interestingly, the second exception came from Roman Catholic prisoners at The Verne and Swaleside. This group was quick to say they were generally very happy with the programme, but noted that they did not feel they could leave the Kairos Weekend to attend Mass (a service central to Roman Catholic beliefs).[5] A woman at Highpoint North mentioned the same problem, but said that she and several other prisoners were eventually allowed to attend. This was specifically a conflict with the Kairos Weekend, however, as at least one prisoner at The Verne was allowed to attend catechism classes during his stay on the Kainos unit, even though the timing of these classes clashed with the follow-up programme agreed to in the Kainos compact.

The final exception was more a perception of restricted religious freedom than an actual experience of such: prisoners from non-Kainos wings tended to be less certain about the scope for religious freedom on Kainos Communities: 'Because you think there would be pressure on you to become a Christian. There would be pressure to push your original religion out' (533). However, this appeared to be a minority view.

The most notable problems with freedom of religion and freedom of expression (Article 10 of the European Convention) again involved Muslim prisoners on the Kainos wing at Swaleside. The views of Muslims interviewed at Swaleside were diametrically opposed to those of Muslims, and indeed of other non-Christians, at Kainos Communities in the other prisons. This latter group stated without fail that their time on Kainos Communities was very positive and that it had strengthened their faith in their own religion. For example, a Muslim at Highpoint South commented that the teaching during the Kairos Weekend 'is not so much to *change* your religion as to *stick* to your religion,' and later about his whole experience on Kainos, 'I want to be a proper Muslim now' (619). The Imam at Swaleside believed that Muslim prisoners on the Kainos wing there also tended to grow stronger in their religion, but that in his view this was due to 'some kind of oppression'. However, he added that 'That was mainly in the past; things are now moving forward, but the stigma is still there' (536).

When the Kainos unit first began at Swaleside, Muslim prisoners on the Kairos Weekend were not allowed to leave the Weekend to attend their prayers. This was even specified in writing but has since been rectified.

One Muslim prisoner on the Kairos Weekend mentioned that he felt pressured to participate in prayers, songs, and 'the bread ceremony'.[6] In his view, even standing for the songs counted as participating in another religion and therefore contrary to his own – yet by not standing he was disrupting the sense of community. This particular prisoner went on to criticize the perceived ignorance of 'even the basics of other religions' (644) on Kainos Communities, such as the fact that referring to Jesus Christ as the Son of God and even the term 'godparent' could be offensive to Muslims. The Imam also noted this as an issue.

Another Muslim at Swaleside said that he did not feel he could express his views during the Kairos Weekend – that this was treated as 'interruptive' (640) – and that the respect of his beliefs seemed insincere. Other Muslims there also felt restricted in discussing their views. The Imam believed that if he were part of Kainos, he would be able to provide support for Muslim prisoners on the wing and help them to address any issues that caused confrontation. The position at Swaleside may be contrasted with Horizon Interfaith at Marion C. I. in the US which has an eight-man 'family group' of Muslim prisoners, along with Christian and Jewish prisoners. Each group receives faith-specific studies from ordained Christian ministers, an Imam and a Rabbi, and each faith leader has equal access to the unit (see Chapter 7).

One Muslim on the Kainos wing at Swaleside said he felt restricted in discussing his views, but commented that this was (at least partially) because they were in prison, where no one could openly discuss, debate, or question. In this sense, is the perceived restriction on personal expression due to the *content* of the programme (specifically the Kairos Weekend) or the *context*? Is it appropriate to introduce people to concepts as personal as religious belief in an environment where they may be less likely to feel free to question the content? One prison governor thought it was appropriate:

> I think [Kainos Community] is a rare opportunity for prisoners to speak about their spirituality without having to feel embarrassed or misunderstood. And I think it has a clear purpose in prison for allowing people to do that given that imprisonment...does tend to expose sides of people's personalities that they weren't aware of before and which if they are not helped to cope with that, they could be severely damaged in prison and afterwards.
>
> (549)

To what extent does this differ from subjecting people to behaviour programmes in prison, in which they have to 'toe the line' in order to fulfill their sentence plans and succeed in applications for parole, especially that this subservient, unquestioning behaviour is usually what is rewarded in prisons (Kendall 2001; Stow 2002)?

Sentence planning in itself posed a particular dilemma for prisons with regard to the Kainos programme. Swaleside, The Verne and Highpoint North have incorporated Kainos into prisoners' sentence plans. Many prisoners and staff wanted Kainos to be part of a prisoner's sentence plan, both so that the prisoner would get credit for participating in a programme focused on changing behaviour and to boost the credibility of the programme throughout the Prison Service.

Kainos is however a voluntary programme and, as such, prisoners were often encouraged to 'try it out', with the option to leave if they decided it wasn't for them. If a move to Kainos is tied in with sentence planning, this means that choosing to leave the unit means failing to complete the agreed sentence plan, which therefore penalizes the prisoner. In discussion, some staff disagreed with the implications of this: a member of the Kainos staff said that people who had incorporated Kainos into their sentence plans but who then decided to leave could then have it removed from their sentence plan without penalty. In contrast, a prison governor commented that leaving Kainos prior to completion, when it was part of a sentence plan, would carry the normal 'price'.

Kainos Communities are meant to offer an opportunity for positive change and, as such, prisoners who participate in them should get credit for doing so. A programme with a religious basis, however, should in no way penalize prisoners for leaving the programme when they choose; any sense of coercion (beyond '[preventing] a prisoner acting fecklessly' (537), as one prison manager phrased it), including having it count against their sentence plans, flags up potential violations of human rights under the terms of the 1998 Act. This is an extremely important issue for discussion between the Kainos Trust and the Prison Service, with the possibility that Kainos programmes, because of their religious basis, should perhaps be granted a special status for sentence planning purposes or be acknowledged formally in some other way.

The prison context of the Kainos Community can also play an important role. While prisoners elsewhere commented that Kainos made them feel more like they were *not* in prison, those at Swaleside tended to see the two as much more closely related. One Muslim prisoner commented that the Kainos Community 'gets tangled up too much with prison politics' (644) – that it was not just about Christian teaching, but that issues such as security categorization and placements on Enhanced workshops were, in his view, used as 'bribes'. The same prisoner commented that prisoners were being told (as part of an orientation session upon entry to the prison) that participation in Kainos improved their chances of Enhanced status and parole. This arose because some prisoners from the Kainos unit present the Kainos programme to others on induction. Other Kainos prisoners subsequently instructed them that such claims about Kainos were misleading and therefore inappropriate.

A Christian prisoner on the Kainos wing at Swaleside appeared to equate prison decisions with life on Kainos as well. He had recently been rejected for recategorization and commented that his relations with prison staff had become worse since being on Kainos because he believed he had been 'promised' things (such as recategorization) which had not come to fruition (645). The pattern therefore suggests that the operation of Kainos Communities in higher security establishments has wider implications than would be the case in lower security prisons.

Another criticism levied at Kainos Communities was the perception that prisoners were being 'brainwashed'. For example, when asked what concerns he would have about joining a Kainos Community, a (Catholic) prisoner on a non-Kainos wing said 'I wouldn't like religion to be forced on me' (566).

Two Muslims interviewed on the Kainos wing at Swaleside agreed with the criticism of 'brainwashing'. One noted that prisoners were encouraged (in his view) to have Bible studies and their own evening courses in Christianity, but said that a comparable Muslim course on the wing was not allowed (a comment the Kainos staff have denied). The prison offered an Islamic studies course, but the prisoner's point was that he did not believe direct comparisons between religions through formal courses or study groups were welcome on the wing. A Christian prison officer on the Kainos wing at Highpoint South supported this view to some extent, saying that the Christian content of the programme can seem 'a bit overt' compared to what would be allowed in, for example, school assemblies. He then commented that they 'never see' representatives of other religions: 'Why shouldn't they be able to come in and give a talk or something?' (624).

Important to note here is that Kainos, as a Christian-based programme, is not equipped to offer alternative religious views, nor is it their place to do so. If alternative views are to be put forward in the same way, then other organizations should be welcome to do so, alongside Kainos or otherwise. To fulfill the criteria for human rights legislation, the Prison Service in England and Wales is required only to ensure that people are free to practise any religion (or none) they choose, and that they have all the facilities they need to do so. Direct comparisons of religions do not necessarily have to take place on the Kainos units, through Kainos or otherwise, as long as people have the opportunity to make comparisons if they wish.

Despite the (infrequent) accusations of brainwashing, the few experiences of conversion were clearly not all one-way. As a prisoner interviewed at Swaleside told us:

I became a Muslim during Kainos. I took part in Kainos to find out what was the right religion for me and I find the Muslim religion for me was the most logical and honest religion.

(354)

Indeed, as conversion was not always one way, neither was religious pressure. One non-Kainos Muslim prisoner wanted to convert to Christianity but was afraid of doing so for fear of reprisals from other Muslim prisoners:

I don't want to go onto [Kainos Community] because, again, next door is my countrymen...I know that if I moved there, they would find out I'd changed my religion from Muslim to Christian and that would be dangerous for me inside prison. Someone might try to kill me in [the prison] if they find out a Muslim changed religion.

(576)

A Pagan (non-Kainos) prisoner believed informal pressure not to practise your own religion while on Kainos may exist, but that:

... you get that anywhere, including [the Enhanced wing]... People try to convert me everywhere. I get that everywhere.

(561)

Another said that he knew nothing about Kainos:

But I don't think I'd change. I'm a Muslim, family's Muslim – you don't change a cow into a sheep.

(564)

Another Muslim prisoner interviewed on the Kainos unit at Swaleside argued that Kainos did not provide rehabilitation, but rather told people how they should think, instilling its own views and expecting people to accept them. A prisoner on a non-Kainos wing at Swaleside commented:

I never wanted to use that word, because 'brainwash' is a very strong word, but through experience I know if you take an uneducated person or a person of below average intelligence and you teach them something, they will adapt to it very, very quickly … A certain level of IQ would question it, but a lot of people don't have that level of IQ. They're happy to go with the flow.

(539)

A woman at Highpoint North believed the Kainos Community did not brainwash people but that the Kairos Weekend did. She commented that the Weekend 'takes advantage of people in a very vulnerable state, and looking for something to fill the gap in their lives.' This perspective was apparent in other interviews as well. Those who were positive about Kainos, however, believed it had more benefits than just 'filling the gap'. When asked what they liked best about Kainos, one prisoner said it was 'being able to talk to people without being laughed at' (608), and another 'That I feel safe about who I am' (611).

In contrast to the more critical comments, none of the other prisoners or staff believed that 'brainwashing' took place on Kainos Communities or on the Kairos Weekend. In fact, another prisoner on the Kainos unit at Swaleside commented that 'Most people here, especially the Muslims, already have a mind of their own', and that people did not have to read things, they were not indoctrinated in any way, and things were not 'forced down their throats' (645). Similarly, a prisoner of another minority religion there commented: 'Even though I didn't agree with certain aspects of what they were saying, it wasn't a problem … even if [I were] Muslim' (643). A Christian prisoner at Highpoint North commented, 'no one tends to *tell* you what to do, but [instead] help you make your own decisions [and] explore options' (608). When asked about brainwashing, a non-Kainos prisoner at Highpoint laughed and said: 'It's a voluntary unit, isn't it? They don't have to stay – they can move away any time they like' (559). A former prisoner interviewed, however, expressed concern that few prisoners were confident enough to leave the room, let alone the unit, when they disagreed with certain practices.

A consistent pattern in the responses was that some people believed the emphasis on Christianity in the programme (and during the Kairos Weekend in particular) to be too heavy, while others said it was less than they expected or even not enough. Clearly the perception depended heavily on personal background and experience of religion prior to contact with Kainos. In a group discussion, one prisoner commented that many people say the only drawback about the wing is the religion, 'but what a terrible thing to say! … [It's] sad that it should come down to that.' An officer commented that he did not like 'people getting hung up on the religious side, because that's *not* what it's all about' (622).

One member of staff raised the question of whether people would be as hostile to Kainos if it were run by a Muslim organization: 'or would it be the PC thing to say it [the Prison Service] was encouraging a minority religion...?' (639). An officer at Swaleside expressed a similar view: 'As soon as people hear the word Christian, they close up' (646).

Of surprise, perhaps, was that despite his criticisms and concerns, the Imam at Swaleside seemed to view the programme as a positive one overall: 'If it was closed it would have a big impact. It would be a loss. Thirty people over six months [would] lose the opportunity to go onto a programme that has good opportunities at the end of it.' (536)

6. Thematic overview

The issues raised by the full-time presence of a charitable organization within a prison, particularly a religiously-based one, are clearly complex and largely subjective. Despite this, several main themes emerge.

First, if participation in Kainos Communities is truly voluntary, this status must be respected.

Second, religion is an intensely personal experience. The manner and extent to which it forms the basis of programmes in prisons – an environment in which people feel less free to question and debate the content of programmes – must be handled with extreme care. People of other faiths must feel supported in their own beliefs, and those of any or no religion should have the opportunity to question and to access information about other views.

Third, differences between prisons, and even within prisons, suggest that much of the success of Kainos programmes depends on the individual personalities involved. Again, this finding emphasizes the need for thorough training and careful recruitment of the civilian staff who run the Kainos communities. Respect of, and relations between, Kainos staff and prison staff and managers are central. Equally, relations between Kainos and the Chaplaincy team, including those of non-Christian faiths, play an extremely important role in the support (and therefore the stability) of the units.

Related to this point is that Kainos Communities seem to differ in their aims and their methods of reaching those aims. Kainos Trustees, staff, and Communities need to be absolutely clear about their philosophy and ensure that others understand their purpose and aims as well. In this way they can work in a more coordinated fashion, with more certainty and support from within their organization and with more coherence and transparency for those outside it.

Equally, the local variation and difficulties with rapid turnover of prison populations suggest that Kainos Communities may not be appropriate for every establishment. The time commitment required for participation, for example, means that Kainos would not be suited to most prisoners in local prisons (those that generally house shorter-term and unconvicted prisoners). The interviews also showed that the implications for prisoners earlier in their sentences, such as at higher security establishments, are likely to differ from prisoners further along in their sentences. The individual circumstances of each prison population *must* be taken into account thoroughly when considering the introduction of a Kainos programme, or indeed any prison-based programme.

Finally, the vast majority of people interviewed for this part of the research who had participated in Kainos were overwhelmingly positive about the programme – much more so than the research team had encountered regarding other types of programmes in prison. With such a diverse range of people interviewed, we could easily have expected a wider range of views and criticisms. The dissenting views were highlighted specifically because they were dissenting, not because they represented the wider feeling. Interviews with prisoners and staff who participated in Kainos gave the overall impression that Kainos Communities offer something different to prisoners, and that most appear to benefit from it, regardless of their religious views:

> *What do you like best about Kainos?*
> It works. It has evolved from the ground floor and was not imposed from above. It brings out the best in everyone involved with it – staff as well as inmates. It has a real sense of community.
>
> (prison officer, 629)

> This is the first rehabilitation I've really seen in prison. Other programmes are imposed *upon* you, but this you have to impose upon *yourself*.
>
> (prisoner, group discussion)

> *What are the advantages to you personally of being on Kainos Community in this prison, if any?*
> I will have a life to live when I get out.
>
> (experienced prisoner, 634)

> *Is there anyone you wouldn't recommend it to?*
> Why keep a good thing from anyone?
>
> (Muslim prisoner, 633)

In saying this, Kainos Communities are not for everyone. Some people will not need the environment Kainos provides, nor are some ready to benefit from it.

7. Conclusions

What broad conclusions can be drawn from this part of our evaluation of Kainos? We suggest the following:

- The general consensus from prisoners, staff, and managers was that no one was actively excluded from participating in a Kainos Community unless they chose to exclude themselves, or if prison staff excluded them for security reasons.

- Opinions from staff about Kainos and its success as a community seemed to depend greatly on the officers' confidence in the individual members of the Kainos staff.

- Some differences in treatment were evident in some of the Kainos Communities. However, living in Kainos Communities often had drawbacks as well as benefits.

- Despite the Christian basis of the Kainos programme, Kainos Communities clearly attracted people from a wide range of beliefs.

- Even the most critical of prisoners said that the Christian basis would not be a problem if Kainos Community were clear in its intentions.

- Almost all the prisoners interviewed and the majority of staff believed the Christian basis of Kainos Community had an impact on prisoners.

- The vast majority of prisoners interviewed on Kainos Communities for this part of the research said they felt free to discuss their beliefs and doubts, to ask questions, and to practise their religion, and that their beliefs were respected, both on the Kainos Community and during the Kairos Weekend, although some exceptions were evident.

In light of these findings, the following considerations should be taken into account in any replication of the Kainos Communities elsewhere:

- If participation in Kainos Communities is truly voluntary, this status must be respected. This means that people should not be located in Kainos Communities unless they specifically request it or at least agree to it after a comprehensive briefing and time to reflect. It also means that they should be able to leave when they wish. Further, prisoners and staff must be clear that, as a voluntary programme, participation in Kainos should be removed from a prisoner's sentence plan should he or she choose not to continue. Because of the religious content of the programme, considerations of human rights demand that a decision to withdraw should be *without penalty*.

- More attention needs to be paid to informed consent prior to participation in the programme.

- Religion is an intensely personal experience. The manner and extent to which it forms the basis of programmes in prisons must always be handled with extreme care.

- The individual circumstances of each prison population *must* be taken into account thoroughly when considering the introduction of a Kainos programme, or indeed, any prison-based programme.

- Much of the success of Kainos programmes depends on the individual personalities involved and their relations with prison staff and managers. Kainos staff need to be carefully recruited and must receive thorough, ongoing training.

- Kainos Trustees, staff, and Communities need to be absolutely clear about their philosophy and ensure that others understand their purpose and aims as well.

- Kainos Trustees, staff, and Communities need to work in a coordinated fashion, with certainty and support from within their organization and with coherence and transparency for those outside it.

Notes

1   Not least at The Verne, which housed a transsexual on the Kainos wing due to this prisoner's vulnerability in a mainstream prison environment.
2   The Kainos Community is not itself multifaith; see 'Faith community or Christian community?' below.
3   Similar in that it was a drug-free wing rather than because it was a community.
4   The Alpha Course, run in churches and adapted for prisons, is an introduction to Christianity designed to encourage conversion (see Chapter 2).
5   Although the Kairos Manual strongly encourages participants to attend their own religious services during the course of the Weekend, the Kainos Coordinator and the Chaplaincy may need to facilitate these services specially

to ensure they do not clash with the time set aside for the programme. In Highpoint South, for example, the Kairos Weekend has been built around Friday Muslim prayers to accommodate Muslim participants.

6   The breaking and sharing of bread in the 'bread ceremony' at the end of the Kairos Weekend is meant to symbolize the people who make up the Kainos Community. While it is not meant to be a Christian ceremony, the symbolism is dramatically similar to the ceremony of the Eucharist (bread and wine) in Christian tradition.

Chapter 7

Navigating by the heavens: Horizon Communities

(formerly Kairos Horizon Communities)

The clearest and most prominent incentive is [prisoners'] contact with free-world volunteers and those social mentors that give them the opportunity to reflect with someone who is stable. The volunteers also have a way of honouring each person and their dignity and holding them accountable – you know, 'I'll be back next week and I hope to see some improvement' on the issues before them. And that I think is so reaffirming. I remember just such an incident here [in Tomoka C.I.], one man walking back to the dorm after a godparent visit on Monday and he said 'I almost *feel human again'*
Mickey Bright Griffin, Co-founder Horizon Communities (2003b)

The Kairos-APAC initiative at HMP The Verne did not only inspire similar developments in the UK, it was also the direct inspiration for a growing number of faith-based units in the US called 'Horizon Communities' which began in 1999 (and were until 2004 known as 'Kairos Horizon').[1] Little has been written about Horizon Communities, and few source documents are in the public domain. This chapter will concentrate on describing the origins, development and key characteristics of Horizon. It will also highlight, where relevant, recurring themes, difficulties and indications (if any) of current effectiveness. The chapter draws on interviews conducted with the founders of Horizon, Ike Griffin (Griffin 2003) and Mickey Bright Griffin (Bright Griffin 2003b), several Horizon programme Coordinators and the Warden of a prison with a Horizon

This chapter was authored by Jonathan Burnside

unit. The chapter also draws on field notes made by Jonathan Burnside during visits to Horizon at Tomoka C.I. in July 2000 and July 2003 and a visit to Horizon at Marion C.I. in July 2003.

Introduction

Although Kairos Prison Ministry International Inc. (KPM) did not become involved in faith-based units until 1999, the seeds were sown some time before. KPM's first contact with faith-based units came in 1991 when the Eckerd Foundation tried to set up an APAC-style unit in the US. Recognizing that the unit would be volunteer-run and aware of KPM's expertise in this area, the Foundation enlisted KPM to help with programme design and volunteer training (Griffin 2003). The project collapsed before it started, however, because of political resistance (see Chapter 8).

The impetus to establish Horizon came not from Kairos itself but from the Florida Department of Corrections (DoC). In March 1997, the DoC published the results of reconviction studies conducted in 1995 on 505 Kairos participants who had attended Kairos at Union Correctional Institution (KPM 1998c; see Chapter 2). They found that prisoners performed better if they had greater exposure to Kairos than if they had not. Other research suggests that the longer prisoners participate in programmes, the better the results (see for example Beech *et al.* 1998; Taylor 2000; Webster *et al.* 2001).

Consequently, the DoC was keen to develop Kairos-style programmes that would engage prisoners over a longer period of time. Rather reluctantly, Griffin pointed the DoC towards the Kairos-APAC initiative that had just started at The Verne. Griffin's reluctance stemmed from the fact that, until that point, the *modus operandi* of introducing and supporting Kairos communities took the form of monthly reunions and 'prayer and share' groups (see Chapter 2). Handing the post-Weekend follow-up over to another entity that would operate in the context of a unit was 'uncharted water' (Griffin 2004).

It was not long, however, before Griffin saw several advantages to operating a 'Kairos unit' over 'stand-alone Kairos'. The first advantage was the presence of a Programme Manager whose encouragement and counsel could promote religious faith and relational skills. The second advantage was the ability of the unit to provide some relief from negative influences found in the general prison population. Writing soon after attending the second Kairos Weekend at The Verne in October 1997, Griffin claimed that:

The project at The Verne is so special because ... [it] offers an incubator for these tender hearts to experience the luxury of resting in a protective womb while they grow. In the prison setting this is unheard of. Normally following a Weekend the men must nurse a tender heart in the midst of the chaos that is prison.

(1997)

The Florida State legislature passed legislation in 1997 directing correctional institutions to establish and maintain liaison with local faith communities. This legislation stated that: 'the Department shall ensure that an inmate's faith orientation, or lack thereof, will not be considered in determining admission to a faith-based programme and that the programme does not attempt to convert an inmate toward a particular faith or religious preference' (Ch944.803 FS). This is a significant document because it *legislates* that such organizations should be non-proseyletizing. It has parallels with the Prisons Act 1952 which prohibits proseyletizing in UK prisons. A non-profit-making Foundation for Partnerships in Correctional Excellence was established. This was a vehicle to provide faith-orientated support for the incarcerated as well as employees of the Department. The DoC investigated various programmes, including Prison Fellowship's (PF's) InnerChange Freedom Initiative (IFI) programme in Texas (see Chapter 8) and the Kairos-APAC project in England. Both made positive impressions, so the DoC decided to concentrate on the faith-based closed community, therapeutic dormitory model for designated trials.

Griffin brought a number of visitors to observe Kairos-APAC in The Verne from Florida, Texas and South Carolina (Lee 2004), so by summer 1998, Florida's plans for faith-based units were well advanced (KPM 1998d). Again it is worth emphasizing the influence of the so-called 'Verne template' (see Chapter 3) upon the initial development of Horizon. It was estimated that each Horizon Community would cost approximately $75,000 to $100,000 per year – considerably cheaper than PF's IFI operation (see Chapter 8).

A new charitable corporation, Kairos Horizon Communities in Prison (Kairos Horizon), was formed to provide faith-based units.[2] The Florida Commission on Responsible Fatherhood provided an initial $10,000 planning grant to the DoC in 1998. A second grant funded the positions of the Programme Manager (or 'Inside Coordinator') and the Community Resource Manager (or 'Outside Coordinator'). This sponsor approved Horizon's entire programme (Kairos Weekend, *Journey*, *Quest* etc.) and proposed that prisoners write twice a week to a family member. Horizon thought this 'a wonderful recommendation' (Bright Griffin 2003b) and although Horizon currently only requires one letter a week to be written, '[we] were always and continue to be startled by the benefits of that requirement' (*ibid.*). Further funding was provided by the Episcopal Church's Presiding Bishop's Fund on World Relief and the local Episcopal Diocese (Bright Griffin 2004). This allowed the first Horizon programme to be launched at Tomoka C.I., Daytona Beach in Florida in November 1999. The Horizon brochure and fact-sheet explicitly stated that the unit was inspired by Kairos-APAC at The Verne (Griffin 2004). But Horizon said it would *not* proceed unless there was – *first* – a local body of Kairos volunteers ready and willing to support the project. Griffin (2003) explains:

> We have refused to go into those prisons where we feel for one reason or another that there is not a good possibility of success. We have been invited into a lot of prisons where we have not started a programme.

Horizon's stated goals are threefold: to enhance personal responsibility, family responsibility and employability (Kairos Horizon 2003).

1. Horizon Communities

Five faith-based Horizon units currently operate in the US. The first was set up at Tomoka Correctional Institution, Florida in November 1999 followed by the first interfaith unit ('Horizon Interfaith')[3] established at Marion Correctional Institution, Ohio in 2000. Three more Horizon units were opened in 2002; Allred Unit (Wichita Falls, Texas), Davis Correctional Facility (Holdenville, Oklahoma) and Wakulla Correctional Institution (Tallahassee, Florida). Davis and Wakulla are both designated 'multifaith' units. We will concentrate on Tomoka, Marion and Davis because they have operated longest and because they illustrate the contrasts between a faith-based Horizon unit, an 'interfaith' unit and a 'multifaith' unit.

(a) Tomoka Correctional Institution, Daytona Beach, Florida

The first Horizon unit opened at Tomoka C.I., Daytona Beach in November 1999. Tomoka C.I. is a maximum-security prison although the presence of Tomoka Work Camp and Daytona Beach Work Release Centre within its jurisdiction means the estate can handle the full range of custody grades from 'closed' through to 'community'. The prison was opened in 1981 and has capacity for over 1,000 male adult prisoners. There are two cell-blocks and five open bay housing units or 'dorms'. The Horizon unit is located on F Dorm.

Two groups of 64 men each are arranged in eight-man family 'cubes'. Horizon at Tomoka is not a formal multifaith unit, as at the other prisons, but from the start it sought to be inclusive, even while the Tomoka Chaplain wanted it to be a Christian unit. From the first class onward at Tomoka, there were always practising Muslims in Horizon, and one class even had a Muslim Encourager (see further below) for a family group made up of a majority of Muslim men.[4] Each group of prisoners follows the same 12-month programme, starting and finishing at different times of the year. One group enters in November of one year, whilst the second group enters in May the following year. This results in a 'graduation' every six months.

For Horizon it is essential that the physical space set aside for the faith-based dorm should not be 'incarceration space' but must be converted into a 'living and learning environment' conducive to study and quiet reflection. The setting in which programmes take place has proved to be an important element in effectiveness in the literature on 'what works' in prisons (see for example Vennard and Hedderman 1998). This may involve 'softening' the existing prison environment, for example, by taking out steel bolted-down tables and benches and installing soft materials on the walls to absorb sound. Tomoka agreed to replace noisy air circulators with ceiling fans so that the environment was quiet enough for programming to take place in the dorm and for prisoners to hear one another in small family groups. Each 'eight-man' family group is housed in four double bunks. This is slightly fewer than in Humaitá where each cube consists of ten to twelve men (see Chapter 1). Standard office wall dividers were introduced to create cubicles for each 'family unit'. Prisoners were also issued with larger lockers because of the extra books and materials they were required to keep. Some bookshelves were also created in the cubes of one of the wings.

This was as far as the institution was prepared to go. Requests for carpeting, a hospitality centre and coffee-making facilities were all refused. Prisoners volunteered to do what they could to further improve the environment. This involved stripping and repainting their bunks, the walls and the communal dorm bathroom. Prisoners are also allowed to display cloth 'banners' made for their Kairos Weekend by Fourth Day communities around the world, both free-world and incarcerated. These frequently contain positive, motivational messages and serve as a visual reminder of care from the outside world.

The 'family group' is identical to the 'table family' forged on the Kairos Weekend. This allows the unit to capitalize on the relational dynamics established during the Weekend, and for prisoners to build on shared experiences and any steps they might have taken towards trust and vulnerability. Allegedly prisoners on Horizon will trust other prisoners within their cube but not those in other cubes. This underlines the importance of maintaining relationships that have been built up during the Kairos Weekend. A Kairos volunteer commented: 'The reason Horizon works well is because prisoners are connecting with the *same* people they met in their Kairos Weekend. The trust is already there. There is continuity in the relationships ... . You have to have continuity in the relationships, people they already know and trust. (Respondent F 2003).

Initially, each cube had a VCR and television, which contrasted favourably with other dorms in the prison where only one television exists per wing of 80 men. However, the televisions were quickly found to be disruptive and too often a source of arguments. They were changed to VCRs and monitors and used for teaching purposes only. Each Horizon wing now has one television, and viewing is restricted to news, sports and a list of programmes mutually devised by the Inside Coordinator and the television committee.

Prisoners can apply to Tomoka from every prison in Florida via their prison Chaplaincy. All of Horizon #1 at Tomoka and most of Horizon #2 were drawn from Tomoka C.I. itself, but the DoC soon decided that it should be open to prisoners from other prisons. Horizon also wanted 'new blood' from other prisons to stop a potential 'power structure' from developing inside the prison. For Horizon #2 there were 1,400 applications from around the State, although a large number did not meet Horizon's few eligibility requirements (see below).

Commencing with Horizon #3, Florida insisted that only 20 per cent of participants should be medium or long-term prisoners (i.e. more than three years remaining on their sentence) and that 80 per cent of participants should be short-termers, (i.e. between one and three years remaining). This was because the DoC wanted to have sufficient numbers for a reconviction study within three years. Accordingly, it was further stipulated that none of these short-termers should be released before the programme was over. This insistence that Horizon should focus on short-term prisoners directly contradicted Kairos's own experience that its programmes worked best with longer-term prisoner populations (see Chapter 2). This proved to be the case. Horizon found that short-term prisoners did not participate at 'anywhere near' the levels of the long-term or longer-term inmates: 'They simply put down their pen and stopped working, particularly if they got anywhere near to the fifth month' (Bright Griffin 2003b). Horizon subsequently negotiated with the DoC to reduce the proportion of short-term prisoners to 50 per cent.

Other entry requirements, this time imposed by Horizon, include no prescriptions for psychotropic drugs that would cause participants to fall asleep and sufficient literacy to cope with reading materials. In practice this means prisoners must be at or above the average grade level in Florida prisons, which is grade seven (roughly equivalent to someone age 12) out of 12 levels.

Each applicant receives a detailed description of the programme and its requirements in order to give their informed consent. Although prisoners are not required to be of any faith, the information stresses that the unit is faith-based, that opportunities for viewing television are limited and that various prohibitions are actively enforced (such as no smoking, foul language, violence or pornography). Prospective applicants are interviewed by their prison chaplain. Successful applicants are also interviewed when they arrive at Tomoka by the Horizon Programme Manager. This second interview is necessary for informed consent because 'any number [of prisoners] have arrived not really very well informed' (*ibid.*). The Assistant Warden, Chaplain and Programme Manager are involved in the selection process. The final decision rests with the Programme Manager so that no one within the prison administration appears to show favouritism or can be blamed regarding inmate selection. Horizon tries to maintain a racial balance and spread of criminal offences. A list of alternates is prepared in case prisoners drop out before start-up, usually because of transfers or health problems.

The daily regime begins, after rising at 5:45 a.m. for breakfast, with silence and devotional practices based on fortnightly seminars. Between 9 a.m. and 3 p.m. prisoners carry out work assignments. Programming takes place on three evenings during the week and every other Saturday, amounting to over 1,200 programme hours during the course of 12 months (Florida DoC 2000). Horizon has brought together a number of programme elements designed both to follow on from the Kairos Weekend and to match the unit's goals of responsibility and employability. In a recent programme review, prisoners identified two types of programming; those that engage with 'personal issues' and those that engage with 'faith'. The 'personal issues' programmes 'really dig into getting honest about one's inner life and its responses to trauma and difficulties' (Bright Griffin 2003b).[5] These include Quest and Bridge Builders: The Way Home and Making Peace With Your Past. The more overtly 'faith' programming include religious training teaching programmes such as Journey, Experiencing God and Crown Financial Ministries (see below). There is some overlap between the two (e.g. Making Peace With Your Past, a Scripture-based programme that addresses living in dysfunctional families).

During the first six months of the programme, prisoners spend one evening with free-world volunteers called 'Outside Brothers' or 'Outside Sisters'. This is Horizon's equivalent of APAC's 'godparents'. The expectations of Horizon volunteers are not as high as they are in APAC, where volunteers are expected to maintain a 'permanent presence' (see Chapter 1), so the relationships may be less intense. Another evening is spent on the 20-week Journey programme, another Scripture-based, small group study. The third evening is spent on the 32-week 'Quest' programme which focuses on relationship and communication skills, anger and parenting from prison. Both Journey and Quest are facilitated weekly by a group of volunteers; one volunteer for each 'cube'. In the absence of a volunteer, the cube 'Encourager' leads the teaching (a Horizon graduate who has undergone facilitator training; see 2(b) below).

After the first six months prisoners at Tomoka begin a six-month programme called Bridge Builders: The Way Home, which deals with addictions. This daily workbook takes the place of contact with 'godparents' but, like the other programmes, is volunteer-led once a week. Following on from the Journey programme, prisoners complete a 12-week programme called Experiencing God, an in-depth experience of Christianity and its basic teachings. Experiencing God runs in US churches, making it easier to raise a team of equipped volunteers. Following on from Quest is the 12-week Making Peace With Your Past that addresses issues of adult children from dysfunctional families. (Some prisons offer counselling, but this is separate from the Horizon year of programming; Bright Griffin 2004).

A final programme, completed towards the end of the year, is the 12-week Crown Financial Ministries, which encourages prisoners to recast their relationship to money in terms of 'stewarding God's gifts'. During the programme prisoners write a will and because most are financially destitute, this is an 'ethical will' of the values that they have learned and want to leave behind should they die suddenly. Bright Griffin (2003b) claims that:

> it raises the pain and really the *shame*, if you will, of having been away from their children but the volunteers work through all that with them and it's really quite a profound experience.

Throughout the year, prisoners also work on computers with self-guided tutorials for Microsoft Office programmes. Horizon also provides school programmes on computer to help those with low education to improve their reading and mathematical skills. Each prisoner is encouraged to prepare a résumé of their work skills and capacities to take with them at the end of their sentence.

The result is a fairly demanding programme that addresses common prisoner needs and deficits. Notably no firm distinction exists between 'faith-based' and 'secular' programming, as appears to be the case with IFI (see Chapter 8).

Throughout the year, there is a morning workshop or seminar every other Saturday. This begins with a study of 12 to 15 spiritual disciplines (e.g. prayer, meditation and fasting) before moving onto victim awareness, parenting and fatherhood seminars. Local clergy or others with expertise in the field lead the workshops. Prisoners conduct devotions every weekday morning after breakfast before leaving for work. Devotions are on the topic of the previous seminar, which changes every two weeks. Prisoners receive a sheet with a further explanation of the subject and questions which they discuss every morning and reflect upon in their small group. Weekly community meetings are also held on a different theme, with each cube responsible for a specific week.

Horizon also provides an eight-week Family Reading Ties programme devised by Bright Griffin for prisoners who are fathers of children aged 13 and under. Prisoners journal questions addressing fatherhood, relationships with their own fathers and family issues. On completion they select one of a variety of children's books to read on tape to their children. This tape and book are sent to the child once permission is received from the child's primary carer. All Horizon prisoners can attend a Family Day held approximately halfway through the programme. Horizon provides a banquet-like meal for prisoners' family members, which Bright Griffin (2003b) describes as:

> *very* unusual in a visiting park when mostly the only food available is out of vending machines ... Love is very present, and the families know that this is very different, and there's a great bonding. Those who don't have family are adopted almost immediately by other large families! It's a beautiful day!
>
> [emphasis original]

There are thus a number of advantages to being on Horizon at Tomoka. Many of these incentives (e.g. study, life in community, increased contact with family) are, as we have already seen in other chapters, disincentives for other prisoners. In addition, some prisoners on Horizon have given up work release and its opportunity to work outside the prison for pay in order to take part in the programme. Bright Griffin (2004) notes that one prisoner, who earned a good wage in the prison industry, gave up this position to serve as an Encourager, costing him hundreds of dollars in lost pay.

Horizon at Tomoka illustrates once again the importance of the Kairos Weekend to building community. Kairos Weekends ran successfully in Tomoka for 17 years prior to the introduction of the faith-based unit. It was initially designed that prisoners would experience the Kairos Weekend first and then enter the Horizon unit. By Horizon #5, however, the Chaplain decided to open the Kairos Weekend to the general prison population. This allowed prisoners housed in restricted accommodation who would never be able to live in Horizon to experience a Kairos Weekend. However the increased competition for places on a Weekend meant that the proportion of men entering Horizon who had attended a Kairos Weekend dropped from 100 per cent to 50 per cent or less. This means that some prisoners finish the Horizon programme without ever experiencing the foundational Kairos Weekend, despite attempts to enable them to attend a Weekend during the year that they are in the unit. These prisoners are not separated but distributed among other participants. Volunteers claim that the capacity of non-Weekenders for change is much lower and that trust is slower to develop (*ibid.*). This again highlights the suitability and value of the Kairos Weekend to building a faith-based unit inside prison.

Horizon strongly encourages the participants to sponsor their wives and female loved-ones for a Kairos Outside (see Chapter 2). In 2002, men in the Horizon programme at Tomoka sponsored 44 women for Kairos Outside.

Encouragers at Tomoka are responsible for a discipline team called an 'Honour Court'. If the Encourager and other members of the cube warn a prisoner that his behaviour is outside the limits of acceptable behaviour for the community, to no avail, the Encourager can arrange for a hearing before this 'Court'. The Honour Court consists of one delegate elected from each cube. Encouragers are not eligible, so the choice is made from among the other prisoners in the cube. So no one prisoner continually plays the role of judge, the position transfers fairly regularly. Any prisoner can appear before the Honour Court either to defend themselves as to the allegations stated against them, or they can bring their own complaints to the Honour Court if they feel that their own Encourager is somehow acting 'out of line', for example, by being partial. Honour Court meets once a week but can be called within a couple of hours' notice if necessary. No member of Horizon or prison staff attends. The authority of the Honour Court is limited. The panel may set certain assignments, such as to write a paper on 'why I get angry and make noise' or 'why I am not participating in this programme'. It has no authority to remove a prisoner from the dorm or from the programme. Should the Court feel this is necessary, the matter is referred to the Programme Manager who will in turn refer it to the Horizon Administrative Committee. This protects the Programme Manager from any potential pressure from prisoners in that he is not seen to be taking the decision independently. The Committee consists of the Programme Manager, the Outsider Community Resource Coordinator, one representative from the Warden's office (e.g. Security) and one representative from the Chaplaincy. This group alone has the authority to remove a person from the programme although the Programme Manager takes this *de facto* decision.

Another way in which Horizon seeks to promote prisoner responsibility is by allowing prisoners to establish their own rules for community living. Although prisoners are very well acquainted with prison rules, Horizon asks them to set their own rules with a view to creating 'an environment that they want to live in, where they will feel safe, where they will be more content [and not] worry about somebody jumping on us at night or attacking us in the shower or anything' (Griffin 2003). Repeatedly, the most popular rules have been: no sex (that is, any form of sex, including open masturbation), no pornography, no drugs, no smoking and no abusive language. When it was pointed out to prisoners that some of these rules are already established in the prison, Griffin says their response is:

> 'Yes, but they happen. In this community we are not going to allow that to happen. The prison rules are laughable because the inmates ... are violating the rules and here, in this community we are going to enforce the rules. We will not allow it to be seen, or known, anywhere that we are living.' And they do .... Since they are their own rules, they obey them.
> (*ibid.*)

In the history of Horizon at Tomoka, prisoners have spoken to the Programme Manager and suggested that a given participant be removed from the programme because they are involved with drugs or sexual behaviour. Such matters first go before the Honour Court and the prisoner is given an opportunity to reform. On these occasions prisoners are said to be effective in keeping such matters to themselves for a fairly short period of time, normally within two to three weeks. After this point, if they have not seen any improvement, they will normally inform the Programme Manager of the issue.

In one case, Horizon prisoners noticed a pattern of drug-dealing behaviour for an individual in the community:

They just suggested to the programme director that he talk with security and have them bring the dogs down to the dormitory at 2:30 in the afternoon next Wednesday. And they brought the dogs down at 2:30 in the afternoon on Wednesday and they encountered a supply of drugs.

(*ibid.*)

This was not seen, as it might have been in other dorms or in other prisons, as 'grassing' on another prisoner. 'Security was overjoyed .... Security said: "You know, this is unheard of" ' (*ibid.*). This act of taking responsibility apparently did much to build trust between prison staff and Horizon prisoners: 'We didn't take a survey at that point but I will tell you that the attitude of many of the officers changed. They could see that perhaps this [Horizon] would work' (*ibid.*). Prisoners have also been removed for other offences, such as speaking to someone with disrespect or for using bad language.

The experience of being on Horizon at Tomoka has inspired some longer-term Horizon graduates to set up their own version of Horizon in a houseblock on a different dorm (D Dorm). Although Horizon has only run for three years in Tomoka this is sufficient for Horizon graduates to form a majority on this houseblock. Here, and entirely without support from Horizon staff, 81 prisoners have spontaneously established their own faith-based regime which is, in effect, an 'alumni' dorm. The graduates have repainted the dorm, requested the office dividers to recreate the family pod setting and organized an Advisory Council with clear roles and responsibilities. Similar prohibitions to those on the parent dorm are enforced, similar meetings are held and there is strong emphasis upon mutual accountability, as noted during a field visit. To date, no funds were provided to make these structural changes. A number of Horizon volunteers visit the alumni dorm to provide fellowship and encouragement but, for the most part, the graduate dorm is independent of volunteer support. After six months of operation an officer reported to Griffin that not a single disciplinary infraction had occurred in this dorm since its opening (Bright Griffin 2004).[6]

This development is highly significant in terms of the pro-social impact of Horizon on the general prison culture. Horizon graduates spoke enthusiastically of the prospect of 'colonizing' the entire prison compound with the values of F Dorm. One Horizon graduate took pride in D Dorm claiming that it was 'better' than F Dorm because it was the result of prisoners' own initiative and did not need to be sustained by outside support. The alumni dorm is indeed remarkable because it shows the value prisoners attach to the Horizon experience after they leave.

Clearly, Horizon was sufficiently valued by prisoners to make them want to replicate the experience. Of even greater significance, it seems that the social mechanisms for building community were sufficiently well-internalized to enable prisoners successfully to challenge and overturn regular 'institutional space'. If imitation is the sincerest form of flattery, D Dorm is the sincerest indication that some of the lessons of F Dorm have been learned. Whether this enhanced ability to 'make community' extends to life outside prison remains to be seen. Even so, the benefits to management and prisoners of a humane prison culture that is established and maintained by prisoner consent should not be discounted. A second alumni dorm was added in 2004.

In March 2001 the Florida legislature mandated the replication of the Tomoka model into six other prisons. Funds were appropriated for these six prison units, although the bulk of the funding was for faith-based alcohol and drug treatment centres in post-release facilities, which lie outside the scope of this chapter. Despite the legislative language mandating that the six faith-based prison units be established on the Tomoka model, the State hired first-time chaplains to oversee them and reduced the role of the Community Resource Manager (or Outside Coordinator) to part-time, low-paid positions. The result is that Horizon at Tomoka has not, to date, been replicated elsewhere in Florida. Horizon at Tomoka was evaluated for its effectiveness on prisoners and their families (Caliber Associates 2004a).[7] The evaluation focused on Horizon classes #1– #5. A processual study found 'increased in-prison productivity, employability and family relationships' although the researchers were unable to investigate these further in the outcome evaluation (*ibid.*: V–64). They concluded that the programme is 'effective at enhancing safety and promising for impacting prison productivity and post-release behaviour among its participants' (*ibid.*: V–66).

A study of the profile of Horizon #1 prisoners at Tomoka by the Florida DoC (2000: 8) revealed that, of the 59 prisoners who completed the 12 month programme, 68 per cent had as their primary offence either 'murder/manslaughter' (44 per cent) or 'sexual/lewd behaviour' (24 per cent). Tomoka has a large number of sexual or sexual-related offenders (20 per cent of the non-Horizon prison population compared to 11 per cent of prisoners in Florida as a whole). However, the proportion of homicide offenders on Horizon was nearly double that of non-Horizon prisoners (22 per cent). This is in keeping with another interesting finding, that whereas 23 per cent of non-Horizon prisoners on Tomoka were serving life sentences, the proportion on Horizon serving life was more than double (53 per cent) (*ibid.*). The reverse was equally true: 10 per cent of non-Horizon prisoners were serving sentences of less than three years compared to only 2 per cent of Horizon prisoners. It seems that although Horizon might have tried to maintain a spread of criminal offences and sentences, the programme was weighted towards the 'heavy' end. It is not hard to see why. Horizon offers a way of 'breaking up' a long prison sentence by providing a highly-structured programme for a 12 month period. Those prisoners for whom the prison is likely to be their home for a considerable period have most to gain from establishing a sense of community. We may conclude that Horizon at Tomoka owes some of its success to the fact that it offers prisoners something they want in a manner appropriate to its setting. Although this might seem obvious, not all faith-based units are as well-adapted to the prisoner population or to their environment (see Chapter 11).

(b) Marion Correctional Institution, Marion, Ohio

The second Horizon unit opened at Marion C.I. (M.C.I), Marion, Ohio in July 2000. M.C.I is a medium-security prison, with a minimum-security camp for adult males and has capacity for 1,800 prisoners. Sentence length ranges from six months to life, although the average sentence is six years. The following account draws on interviews conducted during a field visit to Marion in July 2003, principally with Warden Christine Money (Money 2003) and Jeff Hunsaker, Horizon Programme Coordinator (Hunsaker 2003).

Marion had a poor institutional history prior to Money's arrival in 1996. In the 1980s and 1990s Marion was characterized by conflict and operated under two federal consent decrees (*viz.* judicial oversight). The number of lockdowns increased and yellow lines were painted four-feet apart on prison corridors to separate staff from prisoners. One prisoner who was in Marion in the early 1990s said: 'The place was violent ... awful' (Respondent B 2003). This prisoner was transferred out of Marion and returned a few years ago. 'When I came back ... I didn't recognize the place'. Staff and prisoners alike attribute this shift to the arrival of Christine Money as Warden in 1996:

> Seven years ago this place had a lot of alcohol, drugs ... gang fights, guys getting raped or stabbed. Fights were the order of the day. When Mrs. Money came, within five years you have pretty much what you see right now, i.e. programmes upon programmes, many involving faith. It has changed the nature of the institution.
>
> (Respondent C 2003)

Remarkably, staff and prisoners alike refer to her in an unembarrassed fashion as their personal 'angel'.

Prior to Marion, Money was Warden at Ohio Reformatory for Women (ORW) at Marysville and allowed that institution to hold its first Kairos Weekend. It was also Money's first introduction to Kairos. As Warden she observed the Kairos Weekend:

> I felt that if a group of women could give up eight Saturdays to train for this and three days to come into my prison, the least I could do was turn up and thank them. One of these women was a physician and I thought 'She's given up three days from her practice to come into my prison and do this' (Money, interview).

> I thanked all the volunteers and felt rewarded when I saw the improvements in women's lives who participated in Kairos. I saw women who were hard and bitter soften in the days afterwards (Money 2003).

In 1999, Warden Money flew to England to serve as a volunteer on the first women's Kairos Weekend that took place in Highpoint North.

Due to Money's positive experience with Kairos at O.R.W., when assigned to Marion, she immediately contacted Kairos leadership and requested that the ministry come to M.C.I. (see Chapter 2). Money (*ibid.*) goes so far as to state that: 'Kairos is at the heart of everything positive that goes on in Marion C.I.' Kairos is offered to 42 Marion prisoners twice a year, and there are around 140 applications. At a Weekend in 2003 an additional 12 prisoners in 'protective custody' took part by sitting on a balcony in the prison Chapel. Money notes that although the Kairos Weekend was initially seen as a novelty, 'at some point it became the norm to have Kairos in prisons, and it became acceptable for people to go on Kairos Weekends.'

Following the introduction of Horizon in Tomoka, Money was keen to see Kairos develop a faith-based unit in Marion. This was because: 'A Kairos Weekend lasts for three-and-a-half days, but if you're doing Horizon then you can have a more dramatic impact on people' (*ibid.*). At Marion, Horizon takes the form of a ten-month residential programme. The difference between Tomoka and Marion is that in Marion, Horizon is interfaith.

Horizon Interfaith at Marion developed because Money felt 'very uncomfortable doing something very specific for Christians, because we work in an environment where there are different faiths' (*ibid.*). The three religions represented on Horizon Interfaith are Christianity, Islam and

Judaism. A cloth banner on the wall at the far end of the Horizon dorm reads: 'We submit to the God of Abraham'. The Abrahamic faiths were chosen to reduce complexity. Each group of prisoners is offered faith-specific programming, but the programme is open to all who believe in the potential for personal change.

Horizon Interfaith reflects Money's philosophy that: 'every individual has the capacity to change. It is the obligation of correctional professionals to offer offenders quality opportunities to improve themselves whilst incarcerated. It is critical that the institution be an orderly and safe environment. It is also critical that staff, at all levels, fully participate with the management at the prison' (Marion Correctional Institution 2003b). Money (2003) models an empowering style of leadership and frequently tells staff and prisoners: 'If you can imagine it, we can try it. If it works, we've all gained. If it doesn't work, well, at least we've tried.'

Being a medium-security prison, Marion consists of a mixture of cell-blocks and open dorms. Horizon Interfaith is located on 1 Dorm. Prisoners who have a cell in Marion thus have 'the best of both worlds' because they benefit both from greater privacy and from the increased freedom of movement of a medium-security prison. For such prisoners, there is a sacrifice to be made in moving to the open-barracks dorm of Horizon Interfaith.

The community is organized in eight cubes of six-man 'family groups'. For Hunsaker (Horizon Programme Coordinator at MCI), 48 prisoners is a manageable number to work with every ten months. There are six cubes of Christians, one cube of Jews and one cube of Muslims. For Money (2003), the participation of minority faiths is vital:

> The point of the unit is for people to deepen their own faith commitment whilst learning tolerance and respect for people who are different to you. The interfaith aspect impacts on the institution because it demonstrates for everybody else that people can live together in harmony. They set an example for everybody else.

The interfaith nature of the regime means that an unusual relationship exists between the Kairos Weekend and the faith-based unit. In Marion the Kairos Weekend is not used to open the programme. However, all the Christian prisoners who enter Horizon will have completed the Kairos Weekend at some time in the past and will be active in 'prayer and share' groups. This means that Horizon selects not only those who have an interest in Christianity (as in Kainos) but those who are already 'spiritually active' (Hunsaker 2003). In Marion, Horizon is seen as a 'sister ministry' to Kairos – one that 'raises up' prisoners from existing 'prayer and share' groups in the prison. This means that the relationship between the Kairos Weekend and the faith-based unit is probably used more productively than at any other unit, which is ironic granted that the unit is interfaith.

Prisoners who serve as helpers on the Kairos Weekend conduct much of the recruitment of Christian participants to Horizon Interfaith. Hunsaker (*ibid.*) explains:

> They connect with people who have been on Kairos Weekends and/or sponsor someone on a Kairos Weekend with a view to their going onto Horizon. Part of the skills they learn [in doing this] are Christian-specific [skills, i.e.] discipleship. It is targeted recruitment by prisoners to other prisoners whom they probably already know.

This is a more effective approach to recruitment than occurs in other faith-based units because, presumably, the people who know prisoners best are other prisoners. It is preferable to relying on staff and Chaplains in the home prison because prisoners attach higher value to prisoner testimony. It is also preferable to relying on Chaplains at other institutions, who may give misleading information. As in Tomoka there is a preponderance of shorter-term prisoners rather than longer-term prisoners, which limits the amount of programming (*ibid.*).

The main criterion for selection is motivation: 'they have to want to be part of it, to change and give themselves to it' (*ibid.*). Maintaining a racial balance in each of the Christian cubes is also a key factor. It was known at the outset that there would be a smaller representation of the other faiths: out of currently 1,600 prisoners at Marion, only 40 are practising Muslims. Hunsaker invites the six Christian Encouragers to divide up the Christian prisoners into family groups, or 'cubes' based on their knowledge of the participants, although the Programme Manager has the power of veto. The unit management responsible for all security in the unit of which 1 Dorm is a part also has strategic oversight. Informed consent is achieved by means of an impressively-detailed compact which states the rules of the community (Marion Correctional Institution 2003a). There are over 100 such rules, although some of these are faith-specific. Tomoka C.I. has a similarly extensive compact.

Despite the pervasive influence of Kairos in Marion and a short but established history of Kairos Weekends, Hunsaker (2003) concedes: 'we don't have a significant number of [interested] men who want to be on the programme', citing as a reason the programme's disincentives. In addition to dorm living as opposed to the chance of a single cell, prisoners are not allowed to smoke and experience considerable loss of free time. As in Tomoka, prison rules prohibiting pornography and sexual behaviour, including homosexual advances, are vigorously enforced. 'Not everyone who goes through a Kairos Weekend wants to go through that deeper level of commitment. It's a sacrifice to come into Horizon' (*ibid.*; cf. section 2(d) below).

As in Tomoka, there is considerable self-policing by the community. The first time a participant on Horizon Interfaith breaches a rule (e.g. by smoking) he is warned by a fellow prisoner; on the second occasion a second prisoner or an Encourager will accompany the challenger. On the third occasion, the complainant will refer the matter to the Programme Manager. This system of warnings intentionally follows that laid down in *The Gospel According to Matthew* chapter 18:15–17. The Programme Manager gives the offender a choice between staying and 'working through' the issue or leaving the dorm. Prisoners who have breached rules regarding homosexuality have been allowed to remain on the unit provided there is a willingness to address their behaviour. However, this approach has not found favour with other prisoners on Horizon Interfaith. More serious offences such as possessing a weapon, violence, fights, aggressive action and drug possession result in immediate expulsion. Granted that Horizon Interfaith attracts the more motivated and community-oriented prisoners, it is hardly surprising that the dorm is said to have more 'peace and quiet'. Some officers transferred out of the post of Correctional Officer (CO) on 1 Dorm because 'it wasn't exciting enough' (Hunsaker 2003).

Horizon Interfaith has three stated goals: to become a 'man of faith' in whatever chosen religion; to learn to love in a functioning family; and to learn to be part of and to contribute to the larger community. To this extent there is not much difference between Interfaith and the Kairos Weekend because Interfaith, like the Weekend, is designed to 'raise up leaders within the institution' (*ibid.*). The ten-month Interfaith programme is intentionally structured to try to meet these three goals.

The cycle begins with a three-day programme called 'Opening Doors'. The goal of the programme is to teach prisoners listening and conflict resolution skills (Roeger 2003a). This is thought to be a helpful foundation for prisoners on the unit, especially when the aim of 'living in community' is a relatively new experience for them in the prison setting (Roeger 2004). It is also designed to build trust in 1 Dorm across the three faiths which, as in Tomoka, is a major issue in Horizon Interfaith (Hunsaker 2003). 'Opening Doors' can do this because, unlike Kairos, 'Opening Doors' is a non-religious programme that is open to all prisoners.[8] It is said to be an effective way of providing a common experience for all prisoners, regardless of whether they have taken part in a Kairos Weekend. For this reason, 'Opening Doors' can play a valuable role in prisons or faith-based units that already run Kairos.[9]

'New Beginnings' follows 'Opening Doors'. This takes the network of relationships built up during the previous three days in small groups and aims to bring them together into the single, large group that will inhabit 1 Dorm. Both of these programmes are designed to build community at the outset. First, they aim to develop relationships within each six-man family on the dorm. Second, they aim to forge relationships across several *different* families on 'Opening Doors'. Finally, they aim to create a network of relationships between all eight different families on the dorm with 'New Beginnings'. The combination of 'Opening Doors' and 'New Beginnings' seems to be a serious and intelligent approach to conflict resolution and to building community in prison, and deserves attention by practitioners.

The main curriculum consists of a series of mandatory programmes, as follows, that are held every week. First the Executive Director of the Interfaith Centre for Peace in nearby Columbus leads a Community Building evening. This replaced the Journey programme, which did not work on Interfaith #1 as an interfaith-based activity. The purpose of the Community Building evening is to learn about other faiths based on activities introduced in 'Opening Doors'. The curriculum is unique to Horizon Interfaith at Marion. Some presentations are based around religious holidays. For example at Passover, prisoners share a *seder* together, led by the Jewish community on Interfaith. The evening is intentionally designed to recall 'Opening Doors', so the same volunteers and prisoner facilitators who took part in that programme participate in the Community Building evening. The Community Building evening is designed to teach prisoners the difference between discussion, debate and dialogue. Competitive debate is not permitted, but respectful enquiry in the form of dialogue and discussion is encouraged. The evening thus develops the listening and communication skills introduced by 'Opening Doors'. '[The non-Christian prisoners] thought that the Christians would 'get us in there and try to convert us' (Hunsaker 2003). This does not appear to have happened, however: 'We've not had any racial or religious conflict. It's just not tolerated. It's part of the agreement' (*ibid.*). Tensions do occur within each faith-specific group, but they do not occur openly between the different faiths (Lee 2004).

Horizon Interfaith explicitly seeks to create a link between the correctional institution and the larger community. Outside Brothers programmes provide each participant with a volunteer that visits weekly.

Griffin (2003) goes so far as to say that the Outside Brothers are 'the heart of the programme'. Unlike Tomoka, Outside Brothers at Marion runs for the full programme. Meetings take place 'one-to-one' with prisoners for which the Outside Brothers are trained by Programme Managers and Community Resource Managers. At the end of the programme, prisoners can keep in touch with their Outside Brother by writing. Perhaps surprisingly, the request to continue the relationship came primarily from sponsors and not from prisoners. Outside Brother reunions take place every quarter. It has apparently been far easier to find Christian volunteers to serve as Outside Brothers than it has been for Jews and Muslims (Lee 2004).

Once a week, Horizon prisoners take part in an 'all-day' programme and are exempt from work. Participants who define themselves as Christian are required to go to the Kairos 'prayer and share' groups between 9:00–10:30 a.m. in the Chapel. There they join all those in Marion who have taken part in a Kairos Weekend, not just those on Horizon Interfaith. This is an excellent illustration of how prison management have thought through how to institutionalize the goals of Kairos (see Chapter 2) and to maximize the benefits of the Kairos Weekend. Marion is unique in providing institutional support to the Kairos objective of building strong Christian communities in prison, including those outside the faith-based unit. Significantly, Marion's approach ensures that the Christians on Horizon Interfaith interact with the wider Kairos and Christian community in the prison. This aids recruitment and may help prevent the unit from being seen as a rival 'church' to the prison Chapel.

In the afternoon, prisoners have faith-specific studies led by faith leaders from each tradition, including ordained Christian ministers, an Imam and a Rabbi. Both the Imam and the Rabbi carry out this work under contract, paid for by the State. Christian participants (but not others) have a whole 40-week curriculum ('Credo') for this afternoon series. Horizon Interfaith provides the outline for each week, but volunteers bring their own content and style. There are advantages to using faith leaders from the outside world rather than the prison Chaplaincy. The use of an ordained Christian minister, for example, encourages the church leadership to involve their congregations in supporting the prison. Crucially, prisoners identify them as volunteers rather than as part of the institution, so their contribution is perceived to have greater value. After the faith-specific activities, prisoners take part in a 'Lifeskills' package that includes cognitive behavioural and victim awareness programmes. Horizon Interfaith has abandoned the Quest and Journey programme due to lack of volunteers from outside to run the programmes. Prisoners watch a film or video once a week that has some faith meaning or perspective but is not restricted to explicit Christianity.

Muslim prisoners report that being on Horizon Interfaith provides 'tremendous opportunities to practise [their] faith' (e.g. Respondent C 2003). They use the designated prayer space, which includes an east-facing window, to pray five times a day. Likewise, Jewish prisoners relate that they have been able to celebrate *Shabbat* (Sabbath) more fully than in any other prison they have known. Prisoners from other faith communities on the wing built a *Sukkot* (a traditional shelter used to celebrate the Feast of Tabernacles) in the prison garden. A pond was recently put into the prison garden, which allows Jewish prisoners to observe the *Rosh Hashanah* ceremony of *tashlich*[10] appropriately. One Jewish prisoner explained: 'I have been able to get in touch with my faith more on the inside than on the street. There is persecution of Jews in other prisons [for example, by the 'Aryan Brotherhood']. Horizon Interfaith provides an opportunity to practise my faith in a way that I couldn't elsewhere' (Respondent D 2003). An Interfaith Enrichment Programme provides participants with a view of other faiths and methods of peacekeeping between faiths. Once a year, the men in Horizon conduct an Interfaith conference in which other prisoners receive faith-specific teaching about Christianity, Islam and Judaism.

There is also a series of elective classes. These are not technically mandatory, but prisoners are expected to take at least one elective class per week. Classes take place throughout the week for 45 minutes during afternoon 'count' and are taught by the Programme Manager, outside volunteers, Encouragers and Horizon prisoners. In the past, prisoners have taught each other ancient Greek, Hebrew and have taken significant Bible studies. There are also one-on-one studies in Islam and Judaism. Each class is expected to teach the whole community about their faith. Anyone who wishes to teach a class on a weekend or evening can do so in the dorm dayroom using various group studies and books available in the dorm library. The library is stocked with Christian, Islamic and Judaic materials. The Programme Manager sees his role as not coordinating but facilitating prisoners' development: 'There are no problems in prison that prisoners cannot solve' (Hunsaker 2003). This means that, ultimately, the community on Horizon Interfaith is only as good as its participants want it to be.

Prisoners have a daily programme closely geared to Horizon's overall goals. The most important aspect of the daily routine is the Family Life Meetings that take place at the morning 'count'. Prisoners have 45 minutes to gather in their family groups to try to put some of the prison programming into practice. Gatherings encourage the men to use the skills gained on the Opening Doors programme to listen, share, communicate, express personal desires and work together toward shared goals. Family groups have occasional family meals together. 'The idea is to capture the feel of sitting down at a family table' (*ibid.*). At present in the Christian families, every prisoner receives a copy of the book, *Purpose-Driven Life*, (Warren 2003) which provides them with a structure for the first 40 days. After that the Programme Manager allows them to determine the format for themselves.

The goal is for each prisoner in the family group to be a leader themselves, so staff do not wish to be overly prescriptive. The Community Resource Manager presents 'Lifelines' from the Journey programme in which the speaker discloses his formative life experiences (see Chapter 2). The Manager presents his 'Lifeline' to the whole dorm in order to teach them by example how to do their own 'Lifeline' and to begin to share that with others. This is not mandatory, but it is highly encouraged. Encouragers play a leading role in modelling the necessary vulnerability by making costly disclosures. This allows the programme to access some of the deeper issues prisoners have. Whole dorm 'feasts' are held several times a year in the dorm dayroom.

Like the programme at Tomoka, Horizon Interfaith focuses on 'personal issue' programmes such as anger management, self-esteem, victim awareness and parenting. A Family Letter-Writing programme provides a means for each participant to correspond weekly with his family. Victim Awareness is a ten-week group that examines the impact that crime has upon its victims.

Within a short space of time, Marion is now an excellent illustration of the benefits of running a faith-based unit in a prison that has substantial experience of running Kairos. This means that other Kairos programmes play a key role in the prison. Kairos Torch is designed to meet the needs of younger (18–25-year-old) offenders early in their prison experience (see Chapter 2). Kairos and Horizon Interfaith graduates make important contributions to Torch teams. As with Kairos, the most important work takes place after the Weekend. Marion has held three Kairos Torch Weekends, and adult graduates from Kairos in Marion have mentored younger team members.

Kairos Outside also plays an important role. President Bush in his 2003 'State of the Union' address called upon America to support the families and especially the children of the incarcerated. Marion held the first Ohio Kairos Outside in September 1999. It was also the first Kairos Outside ever to be held, at the Warden's suggestion, *inside* a prison.[11]

There are a number of advantages to holding Kairos Outside in a suitable location inside the prison such as the prison chapel. Family members can spend a significant amount of time in the place where the prisoner is serving his sentence other than the visiting room. Prisoners have the opportunity to decorate the places where the meetings are held and to prepare food. For many, it is the first time they can do something for their family. For some, it opens a door to giving and enables them to carry on giving to their families after the Kairos Outside Weekend. Prisoners also have the opportunity to take part in the closing ceremony and to spend a couple of hours after the Weekend with their family, sharing its impact and having a meal together. This approach has proven to be a time of restoration of relationships between prisoners and their families. One prisoner said it was the first time he had been able to sit and have a meal with his mother in 14 years (Respondent E 2003).

The Weekend establishes a network of relationships not only between prisoners and their families but also between families. Thus a prisoner's mother knows the mother of his best friend inside the prison. Soon, she knows his best friend almost as well as her son does. The mother of one prisoner said that her best friends are now the women she met from Kairos Outside (Respondent F 2003). So far, Marion has held seven Kairos Outsides in the prison. Kairos Outside holds reunions four times a year in the Officers' Dining Room, creating a completely different atmosphere to family visits.

In 2001 the Ohio Department of Rehabilitation and Correction (ODRC) awarded Marion the Excel Award for Best Managed Prison. None of Marion's progressive developments appears to have compromised security – they have indeed enhanced it: no escapes or absconds have been recorded since 1997. In 2002 Marion won an ODRC Excel award for demonstrating the quality of excellence in security. In 2003 Marion won the first American Correctional Chaplains Association's award for Chaplain-Offender Innovative Programmes. It also won the American Corrections Award for Best Faith-based Facility in the United States. Marion is, at present, probably the best illustration of a faith-based unit outside South America.

(c) Davis Correctional Facility, Holdenville, Oklahoma

Horizon expanded outside Ohio with a Multifaith unit that began in September 2002 at Davis Correctional Facility (C.F.) in Holdenville, Oklahoma. (For the difference between Interfaith and Multifaith units, see section 1(b)). Davis is a medium-security prison for Oklahoma prisoners and houses approximately 900 prisoners. Davis consists of eight wings, each housing 120 prisoners. Accommodation is in two-man cells arranged along the wall on three sides with a common area in the centre. All prisoners must come from Oklahoma. Unlike Marion, this is a private prison operated by the Corrections Corporation of America. The following account draws on a recorded interview with Jim Key, Programme Coordinator (Key 2003).

Davis was chosen because of strong support from prison staff and administration. The Warden made a substantial commitment to the programme from within existing staff resources. The role of Programme Manager was provided from half of the Chaplain's time and half of the Unit Manager's time – a role that in other prisons is otherwise wholly funded by Horizon. Unfortunately Davis is located in fairly remote countryside, had limited previous experience of Kairos[12] and lacked an established volunteer base to deliver Kairos Weekends. It is however notable that when Horizon chose to enter an otherwise unfavourable environment on the strength of enthusiasm from senior management it was at significant cost to the facility.

At the time of the interview, Davis was completing Horizon Multifaith #1 and about to commence Horizon Multifaith #2. At the time of writing, Multifaith #2 had graduated and Multifaith #3 was well underway. The Oklahoma Interfaith Council on Prison Ministry (an advisory body to the Oklahoma DoC) was instrumental in helping set up Horizon Multifaith at Davis. Its Christian and Jewish representatives were primarily responsible and recruited support and volunteers from Muslim and Native American groups. Wiccans and Bahai have representatives on the Council, but little community support.

Like Marion, Davis has difficulty gaining sufficient representation from minority faiths. Sufficient numbers of Muslims and Jews in the prison system were available to to take part in a Multifaith unit. The first group of 46 men (Horizon Multifaith #1) consisted of 36 Christian prisoners, six Muslims and four Jews. The number of Jews was smaller than expected because several were lost to other institutions. For Horizon Multifaith #2, Davis included a group of six ceremonial Native Americans. Ninety prisoners applied for Horizon Multifaith #2 compared to around 60 for Horizon Multifaith #1. 'The first time some [people] were sceptical, but since they've had the history on the yard, and the guys that have been in the programme talking to them, we've had great interest' (Key 2003).

Horizon prisoners are not exempt from daytime work, classes or any other activities expected of all Davis prisoners; they give up four evenings per week of free time to participate in the programme. Whilst Key (*ibid.*) accepts that non-Horizon prisoners may perceive Horizon prisoners as benefiting from special privileges, 'the perks really aren't there' beyond the benefits of the programme itself, which is open to all.

Programming takes place on four evenings. On 'Faith Night' prisoners receive faith-specific teaching. Christians participate in the Journey or Alpha programmes, and their respective faith leaders and elders developed similar faith-specific programmes for Muslims, Jews and Native Americans. Volunteer strength consisted of eight to ten Christians, one Muslim, one Jew and one Native American, each of whom taught their respective faith tradition. Faith Nights are also an opportunity for prisoners to observe similarities and differences between faiths.

As at Marion, volunteers called 'Outside Brothers' serve as mentors for each prisoner, whether Christian, Muslim, Jewish or Native American. Horizon Multifaith tries to recruit mentors who reflect the prisoner's own faith, but that is not always possible. As a result, prisoners may be mentored by an Outside Brother of a different faith. This is not seen as a problem because the Outside Brother is 'just ... a person who is primarily interested in getting to know that individual and letting that individual get to know them, regardless of faith' (Key 2003). By the same token it would not be problematic if (hypothetically) a Muslim from the free world were to minister to a Christian prisoner. This is because 'the visitation programme is designed to provide a friend with which to converse .... This is not a ministry time, this is a friendship time' (Key 2004). Davis found volunteer support for Outside Brothers to be slow to start with. Initially only five to eight people were willing to serve as Outside Brothers, so Horizon Multifaith had to hold fairly large group meetings with those people, rather than offer 'one-to-one' mentoring. By the end of the programme, however, volunteer numbers increased to 24, and the ratio was one volunteer to two prisoners. Of these, only one Muslim volunteer and one Jewish volunteer were willing to serve as Outside Brothers; the rest were Christian volunteers. Davis is far removed from Muslim and Jewish population centres. Davis hopes to be in the same position as Marion and to offer 'one-to-one' support for most prisoners, ideally paired with the same faith. For Multifaith #2 it is estimated that volunteers gave over 8,400 hours of their time and drove over 100,000 miles collectively (Kairos Horizon 2004).

Prisoners must also participate in faith-appropriate devotions. (Davis has not had, to date, any prisoners who do not claim any specific religion). Muslims are expected to participate in *Jumah* (a common prayer time) on Friday afternoons, Jews are expected to celebrate *Shabbat* (Friday evening to Saturday evening), whilst Christians are expected to take part in worship on Sundays. Other curricula are character-building (e.g. Quest) rather than faith-specific. Some such as Thinking for a Change are DoC correctional programmes dealing with cognitive-behavioural skills and substance abuse. A further strand is engaging prisoners with their families through letter writing. Trained volunteers deliver all programmes, including those created by the DoC. The total volunteer strength across all the programmes is between 40 and 50.

Key (2003) characterizes Horizon Multifaith as offering 'more community' in contrast to the 'much stronger set of rules and regulations and peer pressure' that is said to be built into conventional therapeutic communities. Key sees the faith-based unit as unique in offering an 'increase in the faith of the individuals'. 'The [conventional] therapeutic community can give them [the prisoners] many of the tools to make changes in their lives, but they don't have the faith that keeps it and sustains it' (*ibid.*).

The prime innovation of Horizon Multifaith at Davis is the introduction of Native American participants. Although this appears to be a departure from the Abrahamic model at Marion, it simply reflects Horizon policy, which is the same in both institutions. This states that if a faith group can provide a curriculum and volunteers to deliver that programme, then that faith group can participate in the unit. This policy meets the requirements of the DoC and equal opportunities legislation. A Native American group is feasible in Davis because Native Americans are a predominant social grouping in Oklahoma. Of course, to comply with equal opportunities legislation, the Multifaith programme must be open to prisoners from any religious faith, although it will be strictly the four faiths in content.

The same applies to Christian programmes. Muslims, Jews and Bahai have all attended Kairos Weekends in Davis, although the content of the Weekend remains Christian. This is unobjectionable provided there is sufficient informed consent. Key (*ibid.*) recalls: '[A Druid prisoner] became one of our strongest Kairos members and he did not give up his Druid beliefs. And I told him, I said: 'You're more Christian than you are Druid!' and he said 'That's not a compliment' and I said 'Yes, it is!' (Laughs). And we've had several Muslims who have not given up their Muslim beliefs. And I told a couple of them the same thing. As a matter of fact, at the end of our ceremony in Kairos we present them with a Cross, and neither of these guys would take the Cross when they went through the programme. But later they came back to help on the continuing programme and they asked for a Cross! (Laughs) And so you never know!' For Multifaith #2 and #3, introductory weekends similar to the Kairos Weekend were conducted for the Jewish, Muslim and Native American groups by their faith leaders (Key 2004). Each faith group had some particular accomplishments; for example the Jewish group established a kosher kitchen, daily prayers, a Hebrew language class and courses facilitated by inmate leaders on Jewish ethics and character development.

Key (2003) accepts that the use of two-man cells was 'an initial problem' in trying to develop a residential community. It was impossible to replicate the six-man units or open dorms of Horizon Multifaith at Marion and Horizon at Tomoka. This underlines the importance of prison architecture to community-building. Several attempts were made to overcome these shortcomings. 'Family groups' of six prisoners were housed in adjacent cells to try to maintain the relational dynamic, and Christian prisoners are kept in the same 'family groups' as their Kairos Weekend. This good practice was established at Tomoka. Key (*ibid.*) noted that the importance of these initial family groupings was not appreciated at first but became apparent as the year progressed. For Horizon Multifaith #2 it was planned to introduce office dividers into the central space. This would allow prisoners to meet in six-man 'prayer and share' groups for an hour, say, during a count. They would also be able to meet there as a family group. However, the prison later ruled this out on safety grounds. Key (2004) describes this as 'a major setback in the essential development of the family identity, and a sense of cohesiveness that was difficult to develop .... Other settings, which were tried in an attempt to compensate, were just not as effective'.

A further aid to 'building community' was the inclusion of Encouragers in Horizon Multifaith #2. This did not happen on Horizon Multifaith #1 because no graduates were available to become Encouragers. The Encouragers developed guidelines based on experience, which are said to be proving 'very valuable' on Multifaith #3 (*ibid.*).

The Kairos Weekend appears to have had a similar effect in Davis as it has in other prisons: 'We bring in people from the outside that are expecting nothing from [prisoners], and this is something [prisoners] can't understand – why a person would come in with absolutely no expectations of getting anything back, to share love with them. That's what blows them away' (Key 2003). Oklahoma does not have a long tradition of Kairos Weekends. The first was in 1994 at the Oklahoma State Penitentiary (OSP), a maximum-security establishment in Oklahoma. Since then there have been 30 men's Weekends and 21 women's Weekends. Key (*ibid.*) claims the first Weekend at OSP worked best because it was a maximum-security prison, and three-quarters of the participants consisted of 'negative leaders'. This is not surprising. As we saw in Chapter 2, Kairos was designed specifically to work in this environment and for this group of prisoners. By contrast, 'when Kairos was pressed into service as part of a faith-based dorm .... you got more of the positive prisoners' (*ibid.*).

Here, Key echoes the experience of Kairos when it was used in the service of Kairos-APAC and later Kainos. It appears to be the case that the different purposes of the Kairos Weekend (quite often retraining negative leaders) and the unit (life in community) often results in Kairos not being targeted on those for whom it was originally developed. At Davis, Key faced the additional complication that 'the population that we were working with to go into the Horizon programme was the honour dorm and so this gave us positive people on the yard to start with' (*ibid.*). This is consistent with our observation that faith-based units such as Kainos tend to attract more compliant prisoners. Key's comment is also consistent with the tendency of prison administrators to 'brand' particular parts of the prison compound as suitable for different types of prisoner. This means that a 'residential community' will not infrequently be located in a part of the prison that previously had a positive reputation. This was true in the case of Swaleside where Kairos-APAC took over a former Drug Treatment Unit. Locating a unit in a place that already has an established institutional history affects prisoner perceptions and it influences who will apply. Key (*ibid.*) hopes Multifaith will 'probably be able to work with more of the negative [prisoners]', but this remains to be seen. It will be essential if Horizon wishes to demonstrate a significant impact on reconvictions. Key (2004) claims that Horizon Multifaith #2 and #3 included more 'negative prisoners', resulting in 'a few more incidents and a few more dropouts, but not to a great extent'.

As in Marion, all Christians must complete the Kairos Weekend before joining Horizon Multifaith. Like the faith-based units in the UK, Davis had no established history of Kairos prior to the introduction of Horizon Multifaith. The first Kairos Weekend in Davis took place at the beginning of Horizon Multifaith #1 in 2002. This means that Davis, unlike Marion, cannot recruit from a pool of existing Kairos graduates, although it can draw on Kairos graduates who arrive at Davis having completed Kairos at other prisons in Oklahoma. Davis runs Kairos Weekends at the beginning of the programme for those who have not experienced it, as happened on Kairos-APAC and early Kainos. Prisoners who join Multifaith having experienced Kairos elsewhere perform the role of 'servants'.[13] This means they share the Weekend with those new to Kairos and all start together.

The main difficulty with setting up a Kairos-inspired unit in an institution with no prior experience of Kairos lies in recruiting volunteers. Davis is located in an isolated area with no established Kairos volunteers. Key (2003) confesses that their 'biggest breakthrough' at that point lay in contacting 'Promise Keepers', a Christian men's ministry that focuses on each individual's commitment to becoming a 'Man of Integrity'. This involves following the 'seven promises' of a Promise Keeper which boil down to a series of commitments to God, their families and their communities (www.promisekeepers.org/; accessed 5 April 2005). Promise Keepers made up the shortfall in volunteers recruited directly from churches. Without the support of Promise Keepers, the development of the unit would probably have been stymied for lack of volunteer support, as occurred in Swaleside, Highpoint South, and Highpoint North and The Verne. However, the use of the Promise Keepers was not without problems. As a 'very evangelistic group' (Key 2004), it is claimed that this resulted in the Outside Brothers visitation becoming a forum for 'evangelizing and proselytizing' (*ibid.*), which was not its purpose.

(d) Allred Unit, Wichita Falls, Texas

The fourth Horizon unit to open and the second Horizon Interfaith was the Allred Unit at Wichita Falls, Texas. The Allred Unit was one of ten prisons selected by the Texas Department of Criminal Justice and offered to Ike Griffin as possible Horizon locations. The first two prisons did not work because Kairos was not active in the institution and the locations were remote from a population base. The Allred Unit was chosen because the Kairos community had been organizing to go into that prison for about a year.

The Allred Unit is a new prison built in 1995 for adult males with a maximum capacity of over 3,600. The Allred Unit is the largest prison in Texas and has the highest security level of all Horizon units. Training for volunteer facilitators and potential inmate Encouragers began in autumn 2002, along with meetings of an Inmate Advisory Council.

Horizon has 48 male prisoners in one wing of a three-wing unit. As in Marion and Davis, representation from minority faiths has been difficult to obtain. In Horizon #2 this included five Muslims and two Jews (Bright Griffin 2004). Another limiting factor was that, before prisoners were moved onto the unit, it was determined that the Muslim Encouragers and Muslim applicants did not meet the required standards for the accommodation. These had recently been changed due to a major escape from another unit.

As in Davis, accommodation is in two-man cells, but programming is conducted in 'cube' family units to aid the relational dynamics. The programme lasts for 12 months, beginning with the Kairos Weekend. Follow-up programmes include Journey, Quest, Experiencing God, Making Peace with Your Past and the Family Letter-Writing programme. It is reported that, during a ten-month period, 44 prisoners had 63 new reciprocated contacts with their families (Kairos Horizon 2003). A number of men sponsored their female loved-ones[14] on Kairos Outside, and prisoner graduation was combined with a Family Day. A team of Outside Brothers and a few Outside Sisters support the participants. Volunteers were initially slow to come forward, but numbers were said to build up as a result of 'word of mouth' (Bright Griffin 2004).

The Allred Unit reports early positive findings regarding Horizon Multifaith. A study of Horizon #1 reported by Assistant Warden James Mooneyham found the following changes in disciplinary rates (DRs) for Horizon prisoners.[15] In the year prior to taking part in Horizon, the number of discipline reports for the 46 Horizon graduates totalled 57. This was reduced to 15 whilst prisoners took part in the Horizon programme and was reduced still further to four in the year following graduation, when prisoners were transferred to another part of the prison. Mooneyham's report claims that these latter disciplinary offences were either for minor or very minor infractions (Bright Griffin 2004). These results are worth closer inspection. The lower DRs during the programme cannot simply result from Horizon's attraction of more compliant prisoners, because a direct comparison is made with their previous behaviour. It is possible that there is a different policy to recording DRs on Horizon in the sense that the community ethos may operate to handle indiscipline 'in house' if possible (cf. disciplinary reports on Kainos; see 1(d), Chapter 5). However, the fact that the trend continues on non-Horizon units suggests that prisoners have acquired greater behavioural control and self-control whilst on Horizon and that they have, to a large extent, been successful in transferring this behaviour to situations outside the original unit.

(e) Wakulla C.I., Tallahassee, Florida

Several months after Governor Jeb Bush signed legislation approving the establishment of a number of faith-based residential units in Florida in March 2001, the DoC Head of Programmes invited Ike Griffin (co-founder of Horizon Communities) to come to Tallahassee, Florida and recommend Kairos communities in Florida that could and would support a Horizon unit. At that time it was believed that Horizon would contract for three of the units while the others would be handled in a different manner. After the terrorist attacks in the US on 11 September 2001, almost all the planning went on hold. It was not until early 2002 that Horizon had the opportunity to bid, not for the whole programme, but only for the position of a part-time Community Resource Manager and only at Wakulla C.I. in Tallahassee. The other five faith-based residential units opened over the course of that year.

Wakulla C.I. is an adult male establishment with capacity for nearly 1,200 prisoners spanning all custody grades. Horizon staff completed all the training in the prison and worked with an ecumenical group in Tallahassee to support a Multifaith unit, which opened in April 2002. The first Community Resource Manager ultimately did not support the multifaith approach and was replaced at the request of the Chaplain. Under those circumstances, volunteer development was slow, but built over the course of the year.

2. General themes

Our overview of Horizon Communities develops recurring themes from previous chapters: the appropriate role of volunteers, serving prisoners and ex-offenders in faith-based communities; equal opportunities; the relationship between the Kairos Weekend and the faith-based unit; the relationship between the faith-based unit and the prison Chaplaincy, and the relevant criteria for expansion.

(a) Role of volunteers

As in APAC and Kainos, outside volunteers seem central to the success of Horizon. There are at least two reasons for this. First, Griffin (2003) estimates that only about 20 per cent of prisoners in the US correctional system receive visits. This means that 'volunteers by their very nature speak volumes to inmates who are by and large very lonely people' (*ibid.*). Second, they are especially effective when it comes to encouraging participation in programmes. Griffin (*ibid.*) notes that:

> [many prisoners] are in prison simply because no mature adult has ever taken them seriously and devoted any time or attention to them during their formative years. So when the volunteers come in and they realize that each of these volunteers could very well be doing something else with their time and they can just imagine all of the things they would like to be doing if they weren't in prison. So they will accept instruction from the volunteers that they would *never* receive from the paid staff of the institution. Even though the paid staff [are] better trained, more professional in their approach and the Chaplaincy of the institution are marvellous … they cannot have the same effect on the lives of an inmate [as] a volunteer who comes in without the training but just speaks from the heart … It doesn't matter what [instruction] you're talking about. It could be faith instruction, it could be secular instruction as to management of personal finances, relationship to money, it could be anger management, learning about relationships, learning about parenting, learning about being a responsible individual, community life.
>
> (emphasis original)

That said, if the volunteer has had experience of wrestling with addictions of whatever sort, that volunteer will have even more credibility (*ibid.*). This is consistent with the experience of Alcoholics Anonymous and similar 'twelve-step' groups where former addicts are used as mentors and examples for those still struggling with addiction. It is also consistent with the finding that peer counsellors instil trust among recovering addicts in prison (Player and Martin 1996; also Eaton 1993; Kendall 1993; Loucks 1998). Such persons may offer a form of 'narrative therapy' or 're-biographing' for prisoners, inviting them to construct 'new' life histories for themselves (e.g. Parry and Doan 1994; White and Epston 1990). Curran (2002: 23) notes that 'often the most painful life experiences can energize, inspire or simply encourage the beleaguered to revise their own life narrative and reconstruct self-identity'.

Bright Griffin (2003b) contends that the greatest incentive for prisoners to come onto Horizon is contact with volunteers: 'Many of the volunteers of course have had traumas and addictions and difficulties that they've overcome and it is ... learning that process from these mentors of overcoming the difficulties of their past that is so instructive'. Bright Griffin's explanation of the value of volunteers in terms of 'accountability to those whose way of life is perceived as desirable' is close to a theory of normative compliance. Bright Griffin (2004) says the point that emerges from discussion and programme evaluation with Encouragers is 'the vital role of the volunteers' who, being non-judgemental, provide 'the safe container' (Bright Griffin 2004) for the work of healing and transformation. Various 'life-skills' programmes are offered at Tomoka, but these are not facilitated in small groups by community people. Bright Griffin (2003b) claims 'the holistic approach and the God-centred approach in this programme [Horizon] offers a measure of respect of much greater depth'. Horizon works in partnership with the National Association of Blacks in Criminal Justice to train volunteers on how to mentor black and white prisoners.

One researcher was present at an annual Volunteers Appreciation Day at Marion in July 2003 in which several prisoners read essays explaining why they valued the contribution of volunteers. One prisoner (Respondent H 2003) commented: 'I know that the best thing about being at Marion [C.I.] is the dedicated core of volunteers'. At the same event another prisoner (Respondent I 2003) described the 'love' shown by volunteers as a 'creative mutuality' that invited prisoners to 'duplicate the selfless love [they give].' If this is correct such volunteers 'leverage the rehabilitation efforts of the prison system' (Bright Griffin 2003a).

(b) Role of serving prisoners

Serving prisoners play a crucial role on Horizon, especially those designated as Encouragers. An Encourager is a graduate of the previous Horizon intake who becomes part of the incoming Horizon group.

His role is to build in a certain amount of accountability and positive peer pressure to mould the men into a 'family group' (Key 2003). Each Encourager lives in a 'cube' with seven other men and should be regarded by them as a stable and trustworthy individual. One of the responsibilities of the Encourager is 'to maintain the atmosphere created by the 'godparents' which is to honour them as full human beings … [who] have the potential to get their life straight and to make good decisions' (Bright Griffin 2003b). In that sense, the roles of Encouragers and godparents are complementary. Encouragers 'work extremely well, but they work extremely well because they have been mentored by outside volunteers and [so] they understand the role of bringing love, attention [and the] affirmation of each individual' (Griffin 2003).

Encouragers are chosen on the basis of their emotional maturity, listening and communication skills. They are of necessity prisoners 'who have considerable sentences … and come to grips with life in prison …. Once they've been through the programme and we see that they have certain talents for leading inmates and for encouraging other inmates we make them Encouragers' (*ibid.*). The Programme Manager selects Encouragers from names recommended by the graduating class. The criteria for a successful Encourager follows guidelines laid down in St. Paul's *First Letter to Timothy* 3:2-10 regarding leadership within the religious community. Once the Programme Manager has established his or her choice for the Encouragers, they present that to the Chaplaincy. The Programme Manager determines the team but the Chaplaincy has the power of veto.

Horizon invests training and 'refresher training' in its Encouragers because 'they are expected to take a leadership role and they are 'on duty' within that cube 24 hours a day, seven days a week, 52 weeks a year' (Griffin 2003). In providing such training, Horizon claims it was 'very careful in also bringing in the heart-centred efforts at leadership and not some other [negative] techniques as well' (Bright Griffin 2003b). Encouragers are themselves 'encouraged' by 'accountability partners' (another Encourager) to whom they report on a regular basis. The Programme Manager is the overall Encourager for the community and has regular meetings with Encouragers. In Griffin's view:

> The Encouragers are *extremely* effective. They are *far*, far more observant than our free-world counsellors. They notice the body language, they notice what's happening in a person's life and they are able to watch them 24 hours a day. So they know the internal and external forces in the life of each person in their pod family. We could not run the programme without the Encouragers
>
> (2003)

The name 'Encourager' was chosen carefully. Until 1968 it was possible for prisoners to exercise physical force over others with the use of firearms. The Supreme Court abolished this in 1968, stating that no prisoner should exercise authority over another prisoner. This was interpreted to mean that prisoners could not exercise decision-making power over others, even if that authority was benign. Hence when Horizon wished to establish positions of responsibility, serving prisoners were styled as Encouragers, as opposed to, say, 'group leaders'.

Griffin (*ibid.*) describes the Encouragers as 'leaders', 'facilitators' and 'peacemakers'. But they are neutered leaders: they have responsibility but no authority. There is a tension between the desire to raise up leaders on Horizon and the DoC perception that positions of leadership for prisoners are undesirable.

(c) Role of ex-offenders

A third issue is the role of ex-offenders, which was a controversial issue in the UK (see Chapter 3). Griffin places great value on employing ex-offenders; it is said that approximately half of Horizon's Programme Managers are ex-offenders. Griffin (2003) defends this on the ground that ex-offenders have 'great credibility among the [prison] population and they understand what the inmates are going through, which is almost impossible for anyone who has not been incarcerated'. However, he concedes that there are risks: 'Ex-offenders quite often have tremendous difficulty with their authority issues and they have developed such strong adversarial relationships with the administration that quite often it's difficult for an ex-offender to lay that down and begin to work 'hand in glove' with the administration' (*ibid.*). Provided those risks are acknowledged and appropriately supervised, Griffin maintains that 'the extra vigilance and the extra care is well worthwhile' (*ibid.*).

Not all agree, however. Hunsaker (2003) is blunt: 'I think you can't have an ex-offender in the position of a Programme Manager. You have the basic distrust of the administration. Two ex-offenders were Programme Managers in Horizon [and] both were locked out by the institution.' The problem with using ex-offenders is that 'there is already built-in distrust of that person, even though they haven't come through that prison' (*ibid*). There may be some symbolic value in employing a person who is apparently 'making good', but for Hunsaker (*ibid.*) the problem of supervision outweighs this: 'Who is that person going to be accountable to? ... The problem is that they've not been trained and they've not had the supervision. We haven't been running long enough to know them long enough to support them in that position'. This squares with Ottoboni's approach to prisoner responsibility in APAC. Offenders and ex-offenders are granted responsibility in proportion to trust earned and personal knowledge of the offender that has been gained over a period of years (see Chapter 1).

(d) Equal opportunities

Horizon, in common with other faith-based prison dorms that opened in Florida in 2002, has attracted criticism on the ground that it 'unfairly gives additional privileges to religious inmates' (Pfankuch 2002). The stakes in this debate are arguably higher in the US than in the UK given the constitutional separation in the US between church and state. In December 2003, Lawtey C.I. in Florida became the first prison in the world since Humaitá in 1984 to house only prisoners who had volunteered for faith-based activities (Pinkham 2003a).[16] Americans United for Separation of Church and State immediately filed a large public records request for prison system records to discover whether its funding, programming and policies were legal (Pinkham 2003b). Interestingly, the fact that Horizon at Wakulla C.I. is multifaith as opposed to Christian-based has not protected it from criticism. Instead of being criticized for favouring 'Christian' prisoners, it is criticized for favouring 'religious' prisoners in general.

Horizon offers a number of incentives to prisoners, notably a 'living and learning' environment with access to religious and non-religious-based programmes and contact with volunteers. However, as noted above, not all these 'incentives' would be viewed as such by all prisoners. Equally, there are a number of disincentives to being on Horizon. Horizon demands programming three nights a week and every other Saturday morning, so prisoners have less free time. Prisoners lose some, though not many, visiting hours and have less freedom to watch television. Prison rules are enforced more stringently on Horizon, and prisoners frequently draw attention to the lack of flexibility in their timetable (Bright Griffin 2003b).

Bright Griffin concedes that, initially, other prisoners viewed Horizon participants as 'getting a perk'. However 'It very quickly became clear that the Horizon men *worked* out there – that as well as their work assignments … they were doing a great deal of inner work, and that this was perhaps the hardest aspect of the programme – that it was not easy, it was not cushy. I believe that [misconception about 'perks'] has generally been dispelled, although it's a misconception that will maintain its prevalence' (*ibid.*, emphasis original).

(e) Relationship between the unit and the Kairos Weekend

A fifth issue is the relationship between the Kairos Weekend and the faith-based unit. As we saw in Chapter 2, a purpose of the Kairos Weekend is to recruit 'negative' leaders so that they will begin to use their 'God-given leadership talents in a new direction' (Griffin 2003). Whereas the Kairos Weekend does not give such prisoners an opportunity to demonstrate those leadership abilities, Horizon aims not only to give them that opportunity but ample time to increase those abilities.

A tension arises from the fact that the recruitment of challenging and disruptive personalities is far more intentional in the case of a short Kairos Weekend than it is in the case of a ten or twelve-month programme such as Horizon. Horizon does not recruit heavily among negative leaders for the simple reason that those who are truly disruptive do not care to volunteer. 'Negative' leaders are far less likely to give up certain privileges to join Horizon for a year than they are to give up privileges for a weekend. Horizon claims that it has received 'quite a number of people who were extremely disruptive going into [the] Kairos [Weekend] but had a 180-degree change in their attitudes' (*ibid.*). Such persons are said to have become excellent Encouragers and participants. But such persons, by definition, are not 'negative leaders' whilst on the programme and would not be allowed to remain if they were.

It thus seems unavoidable that the Kairos Weekend and Horizon have different goals and different prisoners in mind. If that is so then a certain distance between the two may well be beneficial to both, as is the practice at M.C.I.

(f) Relationship between the faith-based unit and the Chaplaincy

A sixth issue is the nature of the relationship between the faith-based unit and the Chaplaincy. This is potentially problematic because, as Griffin (*ibid.*) explains, 'When you start one of these operations, the institution will quite naturally turn to the Chaplaincy and say: "We have a man on staff here and he is the one to run this programme". Horizon offers several different models. There are those in which the Chaplaincy runs the faith-based unit (the later Tomoka, Davis, Wakulla and other non-Horizon units in Florida and in other states) and those where it does not (the early Tomoka, Marion and the Allred Unit). For those running the unit, the latter is preferable; from the Chaplaincy's perspective the former is preferable. For both it is a matter of control and, those running the unit would add, safeguarding programme integrity.

Horizon claims that it experienced difficulties where its units are run by the Chaplaincy. Clearly, the Programme Manager must be under the authority of the prison, but Griffin (*ibid.*) would rather have the Horizon employee under the supervision of the programme director of the prison or the Warden rather than the Chaplain. Bright Griffin (2004) commented that Wakulla C.I. in Florida suffered from a frequent turnover of Chaplains, some with no prior knowledge of Kairos or Horizon. The difficulties in Tomoka were more complex. Initially, the Tomoka unit was under the authority of Horizon subject, of course, to the prison/ Horizon management team. This is because Horizon was funded by a two-year grant from the Commission on Responsible Fatherhood, so the participation of the DoC was limited to making available prisoners and space within the prison. When that funding terminated, the DoC was sufficiently impressed with Horizon that it wished to fund the programme itself and in fact wanted the programme to spread across all of the DoCs in Florida.

Within a short time, however, the DoC moved from providing funds to pay Horizon staff to hiring the Programme Manager directly as a prison Chaplain. This meant that the Coordinator effectively 'switched sides' and became an employee of the DoC and the State rather than an employee of Horizon. When this happened, the day-to-day influence of the DoC on Horizon swung dramatically in the DoC's favour. According to Griffin (2003), the DoC began to exercise its new authority 'to the detriment of the programme'. The institution had a prior claim on the Programme Manager and reduced his time on the dorm to between 40 per cent and 35 per cent. Time to encourage and to counsel prisoners diminished, which placed more responsibility on the Encouragers. On the other hand, if the DoC had not effectively brought the programme under its control, Horizon at Tomoka might have folded completely for lack of money.

This is a recurring problem for faith-based units. Freedom from the controlling influence of the correctional institution is preferable for those running the unit, but this depends on sufficient financial independence which may be impossible to secure. In these circumstances is the 'half a loaf of bread' represented by Chaplaincy control better than none?

The switch at Tomoka from unit control to Chaplaincy control brings into sharper focus what is at stake. It is not simply a matter of 'control' and 'programme integrity' but also a matter of how prisoners perceive the programme. A programme run by an external charity and which symbolizes to them the outside world has a very different resonance from a programme that is run by the DoC. As Griffin (*ibid.*) sees:

there is such an adversarial relationship between the administration and inmates that has built up over years and years and years that that relationship has become central to the culture of the prison. Inmates by and large won't accept a chocolate birthday cake from the institution if it is offered free and delicious simply because it's coming from the institution.[17]

Yet if that programme or individual is paid by an external charity in the free world 'the inmates sooner or later will learn that and they will know that here is an individual coming forward who is not in the enemy camp' (*ibid.*).

In contrast to Tomoka, Marion recognizes the importance of the Programme Manager being paid directly by an external charity and not by the prison, even though the prison in fact sends the monies to the charity. This re-routing of funds may not seem much of a difference, but in the symbolic world of the prison, it matters a great deal because it affects the perceptions and hence the success of the project. It is probably also worth noting that State employees are harder to remove from their position than Horizon employees.

A further reason why Horizon prefers distance from the Chaplaincy is because 'we do not want the Horizon programme to be subject to the theological view of the Chaplain that is perhaps in place. So many of the Chaplains come from such a very fundamentalist background that working interfaith is absolutely impossible' (*ibid.*). Another facet is that 'unfortunately us Christians tend to debate and argue if we have even the slightest difference in theological view. In Horizon we try to find those persons who can be fairly broad in their approach. That type of person can usually get along extremely well with the Warden or assistant Warden in charge of the programme or with the professional staff of the prison but quite often might be looked down upon by the Chaplain for whatever reason [although] not necessarily so' (*ibid.*).

By contrast, Horizon Multifaith at M.C.I. operates under the second model and is entirely separate from the Chaplaincy. The Chaplaincy and Horizon Multifaith both report to the Deputy Director of Special Services who reports to the Warden. The Programme Manager at M.C.I., Jeff Hunsaker, agrees with Griffin that this arrangement is 'a very, very good thing. They [the Chaplaincy] want to control it' (2003). For Hunsaker, the ideal scenario is that Horizon and the Chaplaincy should function as equal partners in religious services in an institution. However, he claims this rarely happens because Chaplains are State employees and, like the DoC as a whole, ultimately seek control over charities such as Horizon Multifaith and its volunteers. Hunsaker feels that the Chaplaincy might try to tell volunteers how to teach the programme or try to teach it themselves and that, either way, one risks losing the value of the volunteer dynamic:

> The Chaplain gets the idea that 'I oversee this programme and you will do what I tell you to do'. It becomes territorial. In my experience I've not found any Chaplains open enough to not want to control things, such as what form the religious teachings take .... It becomes a turf war .... The problem is that most Chaplains are religious services administrators. They don't pastor .... They do all the paperwork, death notices, phone calls to the sick etc.[18] When a programme like Horizon Interfaith [now called 'Multifaith'] comes in they get very leery.
>
> *(ibid.)*

(g) *Type of institution*

Seventh, there is the type of institution in which faith-based units seem to do best. We noted in Chapter 2 that Kairos is best used as a 'mid-stream' experience. The same applies to Horizon: 'The community within the transient situation does not do well' (Griffin 2003). In Marion (and sometimes in Tomoka), prisoners do not enter the faith-based dorm until some time after the Kairos Weekend. This gives prisoners more time to think about and to absorb the Kairos message and, according to Griffin this increases the likelihood of its success:

> Some people, after the Kairos Weekend, 'disappear' in the prison and we worry about them. We don't know what's happened to them and we just know that they don't come back to reunions and so technically they are a dropout. But sometimes they come back two or three years later and just basically say: 'Wow, I finally got it and I want to reconnect with this community and begin to experience a small group work with another inmate who has been through the Weekend and understands what it's all about'.
>
> *(ibid.)*

Ideally this involves starting the unit in a higher-security prison such as Tomoka. During a field visit to Tomoka in 2003, one prisoner explained how he attended a Kairos Weekend and spent 12 months on Horizon without connecting with any of its teaching. One researcher had in fact spoken with this prisoner during this period three years previously. After a period away from the dorm the prisoner returned to help as an alumnus to Horizon. Only at this point did he claim to understand 'what it was all about'. At the time of writing (2004) this prisoner is a driving force on the 'graduate dorm' spontaneously developed by Horizon graduates and mentioned above. This positive development was only possible because Horizon was operating in a maximum-security prison with a non-transient population who had more time than a pre-release population to digest its ethos.

Despite these lessons, the DoC is 'most anxious' (Griffin 2003) to have Kairos in a minimum-security prison in order to socialize prisoners before their release and help them to connect with free-world people. This illustrates the tendency of correctional services to manipulate a faith-based unit to fit their own needs even though it may not be in the best interests of the unit itself. A similar tendency on the part of the Prison Service England and Wales to open Kairos-APAC in settings where it was unsuited was noted in Chapter 2. It is the responsibility of both prison management and those who run the faith-based unit to be clear about its strengths and weaknesses and to exploit those areas where the unit operates best.

(h) Criteria for expansion

A final issue is the identification of appropriate criteria for expansion. Following the apparent success of Horizon at Tomoka C.I., the DoC wanted to expand the programme to other prisons within Florida. Interest also came from outside Florida. By 2003, ten States publicly requested the Horizon programme. However Horizon refused to go into those prisons where they felt, for one reason or another, there was not a good possibility of success.

Horizon has been invited into at least 15 prisons where it has not yet started a programme (Bright Griffin 2004). Even with such restraint, some mistakes were made. Horizon opened a unit for Alaskans in Arizona in the belief that it would find sufficient volunteers to run the programme. Horizon personnel made several trips to Arizona to assess the strength of the local Kairos community. In the end, only 25 of a needed 60 to 80 volunteers were found to drive the long distances necessary to run weekly programmes. One full year was completed after which the faith-based unit reverted to a secular unit. This underlines, once again, the reliance of faith-based programmes upon sufficient volunteer strength.

The broadly successful experience of Horizon enables us to identify the essential preconditions of a successful faith-based programme. The first and most important criterion is that the establishment is proximate to a large population base from which volunteers can be drawn and which can be sustained in the long-term. Large populations are needed because Horizon claims that only 2 per cent of practising Christians are willing to help with a prison population if they live close to a prison. Even larger populations are required if one wishes to work interfaith or multifaith because religions such as Islam and Judaism provide less encouragement for working with prisoners, although Horizon has found that appeals to compassion have quite often been successful.

Second, there must be a willing and supportive institution. This means an institution that will not only welcome the programme but try to help make it a success. It is essential that the Governor or Warden is supportive and informs prison staff of their support so that this filters down 'through the ranks'. That manifests itself subsequently in several ways that can affect future success, including how prison staff deal with volunteers and in dealing with situations in the dormitories themselves. However, it is important that this support is also shared more broadly among other management and staff. If support comes only from the Warden, the programme may fold as soon as he or she leaves because it is too dependent on the strength of a single personality.

Third, there is a need to establish a sponsoring charity that will take on the burden of raising funds from whatever sources are available or to contract directly with correctional services. In the case of Horizon, salaries are required for two full-time staff members: a Programme Manager, a Community Resource Manager to recruit, train and schedule volunteers entering the prison plus approximately $10,000 a year for training, manuals, supplies, and other administrative costs for a total of $110,000 to $120,000 per year. This is approximately one-quarter of the total cost of InnerChange (see Chapter 8). Horizon prefers to employ staff to maintain the programme, despite the value of volunteers. Staff are easier to replace than volunteers, especially if there is an established income stream.

Fourth, there is a need for a suitable 'living and learning environment' in which to base the unit. There is some advantage to establishing it in a dormitory setting. One prisoner on Horizon commented that the 'open plan' dormitory, in contrast to the closed dormitories of The Verne, was critical to building community. The increased visibility of the 'open plan' dormitory is said to make it much more difficult for prisoners to 'withdraw' or 'isolate' from the community. It also meant that prisoners were 'on parade' continually, which was said to promote personal accountability. Horizon participants in Tomoka and Marion also have to make a commitment to get along with at least six to eight other persons in their 'cube', rather than only just their 'celly' (cellmate) in the case of a two-man cell (Allred Unit and Davis) or no-one at all in the case of single cell (e.g. Swaleside). That said, Horizon has also worked effectively in two-man cell-blocks at Allred Unit and Davis, but only because staff were intentional about trying to overcome the architectural limitations.

3. Conclusions

What main conclusions can we draw from this descriptive account of Horizon? We suggest the following:

- Horizon was right not to open units unless there was a good possibility of success and to regard the existence of a body of volunteers as central to that judgement.

- Prison departments frequently manipulate faith-based units to suit their own agenda, even when this is to the detriment of the programme.

- Faith-based units must understand their strengths and weaknesses and stick to their strengths. In Horizon's case that means concentrating on non-transient populations that have time to digest the Horizon ethos.

- The roles of volunteers and Encouragers are complementary. Employing ex-offenders may create difficulties, though these may sometimes be outweighed given sufficient supervision.

- The Kairos Weekend is crucial to building community. Horizon demonstrates that it is possible to have a strong follow-up programme that successfully builds on the Weekend.

- The benefits of running a unit in a prison with substantial experience of Kairos are considerable. But the Kairos Weekend and the faith-based unit have different goals and should maintain a certain distance.

- 'Opening Doors' and 'New Beginnings' deserve attention as a means of promoting conflict resolution and community living.

- Multifaith programmes have been popular but they are heavily dependent on Christian volunteers for their viability.

- Horizon takes considerable trouble to secure informed consent, and this pays dividends.

- Prison architecture is a factor to be considered in identifying whether the environment is conducive to building community.

- Faith-based units may have to choose between maintaining independence from the institution and folding, or accepting direct funding from the institution and losing control of the programme. 'Who pays the piper' is an important issue for prisoners.

- The relationship between the faith-based unit and the Chaplaincy is an area of potential tension which, if left unresolved, can damage the work in that prison and its expansion. Different institutions should perhaps adopt different strategies depending on the personalities involved. 'One size' does not fit all.

Notes

1 The name 'Kairos Horizon' was changed to 'Horizon Communities Corporation' in July 2004 to reflect the independence of Horizon from Kairos Prison Ministry. This separation of identities was felt to be necessary because Kairos aims to present a purely Christian programme, whereas Horizon Communities promotes other religions in addition to Christianity, notably at its Interfaith and Multifaith units (www.kairosprisonministry.org 'Relationship with Horizon').

2 Kairos Horizon Communities in Prisons operated under the corporate governance of Kairos Prison Ministries until 2000, when a separate charitable corporation with its own board of directors was formed and received its formal non-profit status in 2001.

3 Until 2004, Horizon Multifaith units were described as Interfaith units. The term 'Multifaith' replaced 'Interfaith', although the Allred Unit and Marion C.I. are still known as 'Horizon Interfaith'. The term 'multifaith' reflects the belief that, although prisoners are expected to learn about other faiths whilst on the multifaith unit, they are not expected to intermingle those faiths with their own. Rather, they are to be strengthened in their specific faith. During the first 12 months of Kairos Horizon, the Board of Directors devoted some time to discussing whether Horizon was a 'multi-faith ministry' or 'a Christian ministry working in close collaboration with other faiths to support a multi-faith approach to prison ministry.' The latter terminology was decided upon, for, among other reasons within the faith tradition itself, the board and staff were all Christian (Bright Griffin 2004).

4 Bright Griffin (2004) claims that non-Muslim volunteers were always selected with care to be 'godparents' or Outside Brothers to Muslim prisoners, with the result that there were no incidents. One Muslim volunteer was recruited but only attended a few times. The Jewish inmate population in Florida is housed in units in South Florida where there is an organized Jewish support effort in prisons.

5 'Often that trauma includes all kinds of abuse, some of it horrific. The responses of volunteers working in a small group setting, to trauma and difficulties Horizon participants have had, arise from Horizon's 'ministerial' approach and not a counselling approach. None of the volunteers are

psychologists or professional counsellors, but are involved in prison ministry to 'accept the man as he is' and address with compassion the past suffering that might have occurred (as guided by the workbooks – Quest and Making Peace with Your Past) ... The important things to note are that the workbooks are followed ... and that the Horizon participants are living in a 'safe' environment where others are addressing these issues as well, and, finally, compassionate volunteers return weekly' (Bright Griffin 2004).

6 Though in interpreting this and similar claims we must ask 'whether we are witnessing a fundamental reorientation or the results of ... [a] diminution of pressures or temptations'; Toch and Adams (2002: 126).

7 We are grateful to Caliber Associates and Horizon Communities for permission to quote from the study.

8 Griffin (2003) sees Opening Doors as 'an experiential approach to things without the religious teachings [of the Kairos Weekend] ... I think that perhaps that is a very authentic and appropriate way to enter a community. Or to begin a community in an area where you have several mixed faiths and particularly have a small percentage of people who actually profess to be Christian and are not really ready to hear the Christian message at that point.'

9 Kairos is an expressly Christian programme, so not all prisoners on the unit will experience Kairos even in those institutions. Moreover, unless the Kairos follow-up programme is fully implemented, even those prisoners who have experienced it may not know the other prisoners who have.

10 The ceremony is a symbolic 'casting away' of sins over a body of water.

11 Although a Cursillo Weekend for the wives and girlfriends of APAC prisoners was held at Humaitá in 1994 (Lee 1995).

12 Davis started weekly prayer and share groups, monthly reunions, and yearly two-day retreats in 1997 for Kairos graduates from other institutions who were placed at Davis. However the first Kairos Weekend did not take place until the introduction of Kairos Horizon in 2002 (Key 2004).

13 A number of responsible jobs normally taken by outside volunteers on a Kairos Weekend are described as 'servants'. Prisoners of sufficient maturity who have already experienced a Kairos Weekend can also be 'servants'.

14 At present, Kairos Outside is only available for the mothers and female partners of male prisoners.

15 At a Conference of Wardens and Chaplains of the Texas Department of Criminal Justice in Huntsville, Texas, 27th September 2004 (Bright Griffin 2004).

16 This facility opened too late to be considered for inclusion in this book.

17 This illustrates prisoners' need to reject prison staff and the institution as 'acceptable agents of rehabilitation' (Heffernan 1972: 138).

18 A characterization echoed by Beckford and Gilliat (1998: 200): 'American prison chaplaincy is distinctive for being relatively standardized, predictable, equitable and accountable, but the level of provision for religious and pastoral care is also relatively low'. The authors claim this contrasts with the role of prison chaplains in England and Wales.

Chapter 8

Preparing Evangelists: InnerChange Freedom Initiative (IFI)

I am proud to be the Governor of the State that has opened the first Biblically-based pre-release programme in the United States. I believe we ought to add more like it ... now is the time to seek divine help.

George W. Bush, Governor of Texas, June 1997

Introduction

On 21st April 1997, the first Christian-based unit in a US prison was established by Prison Fellowship at Jester II Correctional Unit near Houston, Texas, mere weeks after the opening of Kairos-APAC at HMP The Verne, in England. Known as the InnerChange Freedom Initiative (IFI), the operation at Texas was quickly followed by similar programmes in Iowa (1999), Kansas (2002) and Minnesota (2003). Unlike Horizon, whose immediate roots were in The Verne project in England, the origins of Prison Fellowship lay directly in APAC.

This chapter describes the origins, development and key characteristics of IFI and highlights recurring themes. It draws on recorded interviews with Jack Cowley, National Operations Director of IFI 1997–2003 conducted in April 2004 and with Programme Directors from four IFI units, conducted in August 2003, namely: John Byrne (IFI-Kansas; currently IFI-Minnesota); Phillip Dautrich (IFI-Texas; currently Director

This chapter was authored by Jonathan Burnside

240

of IFI in the UK) and Samuel Dye (IFI-Iowa). This exploration is timely, given that IFI have now expanded to the UK. At the time of writing, the first IFI programme in the UK is scheduled to open in February 2005 at HMP Dartmoor, which will also be IFI's first incursion into a maximum-security prison.

I. Emergence of IFI

By 1990 the US branch of Prison Fellowship and Prison Fellowship International (PFI) had sent a large number of delegations to Humaitá, including Jack Eckerd from the Prison Fellowship US Board of Directors. Eckerd was apparently so moved by what he saw that he was willing either to build or to take over a new prison somewhere in the US to replicate the APAC programme. Through the Eckerd Family Foundation he funded a group, headed by Daniel Van Patten, to investigate the feasibility of replicating the Brazilian APAC programme in the US. This report concluded: 'The APAC programme ... *can* be replicated here in the United States' (Prison Fellowship International 1991; italics original).

The Foundation contracted a firm of consultants in Virginia with the specific task of helping to organize a faith-based community, dorm or prison such as Eckerd had seen in Brazil. At that point it was assumed that faith-based units would work especially well with a high Latin population and a Catholic prison population, as in APAC. This suggests the Foundation's analysis of the core elements of APAC was, at that stage, fairly superficial. There was a willingness to replicate some of the surface characteristics of APAC but not much understanding of its deep structure, its programme elements or its social mechanisms. However, it was also thought that the prison should be located in an urban setting in order to replicate certain aspects of APAC, including the semi-open and open stages of the Humaitá regime. Arizona, California, southern Florida and Texas were all considered as possible locations. The Foundation contacted Ike Griffin of Kairos Prison Ministry Inc. (KPM) to help identify suitable prisons. It was also thought that the unit would be 'volunteer-run' like APAC and so, given Kairos's long experience with volunteers, the Foundation wanted Kairos to train potential volunteers and have substantial input into programme design.

However, the doors remained closed to the Eckerd project. No willing prison was found in a heavily Latin part of the US. A welcome was eventually found in North Carolina, and the Foundation determined to start there. But the timing was inauspicious: its plans coincided with a prison scandal in North Carolina involving the Commissioner and some of the work of the Department of Corrections (DoC). The Commissioner was forced to resign and, rather than risk another controversy, the DoC shelved plans for a faith-based prison.

Eckerd's dream came alive again in the early 1990s when Carol Vance, Chairman of the Texas Department of Criminal Justice (TDCJ), made a visit to Humaitá with Charles W. ('Chuck') Colson, the founder of Prison Fellowship ministries which operates in more than 80 countries. 'Carol fell in love with it, came back and talked to then Governor Bush who had just been elected to office...about a wonderful programme that was happening in Brazil. Governor Bush loved the idea and said: "Let's do it"' (Dautrich 2003). It was in fact a document by Governor Bush's Advisory Task Force on Faith Based Community Service Groups entitled 'Faith in Action: A New Vision for Church–State Co-operation in Texas' that paved the way for the first faith-based unit in the US in 1997 (PFI 2002). Thus it was in 1996 that the Head of Chaplaincy in Texas invited two leading prison ministries in the US, namely Kairos Prison Ministries and Prison Fellowship, to submit a proposal for a faith-based unit similar to APAC. Kairos declined because it was at the time rolling out new ministries in Kairos Torch and Kairos Outside. Bidding for a faith-based unit may also have been seen as a departure from what the Kairos Board saw as its primary purpose, namely holding Kairos Weekends. PF, on the other hand, accepted and spent six to nine months developing what became known as IFI before launching the programme at Jester II, a minimum-security prison.

Although the initiatives at HMP The Verne in the UK and at Jester II in the US began at roughly the same time, they in fact developed 'totally independently of one another' (Cowley 2004). The common factor was the desire to implement some version of APAC. There was very little political opposition to IFI, attributed to the fact that no State funds were involved. 'It didn't get on anyone's radar screens whatsoever' (*ibid.*).[1]

IFI was quick to identify itself with the original APAC (Colson 2000). At a superficial level this connection was easy to establish. In 1988, APAC changed its name to Prison Fellowship Brazil and its founder, Mário Ottoboni, was a Board Member of PFI. Both Ottoboni and the founder of the APAC movement in Ecuador, Jorge Crespo Toral, attended the inauguration of IFI-Texas (Toral 2000). IFI's identification with APAC was also tactical and in some ways opportunistic. Cowley admits: 'We had to base InnerChange on something' because 'most companies, most programmes that move into corrections, have a history somewhere else. And so APAC gave InnerChange the history they needed for credibility within the Department of Corrections. And that's why we used it' (2004). But at a structural level IFI was *not* like APAC: 'there was a distinct difference in the programmes' (*ibid.*), for example, greater emphasis on formal Bible study and greater reliance upon paid staff.

A Senate Bill was passed to recognize IFI within the TDCJ. The then Texas Governor, George W. Bush, enthusiastically supported the programme, two months before it opened. In a key speech Bush said:

> One of my missions as Governor is to encourage people of faith to play a larger role in solving many of society's problems. Government does not have a monopoly on compassion. We ought to recognize that as a society we must be proud of our private charities, churches, synagogues and people of faith who have become involved with our society. Groups with a long tradition are successfully changing lives by meeting the needs of the soul as well as the law. We must encourage them … not only in the prison system, but in all areas of social services delivery .... I am proud to be the Governor of the State that has opened the first Biblically-based pre-release programme in the United States. I believe we ought to add more like it. And we should even consider going a step further: private, faith-based prisons that are for redemptive rehabilitation where the fullness of responsibility rests upon them. We should look at volunteer spiritually-based mentoring programmes as a substitute for jailing non-violent offenders or as a condition of their release .... Our society faces many tough problems. Now is not the time to shun, now is the time to seek divine help.
>
> (1997)

2. Goals

IFI has multiple goals which may be identified as follows (in no particular order): (1) evangelism *to prisoners*; (2) evangelism *to the world*; (3) securing lower rates of recidivism and (4) providing effective aftercare. Each goal has some claim to primacy. This means that the purpose(s) of IFI may seem somewhat confusing to the outsider. However, it is possible to see how, from IFI's perspective, these different goals interlock.

Turning to the first: *evangelism to prisoners*:

> We as a ministry have a desire to equip the people [i.e. prisoners] with a relationship with [Jesus] Christ. That is our firm foundation, and that is where we focus. So the first and important concept is that we evangelize them … [O]ur fundamental concern is the ministry.
>
> (Cowley 2004)

The Programme Manager at IFI-Texas confirms this: 'We want them [prisoners] to come to the light and to see what the true gospel is' (Dautrich 2003). The 'number one' mission of IFI is 'to teach the gospel of Jesus Christ' (*ibid.*). This takes priority over the goal of reducing reoffending. Dautrich admits:

> Yes, you could go through prison, not go to InnerChange and live a crime-free life. That could happen and [you could] go through the anger management, and go through all of the *secular* programmes. But the bottom line is if you have not accepted Jesus Christ as your Lord and Saviour you are not going to the Kingdom of God and you will not enter those gates *per se*. And I hear people say that all the time: 'Look at this person, he conquered his substance abuse' or 'He's not a Christian' or 'He didn't go through a *religious* programme.' And praise God, you know what? If that person can go out and do that – great. But I do know in the end that they are not going to the Kingdom of God if they have not accepted Jesus Christ as Lord and Saviour.
>
> (ibid.; emphasis original)

Evangelism as a goal is noteworthy, especially when compared with the constraints of the Prisons Act 1952 in the UK, which prohibits proselytizing.

However IFI does not see the evangelism of prisoners as an end in itself but as a means to a greater end. This brings us to a second purpose of IFI: *evangelism to the world*. As Cowley (2004) explains:

> Why we do what we do is this. Our culture is moving farther and farther from the Lord....If we can take inmates – and everyone knows that the prison system is failing more that it's succeeding, in other words, inmates come back at a greater rate than they stay out – [and] if we can say to these people – the normal ordinary responsible person – through Jesus Christ this person, this convict, can stay out of prison and live a fruitful life because of his relationship with the Lord, then think what that relationship must be able to do for you. That's InnerChange. That's the hope that comes from it and *that's the purpose of it*.
>
> (emphasis added)

This immediately brings us to what IFI identifies as its unique 'selling point' compared to other faith-based units in prison. Cowley claims IFI is:

a witness to the world. It's not to help the Warden run a better prison – fine, I can do that with the 'God-pods'. It's not in order that a Jewish inmate may understand his Christian brother – we can do that with Horizon. It's to impact, to *evangelize to the world*.

(ibid.; emphasis added)

To that extent, IFI 'offer[s] hope and support to people that aren't in prison' (*ibid.*).

Griffin (2000) describes IFI as 'a Bible college preparing evangelists for the free world'. Cowley agrees: 'We use our guys' testimony a lot, and we want them to stand up. I always told them: 'In five years, when we've got 2,000 people out…I'd like to take all the graduates to the Capitol and say "Look what God has done"' (2004). Likewise, Dautrich (2003) is willing to characterize IFI in Griffin's terms:

> We want the men to be back, productive in their communities … being involved in their nurturing church … Now we're not telling the men to go out and they need to be preachers and they need to do this and that. But they need to go back in and be an example in their community.

It goes without saying that before 'evangelized prisoners' can be a 'witness to the world', they must abstain from offending behaviour. This brings us, then, to the third of IFI's 'primary' goals: reducing reoffending. Allied with this is a concern to provide effective aftercare because this helps to reduce recidivism (Loucks 2004). Cowley asserts: 'Aftercare is the *purpose* for InnerChange' (2004; emphasis original). All IFI programmes are commendably intentional about this: 'aftercare is not an afterthought' (*ibid.*). Dautrich (2003) states: 'we are looking at aftercare from day one'. Upon release IFI offers its graduates a continuing relationship with a mentor, a church and help, if needed, to find a job and housing. Since nearly all of IFI's aftercare is provided by its graduates and by volunteers in local churches, this goal too is inseparable from its wider goal of evangelism.

Two brief remarks may be made regarding IFI's stated goals. The first is that several of its goals (prisoner evangelism, reduced recidivism and successful aftercare) are instrumental in nature. Thus creating a more decent and humane environment in prison, for example, is not valued as an end in itself.[2] The second is that although IFI's *raison d'être* is evangelism, the prime (if not sole) measure of its success is recidivism. The connection between success in evangelism and success in recidivism is that recidivism is seen as 'a by-product of transformed lives. It just so happens that as men mature as Christians, their desires and goals change. Men that complete the programme believe that they can be productive and law-abiding citizens. They pursue that as part of their Christianity' (Byrne 2004). Of course, lower reoffence rates are an important issue for faith-based units around the world, especially those with State funding. However it should be noted that IFI has chosen to invest this issue with far greater significance than other faith-based units. This means we should expect the question of reconviction figures and their interpretation to be an unusually sensitive issue for IFI. This is in fact what we do find (see Chapter 10).

3. Ethos

IFI has a detailed description and rationale of its operations. It describes itself as a '24-hour-a-day, 7-day-a-week,...revolutionary, Christ-centred, Bible-based prison programme' (www.ifiprison.org/channelroot/home/about.htm; accessed 5 April 2005). This 'mission statement' embodies three aspects of IFI's ethos: that it is challenging, overtly Christian and 'Biblical' in emphasis. Each aspect is reflected in comments made by senior IFI personnel. First, its challenging nature: the staff team evaluates prisoner progress once a quarter, and prisoners who are not 'shaping up' are 'shipped out'. Dautrich (2003) candidly explains: '[If] we feel like that [the] person is stagnant, is just kind of, we call "floaters" or just not doing anything, he may be coming to class, he may be going to everything, but just is not grasping what we are trying to teach them, we'll remove that person from the programme.' Byrne (2003) concedes the programme 'can be gruelling...[for] some men that don't have much educational background, [who are] not used to a classroom setting, not used to staying organized and keeping up on their homework'.

Second, its overtly Christian content: 'InnerChange is expressly Christian. *Expressly Christian.* [It] will not be anything else' (Cowley 2004; emphasis original). Third is its Biblical emphasis, which introduces a distinction between 'Biblical' and 'secular' aspects of the programme. The 're-entry' phase at IFI-Texas, for example, is characterized by what Dautrich (2003) describes as 'secular portions, [i.e. prisoners] getting their driver's licence...[learning about] budgeting...those types of things'. Somewhat apologetically Dautrich claims that at this point 'we have gotten away a little bit from the Biblical foundations or the principles in the Bible...the Biblical principles are still there but we are not so much opening up the Bible and going verse-to-verse-to-verse.' This distinction may be of some practical importance. Due to the constitutional separation of Church and State in the US, IFI is permitted to receive State funding for 'non-sectarian' components of the programme but not 'sectarian' components (Cowley 2004). But the distinction may also reflect a perception within IFI that 'less Biblical' elements are of less worth or less value or less effective than those that are clearly 'Biblical' (*ibid.*). Byrne (2003) suggests IFI's 'Biblical' emphasis may be a cultural phenomenon that reflects IFI's origins in the Texan 'Bible belt':

> [T]he volunteers that we recruit tend to be the people in the Midwest and the 'Bible belt' and the people that seem to be attracted seem to be the evangelicals from the churches…. And so I think in a lot of ways the IFI programme is really reflective of the culture.

If so, one might expect the IFI initiative planned for 2005 in HMP Dartmoor, England to show some significant cultural adaptations.

For some both inside and outside prison, the 'culture' that IFI appears to reflect is a cause for concern. Cowley (2004) acknowledges that:

> [The programme] scares people, because – I don't really know why. I think it's gotten mixed up with this Religious Right movement and very conservative, hateful, mean-spirited, sort of: 'We're Christians and if you don't like it, by God we're gonna…' – you know, the whole Crusades thing. But we really did model, try to daily, that Jesus is love. And if a person wasn't ready to accept it, then he should leave
>
> (IFI)

IFI claims to differ from non-religious units by supporting prisoners through 'spiritual and moral transformation' (Brandt 1998: 2). Naturally, the strength of this claim depends on what is meant by 'spiritual and moral transformation': it is not hard to imagine that non-religious units could also claim to share this general aspiration. A clear distinction, however, emerges in the following seminal statement. Brandt claims that:

> [IFI] seeks to 'cure' prisoners by identifying sin as the root of their problems. Inmates learn how God can heal them permanently, if they turn from their sinful past, are willing to see the world through God's eyes, and surrender themselves to God's will. IFI directs members to God as the source of love and inner healing. Members then build on this relationship to recast human relationships built on Biblical insights
>
> (*ibid.*).

247

Hunt (2002: 2) quotes one prisoner at IFI-Kansas who internalized the Brandt approach as follows: 'IFI's curriculum takes the emphasis off of your past upbringing, life experiences or chemical imbalances and puts it directly on you'. IFI claims that this is what makes their programme unique. 'No other programme deals with the issues of the heart, moral convictions or Biblical truths that are addressed in IFI' (*ibid.*: 1). Colson is more blunt: 'InnerChange will show that one can solve the problems of crime through the change of the human heart' (Kershaw 1999: 29). This takes us back, once again, to IFI's purposes of evangelism to prisoners, evangelism to the world and demonstrating lower recidivism. Brandt's statement illuminates the link between IFI's ethos and its goals.

IFI Programme Managers appear to follow the Brandt approach closely. The Director of IFI-Texas remarks: 'I really believe that statement [by Brandt].... I hear all the excuses of why they [prisoners] came to prison and as we relate to them... the bottom line [is] that it was sin in their life. I mean they were turned away from God. Their backs were to Him, they were in the dark' (Dautrich 2003). This perspective also extends to senior prison management where IFI operates. Kershaw (1999: 32) notes:

> The Head Warder [No. 1 Governor] of the Jester prison system... is frank about the evangelical nature of InnerChange. Of course, he agrees, the programme is predominantly about claiming new followers to Christ – that's the whole point. Without Christ, there can be no transformation from sinner to saint.

Translating this ethos into a workable programme proved difficult, however. The first IFI facility (IFI-Texas) hit problems, and the Executive Director of Kairos Prison Ministry (KPM), Ike Griffin, was called upon to visit the unit several times to help. From Griffin's perspective much time appeared to be spent recruiting local churches and inviting them to 'minister' to prisoners. Perhaps inevitably this resulted in a schedule that reflected what the local churches liked doing (preaching 'evangelistic' sermons) in response to their perceptions of prisoners' needs (mainly personal 'salvation'). 'They filled the day with presentations [by churches].... Prisoners were asked time and again, such questions as: "Are you saved? Are you ready for Judgement Day? How do you stand with Jesus?"' (Griffin 2000). There were also difficulties with trying to 'build community' among pre-release prisoners (who already have their attention elsewhere) and a very high population turnover.

Following these early difficulties Cowley – a retired prison Warden from Oklahoma DoC – was brought in as National Operations Director of IFI and 'got InnerChange on track' (Griffin 2000). Cowley had 30 years' experience of running prisons and a progressive reputation. On arriving in Texas, Cowley 'changed almost all of it [the programme]...They had wonderful manuals. I mean, it was very polished, it was very *pretty*, it was very wordy, but there wasn't a lot of substance in the way the programme was being delivered' (2004; emphasis original). It appears that IFI had not really thought through what social mechanisms needed to be in place if the programme were to achieve the goals that had been set for it. As Cowley (*ibid.*) points out: 'Just because it's written [in the manuals] doesn't mean that it's happening'. As a result of Cowley's reforms, IFI 'changed their approach to a more orchestrated curriculum that didn't beat prisoners over the head with religion' (Griffin 2000).[3] Cowley saw IFI as an opportunity to experiment with total institutionalization around faith-based principles:

> Prisons can only be effective as long as environments are created within the walls which replicate the street and allow the men to practise. Traditionally, corrections create environments within prison which are total institutions devoid of really any culture from society in which one would learn how to live when released. InnerChange, as it was explained to me, was an opportunity to use faith-based principles to create environments within the prison to practise those skills which inmates lack, and combine them with mentors and associations with congregations to enable aftercare, which is really the secret to rehabilitation. It was what I always wanted to do – to experiment to see if prisons could in fact work – and 'work' means people leave better than when they came, and not return. And Prison Fellowship had the financial stability in order to pull all of that off.
>
> (2004)

We may question whether the use of churches and Christian volunteers approximates to 'life on the street' for many prisoners. Griffin (2000), for example, comments: 'If you asked [IFI] what their plans are for release, it would have something to do with churches'. Indeed very often prisoners' skills are assessed in terms of their potential benefits to the local church. Byrne (2003) comments: '[E]very kind of gifting that you can imagine is represented in the group of men in an IFI programme. There are guys that are capable of teaching, there are some men that are going to go back to their communities and be leaders in their church, who are going to teach bible studies, there are men that are called to preach.' The problem, according to Griffin (2000), is that 'you then find that the churches don't want them. You have to prepare [prisoners] for what their world will be like'.

249

To sum up, IFI sees itself as different to other units because of its focus on 'Christ-centred' evangelism, Bible study, aftercare, involvement of churches and volunteers and the replication of 'life on the street' in prison. We now turn to consider the implementation of this ethos in three US institutions.

4. IFI Institutions

We begin by briefly outlining the work of IFI in three institutions in the US. These are the Carol Vance Unit, Texas, Newton Correctional Institution, Iowa and Ellsworth Correctional Facility, Kansas. This section draws on recorded interviews with IFI Programme Managers for each of these institutions. A fourth IFI unit opened in 2002 at Lino Lakes Correctional Facility, Minnesota.

(a) Carol Vance Unit, Houston, Texas

IFI-Texas is located at the Carol Vance Unit (formerly known as the Jester II Correctional Unit) near Houston, Texas. It opened in cell-blocks with 26 men in April 1997 and is currently on its twenty-third intake of prisoners. The programme has a throughput of 170 men per session, and 450 have been released so far (Prison Fellowship International Convocation 2003). Colson (2003a) claims that there is 'nothing else like it anywhere in the world' which is an overstatement given IFI's claimed affinity with APAC (see above). Others have described it as 'the most radical experiment in right-wing social policy ever conducted inside a US prison' and characterized it as a return to 'Christian reformism' (Kershaw 1999: 29). The following draws on a recorded interview with Phillip Dautrich, Programme Manager at IFI-Texas (2000 – 2004) in August 2003. Dautrich left IFI-Texas in 2004 to become IFI Director for the UK.

Houston was chosen for IFI-Texas because of the large number of offenders (at least 17,000) due to be released on parole into surrounding counties. To apply, prisoners must be 'minimum-risk' males in the last two years of their sentence and scheduled for release to Harris County, although the programme has recently been extended to include prisoners who will return to the Dallas/Fort Worth area. IFI takes all prisoners except sex offenders. This restriction was part of the local agreement, because the Carol Vance unit is unable to offer appropriate protection for sex offenders and also because the TDCJ already runs a sex offender treatment programme in Texas. Prisoners apply from any of 115 correctional institutions in Texas.

Kershaw (1999: 29) puts the matter too strongly when he claims prisoners 'must be willing to be converted to the word of God'. IFI-Texas participants do not have to be Christians, but 'they must be willing to productively participate in a programme that is explicitly Christian in both content and delivery' (www.ifiprison.org/channelroot/home/aboutfaqs.htm; accessed 5 April 2005). It is also stated that prisoners who practise other faiths are able to participate in this programme, provided, again, they are 'willing to actively participate in a Christ-centred, Biblically-based programme' (*ibid.*).

Recruitment occurs via the TDCJ Programmes and Services and the Chaplaincy department within Texas. Interested prisoners examine an IFI orientation booklet at their assigned unit, and the prison Chaplain decides whether to recommend the prisoner. This means IFI is highly dependent on prison Chaplains making an accurate assessment when choosing to refer. It also means that IFI may risk drawing upon a population of 'chapel boys' or, at the other extreme, troublesome prisoners whom Chaplains would rather lose. Although IFI is in principle open to prisoners from any or no religion, one might expect the Chaplaincy's prominent role in recruitment to slant the intake in favour of professing Christians. Chaplains inevitably tend to have more limited contact with secular populations, especially when the size of the units from which IFI participants transfer (e.g. Allred Unit, Texas) can be as large as 3,600 men. Consistent with this, the proportion of prisoners on IFI from non-Christian faiths has always been small, and the proportion of Muslims taking part is said to be under ten per cent (Dautrich 2003). Even this number is artificially inflated because, in Dautrich's view, the Muslims who have taken part in IFI are 'lapsed Christians':

> The real true Muslims that come there [to IFI] will leave within the first 60 days because they realize that what we are teaching, which is the Bible, goes against everything that they are studying in the Muslim faith. So they will be very honest and they will come to me and they will say, 'Phillip, this isn't for me'. And I give them a couple of days to really think about that before just removing them and if they come back that second or third time we'll send them back to their units.
>
> (*ibid.*)

Recommended prisoners are sent to the unit, whereupon IFI staff conduct a 30-day orientation. This thorough approach to informed consent ensures prisoners understand what is going to happen in the next 18 months. 'Obviously some of them could have just went through [the application form] and filled in the blanks and turned it in. [But] when they get to the programme again, we go A to Z back through what they are expected to do, and at any time they can leave' (*ibid.*). Some claim IFI-Texas is manipulative. For example Kershaw (1999: 30) claims that: 'From dawn to dusk the inmates are manipulated in a relentless process that seems, to the sceptical outsider, to resemble cult-like brainwashing'. This criticism overlooks the fact that prisoners volunteer for the programme, receive detailed information and can leave at any time without penalty.

The selection criteria for IFI applicants is set out in the FAQs of the official IFI website (www.ifiprison.org/channelroot/home/aboutfaqs. htm; accessed 5 April 2005). Dautrich works closely with Programmes and Services (a division of TDCJ) to screen potential participants. First, prisoners must volunteer and be fully aware of the programme's requirements. Second, prisoners must be between 18 and 24 months of their release or parole date, with the exception of selected long-termers. If paroling to Texas they must plan to live in Harris County or surrounding counties: if paroling to other states, they must be released to that state. Considerable care is taken to check the local parole address is valid. This is because some prisoners (e.g. those from North Texas) may falsely claim a local parole address to join IFI and thus receive more visits from friends and family in Houston. Checks are also needed to ensure IFI resources are targeted on local prisoners who can take full advantage of IFI's aftercare. A third criterion is that prisoners must be functionally literate (fourth or fifth grade reading level – equivalent to age 9 or 10) due to the amount of 'homework' given. Fourth, prisoners must have no enemies at the facility site. Fifth, prisoners must not be subject to disciplinary cases within six months of their enrolment to the programme. Finally, and perhaps most importantly, is the prisoner's desire for personal change. The latter two criteria might suggest a tendency towards more compliant prisoners.

The orientation phase allows IFI staff to examine the prisoner's motives and discern 'whether or not the guy really, really wants to be there' (Dautrich 2003). Dautrich claims to be suspicious of what he calls 'the IFI answer [i.e.] "Oh, I love Jesus and praise God, you know". We get some guys that are like that and they are not genuine. We are looking for men that are genuine...that are searching for hope.' This process of selection ensures the programme favours those prisoners most motivated to succeed. Selection is made on the basis of interview:

> We ask [prisoners] why did you come here? Now one of the things I tell the men is that I want their honesty. If a guy comes in and tells me: 'Hey, I am here to get closer to home', if he is honest with me up front I can accept that. Because I know in the end at least

he is honest and he is going to have an open heart to let the Holy
Spirit begin to touch it...
[Interviewer] If somebody said that would you still take them on?
Oh definitely, and I get that answer a lot.

(*ibid.*)

The programme consists of three phases. Phase One lasts 12 months
and emphasizes education, work assignments and 'Biblically-based
life-skills that lay a foundation for Christian growth.' Beginning with
a basic introduction to Christianity called Survival Kit, it moves on to
Brandt's Biblical studies programme which identifies 'sin as the root of
their problem. That is another great class that the offenders really enjoy'
(*ibid.*).[4] Prisoners then move onto the Experiencing God and Search For
Significance programmes to deepen 'their walk with Jesus' (*ibid.*). Phase
Two, 're-entry', lasts for six months and includes community projects,
such as Houston Habitat (building houses for low-income families). Men
with sentences longer than 18 months remain in the programme and are
regarded by IFI staff as 'quasi-staff' who can mentor other prisoners and
begin to lead small groups.

A core element is working with prisoners' families and children.
Prisoners take part in a 'Marriage Without Regret Course' in which
prisoners' families enter the prison once a week to participate. Phase
Three ('aftercare') begins upon parole and consists of regular meetings
with Christian mentors and support groups. The goal is to help offenders
reconnect with their families and communities. This phase lasts for nine
months, although IFI states that true 'aftercare' lasts for a lifetime.

When asked whether IFI-Texas worked its prisoners too hard, Dautrich
(2003) concedes the programme has its casualties:

There is going to be men for example [who] don't have their High
School Diploma or GED, it's tough on them. They get up at 5a.m.,
they go to breakfast, devotion, half the day they are in GED classes,
the other half they are in InnerChange classes, they have about an
hour and a half to two hours to eat, to shower, to do their homework
for the night and then go to evening classes. It's tough, but that is
the choice they made. I've got to get up every morning, I have got
three children, there is not a whole lot of difference.

The question is whether this leads to resentment among prisoners who
perhaps are committed to the programme but who struggle with its
demands. Dautrich states that deciding to remove a prisoner from the
programme is 'one of the hardest things I have to do' but maintains that
this is in the prisoner's best interests:

In one of my days of prayer … God said, 'You know what, I am not just here in this unit [laughter] I am everywhere'. And that is so true and a lot of times [removal] is the best thing that happens to that particular offender. Because he gets in a rut and he gets stagnant and a lot of times it takes to go to the lowest of the low for that particular offender to break, to get them to their breaking point. So removing them from the programme, really, we've probably been enabling that person. So we remove them, they go to another unit, they get a lockdown for a couple of days, and it gives them a lot of time to think. Nine out of ten guys that are removed from the programme, when they get released, Tommie Dorsett [IFI-Texas Director] or myself or one of the counsellors will get a phone call from them saying 'Thank you'. Which totally surprised us, but they thank us because they say: 'You know what I really realize [is] that I had to start leaning on Jesus, instead of start leaning on you or one of the counsellors to solve all of my problems'. So that time alone, they begin to do a lot of reflection, a lot of prayer, and they realize that they had to step it up a notch. So there is no resentment. There may be some resentment at the beginning because obviously no one wants to leave when they are there. But it is an amazing thing, I mean nine times out of ten I get that phone call back just saying: 'Thank you for removing me'.

(*ibid.*)

IFI-Texas has unique rules that contrast with the rest of the establishment. These include a ban on television, except for news. Dautrich claims this removes a potential source of 'negativity' and makes the dorm quieter. There is also a ban on pornography. A complete search for sexually explicit material is made of prisoners' effects upon arrival. Prisoners are removed if pornography is discovered, following an initial 'grace period'. This contrasts with the rest of the prison where certain pornography is allowed. Prisoners can also be removed from the IFI programme if they have more than three unexcused absences from class per quarter. Removal is also automatic for inappropriate relations or confrontations with volunteers ('talking back to a volunteer … is kind of a cardinal sin'; *ibid.*). The DoC will remove prisoners if they are the subject of a disciplinary case (e.g. fighting, use of tobacco).

Each IFI programme is said to provide hundreds of volunteer opportunities. Roles include Clerical assistants, Volunteer Assistant Chaplains, Small-Group Facilitators, Coordinators to identify and recruit local churches, Aftercare Coordinators, Mentors, Tutors (to help prisoners work towards their GED certificates or develop computer related skills),

Residential Biblical Counsellors, Artist Facilitators and Family Support Group Facilitators who hold regular support groups for prisoner's families (www.ifiprison.org/channelroot/home/aboutprogramme.htm; accessed 5 April 2005). Volunteers are recruited directly by IFI staff from local churches and indirectly through other ministries. All volunteers complete a thorough State and IFI-developed screening process. Screened applicants are required to complete a minimum of eight hours' Prison Fellowship and State training before being certified as an IFI volunteer. An additional two hours' basic training in the IFI programme is required for those assigned to advanced or highly specialized volunteer rules such as instructor or mentor (*ibid.*).

Despite this volunteer engagement, IFI is highly staff-intensive. There are 11 paid staff at the Carol Vance unit, including a Director, Programme Manager, Aftercare Manager, Office Administrator, Aftercare Assistant, five Biblical counsellors and one part-time staff Community Coordinator. Operational costs are considerable. It cost an estimated one million dollars to begin IFI in Texas and $400,000 a year to sustain a seven-person IFI team (Griffin 2000). Numerically, IFI-Texas has been highly popular. In 1997 IFI-Texas began with 26 prisoners; a small proportion of the general non-IFI population. By March 2004, IFI-Texas had expanded to include the entire population of 340 prisoners and the unit is now a mixture of open dormitories and cell-blocks. All prisoners on the Carol Vance unit are now IFI participants.

(b) Newton Correctional Facility, Iowa

Following its experience in Houston, PF decided against opening any further units in pre-release centres (Griffin 2000). Accordingly the second IFI unit to open was at Newton Correctional Facility, a medium to maximum-security prison in Newton, Iowa on 1st October, 1999. Once prisoners have completed the 'in-prison' part of the programme, they move to a transitional 'half-way house' prior to going home (www. ifiprison.org/channelroot/home/statesiowa.htm; accessed 5 April 2005). This section draws on a recorded interview with Sam Dye, Programme Director of IFI-Iowa in August 2003.

Newton IFI arose when former state legislator and former parole board member Chuck Hurley heard of the Carol Vance unit in Houston and recommended IFI to his contacts within the Correctional Department and the State Government. Unlike Texas, Iowa did not have a Governor championing faith-based initiatives as part of his personal vision. However, Iowa did have a Director of Corrections, Kip Kowsky, whose path had crossed Colson's and who was thus sympathetic to faith-based initiatives in general and to PF in particular. According to Dye (2003), members of the Correctional Department visited the Carol Vance unit and 'saw that there was promise. Obviously Iowa was like any other state, they had recidivism problems and really IFI is a programme that tells the State: "We will help you reduce your recidivism through our programme" and we [will] do it through a transformational philosophy.' Once again, the pitch was entirely based on the promise of reduced recidivism.

The Iowa DoC decided where IFI could open. Newton was selected because of its central location and proximity to the Des Moines area, the capital of Iowa. Dye (*ibid.*) maintains Newton was a good choice because of its proximity to a large population of potential volunteers and because the Warden at Newton was 'very open for IFI to come'. On the other hand, Newton was a new facility that had been open for only two years. It had few existing PF volunteers in contrast to other prisons in the state. Introducing IFI to a new prison was not thought to have any advantages over introducing it to an established one. Dye explained: 'when IFI comes into a prison it is a totally different culture that you are trying to put in…so you are always going to have the hurdles.' Despite its religious basis, IFI staff claim others in the prison see their programme as a 'treatment' programme and not an 'add-on' to the Chaplaincy. This, they claim, provides greater scope for 'peer relationships with correctional people…. [Y]ou are a core piece of what is going on in the prison, therefore you have greater access, you have greater influence' (*ibid.*).

Newton C.F. has five cell-blocks (A–E), with the IFI unit located in unit E, previously the prison Honour Dorm. The IFI cell-block is a slightly softened version of the Honour Dorm with wooden instead of steel cell doors. Prisoners are held in three-man cells, and each prisoner has the key to his cell. The use of three-man cells instead of dorms is not seen as a hindrance to building community on the grounds that 'they are just there to sleep…[apart from that] they are together all the time' (*ibid.*).

IFI-Iowa recruits by means of advertisements in Iowa prisons, followed up by IFI staff visits. Prisoners are told that it is a Christian programme, but there is no faith requirement. Several Muslim prisoners and one Buddhist prisoner has attended IFI-Iowa which suggests an extremely low proportion of non-Christian faiths participating in the programme. Dye (*ibid.*) states that most prisoners who take part have no particular faith. Prisoners apply from any prison in Iowa. IFI staff travel to interview interested prisoners, as any prison in Iowa is within three hours of Newton. As in other IFI units, the key selection criteria is whether the prisoner wants to change. Prisoners who appear to satisfy this requirement attend an introductory six-hour class where they complete a workbook and are given full details of the programme. If they complete the introductory class satisfactorily, they are placed on a contact list. At any one time, IFI-Iowa has 50–75 prisoners who have completed the introductory list and are waiting to be transferred. DoC criteria require that prisoners are medium-security with no recent assault history.

When prisoners arrive, they take part in a 30-day orientation phase. This provides abundant opportunity for informed consent as the programme is explained in detail:

> We explain our philosophy that the only true lasting change is a change of the heart and we believe that God can put new hearts within us. We go through a basic gospel message, that sin is the issue and we will help you deal with that. At the same time we tell guys: 'You don't have to be a Christian to come but you have to realize that's what you are going to hear'.
>
> (*ibid.*)

Prisoners then sign a contract to become an IFI member. IFI prisoners forego the right to in-cell television. Prisoners can leave at any time without penalty and are transferred back to their previous prison.

For Dye (*ibid.*) the 'correct' incentive to join IFI-Iowa is that prisoners 'have hit bottom and they are willing to give God a chance to change their lives'. However, they recognize that prisoners may have other incentives such as the desire to move to a newer facility or be closer to their families. A disincentive to joining the IFI cell-block from within Newton is the perception in other parts of the prison that it is the 'God pod', so prisoners switching from the general population to IFI can be harassed by former acquaintances.

The IFI-Iowa schedule is highly structured, beginning at 6a.m. and running to 8:30p.m., Monday to Friday. Each prisoner is required to have a job, so in addition to their daily work at the prison, prisoners have five hours of IFI programming per day. Prisoners have a one-hour community meeting and two hours of class daily with their IFI counsellor. The 12-month course is divided into four quarters, each of which is taken by a different IFI counsellor. They also have an additional two hours of evening curriculum delivered by trained volunteers. IFI prisoners are not exempt from regular prison activities, with the result that they have much less free time than non-IFI prisoners.

IFI-Iowa claims that it has recruited and trained over 700 volunteers in Iowa to work with its prisoners. Around 100 volunteers come in per week. Some volunteers lead evening groups, and as many as 40 to 50 volunteers provide one-to-one mentoring during a 'mentor's evening'. Bearing in mind that Newton was a new facility with few existing PF volunteers, this is a remarkable achievement. IFI staff were assiduous in making presentations to churches across the state in the central Iowa area. Dye claims that volunteers are themselves the best recruiters, assisted by IFI graduates; 'Once you come into the prison and you see it, they get won over pretty quick' (*ibid.*). Again, volunteers are crucial. When IFI participants are asked by, for example, State legislators:

> 'What has changed you?'... the overriding thing that happens – and we don't coach them at all, we don't know what they are going to say – [they say] 'I was loved'....[T]he volunteers are the ones that bring that.
>
> (*ibid.*)

The regime is structured to foster relationships between prisoners and volunteers in a number of ways. First, volunteers are allowed to meet prisoners in their living area (the cell-block) and, second, they are allowed to maintain correspondence. This is exceptional: neither practice is allowed on regular prison cell-blocks. Around 60–70 per cent of prisoners are released to central Iowa with the remainder living in outlying areas. Local mentors support prisoners during their time in prison; that mentorship is then transferred to a different area of the State. The new mentor usually visits the prisoner prior to release.

Dye (*ibid.*) concedes that initially non-IFI prison staff perceived IFI-Iowa negatively but claims this has now changed: 'I think a lot of the correctional staff had some fears that we were green, we were not correctional people, we'd be conned, they'd play games with us. After being there three-and-a-half years, they see a great difference in the IFI guys. In fact the unit managers always want our guys to come to their dorm when they are done with IFI because they have such a stabilizing influence on the rest of the population.' Thirty IFI graduates with further time on their sentence to serve are transferred to Rockwell City, a minimum-security prison. It is said that staff at this prison claim that IFI graduates have had a calming influence resulting in fewer disciplinary incidents.

Americans United for the Separation of Church and State has sued Prison Fellowship, IFI and the State of Iowa for violating Church–State separation because it claims that IFI-Iowa accepts State funds to run a Christian unit (Colson 2003b). IFI, however, claims it does not violate the Establishment Clause of the First Amendment to the American Constitution because federal law allows a state to include religious organizations as social service providers. IFI claims it uses 'state monies solely for non-sectarian expenses while private funds are used for all-religious programming' (Earley 2003: 3). Cowley claims that opposition to IFI is really opposition to President George W. Bush's support for faith-based initiatives.[5] 'When Bush started running for President he started talking faith-based initiatives. And then all of a sudden it became very political. And that was really the impetus for the lawsuit in Iowa, [it] was actually Bush's Presidential career. And they'll do anything to discredit that programme' (Cowley 2004). For detractors of faith-based programmes in the US, IFI is an example of faith-based activities that: 'lack constitutional foundation (e.g. prayer and proselytizing) and have become graphic representations of the need to separate Church and State, particularly in cases involving Government funding' (Caliber Associates 2004b: 2). Setting American constitutional anxieties and domestic politics to one side, there is an obvious and non-culturally specific lesson. Faith-based units that benefit (in some measure) from public funds may gain greater credibility and financial stability, but they also invite increased public accountability, scrutiny and criticism.

(c) Ellsworth Correctional Facility, Kansas

The third IFI unit opened in 2002 at Ellsworth Correctional Facility (ECF), a medium-security facility in Ellsworth, Kansas. This section draws on a recorded interview with John Byrne, IFI-Kansas Programme Manager, conducted in August 2003.

The motivation for setting up IFI-Kansas again came from the State DoC. Management from Kansas DoC visited IFI-Texas and were attracted to the Houston model. The selection procedure for IFI-Kansas is very similar to other IFI units. Presentations are made to catchment prisons, and interested prisoners sign up for a six-week orientation Bible study led by a volunteer. Following this, IFI staff travel to Kansas prisons to explain the content of the programme in detail before transfer. The most important issues for them to understand, according to Byrne (2003) is that the programme will not affect the date of their release and that IFI is based on accountability. Prisoners are also told that 'the modality of our treatment is Biblical transformation … and so they are very aware that the teaching will come from a scripture or Biblical perspective' (*ibid.*). In determining who is admitted, the Director draws on the recommendation of the volunteer leading the Bible study together with whether the applicant is 'really desiring change in their life' (*ibid.*).

Feedback on performance during the orientation session is probably a good indicator of likely success on the IFI programme inasmuch as both the orientation session and the IFI programme are heavily geared towards

Bible teaching. Notably, Byrne (*ibid.*) avers that IFI-Kansas appeals more to prisoners who have been in prison more than once because '[they] have a lot of fear about getting out again and know that it is not so easy to make it'.

Byrne (*ibid.*) rejects criticisms that IFI makes excessive demands upon its participants: 'I don't believe that they work hard actually at all, no harder than other inmates…Men that aren't in IFI are also mandated to do other programming [including] substance abuse [and] education…. Every once in a while I hear that some guy quit because the schedule is tough but I don't think that there are many men that quit because of that.' Weekends are free, except for the Sunday morning chapel service.

Byrne confirms the importance of the volunteers to IFI-Kansas and highlights the reciprocal dynamic they engender:

> [T]here is a lot of love that the men in the programme have in appreciation for the people coming in from the outside so I think the volunteers that come in really get overwhelmed [by] how appreciative that the men are. And so that is another aspect of it…to go into an environment and have people so thankful and humble and appreciative [of] your willingness to give your time. And the sense [that] you would think that they are worthy, or you would think that they were valuable enough to take time away from your family. That really gets communicated to the volunteers.
>
> (*ibid.*)

In this way prisoners impact on volunteers just as volunteers affect prisoners. The impact is 'the excitement of seeing what God is doing but also the transformation for the volunteer in being in that environment… [M]any of the volunteers have been impacted by crime and so there is some healing for them as well too' (*ibid.*).

5. General themes

Having considered the operation of IFI in each establishment we turn to consider some general themes.

(a) Role of volunteers

One of the goals of IFI is to make the prison an environment where prisoners can practise pro-social values. Introducing volunteers is said to be key to this. However this led to conflict with those, including prison staff and management, who preferred no change to the prison culture:

They [Jester II] were still running it [IFI-Texas] like a prison. The [prison office] staff was still using profanities....They were still expecting our guys to act like convicts. There was still a closed environment inside the prison....The State liked to point to this innovative programme but when it came right down to day-to-day functions, our guys were still being treated still under the same rules as the general population. In my opinion we were not getting as much out of the programme as was possible because we were still involved in the old convict mentality. So what I wanted to do was totally, as much as possible, push the envelope to again create an environment within that prison that was as much like the street as possible.

(Cowley 2004)

Initially volunteers had to remain with prison staff at all times. By contrast, Cowley:

wanted volunteers to have free rein in that prison. I wanted the mentors to come in any time they wanted to come in. I wanted inmates to stop being strip-searched where visitors could see them. Every time our guys would come in from the fields or from programmes outside of the prison, they were strip-searched right at the gate, in view of everyone, and I said: 'This is *not* the way it's gonna be'.

(*ibid.*, emphasis original)

It took months of perseverance for the institution to cooperate in changing the use of 'institutional space'. Some IFI institutions had difficulty with the very idea that volunteers could be admitted in large numbers:

When we had our grand opening, I told [the Warden] that I wanted the prison opened up to all the visitors, and they just had a fit: 'Oh my God, we can't have street people coming inside the prison'. And I had to go directly to the Director of Corrections, and we had over 500 people inside the prison, which was a first.

(*ibid.*)

Another issue was the Texas DoCJ's prohibition on volunteers of either gender 'hugging' prisoners. 'And I said: "You'd better figure out a way they can do it, because we're going to be breaking policy every day, because we hug inmates"' (*ibid.*). After four hours of discussion a compromise was reached: male volunteers were permitted 'full-frontal hugs' and women were permitted 'side manoeuvres'. Of greater importance was State opposition to how IFI wished to use its volunteers in aftercare. IFI wanted volunteers to acquaint themselves with prisoners for a year as mentors, then to develop that relationship when prisoners were released on probation. However the Department of Criminal Justice said institutional volunteers could not be probation volunteers. IFI regarded the issue as a 'deal-breaker' and threatened to pull out of the facility, whereupon the DoCJ relented.

(b) Role of prisoners

IFI is said to stress accountability. On assignment to the unit each prisoner is given two mentors, one from outside and the other an experienced IFI prisoner. Byrne (2003) claims that peer accountability is 'a whole new mindset for inmates [because] the prison code is essentially "one inmate doesn't tell another inmate how they should live their lives"'. Use is also made of ex-offenders. At IFI-Texas the 'Brother's Keepers' programme allows prisoners who have been released for six months or more to make a one-time visit to the unit as volunteers to encourage IFI participants. After a two-year period they are allowed to return as full-time volunteers if they have a good report from the parole office and letters of recommendation from the pastor of their church and the unit chaplain. At present five prisoners volunteer in this capacity. Initially the State of Texas would not allow this: no prison in Texas permits ex-offenders, after any period, to return to the unit from which they were released. Again, Cowley identified this as a 'deal-breaker' that would result in IFI withdrawing from the prison (Cowley 2004). After 18 months of negotiation permission was finally granted, though the arrangement is unique to IFI-Texas.

(c) Relationship between the unit and Kairos Weekend

As noted above Ike Griffin, then Executive Director of Kairos Prison Ministry, was active with the PF team that established IFI-Texas. Kairos was, from the start, established as the introductory, community-building entry for IFI. Cowley saw Kairos and the Kairos Weekend as an integral part of the IFI programme. According to Griffin (1998), Cowley said at a Kairos Weekend closing ceremony in March 1998 that Kairos was 'the most important ingredient of the project and that it was the only loving visible in what had [by 1998] turned into a very hard-edged and cold project'. A Kairos Weekend is run at IFI-Texas every quarter. Griffin (2003) claims 'they [IFI] do that because they see Kairos as the best method of bringing people into a cocoon of love and acceptance'. KPM established

Kairos Outside at Houston specifically to support the IFI programme and unusually large Weekends are run there for the women of IFI prisoners. When IFI moved to Iowa, PF sought support from Kairos, but because no Kairos ministries existed in Iowa, that ministry is not involved. IFI itself downplays the significance of Fourth Day programmes such as Cursillo and Kairos, claiming its aftercare programme provides an equivalent, if not better, experience. This claim must be treated with some scepticism: Fourth Day programmes are quite specific in terms of their content (an experiential introduction to the Christian faith) and follow-up (regular, disciplined meetings on pre-arranged spiritual topics) and hence should not be confused with generalized claims to 'aftercare'.

(d) Relationship between the unit and Chaplaincy

IFI works with the Chaplaincy in all institutions but is not answerable to it. Instead the IFI Director is answerable to the Warden and the Warden's executive team. In seeking to develop IFI in an institution, Cowley 'pretty much ignored the chaplains and went directly to the Governors through the Departments of Corrections' (2004). In nearly every case IFI's independence led to tensions with the prison Chaplaincy which sought to control it (cf. the experience of Horizon Communities in Chapter 7):

> In the beginning the Chaplains [in Iowa and Kansas] were very supportive but in the end they both left very antagonistic ... 'InnerChange', I kept telling them, 'will build your programme. You'll have more general population inmates involved in religious programming because of InnerChange'. But quite frankly, both had been there a long time, and er ...
> [Interviewer] And this was going to upset the apple cart, really, wasn't it?
> Exactly, exactly! (ibid.)

The exception was IFI-Texas where the only unit for which the Chaplain had any responsibility was IFI, which meant that he was working for InnerChange.

(e) Criteria for expansion

At least four criteria governed IFI's expansion. First, political support: 'we did not go into a State that the Governor did not support the programme' (Cowley 2004). Support from Wardens and Directors of Corrections was also a precondition, especially when the nature of the programme would test that support to its limits: 'It's one thing to say you're supportive and you love the programme, but to operationalize that after *years* of running something one way is still very, very difficult. Change in prisons takes years' (*ibid.*). A second criterion was IFI's refusal to compromise its identity: 'There are some things that are not negotiable. And that if the State is not willing…then the programme will leave. And they have to know that. And that was something that we made very, very clear' (*ibid.*). Expansion was not at any price. Third was the need to be near a large metropolitan area from which to draw volunteers. Fourth was the desire to demonstrate IFI could apply across a range of security classifications (pre-release, minimum and medium). A fifth criterion was securing co-funding from the state:

> After Texas, I wanted the State to start paying for InnerChange….I wanted faith-based programmes to be equal to other secular rehabilitative programmes within the Departments of Corrections around the country. The only respect you get is if you are taking money…you don't have the clout that you need to make the kinds of changes that needed to be made unless they're paying you something for it.
>
> (*ibid.*)

As noted earlier, because of the separation between Church and State, IFI may only obtain co-funding for the non-sectarian part of the programme.

6. Conclusions

What main conclusions can we draw from this descriptive account of IFI? It is important to acknowledge that this description is almost entirely based on the perspectives of senior IFI personnel. In some respects it resembles the perspectives of Kainos staff in the Kainos evaluation (see Chapter 5). Absent from this account are possible contrasting views from non-IFI personnel, IFI prisoners and non-IFI prisoners. This is particularly important to note with regard to a programme that is even more overtly Christian and evangelical than Kainos ever was. With this caveat in mind, we would suggest the following:

- IFI is not simply a 'faith-based' unit; it is 'Christian-based' and expressly so. Its particular focus on 'Christ-centred' evangelism marks it out as unique among all the faith-based units covered in this book.

- IFI's evangelistic goals, which may be encouraged in certain cultural contexts, raise the question of how the programme will adapt to prison environments such as the UK, where proselytizing is forbidden.

- IFI demonstrates the positive role that faith-based programmes can play in resettlement.

- IFI's early evolution suggests there are difficulties with presenting a heavily religious programme that is too reliant on presentations from local churches.

- There is a continuing need for assistance from other Christian ministries (e.g. Brothers in Blue, Kairos) that offer a complementary Christian spirituality.

- Volunteers are once again central to the popularity of faith-based programmes and their perceived effectiveness.

- Faith-based units that attract public funds gain credibility and are less expensive for the faith-based organization to run. But they also invite increased public accountability, scrutiny, and criticism.

- IFI's experience shows that the presence of a faith-based unit invariably creates tension with the prison Chaplaincy.

- Faith-based units involve positive changes to the use of institutional space. They also positively influence relationships in prison, including relationships between prisoners, prisoners and staff and between prisoners and volunteers.

- Faith-based units are thus a significant challenge to prison culture and must 'stand their ground' against institutional control.

- Faith-based units must formulate and retain a clear sense of their identity. The successful unit needs to identify those issues that would significantly compromise its individuality and be willing to withdraw from the prison over those matters if necessary.

Notes

1   No state funds were involved for Kairos-APAC either. However, unlike IFI-Texas, Kairos-APAC did attract political opposition, not least because it was keen to appear on as many different 'radar screens' as possible (see Chapter 3).
2   Cf., for example, Horizon (Chapter 7) and 'New Kainos' (Chapter 11).

3 Ottoboni (2003: 59) notes that 'another usual mistake [of faith-based units] ... is to think that religion itself is enough to prepare prisoners for their return to society'.
4 If it is the case that prisoners 'enjoy' being told this at the outset, it may suggest that IFI is 'preaching to the converted' from an early stage.
5 US President George W. Bush convened a meeting at the White House in only his second week in office with 'a diverse group of religious leaders in order to discuss "faith-based" programmes which have proven their power to save and change lives', (the President's words)' (Hunter 2001).

Chapter 9

Psycho-social impact of Kainos

The aim of Kainos is to help as many prisoners as possible to learn to love, respect and support themselves and others by a combination of community living and the Christian value of loving one's neighbour as oneself
Kainos Community Mission Statement

Introduction

This chapter and the next form the most empirical chapters in this book.[1] This chapter considers the psychological outcomes of the Kairos Weekend and Kainos Programme for participating prisoners in all four Kainos Communities that existed at the time of the research. It also assesses attitudes associated with religiosity in general and Christianity in particular. The following chapter investigates more directly the impact of Kainos Community on reconviction rates. In both cases, Kainos prisoners' attitudes and behaviour were compared to data from similar others. For the psycho-social study considered in this chapter, we drew on an individually-matched control group. For the reconviction study, recidivism data was compared to national reconviction data for those prisoners with likelihoods of reoffending most like those who participated in Kainos (Chapter 10).

This chapter was authored by Joanna Adler

This chapter concentrates on psychological and religious measures. We interviewed prisoners on two separate occasions to assess various aspects of their well-being, psychological state, attitudes towards offending behaviour and their religious perspectives. Baseline data were gathered from Kainos participants ('the research group') and non-Kainos prisoners ('the control group') at both 'Time 1' and 'Time 2'. The first occasion ('Time 1') was prior to the start of the Kainos Programme. Prisoners were interviewed before the start of the Kairos Weekend which, at the time of the research, marked the beginning of the Kainos Programme. Prisoners were then required to take part in the Kairos Weekend and the Kainos Programme to be full members of Kainos Community. It should be noted that most prisoners who took part in the Weekend were already living on the Kainos unit, some of them for several weeks or even months ahead of the Weekend itself. The second occasion ('Time 2') was two weeks following the conclusion of the four-to-six-months Kainos Programme. At both Times 1 and 2 we used a mixture of standardized measures and open-ended, additional questions. The selection and design of these materials is outlined in (Section 2) below.

1. Aims and literature

The Kairos Weekend aims to provide prisoners with an experience of 'Christ's love and forgiveness' with the goal of building strong Christian communities in prisons that will positively affect the prison environment (Kairos UK 1997). Kairos aims to target prisoners who do not necessarily have a strong religious conviction before starting the programme. In particular, Kairos aims to target 'negative leaders', typically prisoners who are in charge of gambling, drugs, gangs and extortion (see Chapter 2). The Kainos Programme aims to offer prisoners a combination of Christian teaching, cognitive behavioural techniques, an experience of community living and a general 'challenge to change'. As well as the Christian focus of the work, Kainos materials speak clearly of desires to build trust, to enhance well-being, and to encourage more pro-social and fewer pro-criminological attitudes in the prisoners who join the community. This chapter reflects how we evaluated those aims.

When we were commissioned to undertake this work, the various members of the team brought different areas of expertise to approach the problem. These included criminology, law, psychology and statistics. Despite some deep personal and professional interests in (varying) religions and indeed in religious jurisprudence, we had not much experience of measuring religious attitudes or their potential effects on personality measures. Clearly, as the intervention is both Christian and cognitive-behavioural in orientation, attitudes towards religion and personal belief were something we needed to measure. Thus when planning this study, we began by exploring the field of research into religiosity. We were at first relieved, then somewhat daunted, to find entire journals devoted to this area (e.g. the *Journal for the Scientific Study of Religion* or *Pastoral Psychology*). Also, nearly a century of work explored both religious belief itself and a host of social scientific approaches to its study (e.g. Allport 1959; Gorsuch 1988; Hester and Paloutzian 1998; King and Crowther 2004; Kwilecki 1988; Leong and Zachar 1990; Strizenec 1992). This may be scarcely surprising to some readers, though it will be news to others. We tried to select well-established and standardized scales. Where necessary, we also contacted scale authors to ascertain their likely reliability within a prison setting. We are particularly grateful to Tom Plante and John Maltby in this regard.

We thought it may be of use to interested readers for us to mention some references for the study of religion, including both those that influenced our design, and those that have been published subsequently, particularly where they reinforce our decisions to use the scales we chose. One of the founders of social psychology, the late Gordon Allport, developed a number of approaches to the study of religion, (Allport 1950). The Religious Orientation Scale (ROS) (Allport and Ross 1967) was published at the end of his career and, despite his own concerns about the need for qualitative as well as quantitative approaches to the study of religion, the ROS has been one of his most influential legacies. Many of the subsequent measures of religiosity use that scale as the starting point. Particular debates in the literature relevant to our research include:

- The respective roles of intrinsic versus extrinsic aspects of religion (e.g. Donahue 1985; Genia 1993; Gorsuch and Venable 1983; Gorsuch and McPherson 1989; Maltby 1999a, 2002; Maltby and Lewis 1996; Morris and Hood 1981).

- The roles of quest in religious orientation (e.g. Batson and Schoenrade 1991a, 1991b; Genia 1996; Williams and Faulconer 1994).

- The relationships between religion and personality (e.g. Carter, Kay and Francis 1996; Francis 1992; Francis 1993a; Francis and Bolger 1997; Francis and Bourke 2003; Francis and Pearson 1993; Francis and Wilcox 1996; Hills *et al.* 2004; Maltby 1999b; Maltby and Day 2004; Maltby and Day 2001; Maltby *et al.* 1995).

- The relationships between religious orientation and mental health (e.g. Exline, Yali and Sanderson 2000; Frenz and Carey 1989; Hackney and Sanders 2003; Jackson and Coursey 1988; James and Wells 2003;

Kunst 1999; O'Connor, Cobb and Connor 2003; Thoresen and Harris 2002; Williams and Faulconer 1994).

- The possible roles of religion in coping (e.g. Ganzevoort 1998a; Ganzevoort 1998b; Harrison *et al.* 2001; Maltby and Day 2003; Pargament, Koenig and Perez 2000; Pargament *et al.* 1992; Pargament *et al.* 1998; Siegel, Anderman and Schrimshaw 2001; Wong-McDonald and Gorsuch 2000).

- The relationships between religion and psycho-social behaviour and well-being, including to a very limited extent, delinquency (e.g. Benda 1995, 2002; Kloos and Moore 2000; Longo and Peterson 2002; Trimble 1997; Watson *et al.* 1986).

- Attitudes and orientations towards Christianity (rather than religion in general) (e.g. Francis 1993b; Hall, Tisdale and Brokaw 1994; Joseph and Lewis 1997; Lewis *et al.* 1998; Maltby and Lewis 1997).

- Finally, but possibly most importantly to this section of our work, ways of best measuring religion have been continuously debated, and there have been a number of useful literature reviews, meta-analyses and so forth which inform the debate as to exactly what is measured, and how reliably (e.g. Deconchy 1987; Exline 2002; Francis *et al.* 1995; Hunsberger 1991; Idler *et al.* 2003; Lewis and Maltby 1997; Maltby and Lewis 1996; Pargament 2002; Sherman *et al.* 2000; Slater, Hall and Edwards 2001; Strizenec 1997; Trimble 1997).

2. Research design and materials

The construction of interview protocols and selection of standardized materials was informed by the literature discussed above and elsewhere in this book. Materials were also produced to satisfy the commissioning specifications identified by the Home Office, Kainos and the Prison Service. The final research tool was a 16-page structured questionnaire followed by a short structured interview. To ensure that the research instrument would evaluate the main aims of the Trust, we also made careful consideration of their literature. We also made close observations of Kairos Weekends held at Swaleside (May 2000) and Highpoint South (July 2000). The design of the research instrument was further influenced by information gained from Kainos project coordinators' reports from each prison, an early field trip to The Verne (July 1999), comments and reports written by other observers and evaluators and a study of additional Kairos and Kainos programme materials, insofar as these were available. Having deliberately conducted our pilot research quite broadly, we were able to refine our materials following separate pilots at Swaleside, Highpoint North and Highpoint South.

Having identified the aims of the Kairos Weekend and Kainos (see 1 above), the research instrument was specifically developed to test the impact of Kainos in each of the following areas:

- *Dysfunctional attitudes* – elements of Kainos, including the Kairos Weekend, 'godparenting' evenings, counselling, prisoners' meetings and individual programmes, utilize strong cognitive behavioural techniques.

- *Attitudes to criminality* – Kainos claims to offer prisoners a 'challenge to change', and prisons add value by preventing recidivism. Thus, this is possibly the single most prominent attitude of interest to the Home Office.

- *Self esteem* – elements of Kainos, including the Kairos Weekend, 'godparenting' evenings and counselling, are designed to encourage feelings of self-worth.

- *Anxiety* – Kainos espouses a policy of psychological support.

- *Quality of relationships in prison* – Kainos claims to offer a community experience.

- *Orientation to religiosity* – Kainos claims to be a religious-based community.

- *Attitudes towards Christianity* – the Christian religion is central to both Kainos and the Kairos Weekend.

The final questionnaire consisted of 129 items. The first 21 items were designed to provide descriptive, demographic data about the sample. The remaining 108 were designed to measure the impact of Kainos on attitudes and behaviour in light of its goals and methods. Only items in which one might expect a change between Time 1 and Time 2 were included. In refining our materials, we wished to maximize their reliability and validity whilst keeping the number of questions to a minimum. We were aware that their implementation would take some time. Wherever possible, we thus used standardized measures in cut-down versions that had themselves been previously assessed for reliability (Katz 1997). The following scales were chosen after piloting and in consultation with the Home Office, Kainos and the Prison Service. In citing additional references to these scales, we have again selected those that should be of most use to readers. Therefore some of the following references were published after we completed the research in 2001:

- Beck Dysfunctional Attitudes Scale (BDAS) (17 items; Beck *et al.* 1991).
- Crime-PICS II (Frude, Honess and Maguire 1998).
- Francis Attitudes towards Christianity scale (Francis 1993b; Francis *et al.* 1995; Lewis and Maltby 1997; Lewis *et al.* 1998).
- Maltby Orientation to Religiosity Scale (Quest sub-scale dropped; Maltby 1999a, 2002; Maltby and Lewis 1997).
- Rosenberg Self-Esteem Measure (four items; Rosenberg 1989).
- State Trait Anxiety Index (STAI) (nine items; Spielberger, Gorsuch and Lushene 1970).
- Santa Clara Strength of Religious Faith (SCSORF) scale (Lewis *et al.* 2001; Plante and Boccaccini 1997a, 1997b).

In addition, 18 questions derived from Liebling *et al.*'s *Evaluation of Incentives and Earned Privileges* (1997) were replicated by kind permission, to measure changes in the quality of prisoners' relationships.

The reliability of all scales used within our prison sample was generally acceptable and is discussed in Section 6(b) below.

Some concern was expressed at the design stage that prisoners would not appreciate being asked questions about religion. In the event, non-religious prisoners did not object, and religious prisoners were pleased to answer questions about an area of their lives that was commonly overlooked. No non-Christian prisoner objected to answering the Francis Attitudes towards Christianity scale.

The questionnaire was followed by some open-ended questions with supplementary follow-up questions, as necessary. These questions helped to make sense of the findings from the more qualitative study (see Chapters 4–6) and were a means of triangulation.

Time 1 Kainos prisoners were asked:
'Why did you want to come onto Kainos Community?' and
'What are your expectations of the Kairos Weekend?'

Time 1 non-Kainos prisoners were asked:
'What is your understanding of what Kainos is and what it does?' and
'Have you ever thought of joining Kainos?'

Time 2 Kainos prisoners were asked:
'What did you think about the Kairos Weekend?' and
'What did you think of the follow-up programme?'

There was no need to repeat questions for the non-Kainos sample at Time 2.

3. Fieldwork, interview schedule and procedure

Governors at each of the four prisons received separate letters from the Prison Service and Research Team in advance of all planned research (including research reported in Chapters 5, 6, 7 and 10). The various studies were introduced and assistance requested. Jonathan Burnside made a brief presentation to Kainos and some prison staff at the annual Kainos Community Conference in September 2000. Whilst on site, contact was made with senior management, Senior Officers (SOs) or Principal Officers (POs) of relevant wings and Kainos Coordinators to explain the research and answer any queries.

The information collected covers the period 18th September 2000 (start of Time 1 at Highpoint North) to 19th April 2001 (end of Time 2 at Highpoint South). The first phase of the fieldwork (Time 1) took place between 18th September 2000 and 23rd January 2001. The order in which establishments were visited (Highpoint North, The Verne, Swaleside and Highpoint South) followed the chronological order in which Kairos Weekends were held. As noted in Section (2) above, this is because the Kairos Weekend marked the start of the programme, and all Time 1 interviews had to be completed by this date. Highpoint North held the first Kairos Weekend (5th–8th October 2000), closely followed by Swaleside (12th–15th October 2000). Progress at Highpoint North was severely hindered by a UK-wide petrol crisis in September 2000.

A total of 330 interviews were carried out, the shortest of which took 15 minutes, although the median length was 40 minutes. Nine participants required a prisoner to translate, and each of these interviews took up to two-and-a-half hours to complete. Five of the seven prisoners at Time 2 (two dropped out) had the same translator at Time 1.

Prisoner interviews were scheduled in consultation with staff and prisoners to cause minimum disruption. The number of interviews, and limited amount of fieldwork time available, meant making maximum use of time on site, usually entering the prison before first movements and departing after final lockup. Interviews were conducted during weekdays, evenings and weekends. The longer hours assisted with staff and prisoner cooperation, particularly on the Kainos units, where our presence was initially regarded with some suspicion. Most interviews took place in senior staff offices, interview rooms and casework offices, although a small number took place at prisoners' places of work or education. At Swaleside, some interviews took place on an open landing, which provided good opportunities for observation.

On the Kainos unit, we often spent time between interviews in informal discussions with staff and prisoners. Even during lockup, we had opportunities to converse with prisoners who were released to perform specific, trustee tasks (e.g. painting). On the non-Kainos wing, we had opportunities for informal discussions with staff. Non-Kainos prisoners were less willing to engage in discussion than Kainos prisoners probably as they had less interest in the subject and the outcome of the research. These exchanges and impressions were an additional guide to our analysis and writing-up. Interviews progressed more efficiently on the Kainos wings than on the non-Kainos wings due to the higher degree of prisoner co-operation. Delays took place on non-Kainos wings with a higher refusal rate.

4. Sample numbers

A total of 330 interviews were conducted with 216 prisoners as part of this study. Table 9.1, below, shows the breakdown and clearly indicates a problem with participation rates for the Time 2 control group. From the Kainos sample, 29 fewer people participated at Time 2, but from the non-Kainos sample, this increased to 73. In both cases, some of these lost participants were due to the Prison Service moving prisoners onto other prisons, but some loss was through withdrawal from the research. This was something we addressed in analyses and will be discussed in Section (7) below. Tables showing prisoners' stated reasons for declining to take part are given in Burnside *et al.* (2001).

There are several possible, generalized reasons for the elevated Time 2 refusal rates within the control group. Firstly, Kainos participants had a greater interest in taking part in a Kainos study at Time 2 than the control group, though many non-Kainos prisoners were reluctant to take part even at Time 1. Fifty-two of the original matches chosen to participate in the control group declined to take part at Time 1, citing lack of interest in Kainos or the research (e.g. 'there's no brownie points'). Secondly, there was anecdotal evidence that some Kainos participants felt pressured by Kainos Coordinators to take part at Time 2 even though they were told, and said they understood, that interviews were strictly voluntary. The control group, by contrast, received no such prompting from staff. A third explanation may be that the research group was in general more compliant than the control group, and there is some evidence to suggest that this was the case.

Table 9.1 Sample numbers and interviewers for attitudinal study

	Highpoint North	The Verne	Swaleside	Highpoint South	n
Time 1					
Research group	17	36	30	24	*107*
Control Group	18	36	30	25	*109**
Total					*216*
Time 2					
Research group	12	26	25	15	*78 (–29)*
Control Group	8	13	15	N/A	*36 (–73)*
Total					*114*

*The matched control group was slightly larger than the research group at Time 1 because individual matches were made for two Kainos prisoners at Time 1 who declined to take part.

The fact that a number of Kainos prisoners were unavailable at Time 2 suggests that a number of prisoners were accepted who were not in the best position to take advantage of the programme. Several prisoners dropped out during the Kairos Weekend, or left immediately afterwards, or had requested transfers to other prisons. In all fairness, little can be done to prevent such attrition. Some prisoners will invariably decide that Kainos or the Kairos Weekend is 'not for them', and it is in the nature of a voluntary (in particular, a *religious* voluntary) programme that they should be free to go. Nor is it advisable to discourage prisoners from making applications to transfer before joining Kainos.

5. Individual matching

We tried to select a control group that was as close as possible to the research group. In each establishment, a printout was requested of the total population in the prison on the first day of fieldwork. Data was collated on each prisoner in the research group on the following variables: age, sentence length, main offence, marital status and previous custodial sentences. At Swaleside, information was also provided on previous convictions, but this was discounted because it was not reliable (e.g. the computer system registered no previous offence whilst at the same time noting that the subject had previously received a custodial sentence). Individual matches were then made to form the control group.

The closeness of the match between research and control groups at Time 1 and Time 2 is set out in Tables 9.2 and 9.3 below.

6. Descriptive data findings and discussion

(a) Comparison of Kainos and control groups

This section concentrates on the key dependent variables rather than demographic similarities. For figures that illustrate the age range, sentence ranges, etc. in more detail than the information presented in Tables 9.2 and 9.3 see Burnside *et al.* (2001). As can be inferred from the control matching information above, there were no significant differences between the research and control group on demographic indices. Research and control groups were similar in the extent to which they participated in educational courses (68 per cent and 65 per cent respectively), although there was some difference in terms of skills courses (23 per cent and 35 per cent respectively) and behaviour courses (28 per cent and 48 per cent respectively). The relative lack of experience of skills and behaviour courses among the research group may be explained by the number of Kainos participants join Kainos Community from induction.

Although participants were not matched directly for ethnicity, they were broadly similar. Figures for the two groups are as follows, with research first and control in parentheses: White 57 per cent (59.8 per cent), Black 29 per cent (34.5 per cent), Asian 3.7 per cent (2.7 per cent) and Other 10.3 per cent (2.8 per cent). This suggests that Kainos attracted a mix of ethnic groups and thus limited the potential for racial discrimination.

By contrast, Figures 9.1 and 9.2 (below) show that the research and control groups diverge on the unmatched variable of religious belief. Categories of religious belief include the 'Theist' which refers to a 'general believer in God'.

The proportion of research group prisoners describing themselves as Christian was 62 per cent, compared to 38 per cent who described themselves as non-Christian. These figures were nearly reversed for the control group, of whom only 34 per cent described themselves as Christian, compared to 66 per cent who described themselves as non-Christian. This suggests that Kainos attracts Christians as opposed to non-Christians at a rate of nearly two-to-one. This is not surprising in

Table 9.2 Comparison of Research and Control groups in each establishment at Time 1

Time 1	Highpoint North		The Verne				Swaleside		Highpoint South	
UK/foreign	UK and foreign		UK nationals		Foreign nationals		UK and foreign		UK and foreign	
Research/Control	R	C	R	C	R	C	R	C	R	C
	n = 17	n = 17	n = 22	n = 22	n = 14	n = 14	n = 30	n = 30	n = 24	n = 24
Mean age (years)	30.23	34.1	35.0	33.7	32	32.2	34.3	35	32.9	31.9
Previous custodials	7 (49)	5 (43)	N/A	N/A	N/A	N/A	3 (5)	6 (4.7)	10 (60)	11 (47)
Sentence (av. months)	54.6	47.6	63.2	58.55	68.57	67.3	130.5	124	40.0	40.3
Number serving life	0	0	3	3	0	0	5	6	1	1
Main offence:										
Murder/manslaughter	0	0	4	6	0	0	5	5	0	1
Other violence	3	4	5	6	1	0	5	5	5	3
Drugs	10	11	8	6	9	14	18	17	10	9
Sex	1	0	0	0	0	0	2	2	1	2
Property	1	2	5	4	0	0	0	0	7	9
Other	2	0	0	0	0	0	0	0	1	0
Holding warrants	0	0	0	0	4	0	0	1	0	0
Marital status:										
Single	10	12	13	13	9	10	16	19	18	19
Married	4	2	5	4	1	4	7	8	5	3
Divorced	2	2	3	4	1	0	4	3	0	0
Wid/sep/cohab	1	1	1	1	3	0	3	0	1	2

277

My Brother's Keeper

Table 9.3 Comparison of Research and Control groups in each establishment at Time 2

Time 2	Highpoint North		The Verne				Swaleside		Highpoint South	
UK/foreign	UK and foreign		UK nationals		Foreign nationals		UK and foreign		UK and foreign	
Research/Control	R	C	R	C	R	C	R	C	R	C
	$n=12$	$n=7$	$n=16$	$n=8$	$n=10$	$n=5$	$n=24$	$n=14$	$n=15$	$n=$N/C
Mean age (years)	28.3	32.4	32.4	34.6	38.8	35.8	35.5	35.1	33.9	–
Previous custodials	4 (8)	3 (17)	N/A	N/A	N/A	N/A	1 (5)	1 (1)	4 (16)	–
Sentence (av. months)	70.4	61.7	56.1	69.8	73.2	65.4	134.8	157.5	44	–
Number serving life	3	2	0	0	5	6	1			–
Main offence:										
Murder/manslaughter	0	0	3	3	0	0	4	5	0	–
Other violence	2	3	4	2	1	0	3	1	3	–
Drugs	9	4	5	2	8	5	16	8	7	–
Sex	1	0	0	0	0	0	1	0	1	–
Property	0	0	4	1	0	0	0	0	3	–
Other	0	0	0	0	0	0	0	0	1	–
Holding warrants	0	0	0	0	1	0	0	0	0	–
Marital status:										
Single	8	4	10	4	6	4	13	9	12	–
Married	2	1	3	2	1	1	4	3	3	–
Divorced	2	2	2	2	0	0	4	2	0	–
Wid/sep/cohab	0	0	1	0	3	0	3	0	0	–

Notes to Tables 9.2 and 9.3:

- Previous custodial sentences are presented as the number of persons with previous custodial sentences, followed by the total number of previous custodial sentences in brackets.

- N/A signifies that this information was not available on the local prison database.

- The size of the foreign national population at The Verne (approximately 40% of the total prison population) justified splitting that part of the research group into two sub-groups. However, although we could match according to whether the prisoner was a UK or foreign national, it proved impractical to match by country, or even by continent. Countries represented in the research group included: Canary Islands (1), Cayman Islands (1), Cyprus (1), Czechoslovakia (this was on the system as such, we do not know if the prisoner was Czech or Slovakian) (1), Eire (1), Ethiopia (1), Germany (1), Ghana (2) and Jamaica (4). Countries represented in the control group included: Colombia (1), Guatemala (1) and Jamaica (12).

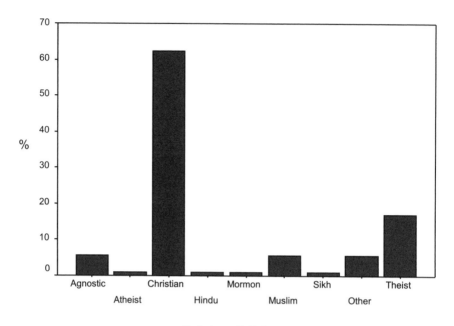

Figure 9.1 Kainos group's religious beliefs (Time 1)

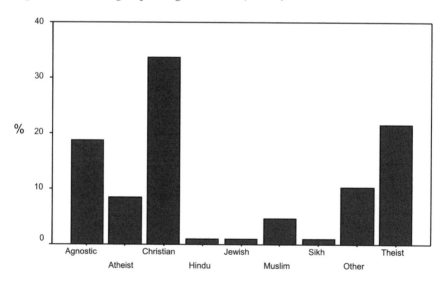

Figure 9.2 Control group's religious beliefs (Time 1)

view of the nature of the regime. However, it undercuts the claim that Kainos prefers or actively targets more disruptive people and does not particularly wish to have already committed Christians.

Similarly, in terms of overall religiosity, the research group included a larger proportion of believers than the control group. Of those in the research group, 93.5 per cent said they were believers of one sort or another (Hindu, Sikh, Theist, etc. as well as Christian) compared to only 6.5 per cent who described themselves as atheists or agnostics. By contrast, 73 per cent of those in the control group said they were believers compared to 27 per cent who described themselves as atheists or agnostics. Again, this is not surprising in view of the nature of the regime (although the generally high levels of belief may be of interest). However, it appears that whilst Kainos may claim that their community is suitable for the avowedly non-religious, few prisoners seem to agree.

One final descriptive finding worth noting here is that 83 per cent of Kainos prisoners at Time 1 say they would like to remain on Kainos units, and 62 per cent say this would be the case even if it meant they would not be able to progress to a lower security category prison.

(b) Techniques employed in hypothesis testing

Questionnaire items were coded and analyzed using SPSS. The measures used in the study were tested for internal reliability using Cronbach's alpha. This is a measure of the consistency between the items used to measure a construct. The acceptable range is normally considered to be between 0.6 and 0.9. Most of the scales used were between 0.7 and 0.9 (i.e. highly acceptable) but there were some outside that range.[2]

The study utilized two main independent variables: Time (Time 1 vs. Time 2) and Condition (Kainos vs. non-Kainos prisoners). The overriding hypothesis was that Kainos participants would show improvement on the dependent variables (well-being, pro-social attitudes, anti-criminality, religiosity, etc.) between Time 1 and Time 2 whilst the control group should not show such improvements. To test this hypothesis, a 2 × 2 (Time × Condition) mixed-model analysis of variance was performed on each dependent measure. Three-way Analyses of Variance (ANOVAs) were also conducted to check the control measures and to see whether age, marital status, institution and so forth had an effect on the findings.

Finally, to check whether any important differences existed between participants who stayed in the research and those who did not, we ran a 2 (Kainos vs. Non-Kainos) × 2 (Stayed vs. Dropped-Out) Multiple Analysis of Variance (MANOVA) on the dependent variables in the main analyses. This allowed for two important tests within one set of analyses: firstly, to test for any general differences between those who stayed and those who dropped out, regardless of whether they were Kainos prisoners, and secondly to test for any statistically significant differences between Kainos participants who stayed or dropped out and non-Kainos participants who stayed or dropped out.

7. Results and discussion

Descriptive data for all dependent variables at Time 1 and Time 2 from both research and control groups is summarized in Tables 9.4a–c below. Figures showing significant differences between Time 1 and Time 2 are in bold type. The data have been split into three tables simply for clarity of formatting: Table 9.4(b) is merely an extension of Table 9.4(a) and so on.

The key to interpreting the tables is as follows: where Lickert-type scales (where participants respond using a sliding scale such as 1–5) were used, and in particular, where response bias had been minimized by varying which end was positive and which negative, the necessary items were reversed so that the scores for each scale are unidirectional, within the tables presented below. More information on how to interpret the significant findings is presented after each table.

The findings may be summarized and interpreted as follows:

(a) Attitudes Towards Crime

In terms of general attitudes towards offending, Kainos participants seemed to develop more anti-offending attitudes over time, moving from a more neutral position towards a tendency to disagree with crime-supporting statements. This 'anti-offending' tendency was not markedly different from that of non-Kainos prisoners but is in the right direction. The pattern suggests the improvement in crime-related attitudes for Kainos participants only; non-Kainos participants did not seem to show such changes. Kainos therefore seems to have some positive influence on general attitudes towards offending.

In terms of prisoner evaluations regarding how worthwhile they considered crime to be, Kainos prisoners did not vary significantly from non-Kainos prisoners, nor did the two groups vary significantly over time. However, Kainos participants seemed to show more positive changes in their attitudes over time compared to non-Kainos participants, who seemed to show no change. Kainos participants became more likely to differ and disagree with pro-crime statements over time, whereas the non-Kainos participants seemed not to shift in their attitudes towards crime. Thus, Kainos appears to have some positive effect on participants' evaluation of crime as worthwhile.

Table 9.4a   Outcome measures for research and control groups

Mean (Kainos)	S.D. (Kainos)	Variance (Kainos)	Measure	Mean (Control)	S.D. (Control)	Variance (Control)
3.59	**0.62**	**0.38**	**PICSG (General Attitudes to Criminality)** Time 1	**3.50**	**0.63**	**0.40**
3.87	**0.55**	**0.30**	**PICSG Time 2**	**3.61**	**0.61**	**0.37**
3.59	0.79	0.63	PICSA (Anticipation of reoffending) Time 1	3.49	0.82	0.67
3.85	0.68	0.47	PICSA Time 2	3.60	0.76	0.58
3.57	1.20	1.44	PICSV (Victim hurt awareness) Time 1	3.40	1.20	1.44
3.58	1.32	1.74	PICSV Time 2	3.44	1.37	1.87
3.53	**0.72**	**0.52**	**PICSE (Evaluation of crime as worthwhile)** Time 1	**3.40**	**0.86**	**0.74**
3.80	**0.66**	**0.43**	**PICSE Time 2**	**3.48**	**0.81**	**0.65**
3.55	0.52	0.27	Total BDAS (Dysfunctional attitudes) Time 1	3.54	0.57	0.32
3.71	0.54	0.30	Total BDAS Time 2	3.74	0.47	0.22
3.69	0.68	0.46	BDAS Vulnerability Time 1	3.63	0.65	0.42
3.73	0.71	0.50	BDAS Vulnerability Time 2	3.79	0.57	0.32
3.68	0.86	0.75	BDAS Need for approval Time 1	3.92	0.69	0.48
4.05	0.87	0.75	BDAS Need for approval Time 2	4.12	0.58	0.34
3.56	0.84	0.71	BDAS Success vs. Perfectionism Time 1	3.50	0.93	0.86
3.68	0.95	0.90	BDAS Success vs. Perfectionism Time 2	3.67	0.97	0.95
3.11	0.78	0.60	BDAS Imperatives Time 1	3.12	0.87	0.76
3.23	0.80	0.63	BDAS Imperatives Time 2	3.25	0.67	0.44
2.04	0.55	0.31	Rosenberg (Self-esteem) Time 1	2.07	0.45	0.21
1.86	0.56	0.31	Rosenberg Time 2	1.94	0.62	0.39

Notes:

- For the Rosenberg self-esteem measure, a mean of 2 signifies agreement with statements about self-worth, less than 2 signifies strong agreement and more than 2 shows progressive disagreement.
- For the Dysfunctional attitudes (BDAS) and Crime-PICS scales, a mean of 3 signifies neutrality, less than 3 shows agreement with dysfunctional attitudes and crime-supporting statements whilst more than 3 signifies progressive disagreement.

Table 9.4b Outcome measures for research and control groups continued

Mean (Kainos)	S.D. (Kainos)	Variance (Kainos)	Measure	Mean (Control)	S.D. (Control)	Variance (Control)
2.80	**0.81**	**0.66**	**STAI State (Anxiety) Time 1**	**2.87**	**0.72**	**0.51**
3.05	**0.73**	**0.53**	**STAI State Time 2**	**2.85**	**0.76**	**0.58**
3.06	0.60	0.36	STAI TRAIT (Anxiety) Time 1	2.99	0.55	0.30
3.06	0.55	0.30	STAI Trait Time 2	2.93	0.59	0.34
2.24	**1.03**	**1.06**	**Relationships between Staff and prisoners**	**2.47**	**1.09**	**1.19**
1.97	**0.97**	**0.93**	**Relationships between Staff and prisoners (2)**	**2.70**	**1.07**	**1.16**
2.15	0.93	0.87	Relationships among prisoners	2.57	1.07	1.15
2.16	0.93	0.87	Relationships among prisoners (2)	2.50	0.99	0.98
2.00	0.88	0.78	Get on with officers on your unit	2.10	0.95	0.90
1.90	0.87	0.75	Get on with officers on your unit (2)	2.26	1.27	1.61
1.85	1.04	1.08	Get on with personal officer	1.97	1.03	1.05
1.88	1.15	1.33	Get on with personal officer (2)	2.13	1.01	1.02
1.94	0.91	0.82	Get on with other prisoners	2.16	0.90	0.81
1.89	0.86	0.74	Get on with other prisoners (2)	2.18	0.90	0.82
2.73	1.00	0.99	How much trust for officers	2.80	1.08	1.16
2.53	0.93	0.87	How much trust for officers (2)	2.97	0.89	0.79
3.07	0.87	0.75	How much trust for other prisoners	3.37	0.80	0.63
2.96	0.93	0.86	How much trust for other prisoners (2)	3.49	0.66	0.43
2.61	**0.96**	**0.93**	**Morale amongst prisoners**	**2.98**	**1.01**	**1.02**
2.22	**1.04**	**1.08**	**Morale amongst prisoners (2)**	**3.00**	**0.94**	**0.88**
1.64	0.66	0.44	Do you feel safe from being injured by other prisoners	1.83	0.85	0.73
1.47	0.64	0.41	Do you feel safe from being injured by other prisoners (2)	1.81	0.86	0.73
1.49	0.71	0.50	Do you feel safe from being bullied by other prisoners	1.54	0.77	0.59
1.32	0.63	0.40	Do you feel safe from being bullied by other prisoners (2)	1.58	0.87	0.76

Notes:
- For that State Trait Anxiety Index (STAI), a mean of 3 signifies agreement with the feeling expressed, less than 3 heads toward disagreement and more than 3 shows strong agreement.
- Questions about the quality of prisoner relationships were a mixture of four and five-item scales. In all cases, the lower the score, the better the quality of the relationship.

Table 9.4c Outcome measures for research and control groups continued

Mean (Kainos)	S.D. (Kainos)	Variance (Kainos)	Measure	Mean (Control)	S.D. (Control)	Variance (Control)
1.64	0.77	0.59	Do you feel safe from threatening by other prisoners	1.64	0.78	0.61
1.42	0.61	0.38	Do you feel safe from threatening by other prisoners (2)	1.64	0.83	0.69
2.12	0.82	0.67	Do you think prisoners behave well	2.50	0.85	0.72
2.01	0.89	0.79	Do you think prisoners behave well (2)	2.44	0.89	0.80
1.54	0.65	0.42	Would you describe yourself as well behaved prisoner	1.57	0.60	0.36
1.41	0.76	0.58	Would you describe yourself as well behaved prisoner (2)	1.47	0.61	0.37
1.86	0.78	0.61	Does prison deliver support when you need it	2.01	0.74	0.55
1.79	0.71	0.50	Does prison deliver support when you need it (2)	2.12	0.81	0.65
1.51	0.72	0.52	Can you be yourself in prison or do you wear a mask	1.60	0.80	0.64
1.37	0.63	0.39	Can you be yourself in prison or do you wear a mask (2)	1.53	0.74	0.54
2.93	**0.76**	**0.54**	**SCSORF (Religious orientation) Time 1**	**2.45**	**0.97**	**0.95**
3.16	**0.80**	**0.65**	**SCSORF Time 2**	**2.27**	**1.02**	**1.03**
2.85	**0.66**	**0.44**	**ROS (Religious orientation) Time 1**	**2.47**	**0.92**	**0.84**
3.05	**0.83**	**0.69**	**ROS Time 2**	**2.32**	**0.91**	**0.83**
3.17	**0.56**	**0.32**	**FRANCIS (Attitudes to Christianity) Scale Time 1**	**2.82**	**0.83**	**0.69**
3.40	**0.63**	**0.40**	**FRANCIS SCALE Time 2**	**2.75**	**0.83**	**0.70**

Note:
- For SCSORF, ROS and Francis scales, a mean of 3 signifies agreement with pro-religious or pro-Christian views, less than 3 heads toward disagreement and more than 3 shows strong agreement.

A degree of caution should be exercised over these positive findings because of the 27 per cent attrition among the Kainos sample between Time 1 and Time 2. A logical *post hoc* hypothesis would be that those who dropped out were the ones who were most pro-crime. When tested, the results indeed showed significant differences on the Crime-PICs measures between the original Kainos sample and those who stayed in the study to the end. Kainos participants who stayed in the study were more likely to have held anti-crime supporting views and believed themselves less likely to reoffend at the start of the research. Thus overall, we have to conclude that Kainos had no significant effects on the two PICS sub-scales (PICS A: Anticipation of reoffending; PICS V: Victim hurt denial).

(b) Psychological well-being

Similarly, our findings indicate that Kainos had no significant effects on Dysfunctional attitudes, Self-esteem or Anxiety. However, the results on the STAI do suggest an improvement that is tending towards significance. There were no significant differences between Kainos and non-Kainos participants in terms of state anxiety (current rather than general feelings of anxiety) at either Time 1 or Time 2. However, over time, the Kainos participants felt marginally more secure and less nervous, whereas there were no differences over time for the non-Kainos participants. Kainos participants moved from saying they felt more than 'somewhat' secure to saying they felt 'moderately' secure. Thus, Kainos seems to make its prisoners feel safer over time (and in this case, we did not find differences between those who stayed and those who dropped out from the Kainos sample). The results for non-Kainos prisoners seem to suggest a decrease (albeit statistically non-significant) in feelings of security.

(c) Quality of relationships in prison

Non-Kainos participants indicated poorer relationships with staff than did Kainos participants. There was also a marginal improvement in relationships between staff and Kainos prisoners over time but not among non-Kainos prisoners. Kainos prisoners moved from saying that relationships were poorer than 'fairly good' towards saying that they were better than this. These findings suggest that relationships between staff and prisoners are better in Kainos compared to the general prison sample in this study. This should again be seen in the light of our discussion of attrition, below.

The data also suggest that religion may moderate the effects found. It seemed to be the case that for Kainos prisoners, behaviour among Christians seems to improve over time (moving from better than 'fairly good' towards 'very good') whereas for non-Kainos prisoners, behaviour among Christians seems to deteriorate slightly over time (slipping from 'very good' to better than 'fairly good').

There was also an improvement in morale among Kainos prisoners over time but no significant changes among non-Kainos prisoners. Kainos prisoners moved from a 'better than neutral' position to saying that morale was just less than 'fairly high'.

Kainos had no significant effects on any other dimensions of relationships in prison. These included: general quality of relationships among prisoners; interviewees' personal relationships with officers, personal officers and other prisoners on the wing; trust of both officers and prisoners; perceptions of safety from being injured, bullied or threatened; being treated with respect; whether prisoners behave well on the Community; perceptions of their own quality of behaviour; support from staff; the ability to 'drop the mask' and prisoners' relationships with their partners and/or families. This may have been due to something of a ceiling effect. On the whole, their assessments of the quality of relationships ranged from fairly good towards very good. Therefore, further improvements may have been difficult to achieve or measure.

(d) Religious orientations and beliefs

Results from the Santa Clara Strength of Religious Faith (SCSORF) Scale showed that Kainos participants state more pro-faith views than non-Kainos participants at both Time 1 and Time 2. In this scale, the questions centre on how important a role faith plays in the respondents' lives. Kainos group's responses tend towards agreement with pro-religious statements at Time 1, whilst responses from the control group tend towards disagreement. This suggests that individuals who participate in Kainos are more likely to identify themselves as having faith, compared to non-Kainos participants. In addition, Kainos participants state more pro-religious views over time compared to non-Kainos participants. At Time 2, the responses of Kainos participants headed towards strong agreement whilst non-Kainos responses moved in the opposite direction towards greater disagreement. We conclude that, based on this measure, Kainos seems to be associated with an increase in prisoners espoused religious beliefs, over Time, possibly reinforcing the already favourable religious attitudes that the Kainos prisoners expressed at the outset.

There was some variation between the different religious scales but largely in the control group findings. Unsurprisingly, pro-religious attitudes in one scale matched similar pro-religious attitudes in the next. So, the Maltby Religious Orientation Scale further supports the pattern of results from the SCSORF. The Maltby scale is the one most closely derived from Allport's Religious Orientation Scale and had been well validated on British as well as North American samples. Following pilot testing, we were left with just the Intrinsic sub-scale of this measure. It asks about religion rather than faith and assesses how central religion is to respondents' lives. Again, Kainos participants state more pro-religious views than non-Kainos participants at both Time 1 and Time 2. Kainos participants tend towards agreement with pro-religious statements at Time 1, whilst non-Kainos prisoners tend towards disagreement. In addition, Kainos participants state more pro-religious views over Time compared to non-Kainos participants. At Time 2 Kainos responses moved closer to strong agreement, whilst non-Kainos responses headed in the opposite direction.

Similar results were again found using the British measure of attitudes towards Christianity, involvement in church life and so on (the Francis Attitudes Towards Christianity scale). Kainos participants state more positive attitudes towards Christianity than non-Kainos participants at both Time 1 and Time 2. Kainos responses tended towards strong agreement with the statements at Time 1 whilst non-Kainos responses tended towards agreement. In other words, both groups tended to agree with the attitudes on the scale and were positive towards Christianity, but the Kainos group agreed strongly. Kainos participants stated more positive attitudes towards Christianity over time when compared to non-Kainos participants. At Time 2, Kainos responses moved closer to strong agreement whilst non-Kainos responses slipped away a little from agreement towards disagreement.

Thus far we can say the Kainos group seemed positively affected by the programme, though not as definitively as might have been desired. In this context, we should note that none of the variables suggested Kainos participants were significantly adversely affected compared to non-Kainos participants.

Three-way ANOVAs were also conducted to check the control measures. A number of variables were tested to see whether they had any effect on the findings including age, institution, marital status, religious beliefs, ethnicity and number of previous sentences. There was no consistent pattern to any of these variables to suggest they might moderate or mediate the observed effects of Kainos. Therefore, Kainos appears to be the effective agent in bringing about change.

Other factors could contribute to some of the differences. One is the length of time spent living on the Kainos units. As mentioned in (1) above, some prisoners spend a period of time living on Kainos before taking part in the Kairos Weekend and the follow-up programme. The length of time spent on Kainos for those who officially started and completed the programme within our sample varied from 15 weeks to 77 weeks (just over one-and-a-half years). The average was 33 weeks (just over eight months). A further test was run to measure any relationship between the significant effects noted above and the length of time spent on Kainos. This was to see whether any benefits were gained from living in a Kainos Community milieu, even without direct intervention and formal programmes. No relationship was found.

The power of the attitudinal effects of Kainos is, however, somewhat diluted when we explored attrition rates. Tests were run at the most conservative estimate of significance (0.05) to check if any features might characterize non-participants in research and control groups at Time 2. Although no attrition-related differences were found on the majority of scales, there were significant differences between those who stayed and those who dropped out from the study (regardless of research condition) on the following variables: BDAS (total and imperatives), Crime-PICS (sub-scales G (general attitudes to criminality), A (anticipation of reoffending) and E (evaluation of crime as worthwhile)) and item F12 ('Do you feel you are treated with respect in here by other prisoners?') as summarized in Table 9.5. The scores should be interpreted here in the same ways as they were in Tables 9.4a–c.

Essentially, this table shows that those who stayed in the study at Time 2 (Research and Control) were more likely to have a more positive view of life, hold non-crime supporting views and feel they were more likely to be treated with respect than those who dropped out.

A test was also run to see whether there were important differences between Kainos participants and non-Kainos prisoners in terms of attrition. Significant results were found for Crime-PICS G (general attitudes to criminality) and Crime-PICS A (anticipation of reoffending) and several items relating to prisoner relationships (relationships between staff and prisoners and prisoner morale).

Table 9.5 Significant effects of attrition (research and control)

Stayed mean	SD	Measure	Drop-out mean	SD
3.71	0.49	Total BDAS	3.46	0.48
3.34	0.72	Total BDAS (Imperatives)	2.93	0.84
3.68	0.56	PICS G	3.38	0.65
3.69	0.68	PICS A	3.34	0.95
3.62	0.79	PICS E	3.27	0.87
1.75	0.73	Do you feel respected by other prisoners (F12)	2.14	0.89

Table 9.6 demonstrates that Kainos participants who stayed in the study were more likely to hold non-crime supporting views, believe themselves less likely to reoffend and were more likely to get on with officers on their unit. There were no significant differences on these measures between the control group of non-Kainos prisoners who stayed and those who dropped out, or were unavailable at Time 2.

The results also suggest that Kainos participants who stayed were more likely to trust officers on their unit compared to those who dropped out. This was reversed for non-Kainos prisoners, with those who stayed appearing to trust officers less than those who dropped out, or who were moved on and so forth. This may imply that, within the control group, those who stayed were overly negative on this item. In contrast, those who stayed in the research group were overly positive. This might explain any apparent effect of Kainos at Time 1 and Time 2 on this particular item. It is also possible that these attitudes are themselves associated with why a prisoner is moved on, or stays on a particular unit.

This idea may be reinforced as the Time 1 data indicate that Kainos participants who stayed were more likely to believe prison supports their needs, when compared to those who dropped out. Again, this was reversed for non-Kainos prisoners, with those who stayed appearing to feel prison did not support their needs compared to those who dropped out. Again, this also suggests that those who stay in the control group may be motivated to participate through grievance and are overly negative, whilst those who stay on the research group are overly positive. There is another possible interpretation though, which is that both sets of findings may be partly explained on the grounds that more pro-social officers apply to join Kainos than the non-Kainos wings. In other words, something is qualitatively different about the officers on those wings. So, for example, it may be that the appropriate response for each group is: trust on Kainos and distrust off Kainos.

Overall, based on those differences that are significant, those who stayed as part of the research group at Time 2 are generally more positive and less crime-prone than those who left. Finally, there was only one difference between those who stayed and those who dropped out for non-Kainos participants. This was on the BDAS Success *vs*. Perfectionism sub-scale. Here, it seems that for non-Kainos participants, those who dropped out were more likely to have maladaptive thinking concerning success and perfectionism. There were no such differences for Kainos participants.

Table 9.6 Significant interaction between condition and dropout

Stayed mean (Kainos)	SD (Kainos)	Drop-out mean (Kainos)	SD (Kainos)	Measure	Stayed mean (Control)	SD (Control)	Drop-out mean (Control)	SD (Control)
3.79	0.50	3.17	0.68	PICS G	3.51	0.62	3.47	0.63
3.83	0.57	3.10	1.06	PICS A	3.45	0.78	3.44	0.90
3.50	0.92	3.66	0.51	BDAS (Perfectionism)	3.90	0.63	3.31	0.91
1.68	0.86	2.33	0.98	Get on with unit officers	2.00	0.90	1.74	0.82
2.41	1.04	3.08	1.08	Trust for officers (F6)	2.95	0.97	2.32	1.08
1.58	0.71	2.17	0.58	Support from prison (F15)	2.19	0.60	1.77	0.76

8. Conclusions

What main conclusions can we draw from this empirical evaluation of Kainos? We suggest the following:

- Kainos may have some effect in reinforcing religious beliefs and the pro-social and anti-criminal attitudes of those who participate in the community. Living in the community was also related to marginal improvements in prisoners' psychological well-being.

- Throughout, Kainos participants are more religious and have more positive attitudes towards Christianity than non-Kainos prisoners.

- Whilst on Kainos, participants become more religious and develop more positive attitudes towards Christianity compared to non-Kainos participants.

- Whilst on Kainos, participants feel somewhat more secure and less nervous compared to non-Kainos participants.

- Whilst on Kainos, participants' relationships with staff seem to improve marginally, although this finding should be interpreted with caution.

- Whilst on Kainos, participants said their morale improved.

- Although Kainos seems to have some positive influence on these dimensions, no effect was found for the other measures. In many cases, no differences existed between Kainos and non-Kainos groups at Time 1 and Time 2.

- None of the dependent variables suggested participating in the community adversely affected Kainos prisoners. Where differences were discerned, they were always in positive, desirable directions.

- Our overall conclusion from this part of the research is that Kainos has some modest, desirable effects on participants' attitudes and beliefs over time.

Notes

1   We are grateful to G. Tendayi Viki, who contributed to the original data analysis on which this chapter is based (see Burnside *et al.* 2001).
2   The uncut and previously standardized religiosity scales were actually closer to 1 than is normal (ranging from 0.93 up to 0.98, implying that some of the items may conceptually be too close to each other). In the other direction,

two of the sub-scales were only marginally reliable at 0.5. These were both sub-scales of the Dysfunctional Attitudes Scale. However, when taken as a total scale, the reliability scores for the DAS, at both Times were entirely satisfactory (0.80 at Time 1 and 0.79 at Time 2). For a full breakdown of the Cronbach's alpha scores at Time 1 and Time 2, see Burnside *et al.* (2002).

Chapter 10

The impact of Kainos and Christian-based units on recidivism

[T]he world is concerned about seeing our guys stay out of prison. And so we know that if a person is living, following his Christian beliefs to the nth degree, that he will not re-offend. ... It's in the numbers. That's the culture we're living in today, so to have success we gotta have more guys that stay out than go back

Jack Cowley (National Operations Director of IFI 1997–2003)

Introduction

This chapter presents and discusses the impact of Kainos Community on reconviction rates. The Kainos reconviction sample (see section 2(a)(i) below) comprises all those who took part in the Kainos Programme at HMPs The Verne, Swaleside, Highpoint North and Highpoint South since their inception and who were discharged from the prison system prior to October 1999. The main outcome measure used is reconviction within two years of release. The methodology for the evaluation involves a careful assessment of reconviction rates for the Kainos sample and controlled comparison with prisoners having similar characteristics released from the prison system over the same time period.

This chapter was authored by Gerry Rose

294

I. Impact of Christian-based prison programmes on recidivism

We begin by reviewing previous studies relating to the impact of Christian-based prison programmes upon recidivism, since much can be learned from the existing research literature. We have concentrated on those studies that have used recidivism after release from prison as an outcome measure. Such research has generally been based on rearrest or reconviction data over a period of one or two years after release. The key question is whether Christian-based programmes have demonstrably shown reductions in recidivism.

The number of previous studies is in fact quite small; we have omitted research where insufficient information is available for an assessment.[1] Our coverage is consistent with that of Johnson et al. (2002), whose systematic literature review provides a recent and comprehensive coverage of existing research in this field.[2] The research studies reviewed here are as follows:

- Johnson et al. (1997). A secondary analysis of data on the impact of the Prison Fellowship programme in selected New York State prisons. The data are from 1994.

- Johnson's comparison of two Brazilian prisons (2002), one of which was Humaitá, described in detail in Chapter 1. The data are from the late 1990s.

- Evaluation of IFI-Texas, which is described in Chapter 8. This was first published as two reports from the Texas Criminal Justice Policy Council (Fabelo et al. 2002; 2003) and subsequently reported on in more detail by Johnson with Larson (2003). The data are from the late 1990s.

Our review considers the results of each study and assesses its methodological adequacy – i.e. its 'internal validity' (Cook and Campbell 1979). 'External validity' – that is, the extent to which results might be generalized to other contexts – will be considered in the conclusions to this chapter. All of the faith-based programmes considered in the research studies are, in fact, explicitly Christian-based, being run either by APAC or IFI.

(a) Johnson et al.'s study of Prison Fellowship in New York State

This substantial article (Johnson et al. 1997) is based on a secondary analysis of data from a 1994 study of the Prison Fellowship (PF) programme in New York State prisons. The sample of prisoners had been released between January 1992 and April 1993. Two outcome dimensions are investigated: institutional adjustment and recidivism. We shall deal only with the latter here.[3]

The research design is as follows. Four prisons from the earlier study are selected – these are regarded as the only prisons with adequate record keeping on the extent of PF participation. The 'experimental group' comprises 201 PF participants from these four prisons. A matched comparison group was then set up by selection from a pool of 40,000 ex-prisoners (excluding known PF participants). Seven variables were matched (age, race, religion, area of residence, military experience, sentence and security classification) and each member of the PF group was assigned an individual non-PF match. The 'non-PF' comparison group were 201 releasees from New York prisons generally, rather than the four selected prisons. Johnson *et al.* (1997) shows that the PF and non-PF groups are similar for three of the matched variables (age, race and religion) as well as marital status and years of education. No figures are given on sentence or security classification, but we shall assume the two groups are also well matched on these important variables.

The nature of overall PF participation is assessed, and the PF group is classified into three sub-groups depending on the extent of exposure to PF programmes: low participation (99) medium (80) and high (22). This classification is central to the subsequent data analysis.

The outcome measure of recidivism is 'any arrest during a one-year post release period'. The authors clearly recognize the limitations of this indicator, but it is the only measure realistically available on the groups studied. Within the whole PF group, 37 per cent were arrested in the year, compared to 36 per cent of the comparison group (1997: 154).

Johnson and colleagues then break down the recidivism rates for the three PF subgroups according to the extent of PF participation. If we group the whole of the non-PF group together, which is justified since the recidivism rates are not significantly different between the three non-PF subgroups,[4] the recidivism rates can be set out as in Table 10.1, below.

A statistical test comparing the four individual groups (i.e. columns 1 to 4) in Table 10.1 shows that the differences are statistically significant – that is, they are unlikely to be due to chance alone.[5] The most important point, however, is that the differences between the groups in the table are clearly due both to the lower rearrest rate for the high participation group *and* the higher rate for the medium participation group. Indeed, if the data for these two groups are amalgamated, the rearrest rate is 38.2 per cent (39 out of 102), which is close to both that of the PF low participation and comparison groups, and not significantly different from either.

Table 10.1 Recidivism rates for the three PF groups and the comparison (non-PF) group*

	Comparison group	PF low participation	PF medium participation	PF high participation	Whole PF group
Recidivism (arrest) rate	35.8%	36.4%	45.0%	13.6%	37.3%
Numbers	72/201	36/99	36/80	3/22	75/201

*Johnson et al. (1997): study of Prison Fellowship (PF) participants in New York State.

If it is to be argued, as Johnson et al. do, that we have real differences here, the patterns are rather tricky to interpret. They require us to believe not only that high participation has a strong positive effect but also that slightly less (medium) participation has a negative effect. It would be difficult to produce a sound theoretical justification for such an argument. The authors do not comment on the higher rearrest rate for the medium PF group.[6]

The rearrest analysis in Johnson et al.'s Table 2 is expanded in their Table 3 (1997: 158), where an additional variable is introduced – risk level – presumably based on criminal history, and categorized as low, medium and high risk. So rearrest rates are now shown according to PF participation category and risk level.[7] The authors' discussion following from their Table 3 (using a likelihood ratio chi squared approach) is somewhat difficult to follow. At this stage the three categories of PF participation are still used, but the variable is referred to as 'bible study participation', a term which is retained for the authors' Table 4, which draws on the results of a logistic regression with arrest as the dependent variable and six independent variables including 'bible study'. In fact, Table 4 is not at all clear: it gives no details of the sample size or whether the comparison group is still included; we are not told how 'bible study' is coded, what variables were excluded by this 'best fit' model, or whether interaction effects were tried out; no significance levels are given for the coefficients tabulated.

It is clear, however, that the 'risk' variable is very important in analyzing recidivism. In an attempt to explore further the data in Johnson et al.'s Table 3, we have used logistic regression modelling for rearrest, taking the independent variables as: risk (low/medium/high), main group (PF/non-PF) and participation (low/medium/high). This follows the logic of Table 3 exactly, but simply applies more rigorous statistical methods to the data. We found that only the risk effect was significant. Once risk is controlled for, the effects of main group (PF or non-PF) and extent of participation were statistically insignificant, as were all interaction effects between risk, group and participation. Other logistic regression models were also tried on the same data, by grouping all of the non-PF comparison group together, and the same results were obtained (for further details see Appendix A). Further analysis showed the 'risk' variable is by no means evenly spread between the various subgroups, and this may largely account for the differences observed in patterns of rearrest rates (as in our Table 10.1 above).

What can we conclude from this review of Johnson *et al.*'s study? The research is quite complex, and even when we confine attention to the analysis of recidivism there are a number of strands. The main point is that our reanalysis of the data does not support Johnson *et al.*'s argument that 'inmates who were most active in Bible studies were significantly less likely to be rearrested during the follow-up period' (1997: 145). It is clear how the authors have been drawn to this conclusion, but it fails to take account of the 'counter-intuitive' higher rearrest rates among medium-level PF participants. Moreover, when prior risk is controlled, the effect of high PF participation seems to disappear. Our reanalysis shows the likelihood of recidivism for the Prison Fellowship group (as measured by rearrest within a year after discharge from prison) was not significantly different from that of released New York State prisoners with similar backgrounds, no matter whether exposure to the PF programme is high, medium or low.

(b) Johnson on two Brazilian prisons

This short article compares two Brazilian prisons – Humaitá and Braganca – that are 'considered to be exemplars in a country facing an array of correctional crises' (Johnson 2002: 7). Humaitá, which was taken over by a body of Christian volunteers called APAC in 1984, is the first and to date only correctional facility in the world to fully adopt a Christian-based therapeutic regime (see Chapter 1). Braganca is another innovative prison, self-sustaining through contracts for work undertaken by prisoners, and run by a public-private partnership.[8] Both regimes are claimed to be effective in reducing recidivism, but Johnson's is the only known study to examine these claims based on empirical data.

Johnson's abstract (2002: 7) summarizes the findings as follows:

(1) the three-year recidivism rate of prisoners from both facilities is extremely low by any standard (16 per cent Humaitá and 36 per cent Braganca), (2) the recidivism rate for former Humaitá

prisoners was significantly lower than that found for Braganca prisoners, (3) Humaitá's lower recidivism rate holds among high as well as low-risk prisoners, (4) inmates from the faith-based prison were charged with significantly fewer arrests during the three year follow-up period, and (5) where disposition data were available, former Braganca prisoners were significantly more likely to be reincarcerated than former prisoners from Humaitá.

The study sample for each prison was all those released from the institution in 1996 (Humaitá 148; Braganca 247). The research design involved tracking these releasees through to the end of 1999 using official records. Recidivism was defined as rearrest within three years of release.

It is clear from the article that official records on arrests, convictions and criminal careers are somewhat problematic in Brazil's São Paulo state. It seems that data on rearrests after prison or other forms of sentence are not readily accessible by researchers, and this is clearly a crucial problem for the study. In the circumstances, Johnson does well to bring together such data as can be obtained on rearrests, type of offence and so on. The source of criminal career data is the Department of Criminal Identification in São Paulo, although the database was accessed through collaboration with the police. The difficulties with the data can be seen at many points in the article, and result in a number of problems, the most important of which are:

- A total number of 395 prisoners were included in the research samples. Data on offence was available for 348 prisoners. Recidivism data was available on only 182 individuals,[9] so over half are omitted from any recidivism analysis. Whether this high 'attrition rate' produces any bias in the analysis, it is indicative of serious problems with the reliability and coverage of the official database.

- Differences between the Humaitá and Braganca samples are analyzed in an attempt to control background factors related to recidivism. Much of this analysis is unsatisfactory since key background factors (e.g. prior criminal history, age) are not considered, presumably because they were unavailable. Studies of recidivism do not generally show that the background variables used in Johnson's article – offence type and time in prison – have much effect. This probably explains why the measure of risk (based on offence severity, and categorized as high or low) is only weakly related to rearrest in Johnson's Table 1. The total number in this table is reduced to 167,[10] due to the attrition problems outlined above.

- The main problem with Johnson's findings is the statement that 'the recidivism rate of prisoners from both prisons is remarkably low *by any standard*' (italics added). With no standard to make comparisons, is this argument justified? If these were *true* rearrest rates, perhaps there is a case to be made, but the arrest rates are calculated from a database that is clearly problematic. We need to consider how complete the Department of Criminal Identification database is, both in terms of coverage of individuals and their criminal histories – a point discussed in more detail below. The difference between the two prisons in arrest rates after discharge (16 per cent Humaitá and 36 per cent Braganca, statistically significant at p< .01), is a more soundly-based finding, since the same data problems are likely to affect both groups.

In his conclusions, Johnson is careful to acknowledge the methodological problems with the study, but he does not recognize the full effect of these problems. Johnson is to be commended, too, for having considered several different indicators of recidivism (time to rearrest, reincarceration rate etc.), but unfortunately the data for these other measures are also affected by high attrition rates and other methodological problems.[11]

Really, we have no idea what a standardized measure of the three-year rearrest rate would be for ex-prisoners in São Paulo state *as measured from the existing Department of Criminal Identification database*. What we do know from the UK is that databases of criminal histories require very good record keeping if arrests and convictions are to be reliably linked to the histories of individuals, and that much time and money needs to be invested in the integrity of the database. Ex-prisoners usually have substantial prior criminal records, so when only 46 per cent can be traced from the database, we should be very wary of issues of completeness and coverage. There is, however, a good indication of a difference in recidivism rates between the two prisons, which is a positive finding for the Humaitá programme.

(c) Studies of IFI-Texas

The evaluation of the InnerChange Freedom Initiative (IFI) programme in Texas is dealt with in three separate publications. The first two are reports issued by the Texas Criminal Justice Policy Council (CJPC) (Fabelo *et al.* 2002, 2003).[12] The third publication – Johnson (2003) – is a more detailed report based on the same project and adds an expanded process dimension to the evaluation.

Fabelo *et al.* (2002) provides a good overview of the IFI programme, the plan for the evaluation and the details of the research design; results and findings are given in Fabelo *et al.* (2003). We shall discuss these two publications together. The main CJPC researchers were Eisenberg and Trusty, but Fabelo (CJPC Director) contributed important introductions and summaries to the two reports.

The IFI-Texas programme is run at the Carol Vance Unit – a pre-release prison in the Houston, Texas area – and at the time of the study provided 200 places, about half the capacity of the Unit (see Chapter 8). The study tracks the two-year post-release recidivism rates for prisoners who entered the IFI programme from April 1997 to January 1999, and who were released from prison prior to 1st September 2000. The evaluation is well-designed and involves comparison of IFI participants with substantial groups of prisoners who were eligible for IFI but did not participate. The participant group (N = 177) is split into two main subgroups – those who completed the whole programme and those who did part of it. There are three comparison groups: the first two comprise volunteers (N = 560) and those screened for IFI who were not accepted (N = 1,083), and the third is a matched group from other prison inmates (N = 1,754).

The research covered both outcome and process evaluation.[13] We focus here on the outcome research, based on recidivism within the two years after release and measured by (a) rearrest within the two years and (b) reincarceration within that time. Fabelo *et al.*(2003: *ii*) summarize the outcome results as follows:

> Results for the completers [8 per cent recidivism rate, based on reincarceration] were mitigated by the high recidivism rates of offenders who did not complete the [IFI] programme. Non-completers had a 36 per cent recidivism rate after two years compared to the 19 per cent to 22 per cent for the comparison groups. Therefore, the overall recidivism rate for [IFI] participants (completers and non-completers) was slightly higher (24 per cent) than for all comparison groups.

This is a very odd finding and appears to make little sense theoretically: if exposure to IFI is so beneficial to the completers, why should partial exposure to IFI make things worse?

The explanation is really quite simple. The completers are elsewhere referred to as graduates and are defined (Fabelo *et. al.* 2003: 11) as follows:

Graduation is defined by [IFI] as:
• Completion of at least 16 months or more in the programme;

- Completion of 6 months of aftercare;

- Hold a job and have been an active member in Church for the previous 3 months;

- Have verification from the Parole Officer, Mentor, Sponsor, Response and Faith Community Coordinator, and [IFI] staff regarding satisfactory completion of aftercare requirements.

It is evident that the criteria for being a completer/graduate are not based solely on the experience of IFI in prison, but also involve compliance *after release*, especially during the first six months of aftercare. It is no surprise, therefore, that this group has lower recidivism rates than expectation. By contrast, the 'non-completers' comprise those who have experienced the IFI programme but are less compliant in the six months after release, for example because of early reconviction or avoiding aftercare requirements, and may be expected to have higher recidivism rates.

One lesson here is clear: the research team should set the criterion for the 'experimental group'. It is not acceptable for the programme organizers to choose a particular subgroup and define that group as 'graduates' for the purposes of evaluation. It is fortunate that the report makes these flaws in the research design clear to the reader. Surprisingly, the authors themselves have not recognized the fundamental importance of this point.

The main figures for two-year recidivism are shown in Table 10.2. If we compare all IFI participants with any of the three comparison groups, the differences are fairly small, and any differences are marginally unfavourable to IFI. The differences between graduates/completers and non-completers are evident for both criteria of recidivism but are of course accounted for by the flawed selection of the 'graduate' group indicated above. Our main conclusion is that, on the basis of this reanalysis, IFI makes no difference to recidivism rates.

Additionally, the non-completer group is very mixed, as the footnote to Table 10.2 indicates. To investigate this further, we can refer to the later report by Johnson (2003), since here the recidivism rates for IFI participants are broken down by more detailed subgroups according to time spent in the programme and whether early parole was granted.[14] This analysis produced a very odd finding, not highlighted in Johnson's report. As we show in Table 10.3 below, the 51 IFI non-completers who are paroled early have very high recidivism rates (62.7 per cent rearrested and 47.1 per cent reincarcerated within two years). These rates are approximately twice as high as those of the comparison groups in

Table 10.2 IFI study: Recidivism outcome results*

Group	Per cent arrested within 2 years of release	Per cent incarcerated within 2 years of release
IFI total		
Completed IFI (graduates, *N* = 75)	17.3%	8.0%
Did not complete (*N* = 102)	50.0%	36.3%
All IFI Participants (*N* = 177)	36.2%	24.3%
Comparison Groups		
Match (*N* = 1754)	35.0%	20.3%
Volunteer (*N* = 560)	29.3%	19.1%
Screened (*N* = 1083)	34.9%	22.3%

*Based on Fabelo *et al.* 2003: 21–23.
**The 102 are made up as follows: 48 'removed' from IFI (24 dropped out; 19 removed for discipline reasons; 4 removed at request of staff, 1 on medical grounds), and 54 'parole/mandatory release' (38 spent < 16 months in the IFI programme and 16 spent > 16 months in the programme).

Table 10.3 IFI study: Recidivism of the IFI group: three subgroups compared

IFI Group	Percent arrested within 2 yrs of release	Percent incarcerated within 2 yrs of release
Completed IFI ('graduates', N = 75)	17.3%	8.0%
Did not complete – paroled early (N = 51)*	62.7%	47.1%
Did not complete – other reasons (N = 51)	37.3%	23.5%
All IFI Participants (N = 177)	36.2%	24.3%

*Johnson, 2003: 20, Table 6

Table 10.2. The other 51 IFI non-completers have recidivism rates not too different from the comparison groups, yet 48 of these are presumably the prisoners 'removed' from IFI.

The patterns these data show are a major puzzle for interpretation, and *if correctly reported* should lead to further investigation of the dataset. Clearly, there is no theoretical reason why IFI involvement followed by early parole should lead to such a substantially *increased* risk of recidivism. Indeed, the decision of the parole board in such cases would normally be based on the chances of reoffending being low. It is strange the research team has not followed up these points.

Setting aside these particular criticisms, it seems that more might be learned from this project by reconsidering what is the most appropriate total IFI participant group for the study. The 'experimental group' should surely include (at least) IFI 'non-completers' who spent time in the programme but were not removed and did not drop out. As we understand it, these individuals had the same experience of the IFI programme as 'graduates' *up to the date of release.* A legitimate total group for outcome evaluation in this study might then be defined as the 75 'graduates' plus these additional participants (who might number as many as 54).[15]

(d) Reviewing the research findings: controversy and debate

In addition to the individual studies analyzed above, there has been one important publication based on a systematic review of the literature (Johnson *et al.* 2002). This report – entitled *Objective Hope* – is broadly based, covering the whole range of recent empirical research on the effects of both 'organic' religion and faith-based organizations (termed 'intentional religion'). Nearly 800 research publications are reviewed, the bulk of which investigate the effects of organic religion (e.g. church involvement) on health or well-being outcomes (e.g. mortality, alcohol use, educational attainment, self-esteem). The 25 studies of initiatives by faith-based organizations (FBOs) are listed in Johnson *et al.*'s Table 2 (2002: 38).[16] Although the number of publications is small, *Objective Hope's* conclusions focus closely on the effects of intentional religion. The authors are scrupulous in pointing to the methodological shortcomings in some of the research and making recommendations for better quality in future research. But they are cautiously optimistic in arguing 'what we do know about their effectiveness is positive and encouraging. FBOs appear to have advantages over comparable secular institutions in helping individuals overcome difficult circumstances (e.g. imprisonment and drug abuse)' (*ibid*: 21).

This optimistic stance continued when Johnson's IFI evaluation was published (2003). In a University of Pennsylvania newsletter (2003), John DiIulio, a CRRUCS adviser, University professor and former Prison Fellowship board member was quoted as saying 'This excellent study suggests that this faith-based programme works in that, two years after release and counting, it benefits most prisoners who make it all the way through ... More research is badly needed, but the first statistical findings are encouraging.' The IFI report was, in fact, officially launched at a White House roundtable discussion in June 2003, which is indicative of the degree of political interest shown by George W. Bush's administration. On taking office, President Bush established a White House Office of Faith-Based Community Initiatives to help religious groups compete for an estimated 5.5 billion UKP in federal funding (see Loconte 2001). In the US press there was much comment around this time about the merits and legitimacy of IFI's programmes in prisons (e.g. *Dallas Morning News* 2003; Goodstein 2003).

However, criticism of the IFI evaluation followed rapidly. In an important article entitled 'Faith-Based Fudging: How a Bush-promoted Christian prison programme fakes success by massaging data' Kleiman (2003) argued that the results reported for the IFI evaluation were misleading due to selection bias in setting up the experimental group. Kleiman essentially makes the same critical points about the research design as those made earlier in this chapter, concerning bias in selecting the IFI 'graduates'. Kleiman writes:

Here's how the study got adulterated ... InnerChange started with 177 volunteer prisoners but only 75 of them 'graduated'. Graduation involved sticking with the programme, not only in prison but after release. No one counted as a graduate, for example, unless he got a job. Naturally, the graduates did better than the control group. Anything that selects out from a group of ex-inmates those who hold jobs is going to look like a miracle cure, because getting a job is among the very best predictors of staying out of trouble.... The InnerChange cheerleaders simply ignored the other 102 participants who dropped out, were kicked out, or got early parole and didn't finish. Naturally, the non-graduates did worse than the control group. If you select out the winners, you leave mostly losers.

What response did these criticisms bring from Johnson or from CRRUCS? If Kleiman had got it wrong, one could have expected an explanation and a defence of the research design and data analysis for the IFI study, but this has not appeared – at least not in any straightforward way. A later University of Pennsylvania newsletter makes no mention of selection bias problems, except perhaps to urge more caution in interpreting the results. It quotes Johnson as saying: 'The Texas programme might be biased ... because recruits were selected for their suitability – they had to be able to read and couldn't be sex offenders – rather than being a true random sample. And [he] would be more comfortable with data that looked at recidivism rates over three years after release rather than just two.' (University of Pennsylvania 2004).[17] These comments simply miss Kleiman's main point, which is confirmed and elaborated by our own analysis.

(e) Contentious research findings

To those unfamiliar with applied social research, it may seem odd that research findings can be so contentious – but in fact this is typical rather than unusual. Indeed, one textbook on social research methods, appropriately titled *The Limitations of Social Research* (Shipman 1988) is organized entirely around controversies in the field of education; Shipman's review of these controversies shows the interplay of values, interests and politics in determining the way in which research results can be argued and interpreted. Weiss (in Bulmer 1986) says: 'the use of social science research in the sphere of public policy is an extraordinarily complex phenomenon' and suggests seven possible models for research, many of which involve quite complex interplay between sponsors, interested parties and the researchers. Similarly, Robson (1993: 183) states:

> It is almost inevitable that an evaluation will have a political dimension … [i]nnovations, policies and practices will have their sponsors and advocates … critics and sceptics. … the existence and the outcomes of an evaluation research project are likely to be of interest to a range of 'stake-holders'– national and local government, both politicians themselves and bureaucrats, the agencies and their officials responsible for administering the programme or policy; persons responsible for direct delivery; the clients or targets of the programme and groups such as unions responsible for looking after their interests; possibly taxpayers and citizens generally. It would be highly unlikely for the interests of all these groups to be identical, and … whatever the results and findings of an evaluation, some will be pleased and others not.

Thus the several groups that have an interest – often a partisan interest – in a particular research study may well differ in their views of what the results are or what they mean.[18]

These sources help to give a perspective on the differing interpretations of studies of faith-based initiatives in prisons. We have the usual range of interested parties – national/state government, politicians and bureaucrats, agencies responsible for instigating programmes and policy, agency personnel and so on. Those running faith-based programmes naturally believe in positive outcomes as a result of their work. They hope for evidence of reductions in recidivism as one major way of demonstrating the effect they have on the future lives of participants and may well select findings from research results that suit their case.[19] Politicians and bureaucrats may also be highly selective, although their agenda will be different; examples are given in Chapter 11.

2. The Kainos study: an analysis of two-year reconvictions

We turn now to the impact of Kainos Community on reconviction rates. This analysis of recidivism was undertaken as part of a wider evaluation of Kainos for the Home Office, Kainos and the Prison Service, the results of which have already been outlined in Chapters 4–6 and 9. In this chapter we analyze the patterns of recidivism of released prisoners who have been participants in Kainos programmes, using reconviction as the criterion.

Reconviction patterns were studied for all Kainos participants released from prison between late 1997 and October 1999. The majority of these prisoners were from The Verne (which had the longest-running Kainos Community), with some participants from Highpoint North and Highpoint South.[20] For the initial project, this group – the 'Kainos reconviction sample' – was followed up for a year from release date, but additional research extended this tracking period to two years and is the basis for the analysis below.[21] The reconviction sample was necessarily restricted to British nationals; foreign prisoners are usually deported after release, and are therefore not 'at risk' of reconviction in England and Wales. Information on court appearances and reconvictions was obtained from the Home Office's Offenders Index (OI), the official national database for research on criminal histories.

The analysis of reconviction rates is an intrinsic part of research evaluating the relative effectiveness of 'treatments' or sentences of offenders (Colledge *et al.* 1999; Goldblatt and Lewis 1998), and an extensive literature exists on the methodology of the approach (e.g. Lloyd *et al.* 1994). Central to any reconviction study is how comparisons are made between the reconvictions of the sample and the 'expectation' of their performance (Colledge *et al.* 1999). In most studies a comparison group is defined, but it is rare for this group to be matched to the 'experimental group' or sample in any exact way.

Consequently, in most analyses of reconviction rates, criminal histories and other background factors (age, sex etc.) must be taken into account by using 'statistical control' even when a comparison group is involved. Much of the research on these topics is related to the development of 'prediction scores' for the risk of reconviction. Essentially, a prediction score assesses the likelihood of a reconviction within a given period (usually two years) for offenders of a specified age, sex and criminal history. In England and Wales, the established scoring method is OGRS (Offender Group Reconviction Scale), developed by the Home Office, predicting the likelihood of reconviction within two years from date of sentence, or release from prison. The second version, OGRS2 (Taylor 1999) takes account of more details of criminal history than OGRS1 (Copas and Marshall 1998), though the logic of the approach is the same. We have adapted the general approach of OGRS to the needs of the current reconviction study in ways that are described below.

(a) The samples

(i) Kainos reconviction sample (KRS)
Data identifying offenders who had participated in the Kainos programme in The Verne, Highpoint North and Highpoint South were assembled by liaison with local Kainos coordinators and through subsequent checks via official prison records. Data were required on name, sex, date of birth, date of court appearance (when sentenced), and date released from the prison system (which had to be before 1 October, 1999). Identification numbers for the national criminal records database were available for most of the sample, and were also noted.

A list of 97 offenders was submitted to the Offender's Index (OI) for matching with OI records. The first attempt yielded only 61 unambiguous matches, but after a second attempt, the number of valid matches was increased to 84 offenders, who comprise the Kainos reconviction sample (KRS).[22] The characteristics of these offenders will be described below.

(ii) The Comparison sample (CS)
The Comparison sample (CS) was designed to consist of prisoners discharged from institutions similar to those that had Kainos Communities and over the same time period – but otherwise to be as large as possible to increase the statistical power of the research design. The sample was therefore drawn from all sentenced prisoners released from prisons in England and Wales in 1996 and 1997. This was the most recent cohort of ex-prisoners for which an OI database had been assembled, linking data on release from the prison system to OI criminal histories. This sample is utilized for Home Office Research, Development and Statistics (RDS)

research, including studies of reconviction, and we are grateful to the Home Office for access to it. For the purposes of basic comparability with the Kainos sample, we restricted the CS to: adult ex-prisoners; British nationals; having served sentences of six months to fifteen years; released from medium and low security male prisons ('Cat C' and 'Cat D'), or female prisons (excluding local prisons). Selection by the OI based on these criteria initially yielded a total of over 16,000 cases, but after imposing these restrictions, the final Comparison sample comprised 13,832 ex-prisoners.

(iii) Data on the two samples

Comparable data were supplied by the OI for the two samples, including: sex; dates of birth, first court appearance and court appearance for which imprisoned; criminal history, including number of court appearances and type of offence; OGRS1 and OGRS2 prediction scores; and date of first reconviction after release (where applicable).[23] These data provide the basis for the detailed analysis of reconviction rates below.

We begin, however, by comparing the profiles of the Kainos sample and the Comparison sample, as follows:[24]

- *Gender.* The Kainos sample has a higher proportion of females (18 per cent) than the Comparison sample (12 per cent).

- *Age.* At the beginning of the sentence the age profile of the two samples is similar, with just over 40 per cent of each sample aged 30 or more. However, by the stage of release from prison, the Kainos sample has an older age profile: 36 per cent were aged 35 or more, compared with 26 per cent for the Comparison sample. This difference is largely a result of longer sentences among the Kainos sample, which we comment on below.

- *The criminal histories* of the two samples also show differences: the Kainos sample have slightly higher average numbers of previous convictions, but the convictions are spread over longer periods. The average rate of offending during the course of the criminal history is very similar for the two groups (0.82 and 0.80 court appearances per year respectively). This is an important point, since the rate of offending is very closely related to risk of reconviction (Copas and Marshall 1998).

- The key measure of *criminal history* is, however, provided by OGRS score. Using the first version, OGRS1, 49 per cent of the Kainos sample were predicted as reconvicted within two years, a figure very close to that for the Comparison sample (48 per cent). For OGRS2, the figures are a little more separated, with a 3 per cent difference between the KRS (47 per cent) and CS (44 per cent). Nonetheless, on either version of OGRS the difference is small, indicating that the overall criminal history profile of the Kainos sample is fairly close to that of the Comparison sample.

- The biggest difference between the Kainos sample and the Comparison sample is *in time spent in prison since sentence.* The average time in prison was 25.9 months for the Kainos sample, nearly twice as long as the figure for the CS at 13.7 months. This indicates that the Kainos sample have served substantially longer sentences than the offenders in the Comparison sample.

(b) Reconviction rates

For this study the most important data on the two samples are the two-year reconviction rates. The rate for the Kainos sample is, at 36.9 per cent, nearly 6 per cent less than the rate for the Comparison sample at 42.7 per cent. A simple statistical test on this finding shows that a difference of this magnitude is highly likely to arise by chance alone in a sample of this size;[25] in statistical terminology it is certainly 'non-significant'. Of course, this bald comparison takes no account of criminal histories or other characteristics of the two samples. The Kainos sample is in many ways similar in composition to the Comparison sample, especially on basic aspects of criminal history. On the other hand, the gender balance in the Kainos sample is more even, at time of release from prison Kainos sample offenders are older than the Comparison sample, and they have served longer sentences. We now turn to an analysis which takes all these factors into account.

(i) The Comparison sample as a 'standard'

The rationale for the Comparison sample (CS) is that it acts as a 'standard' against which the results for the Kainos reconviction sample (KRS) can be assessed. One way to approach this task systematically is to 'recalibrate' a risk score for two-year reconviction using the OGRS approach, using the variables that are the core of the CS data. Expected rates of two-year reconviction for released prisoners can then be calculated; in short, the observed reconviction rates of the Kainos sample can be compared with expectation.

Following the methods in Copas and Marshall (1998), the 'recalibration' was undertaken, and a 'two-year reconviction risk score' (TYRRS) was produced. Appendix B gives a brief account,[26] and further details are available in a separate technical paper prepared for the Home Office

RDS (Rose 2001). The TYRRS is thus a prediction of risk, analogous to an OGRS score, based on a large sample (the CS); however, unlike OGRS it is not intended to be of general utility outside the confines of this study.

As a further refinement, the TYRRS was developed in two forms:

- TYRRS1 is a prediction of the two-year reconviction risk for released prisoners based on the comparison sample as a whole, and takes no account of prison establishment;

- TYRRS2 also takes account of whether the offender has been released from the Verne, Highpoint North or Highpoint South.

There are only minor differences between the two versions of the score, although TYRRS2 is utilized for sections of our results where distinctions are made between establishments.

(ii) Reconviction rates compared with expectation

The results for the Kainos sample as a whole are shown in Table 10.4. For a sample with the characteristics of the KRS, the TYRRS1 scores predict 43.1 per cent of offenders would be reconvicted within two years, and the TYRRS2 analysis predicts 42.4 per cent. As we have seen, the observed two-year reconviction rate is 36.9 per cent (31 out of 84). In broad terms, this is some 6 per cent below the predicted rate, representing five fewer reconvictions than would be expected on the basis of the known characteristics of the KRS. However, this is a small 'improvement', and in purely statistical terms it is not significantly different from either of the predictions.[27] This means that the observed reduction of 6 per cent in reconviction rates is well within the range of variation expected by chance alone in a sample of this size, rather than indicating an effect of Kainos participation on reconviction. On the basis of these results there are no clear statistical grounds for concluding that Kainos Community prisoners have reconviction rates that are any lower (or higher) than would be expected for released prisoners as a whole.

The results shown in Table 10.4 do not, however, rule out the possibility that a sub-group within the KRS may have a significantly lower reconviction rate than expectation. Table 10.5 breaks down the sample by establishment – and also within one establishment (The Verne) by a simple two-fold division based on amount of exposure to the Kainos programme.

In percentage terms, the biggest difference is for those with the higher level of exposure to the Kainos programme at The Verne, where the 25 per cent actual reconviction rate compares with 37.5 per cent predicted

Table 10.4 Actual and predicted two year reconviction rates for Kainos
Community prisoners

	Total number	Reconviction rate	Number reconvicted within two years
Kainos sample	84	36.9%	31
TYRRS1 score prediction	84	43.1% predicted	36.24 expected
TYRRS2 score prediction	84	42.4% predicted	35.58 expected

Table 10.5 Actual and predicted two-year reconviction rates for Kainos
Community prisoners, by groups based on establishment

Kainos sample: establishment and group	No. of cases	Predicted reconvictions: TYRRS1 scores		Predicted reconvictions: TYRRS2 scores		Kainos sample: actual two year reconvictions	
		Percent	Expected number	Percent	Expected number	Percent	Actual number
The Verne (all cases)	56	45.7%	25.58	45.1%	25.27	41.1%	23
The Verne Lower exposure	32	51.5%	16.47	50.9%	16.28	53.1%	17
The Verne Higher exposure	24	37.9%	9.10	37.5%	8.99	25.0%	6
Highpoint South (Male)	13	47.7%	6.20	50.9%	6.62	46.2%	6
Highpoint North (Female)	15	29.8%	4.46	24.6%	3.70	13.3%	2
All cases	84	43.1%	36.24	42.4%	35.58	36.9%	31

– which equates to six reconvictions for the 24 individuals, rather than
the nine expected. This is the strongest suggestion in the data of an
improvement over expectation, but it can be no more than a suggestion,
since the numbers involved are small. Overall, the findings from Table
10.5 are that, for each group of offenders, the number reconvicted is
close to the figure expected, based on either of the TYRRS scores. Testing

confirms that none of the differences approach statistical significance, so once again the patterns could have arisen through chance variations in a sample of this size.[28]

(iii) Comparison with reconviction data from the Verne
Kainos staff at The Verne maintain a database which monitors reconvictions that result in a return to the prison system, using data available within the Prison Service. All but one of the 56 KRS members from the Verne appeared on the Verne's own database. The reconviction data from the OI were therefore compared with the information from The Verne for 55 cases. Overall, there is a high level of consistency between the two data sets,[29] and the findings of this comparison clearly strengthen the belief in the reliability of each set of data.

3. Discussion of the Kainos reconviction analysis

The results clearly indicate that although the two-year reconviction rates for the Kainos sample are reduced compared with expectation, they are not significantly lower than predicted for released prisoners with these characteristics. What conclusions should we draw from this finding?

First, the small number in the Kainos sample places limitations on the research. In order to demonstrate that the Kainos programme had a significant effect on the two-year reconviction rate – at least at the 95 per cent confidence level conventionally accepted in statistical analysis – it would be necessary for the observed rate to be reduced from the 43 per cent 'expected' to 32 per cent in the KRS. In round figures this means that out of the 84 cases, the number reconvicted within the two-year period would need to be as low as 27, rather than the 31 observed. In percentage terms, a reduction of just over 10 per cent in the reconviction rate is needed in order for the 'effect' to be detected as statistically significant, given a sample of size 84. Smaller effects – for example of the order of 5 per cent or 6 per cent – can be reliably detected only by studying a larger sample.[30]

Second, do any other aspects of the design of the reconviction study or its implementation cast doubt on the validity of the findings? In common with most studies on reconviction, the research design is 'quasi-experimental' (Campbell and Stanley 1966), and there will be a number of potential 'threats to validity'. One design problem is that members of the Comparison sample were released from prison in 1996/97, whereas the Kainos reconviction sample were mainly discharged in 1998/99. Although data on trends in reconviction rates are necessarily published several years in arrears, and the latest available figures for released prisoners are for the first quarter of 1996 (Kershaw *et al*. 1999), there seems to be little evidence of major trends over time. Further, the magnitude of any change in reconviction rates over the period from 1996/97 to 1998/99 would have to be unprecedented in order to threaten the findings of this chapter.

Many other aspects of the research design were tightly controlled, for example the strict comparability of the data source (the OI) and standard format of data for each sample. Naturally, this does not mean the data are totally reliable as measures of criminal history, but it does mean that any imperfections are common to the data for both samples. The restriction of the study to British nationals reduced the size of the Kainos reconviction sample but enhanced the validity of the study. The representativeness of the Comparison sample is clear since it is, in effect, the population of all eligible releasees in the 1996/97. The Kainos sample also started with a 'population' of all eligible participants, but the size was reduced to 84 by the need for information on participants and subsequent matching problems with the OI data. However, it is doubtful whether this process has threatened the representativeness of the Kainos sample.

4. Conclusions

What main conclusions can we draw about the impact of Christian-based prison programmes on recidivism from this literature review, and from the analysis of reconvictions among Kainos participants? We suggest the following:

- Although much has been written about Christian faith-based programmes in prison, only a handful of previous studies of recidivism among groups of participants are academically acceptable, i.e. where the research has resulted in peer-reviewed publications. We have assessed the three identifiable research studies and all publications based on them. They are: two research studies on programmes in the USA (Prison Fellowship in New York State, and IFI-Texas); and one piece of research on Humaitá prison in Brazil.

- Claims made for the reduction of recidivism among released prisoners who have experienced faith-based programmes have generally been exaggerated, and our conclusion is that no previous study has shown an effect that can be substantiated. A detailed scrutiny of the methodology of each of the three previous studies has shown flaws both in research design (most commonly a 'selection bias' in defining the key group of participants) and in data analysis (for example, not controlling on 'risk factors' for recidivism). Thus, unfortunately, 'internal validity' is poor for each of the three previous studies.

- The methodology used in our own study of Kainos Community was much more rigorous than the previous research reviewed, involving a large comparison group and a multivariate analysis of background factors from a standardized data source (Home Office, Offenders Index). Our research, based on a sample of Kainos Community participants in three English prisons, showed a marginal decrease in recidivism (as measured by reconvictions over two years), but this decrease was too small to be statistically significant. However, our sample of Kainos participants numbered only 84 in total; a more definitive assessment would need to be based on a larger sample, which will be possible in the future when enough Kainos participants have been released from the prison system.[31]

- Taking our own study in conjunction with the earlier studies, can any summary statement be made about the impact of Christian-based prison programmes on recidivism? It must first be observed that the 'external validity' – that is, the possibility of generalizing from the results of any one individual study (whether positive, negative or zero) to other settings – is limited. Account must of course be taken of the exact nature of the programme, the selection of participants, as well as the location (the prison, the wing or unit) and the broader social context (the state, society etc). For example, for the Kainos study the factors discussed in Chapters 5–8 would first need to be considered.[32] More broadly, we have the problem of how to generalize from a total of only four studies, in disparate settings (and countries), where the programmes differ very significantly, and where the results are (on our analysis) almost entirely 'null findings'. Although there are no major inconsistencies between these 'null' results, it is too early to conclude that faith-based programmes can have no effect on recidivism; rather, no such effect has yet been demonstrated.

- Given the large-scale investment in faith-based programmes currently (especially in the USA), the need is for more research – and better quality research – on recidivism outcomes. Claims made by proponents of faith-based organizations about the effectiveness of programmes in reducing recidivism should not be taken at face value[33] (see Chapter 11). Good quality studies of recidivism are not easy to undertake: they should be carried out by independent and well-qualified researchers, and peer reviewed before results are released. Ideally, an accredited organization such as the Campbell Collaboration[34] might monitor the results of studies and help in assessing their quality.

Notes

1 For example, Florida has faith-based programmes in some 20 prisons; it appears that evaluations have been carried out in at least two institutions, but few details are available.

2 Johnson *et al.*'s report lists some 25 evaluation studies of the impact of 'intentional religion'. Six of these are based on former prisoners, and of these only three focus on recidivism.

3 The article argues that PF participation has no effect on institutional adjustment, although they acknowledge there are significant problems with the data.

4 In Johnson's Table 10.3 (1997) each PF subgroup is compared with its matched non-PF subgroup. A statistical test comparing the arrest rates for the three non-PF subgroups, however, shows $\chi^2 = 0.735$ (2 d.f.), $p = 0.692$, indicating that the rates are not significantly different. In these circumstances, the whole comparison group can be considered together – as in our Table 10.1 and statistical power in comparing with PF subgroups is maximized.

5 $\chi^2 = 7.49$ (3 d.f.) $p = 0.058$, so the differences shown in Table 10.1 are statistically significant at $p < 0.10$, but not quite at $p < 0.05$.

6 Although the rearrest rate for the medium PF group is 9 per cent higher than for the comparison group (45 per cent *vs.* 35.8 per cent), considered on its own, the difference is not significantly different.

7 There are 401 cases included in Johnson's *et al.'s* Table 10.4, compared with 402 in Table 10.3; one member of the comparison group is absent, presumably due to missing data.

8 Later information indicates that Braganca was originally an APAC prison (Creighton 2001: 21) although Johnson does not mention this.

9 There was no data on rearrest for 213 individuals – stated to be 46 per cent (Johnson 2002: 9) but in fact comprising 54 per cent of the 395 ex-prisoners.

10 The *n*s in Johnson's Table 10.1 are: LoRisk/Humaitá = 34, HiRisk/Humaitá = 41, LoRisk/Braganca = 50, HiRisk/Braganca = 42, totalling 167. This is the effective total sample size for the most important parts of the recidivism analysis.

11 For example, Section 3 of Johnson's findings (on the aggregated number of rearrests) is wrongly based on all prisoners rather than just those arrested. The appropriate indicator is the number of rearrests per 'arrestee'. Section 4 looks at the reincarceration rate, but the analysis suffers so much from data loss that it is really not worthwhile. The same comment applies to section 5 on the severity of rearrest offences (Johnson 2002: 9).

12 These reports are available from the Criminal Justice Policy Council website: www.cjpc.state.tx.us (accessed December 2004).

13 Johnson (2003) gives a much more extensive coverage of the process evaluation.

14 An 18 month recidivism period (months 7 to 24 inclusive) is also considered for one tabulation, in an attempt to control statistically for the selection effect of the graduate group.

316

15 On the basis of the groups Johnson (2003) distinguished, non-completers paroled early would be included. Naturally, the counter-intuitively high recidivism rates reported for this subgroup would need to be carefully checked.

16 Only three of these involve prisoners as the research sample and recidivism as the outcome variable. Two have been discussed above, but we have been unable to obtain a copy of the report for the third (Florida Department of Corrections 2000).

17 At one point, Kleiman (2003) writes that Harvard public policy professor Anne Piehl, who reviewed the [IFI] study before it was published, calls this instance of selection bias 'cooking the books'.

18 A policy-relevant applied social research project will usually have many 'interested parties'. Based on Robson's analysis we can list the following: researchers; participants and respondents (with subgroups such as management/workers or staff/inmates); sponsors, clients and funding organizations; policy actors – i.e. policy makers, bureaucrats, politicians, government; practitioners; interest groups; journalists and public opinion. For any given research study or research programme, the list of interested parties is unlikely to be so long or so complex, but nonetheless there will be a number of groups for whom the research and its findings are important in practical or political terms. There are likely to be implications for how the research is conducted and how the results are understood and used.

19 Two examples relating to the current project on Kainos Community are given in the Conclusions to this chapter.

20 Although Kainos Community was running in Swaleside over this period, no Swaleside participants had been released from the prison system by October 1999.

21 In Burnside et al. (2001) the follow-up period was therefore one year. We are grateful to Kainos Community for permission to use the two-year follow up reconviction data presented in this chapter, prepared by Gerry Rose for Kainos in July 2002. The data for the first year after release is occasionally referred to for comparison.

22 Difficulties included aliases or name changes (more likely for females), and at the second stage more prominence was given to matching the CRO number. Considerable effort was expended in order to match as many cases as possible with OI records since it was crucial to maximize the useable number in the Kainos sample.

23 The data were in an identical form for each sample, although two variables – length of sentence and establishment from which released – were available only for the Comparison sample.

24 Further details are given in Burnside et al. (2001).

25 The χ^2 value was 1.17, with a probability value very close 0.30.

26 The method used was a logistic regression (Colledge et al. 1999) for the CS data, with 'reconviction within two years' as the dependent variable and the OGRS predictor variables as independent variables (see Appendix B).

317

27 χ^2 values are 1.3327 (1 d.f.) for comparison with TYRRS1 predictions, and 1.0238 (1 d.f.) for TYRRS2 predictions. Neither approaches significance at the 5% level.

28 χ^2 values for the ten tests (all on 1 d.f.) range from 0.012 to 1.9371 and none approaches statistical significance at the 5 per cent level.

29 For the 32 with no recorded OI reconvictions, none were recorded as returns to prison. Fourteen of the 23 with reconvictions were shown on The Verne database as returns to prison. For the remaining nine cases, the OI records of reconvictions were examined; in eight cases, the reconvictions resulted in non-custodial sentences only, and in one case a custodial sentence had been imposed.

30 A sample of size 265 would be needed to detect an effect size of 6 per cent; for a 5 per cent effect size, the sample would need to be 380. For further discussion, see Burnside *et al.* (2001).

31 Kainos Community continues to monitor returns to prison for released participants from The Verne. A memorandum from Kainos (2004) notes that on the basis of November 2004 management information, for 186 'Kainos graduates' released up to 2002, the percentage recommitted to prison within two years was only 14.5 per cent. Comparison with a control group is of course needed if a claim of an effect is to be substantiated, and this is acknowledged in the memorandum although no further research had been commissioned at that time. The memorandum also quotes selectively from our own reconviction study by picking out only the most positive reconviction results from Table 10.5, for the higher exposure group at The Verne (n = 24); no mention is made of the remainder of the reconviction sample at The Verne or elsewhere.

32 As Yin emphasizes, each research project must be considered as a case study; he uses the term 'analytic generalization' to refer to the way in which external validity may be addressed (1994: 30–32).

33 For example, in an article published in *Christianity Today* Magazine (Dec 17, 2001) Kainos Community, commenting on the early results of the current study (based on reconvictions within a year from release) 'says that once released from prison, former inmates of the Christian wings – who volunteer for the programme – have a short-term reoffending rate of 23 per cent. The charity accepts a prison service finding that the general prison population has a reoffending rate of 26 per cent after one year.' Ian Aldred, Chairman of Kainos Community, is then quoted as follows '*In no way does this mean the Christian wings have failed. Three per cent is an enormous improvement in lives changed and money saved [when ex-convicts are sent to jail again].*' (italics added). This rather misses the point that the two rates are not significantly different.

34 The international Campbell Collaboration 'is a non-profit organization that aims to help people make well-informed decisions about the effects of interventions in the social, behavioural and educational arenas.' (www. campbellcollaboration.org, 2004). Clearly, this is a very broad remit, and much of their current work focuses on systematic reviews of the literature, which depend on having a large number of studies on the same effect.

Chapter 11

Keeping faith in prison: the promise of faith-based units

A prison sentence is not passed in order to deprive a man of his religion. Kainos might be one element helping to drag British prisons from their scandalous condition

Christopher Howse (2001)

This chapter looks ahead to the promise of faith-based units. It brings the Kainos story up-to-date and highlights the main themes and lessons from previous chapters. It also looks at new programmes that have been established in the UK and around the world and a concluding comment on what such units might mean for prisons at the start of the twenty-first century.

1. Curtains for Kainos?

The Kainos evaluation (Burnside *et al.* 2001) was broadly positive and recommended, at the very least, that those Communities which had strong support from local management should be allowed to continue. The Prison Service's initial response, however, was negative. In the House of Lords, Lord Rooker reported for the Government in the following terms:

This chapter was authored by Jonathan Burnside

319

Whilst [the evaluation] has shown some modest, positive effects on prisoners' attitudes and behaviour, the research found that the programme had no impact on reconviction rates in the 12 months after the prisoner's release. In the light of that the Prison Service decided as a matter of policy that it would not be right to continue the programme.... It said that it would take a similar approach with any faith-based offender treatment. I understand that this was done in the light of the evaluation and other available information, including the views of the Chaplain-General and the Muslim adviser [to prisons]'.[1]

In its own statement the Prison Service also highlighted the reconviction findings, adding:

In the light of the research findings, and taking account of a wide range of views, the Prison Service decided it would not be appropriate to provide public money for religiously-based offender units in prisons.

(Carter 2001: 1)

Ken Sutton, Prison Service Director of Resettlement, subsequently informed prison governors that: 'it would not be appropriate to provide public money at either local or central level to support [Kainos] or other religious-based intervention[s]' (Johnston 2001a: 18). (In fact the Prison Service did not provide any public money for Kainos at the time of the research). Elaborating further, Sutton claimed the Prison Service management board was 'particularly concerned about intensive religious-based interventions and would not want Kainos to be extended' (ibid.).

It was curtains for Kainos. The Communities were set to close in March 2002 (ibid.), although Kainos would continue at HMP The Verne until August 2002 (Carter 2001: 1) to give the prison time to sort out its dormitory accommodation.[2] The Prison Service agreed to limited funding during this wind-up period to enable Kainos to make an orderly exit (Aldred 2004).

However, the decision to close Kainos could not be justified on the basis of the research. This would have been difficult, because the decision ran counter to the main recommendation of the Kainos evaluation, to some positive findings from the attitudinal study and to the largely positive results of the processual study. Instead the reconviction figures were singled out as providing partial authority along with 'a wide range of views' of which the opinions of the Chaplain-General and the Muslim Adviser to Prisons received honourable mention.

When the Kainos evaluation was commissioned, great play was made of the importance attached to religious freedom and equality of opportunity. Oddly, the finding that Kainos seemed to adhere to the spirit and the letter of equal opportunities legislation received no publicity.[3] Instead, Ken Sutton informed Governors that the Prison Service Management Board was 'particularly concerned about intensive religious-based interventions' (Johnston 2001a: 18). What concerns were these that were not considered by the evaluation?

Both statements were studiously neutral regarding the faith-specific nature of Kainos. But the admission that the Muslim Adviser to Prisons was influential in the final decision rather spoiled the effect, as was clear from the press reaction. Critics of the Prison Service immediately seized upon the decision as evidence of 'bureaucrats over-reacting to Muslim concerns' (Aitken 2001: 26);[4] a chaplain at one of the affected prisons described it as 'genuflectuating towards the altar of multi-faith political correctness' (ibid.), and an MP on the floor of the House of Commons suspected the decision was 'an irrational reaction to Muslim opinion following the events of 11th September'.[5] The Prison Service was forced to respond to allegations of 'Muslim pressure' (Johnston 2001b) and denied the decision to close Kainos was 'a gesture to multi-faith working' (Carter 2001: 1).

Even so, the Government (via Lord Rooker) and the Prison Service did not speak in one voice. The Prison Service's claim that: 'it would not be appropriate *to provide public money* for religiously-based offender units in prisons' (ibid.; emphasis added) was rather different to Lord Rooker's claim that it was wrong *as a matter of policy* to continue the programme. If it was simply a matter of not providing public money, then surely Kainos or any other 'religiously-based offender unit' could continue, providing they raised their own funds. This had been the position since 1999 anyway. If it was wrong as a matter of policy to continue the programme, then the question of who funded Kainos was irrelevant.

The opacity of the Prison Service's decision left it open to criticism, not all of it well-founded. Jonathan Aitken, himself recently released from prison, wrote a leader article in *The Daily Telegraph* criticizing the decision (2001). Unfortunately Aitken did not take account of the basic findings of the Kainos evaluation, which hardly helped his point. His claim that the reoffence rate of 22 per cent was 'far better than the national average' simply ignored the findings of the non-Kainos control group.

Uninformed though it was, Aitken's article sparked a wider debate among practitioners, the general public and Members of both Houses of Parliament. Fortuitously for Kainos, a Prisons Debate was scheduled in the House of Lords in November 2001, and the Earl of Dundee and Lord Hylton took the opportunity to question the Prison Service decision. The Lord Bishop of Wakefield erroneously claimed the Kainos evaluation had 'proved inconclusive' before admitting that he had not, in fact, seen the study.[6] Lord Dixon-Smith tackled the perceived 'Muslim backlash':

> ... it was disturbing to learn that programmes based on Christian principles might be frowned on because the [Prison] Service could not be seen to take a position in favour of a particular religion. I am sure that the correct response to that is ... to offer other religions the opportunity to work with prisoners in a similar fashion. Not the least of the problems faced by prisoners is that most of them have nothing to believe in. That too is something they need.[7]

Lord Rooker repeated his claim that 'following an independent evaluation the programme was found not to do the job intended. That was the reason for abandoning it'.[8] But this could only be on the basis of a very narrow definition of success. 'Independent evaluation has demonstrated – I paraphrase – that it did not work. It did not work ... as regards reconviction in the 12 months after people left. I do not know whether there are any more figures available.'[9] There were, however, important respects in which the programme could be said to 'work' and for which figures were available.

A rare voice of reason came in the form of *Daily Telegraph* columnist, Christopher Howse:

> One answer to objections from Muslim prisoners ... would be to let them, too, organize their own religious life, if there is someone to start them off. In the meantime, Christians should not be prevented from living according to their beliefs. A prison sentence is not passed in order to deprive a man of his religion. Kainos might be one element helping to drag British prisons from their scandalous condition.
>
> (2001: 27)

In the House of Commons Mark Hoban MP, unusually, took the trouble to quote from the actual evaluation: 'Independent research has described the wings as "a signpost to the Prison Service in terms of promoting standards of decency, humanity and order in prisons" '.[10] Hoban described the Prison Service's reasoning as 'confused':

Lower reoffending rates have been described as statistically insignificant but the fact that the Kainos wings have only had a short time to work has been ignored. Their purpose seems to have been misunderstood by the Prison Service, although they have received the support of governors, staff, the Prison Officers Association, Boards of Visitors (BoV) and inmates themselves, all of whom want the wings to continue their excellent work.[11]

He then asked the Minister for Prisons to reconsider the decision.

As a result of all this publicity, the Prison Service received hundreds of letters from concerned practitioners and laypersons. Freda Fisher, Chair of the Board of Visitors at The Verne exchanged letters with Director-General Martin Narey challenging the decision in view of the positive effect of Kainos on D Wing and the prison as a whole (Aldred 2004). In its Annual Report, the BoV noted: 'Many of the prison officers have brought to our attention their concern at the possible closure of the programme, even asking us to express their views to the Minister and the Prison Board' (2001: 2). The BoV also claimed that Kainos saved the Prison Service around £88,000 per year, including the salary of a night patrol officer (Kainos 2002: 22), cheaper than the cost of the Kainos programme itself. The Annual Report stated that: '[T]he Kainos wing continues to flourish and prisoners from other prisons continue to apply to come on the programme. Prisoners are only on the wing because *they want to be there*' (2001: 3; italics original).

There was also strong support for Kainos Community at the level of individual Prison Governors and Area Managers, particularly at The Verne (Aldred 2004). Martin Narey sought to respond to some of these criticisms in *The Daily Telegraph* , where he repeated the mantra that Kainos was a 'failed'[12] programme and, consistent with the Ken Sutton memo, expressed concern about 'religious pressure' even though the Kainos evaluation had made it clear these were isolated instances. Hebbern (2001), a Principal Officer on the Kainos unit at The Verne, vigorously refuted his claims, saying that: '[the Prisons Board] seem hopelessly out of touch with what is actually happening on the ground. I am really concerned for the future of this wing as it is in real danger of descending into violence and anarchy again.'

To conclude, responses to the future of Kainos were strikingly partisan. The same clichés for and against Kainos were recycled with little regard to the details of the evaluation. Supporters dubbed Kainos Communities 'islands of hope in the ocean of reoffending despair' (Aitken 2001: 26), and the Christian media happily followed this line, word-for-word in places.[13] So too did prison chaplains. A former chaplain at HMP Swaleside peddled the myth that: 'Without question, Kainos have been effective in reducing the reoffending rate in the wings from the national average of over 60 per cent to around 20 per cent' (Hogarth 2001: 1). The Earl of Dundee offered the extraordinary claim that 'Regarding reduced prisoners reoffending, arguably it has even indicated *better results than any other prisoner scheme or process*' (italics added).[14] They also revitalized old claims that Kainos 'take[s]...the negative leaders' (*ibid.*: 1) and was 'often used as a last resort for the most violent prisoners in the system'[15] which the evaluation had refuted. At the same time, the Prison Service harked back to earlier allegations about religious coercion which the evaluation had since investigated. The subject of Kainos was enough to trigger knee-jerk reactions from supporters and sceptics alike, regardless of the findings uncovered. Perhaps the issue was not 'religion and rehabilitation' at all. To some extent Kainos may simply have been a focus for the ambiguous feelings of many in a postmodern society of how to respond to Christianity in public life.

Reflecting on the Prison Service's response to the evaluation, a former prison Governor with experience of Kainos comments:

> Kainos takes a big risk....In a fear-ridden, highly political, highly centralized and controlled service, where the main performance indicator is invisibility ('coming off the front page' was how Martin Narey described his major contribution) you don't take risks. Kainos paid the price. It raised the money for [an] evaluation which appeared to show little effect on reconviction in what was then the short-term, and the Prison Service, which had good grounds to be fearful of showing any partisan support for one religion against another, wished it good riddance. I thought that hasty, and wrong. Hasty in that the full evaluation spoke of much that was very worthwhile, and much that could be tweaked to make more of what it offered. Wrong in that the argument seemed to throw out spiritual development along with improved prospects of avoiding offending.
>
> (Respondent J 2003)

2. 'New Kainos'

This ambiguity was underlined when, just before the first of the Kainos wings was due to close in March 2002, the Director-General of the Prison

Service informed Kainos that he was 'content for it to continue'. Kainos Trustees were invited to submit new proposals to continue its work, but such proposals had to be on the basis that Kainos Community would not seek Prison Service funding. At the same time, the Director-General expressed concern about its 'evangelical slant' (Johnston 2002), although what he meant by this was unclear.

The reprieve came too late to save the Communities at Highpoint North and South. Insufficient funding and staff uncertainty resulted in the decision to withdraw from these establishments by April 2002. In the case of the men's unit at Highpoint South, Prison Fellowship agreed to take on the Kainos Community staff and develop their own programme called 'Compass' (see section 3; below). However, Prison Fellowship declined the offer of the women's prison.

Kainos Trustees requested a new programme from its Coordinators at Swaleside and The Verne that would meet the problems identified in the evaluation and would give 'clarity, uniformity and clear structure' to the programme (Kainos 2002: 2). The evaluation enabled Kainos to address its weaknesses (Phillips 2003), and the Prison Service accepted its new proposals in August 2002. Like other non-accredited programmes, Kainos had to demonstrate that it satisfied the requirements of Prison Service Order (PSO) 4350 regarding Effective Regime Interventions (HM Prison Service 2002).[16]

Kainos described itself as 'a completely revamped programme' (Kainos 2002; see generally http://www.kainoscommunity.com; accessed 5th April 2005). It is thus necessary to distinguish between 'Kainos' as it existed between 1999 and 2002 and 'New Kainos' to describe the new programme which has existed since 2002. 'New Kainos' continues to operate in HMP The Verne and Swaleside. A new Kainos Community opened in HMP Parc, in Bridgend, in 2005, although no details were available at the time of writing.

'New Kainos' operated under several formal restraints. The first obvious constraint was the requirements of the research-based criteria for 'what works' in prison programmes (see for example Rex *et al.* 2003). Another was that Kairos UK (the body responsible for Kairos Weekends in the UK) decided to stop running Kairos Weekends for Kainos Community, believing the association and similarity of name had damaged Kairos enough.

The main changes in the Kainos programme included, first, the introduction of a 'Good Neighbour Weekend' to replace the Kairos Weekend. The pilot for this was launched at The Verne in April 2003 and takes place every six months in both Kainos Communities. As the name suggests, the theme is 'how can people live in harmony with one another, promoting tolerance, promoting good neighbourliness' (Phillips 2003).

'New Kainos' consists of a three-stage programme: 'induction' (approximately 10 per cent of the whole); 'main' (approximately 60 per cent); and 'reinforcement' (approximately 30 per cent), each with specific objectives. In the absence of the Kairos Weekend and follow-on programmes, there is no common entry and exit point. Prisoners enter Kainos at different times, and every prisoner is at a different stage. A flexible entry point has the advantage over a fixed point in that prisoners need not wait for the next cycle to start. That said, the prisoner who arrives just after a Good Neighbour Weekend has to wait six months for the next one, although he can take part in programming in the meantime. There is no common exit point either: a prisoner completes the programme when he has completed all recommended interventions. The minimum time for completion is six months, although the preferred amount of time is between 12 and 18 months. A flexible exit point has the advantage of keeping a prisoner longer on the programme in order to readdress areas on which the prisoner had either failed or not fully grasped. The disadvantage is that prisoners do not experience the solidarity that comes from beginning, journeying and completing a programme together. Although 'New Kainos' is ostensibly a Community, each prisoner in fact pursues an individual programme, and its prisoners are less naturally joined to the same objective.

A further major change is how 'New Kainos' has tried to 'broaden the spectrum of addressing improvements and behaviour of the men in terms of improving their social skills'. This gives 'New Kainos' 'a broader brush stroke' (Phillips 2003). At HMP The Verne, Kainos participants are required to take part in a number of 'core interventions' as follows: spur/dormitory meetings, community meetings, 'social development evenings', 'life values discussion groups', 'community building' (communication skills), and 'change workshops' (promoting confidence and self-worth). Other interventions run by Kainos include a 'focus workshop' (cognitive skills), 'victim awareness', 'relationships', 'Genesis workshop', 'Boundaries workshop', and 'Health Wise' (Phillips 2005). The 'life values discussion group' is a workshop based on the Ten Commandments and adapted from a popular series (John 2000, 2001).

The 'social development evening' is a repackaged version of what used to be called 'godparenting' evenings and is a more accurate description. Kainos volunteers do not have the same role as APAC's 'godparents'. Volunteers simply take part in an 'environment for social interaction' which allows prisoners to 'develop social interpersonal and communication skills' (Kainos 2002). Events such as spur/dormitory meetings and other community meetings are similar to 'prisoner council' meetings that occur in prisons elsewhere in the country (Solomon and Edgar 2003).

'New Kainos' claims these interventions represent its attempt to build on the modest, though positive, findings from the attitudinal part of the research (see Chapter 9). However, some of its claims are open to question. For example, it claims that:

> The supportive environment on KC [Kainos Community] and the value that is placed on new social attachments in the social development evenings *in most instances results in a changed self-identity and normative compliance.*
>
> (Kainos 2002; italics added)

However, our research did not find evidence of such widespread transformation. Indeed, the attitudinal study reported that for a number of indices, Kainos Community had *no* statistically significant effect (see Chapter 9). The 'New Programme' also claims that:

> The outlook of the participants on the programme changes with regards to victim hurt ... when they begin to see that the 'volunteers' who come to see them on a regular basis are 'people'.
>
> (Kainos 2002)

However, the evaluation actually found that Kainos Community had *no* significant effects on the Crime-PICS sub-scale 'Victim Hurt Denial' (PICS V); (see Chapter 9).

A very large number of the Kainos interventions claim their aim is to enable prisoners to develop respect for themselves, self-worth or self-esteem (e.g. social development evenings, focus workshop, life values discussion group, restoring relationships, and change workshops) (Kainos 2002). However, the evaluation found that Kainos had no significant effects on prisoners' self-esteem (see Chapter 9). It may be that 'New Kainos' will succeed where the previous programme failed, but it is somewhat surprising to see heavy investment in an area where Kainos has not previously had a record of success. Programme developers might think constructively about the potential engines for change by which, for example, a 'focus workshop' might increase 'self-esteem'.[17] Without this, the hope of improvement may be rather optimistic.

In addition, 'New Kainos' places great emphasis upon reconviction findings as its primary outcome. Yet only a few of its programmes actually claim to have 'reducing reoffending' as their aim (i.e. the 'focus workshop', 'relationships' and Sycamore Tree), and it is far from clear that any of these programmes, either individually or collectively, can bear the weight of this expectation. It may be that 'New Kainos' expects to lever positive effects upon reconvictions by some other route, but this is not identified or explained.

'New Kainos' should not assume that any positive effect it may have will automatically translate into improved reconviction figures. It is in the interests of a voluntary agency such as Kainos to make sure that expected outcomes translate into actual outcomes and that these actual outcomes measure what the organization sees as its strengths and achievements. If the organization's stated aims are not clearly and closely related to the programme and its assessment, then either its aims, programme or assessment have not been properly thought through.

'New Kainos' succeeded in addressing some of the internal weaknesses identified by the evaluation. Prisoners are now given an application form, compact, questionnaire and relapse assessment form as well as a *Resident Information Guide* that covers programme history and expectations. The booklet is explained to the newcomer by a participating prisoner and followed up by a staff interview. This aids informed consent. Kainos continues to attract prisoners from other faiths including Buddhism, Hinduism, Islam and (on one occasion) Satanism.

Notably, 'New Kainos' expressly denies it is a religious programme: 'Although the programme is run on Christian principles, *it is not a religious programme*' (Kainos 2002; italics added). This claim reminds us of Kainos's tendency, at the time of the evaluation, to describe itself as two things at once ('Christian but not Christian'). We saw in Chapters 5 and 6 that Kainos was criticized for this ambiguity, which risked misunderstanding and suspicion. Interviews conducted as part of the Kainos evaluation called on Kainos to be clear about its identity. Even the most critical of prisoners said that the Christian basis of Kainos would not be a problem if Kainos were clear in its intentions.

Based on literature 'New Kainos' provided to the Prison Service (Kainos 2002) and to prisoners (Kainos undated), 'New Kainos' comes across as less openly Christian than was the case at the time of the evaluation,[18] although this may not be the case in reality. It may even be that the actual programme is at least as Christian as it was before, if not more so. For example, anecdotal accounts about the 'Good Neighbour' weekend suggest that it is strongly Christian, but the literature only describes the weekend as an exercise in 'neighbourliness'.

The religious basis of the programme, as described in the literature, is extremely vague. The closest it comes is to say that it is 'run on Christian principles'. For 'New Kainos', 'Christian principles' are defined as wings that are safe for introspection[19] and where prisoners 'develop life skills and grow through 24-hour community living' (Kainos n. d.). At this level of generality it becomes hard to distinguish between the 'Christian principles' of 'New Kainos' and those of the Prison Service itself. For example, 'New Kainos' states that its primary aim is to create 'a safe[20] living environment where prisoners can improve their social functioning and employability' (Kainos 2002) whilst its secondary aims include 'training in social development', 'right living' and 'restoring family links'. This is very similar to the Prison Service's Statement of Purpose, which states: 'Her Majesty's Prison Service serves the public by keeping in custody those committed by the courts. Our duty is to look after them with humanity and help them lead law-abiding and useful lives in custody and after release.' This vague definition of 'Christian principles' is in keeping with Kainos's claim that it is not a religious programme.

At the same time, the logo on the front page of the Kainos Community Programme describes Kainos as 'Christian rehabilitation programmes for prisoners' (Kainos 2003). There is also a reference to Kainos as 'a Christian-based community' (Kainos 2002: 26). It also appears that Chaplains are involved in prisoner applications, interviews and 'spiritual matters'; there are references to Prison Fellowship programmes and there is the use of the Ten Commandments as a basis for the 'life values discussion groups'. Prisoners are also questioned about their religious belief, including: 'Do you believe in God (or a power greater than you)?' (Kainos 2002: 29).

'New Kainos' thus needs to be clear about its identity when distributing materials about itself to the Prison Service and to prisoners. This is very important from the point of view of informed consent. This is because decisions within the Prison Service and by prisoners are made on the basis of materials that Kainos provides. This is particularly important if the Kainos programme is integrated with sentence planning (cf. Kainos 2002: 3, 25) because prisoners will be penalized for withdrawing from the programme. If Kainos is not clear about its identity, this has human rights implications.

3. Comparing faith-based units

This book has surveyed a range of faith-based units and their implementation in different parts of the world. Table 11.1 compares each facility according to selected criteria.

Table 11.1 allows us to move beyond the detail of specific programmes to draw some conclusions of a general nature.

Table 11.1 Comparison of faith-based units according to selected criteria

	Non-violent environment	24-hour 'community'	Restoring family ties	Assuming family responsibility	'Prisoner Councils'	Helping run prison	'God-parents'	Volunteer Visits	Cursillo Kairos/	Compulsory Christian faith-group programmes
S. America										
APAC (i.e. 'full control')	✓	✓	✓	✓	✓	✓	✓	✓	✓	✓
N. America										
'Horizon'										
at Tomoka	✓	✓	✓	×	✓	×	×	✓	✓	✓
at Marion	✓	✓	✓	×	✓	×	×	✓	✓	✓
at Davis	✓	✓	✓	×	✓	×	×	✓	✓	✓
at Allred	✓	✓	✓	×	✓	×	×	✓	✓	✓
'IFI'										
IFI – Texas	✓	✓	✓	✓	n/k	×	×	✓	n/k	✓
IFI – Iowa	✓	✓	n/k	n/k	n/k	×	×	✓	n/k	✓
IFI – Kansas	✓	✓	n/k	n/k	n/k	×	×	✓	n/k	✓
England										
Kairos – APAC (1996–99)	✓	✓	×	×	✓	×	×	✓	✓	✓
Kainos (pre-Report) (1999–2001)	✓	✓	n/k	×	✓	×	×	✓	✓	✓
'New Kainos' (2002–present)	✓	✓	✓	×	×	×	×	✓	×	n/k

	Compulsory Moral Education	Christian therapy	Creative self-expression/ 'labour therapy'	General re-settlement	Specialized Professional Training	Voluntary work in prison	Voluntary work for wider community	General relationship and communication skills	Remedial Education
S. America									
APAC (i.e. 'full control')	√	√	√	√	√	√	√	√	√
N. America									
'Horizon'									
at Tomoka	√	×	×	×	×	×	×	√	×
at Marion	√	×	×	×	×	×	×	√	×
at Davis	√	×	×	×	×	×	×	√	×
at Allred	√	×	×	×	×	×	×	√	×
'IFI'									
IFI – Texas	√	×	×	√	n/k	n/k	√	√	√
IFI – Iowa	√	×	×	√	n/k	n/k	n/k	n/k	n/k
IFI – Kansas	√	×	×	n/k	n/k	n/k	n/k	n/k	n/k
England									
Kairos – APAC (1996–99)	√	×	×	×	×	×	×	n/k	×
Kainos (pre-Report) (1999–2001)	√	×	×	×	×	×	×	√	×
'New Kainos' (2002–present)	√	×	×	×	×	×	×	√	×

First, it is clear that whilst some characteristics of faith-based units are common to all or to most, other characteristics are shared by only a few or hardly any. All the faith-based units considered in this book aspire to create a non-violent environment and a 24-hour 'community' involving visits from volunteers, compulsory moral education and practising general relationship and communication skills. Nearly all have compulsory programmes relating specifically to the Christian faith, seek to restore family ties, and have 'prisoner councils' of some description. Some offer Fourth Day Weekends and associated follow-up programmes. Several offer assistance with remedial education and general resettlement. A few go further than merely seeking to 'restore family ties' and actively try to enable prisoners to assume family responsibilities. A few actively encourage creative self-expression and voluntary work for the wider community. Only APAC is intentional about offering 'godparents', real responsibility for 'running' the prison, specialized Christian therapy and professional training that continues upon release. It is thus clear from Table 11.1 that APAC is the most rounded example of a faith-based unit, covering all 19 indices. This rounded picture reflects the fact that APAC was the product of a long period of trial and error during which volunteers and administrators became attuned to the particular needs of participating prisoners.

Second, it is notable that the primary differences are between *organizations* rather than between *establishments* run by the same organization. Horizon programmes are different to IFI on certain issues (including general resettlement, remedial education and assuming family responsibility). But at the level of programme characteristics, there is not much difference *within* the different 'Horizon' or IFI programmes, even though establishments vary from pre-release to a medium/maximum security prison. This suggests that the character of the faith-based unit is more likely to be determined by the parent organization than by the overall climate of the individual prison, important though that is. This in turn suggests that, subject to gaining access to the prison and the need to adapt to local conditions, sponsoring organizations have a great deal of choice over what kind of programme they wish to implement. It is up to them whether they wish to offer any of a range of dimensions associated with certain faith-based units, including Christian therapy, remedial education, specialized professional training, creative self-expression and so on. It follows too that the tone and style of each type of faith-based unit will reflect the interests and preferences of its founders and, in turn, their support base. Some faith-based units are clear their identity is solely Christian ('InnerChange is expressly Christian. *Expressly Christian. Will not be anything else. Will never be anything more than Christian*';

Cowley 2004) whereas Horizon seeks to offer interfaith and multifaith communities and literature provided by 'New Kainos' claims that it is not a 'religious' programme at all (Kainos 2002).

Yet even among those who wish to offer a purely Christian or Christian-based programme, there is variety about how this might be done.[21] There are those who believe that the prime justification for an intervention is 'evangelism' (IFI; see Chapter 8) and that programmes should have a clear 'Biblical' basis (IFI again),[22] on through the spectrum to those who wish to promote general Christian teaching (APAC) and thence to more general Christian values, e.g. quality of relationships (Horizon) that in turn shade into general 'humanitarian' but less clearly Christian concerns, e.g. health and safety ('New Kainos'). It probably goes without saying that the most effective faith-based unit will be one that covers as much of this spectrum as possible. Few faith-based units are likely to address all of these different interests and concerns, and so there is a continuing need for a 'mixed economy' when it comes to faith-based units. This is true even for those based on a particular faith. For this reason it is welcome that 'New Kainos' is no longer the only faith-based unit in England and Wales and that 'Compass' and IFI UK are providing additional choice. There is no reason why these initiatives cannot be joined, at the national level, by other organizations, providing they meet with the approval of the Prison Service. Likewise, at establishment level, a faith-based unit in a given prison can benefit from the involvement of other Christian prison ministries, whether Prison Alpha, Kairos, Prison Fellowship or the Chaplaincy itself.

Several practical recommendations may be drawn from Table 11.1. The first is that since APAC is apparently the most rounded faith-based unit yet developed, those seeking to develop or implement a faith-based unit should do all they can to internalize the standards set by APAC and the experience of its founders. The second is that Table 11.1 provides faith-based units with indicators of possible future development. Common characteristics are grouped on the left-hand side of the Table, declining towards those that are rare or unique on the right. Faith-based units with elements located predominantly on the left of the table can learn from those with characteristics predominantly on the right. Faith-based units that currently manage to cover half, or less than half, of the elements covered by APAC may gain a broad sense of how they might develop in future. The need to develop *across* a range of indices does not, of course, exclude the need for further development *within* individual elements: 'volunteer visits' and 'prisoner councils' may both exist, but there can be wide variations in terms of best practice.

4. Common themes

This section draws together common themes from each of the faith-based units. This is important in the light of the global expansion of faith-based units, as it is likely that some of these issues will recur in future.

(a) The primary role of correction agencies

A recurring theme is the role of corrections in initiating faith-based units. It is usually assumed that such units come into being as a result of pressure from Christian groups. However it is more often the other way around, with Christian prison ministries capitulating to the desires of prison departments. IFI and Horizon were both founded because senior management in Departments of Corrections wanted the support of PF USA and Kairos respectively. At the time, neither PF USA nor Kairos were actively seeking to extend their ministries into this area. In South America, APAC gained control of Humaitá prison at the request of local authorities, who could think of no alternative. In the UK, Kairos-APAC began at The Verne because its Governor challenged staff to come up with a viable use for D-Wing and 'Compass' was requested at Highpoint South by prison staff.

But whilst the initial approach may have come from prison departments, Christian organizations have been quick to respond, relying at times on the expertise of others to secure access. Kairos-APAC heavily referenced the success of both Kairos and APAC (Griffin 1999a) whilst IFI made use of its association with APAC to provide the Texas DoC with a credible history. The formation of faith-based units in prison has been the product of initiative and risk on both sides. The same appears to be true when it comes to expansion. Kairos-APAC in England was proactive about expanding, but the Prison Service offered considerable encouragement. In the US, following the success of Tomoka C.I., the DoC wanted to expand Horizon to other prisons within Florida. Pressure to expand also came from DoCs in other states: by 2003, ten States had publicly requested the programme.

The willingness of corrections departments to turn to community-based agencies for help means it is likely faith-based units will have a continuing role in prisons. To that extent, the long-term future of religious units is likely to depend as much on the perceived shortcomings of the modern prison environment as on the intrinsic value of the units themselves. Voluntary agencies encouraged by prison departments to open or expand must therefore consider whether it is in their long-term interests to do so. Kairos-APAC opened in unsuitable locations rather than lose the opportunity. By contrast, Horizon refused to enter those prisons where it was felt, for one reason or another, there was not a good possibility of success. There are times when it is better to say no.

Corrections agencies are not only proactive in seeking to establish faith-based units but also tend to seek control of such units when established. Sometimes this is to the detriment of the programme. For example, APAC's five phases were not always used in the manner for which they were intended. Between 1979 and 1983 judges assigned prisoners directly to semi-open or open conditions without requiring that they should first graduate from closed conditions. Ottoboni (2003) claims this resulted in a lack of discipline among prisoners and greater reoffending on release. Another example is the insistence of the Florida DoC that 80 per cent of Horizon participants should be short-term prisoners, even though this was not the group the programme was designed for. Griffin (2004) claims only the Ohio Dept. of Rehabilitation and Corrections 'had the wisdom to realize the importance of maintaining a collaborative approach' with respect to Horizon's role at Marion C.I. All other DoCs sought to manage the programme 'from the control inherent to Corrections' (*ibid.*). This is despite the fact that 'one of the best defences a Department of Corrections has against critics is to maintain programmes run by others who are responsible for programme content' (*ibid.*). Kairos Prison Ministries has experienced widespread demand for Kairos even from prisons with relatively short-term populations. Similarly, during Griffin's years as Executive Director of Kairos (1990–2001), US DoCs were 'most anxious to have Kairos in a minimum security prison which is pre-release in order to maybe socialize the inmates…[even though] Kairos really does not work well in that setting' (Griffin 2003). The dominant role of corrections in instituting and reshaping faith-based units means that it is advisable for faith-based organizations to have and to maintain a clear sense of their strengths and identity.

(b) Political pressure

Of all the faith-based units surveyed in this book, APAC and IFI have probably experienced greatest political opposition. Both Kairos-APAC and Kainos were subject to negative publicity, but compared with APAC and IFI it was less serious. Opposition to APAC focused upon its generally liberal character rather than its Christian identity. By contrast, opposition to IFI has centred mainly on its Christian identity and the claim that IFI-Iowa uses public monies to promote the Christian faith in prison (see Chapter 8). In the UK, criticism of Kairos-APAC and Kainos centred around the claim that Christianity was given favoured status by the Prison Service, in addition to allegations of 'proselytizing' contrary to the Prisons Act 1952.

By contrast, Horizon has met with relatively little political opposition beyond the allegation, common to religious-based units, that it 'unfairly gives additional privileges to religious inmates' (Pfankuch 2002). During the planning stage for Horizon at Tomoka, Florida changed from a Democratic to a Republican Governor. However both regimes approved the Horizon development and were 'very much in favour' (Bright Griffin 2003b). Cowley (2004) suggests Horizon is less politically charged than IFI because Horizon implemented multifaith regimes, whereas IFI has remained solely Christian: 'Interfaith was easier to establish within prison systems than expressly single-faith based. But let me tell you, politically, Ike chose the less … er …' [Interviewer]: *'Controversial route?'* [Interviewee] … 'Right.' But whilst it may be the case that Horizon has evaded political opposition by playing the multifaith card, it has run into opposition among some of its own supporters who favour an exclusively Christian approach. This is the exact reverse of IFI's position. IFI has remained solely Christian and has not risked conflict with grassroots supporters.

Political opposition places an additional pressure on faith-based units which, by virtue of their innovative nature, require a long period of slow development in which to mature. It might therefore be advisable for faith-based units to avoid premature publicity or rapid development at too early a stage.

(c) Location, location, location

What might be the elements of a successful faith-based intervention? First and foremost, there must be a willing and supportive institution, that is, one that will not only welcome the programme but try to help make it a success. It is essential that the prison Governor or Warden is supportive and informs prison staff of their support so this filters down 'through the ranks'. That manifests itself in several ways that may affect future success, including how prison staff deal with volunteers and situations in the dormitories themselves. It is important that this support is also shared more broadly among other management and staff. If support comes only from the Governor or Warden, the programme may fold as soon as he or she leaves because it is too dependent on the strength of a single personality. This is important in institutions that have very frequent changes of managerial staff, especially in the UK. It might thus be desirable to have support from the senior management and the full Chaplaincy Team (not just the prison Chaplain). A successful unit needs to have suitable physical space within the prison, with as much communal space as possible. It is also preferable to have prisoners who have a sufficiently long sentencing profile to allow maximum benefit from the programme. A faith-based unit that wishes to be successful also needs local volunteers, preferably those who are already involved in prison ministry. Finally, it is beneficial to have a sufficiently local establishment to facilitate the development of family and community ties.

Attempts have been made to establish faith-based units with only a few of these elements in place but such units have struggled. It is possible to set up a faith-based unit that lacked certain key elements, provided there are strong compensatory factors. Yet even here there are major risks. Horizon, for example, decided to establish a unit in a remote location (Davis C.F.) with no previous experience of Kairos. The gamble was taken because senior management agreed to invite Horizon at significant cost to the institution. Even so, the unit would have foundered but for the Promise Keepers' men's movement whose volunteers provided a lifeline. Kairos-APAC's decision to open faith-based units in unfavourable environments such as Highpoint North and Highpoint South on the strength of more limited commitment from senior management created problems for that organization from the outset.

It might in the future be possible to plan faith-based units in several prisons within striking distance of each other. Ideally, each establishment would represent a different security classification. Prisoners serving long sentences could begin in a high security prison and progress through to lower security prisons, all the while retaining a continuing relationship to the community. This was discussed in England and Wales at a North West Area Chaplaincy meeting in 1999 and deserves further consideration. To some extent this already happens in England and Wales when 'New Kainos' prisoners transfer from HMP Swaleside (a higher security prison) to HMP The Verne (a lower security prison). However the number of prisoners who do this are small, the prisons are located in different parts of the country, and there is no continuity of community.

A further issue is where the unit is best located within the prison itself. We noted a recurring perception among staff and prisoners that participants in faith-based units 'get a perk'. Prisoners complaining about 'fancy carpeting' and other treats they believed were on the faith-based units dogged the development of Kairos-APAC and Kainos in England and Wales. Physical conditions at The Verne were indeed originally better on the faith-based unit than elsewhere in the prison at first, though this has now reversed. At Swaleside, this is arguably still the case, but due more to its calmer environment than to any physical 'perks'. At Highpoint North, Kainos was noted for its calmer atmosphere but also for the fact that women retained open access to the facilities on the spurs after lock-up. On Horizon the (mis)conception of the 'cushy number' maintains its prevalence even though it may become clear over time that participants do a great deal of difficult 'inner work' (Bright Griffin 2003b). Such comments may be forestalled by deliberately locating the unit in a less desirable part of a prison. It can be a visible statement to the rest of the prison that those who choose to take part do so primarily because of the programme's content and ethos.

If the programme is located in a harsher physical environment and is successful, the contrast is greater than if it succeeds under more favourable conditions (cf. APAC). Against this approach is a tendency on the part of prison administrators to locate faith-based units in parts of the prison that already have a reputation for being 'progressive'. This was the case in several prisons where faith-based units were established in a former Drug Unit (HMP Swaleside) or 'honour dorm' (Newton C.F. and Davis C.F.).

There may be value in locating faith-based units in open dorms, which can help to build a sense of community, as at Humaitá, Carol Vance Unit (since 2004), Marion C.I., The Verne and Tomoka C.I.. Faith-based units have been successfully established in cell-blocks housing either single or two man cells (Davis C.F., HMP Highpoint South, Newton C.F., Carol Vance Unit (1997–2004), HMP Swaleside). However, such units have had to work harder at creating a sense of community, for example, by creating highly structured and active regimes that discourage prisoners from 'hiding-out' in their cells and by maximizing the use of common areas. Some maintain that cells are beneficial insofar as they allow men to have some time away from the community (Dye 2004).

(d) Processual issues

A common practice to all faith-based units surveyed in this book is to recruit on the basis of prisoners' desire for personal change and thus to select those most motivated to succeed. Data from the Kainos evaluation suggested that Kainos may, in addition, have tended to take more compliant prisoners with a lower risk of reoffending. The same may also be true of other faith-based units, to judge from their selection criteria (e.g. not accepting prisoners who are the subject of any major disciplinary cases). Other factors that may lean in favour of more compliant prisoners include a reliance upon Chaplains in making referrals (IFI-Texas) or the fact that the unit was located in a former 'honour dorm' (Davis C.F., Newton C.F.) or Drug Unit (HMP Swaleside), or simply prisoners having more to lose if they were removed from the unit (see Chapter 4). One of the implications of this strategy is that whilst it may help to create 'calmer' environments it also means that, as in the case of Kainos, the predicted reconviction rates of such participants is likely to be lower than the national average. This in turn makes it harder for the faith-based unit to demonstrate a significant impact on reconviction rates because the predicted figure is relatively low to start with.

Another common theme is the tendency to recruit from professing Christian or Christian-sympathetic prisoners. This is not surprising given the Christian basis of all the faith-based units covered in this book. Although it is true that a number of prisoners are recruited from a wide variety of faiths, the number of non-Christian prisoners is generally low and, in some units, remarkably low (e.g. IFI-Iowa).

In the case of multifaith units, this may reflect the low number of representative faiths in the prisons as a whole and a lack of support from faith-specific volunteers outside the prison. In the case of Christian-based units, such low numbers may reflect the degree to which the unit has been successful at communicating its Christian identity. Prisoners know what it stands for, and they self-select accordingly.

A clearly-communicable identity is crucial for informed consent. Lack of clarity and proper communication runs the risk of resentful prisoners who may justly feel their religious conscience has been violated, especially when mandatory religious events are involved. The successful unit needs to ensure it has appropriate strategies for informed consent. This may include an initial interview, detailed compact, induction (by staff and fellow-participants) and follow-up interview. Prisoners should not be obliged to take part in otherwise mandatory, faith-specific exercises if they have previously identified themselves as not belonging to that particular faith. They should also be allowed to leave a religious-based programme at any time without penalty.

Several faith-based units in different parts of the world (Marion C.I., HMP Highpoint North) reported prison staff bidding out of their post as a Prison Officer or Correctional Officer because life on the unit had calmed to such a degree their job was no longer 'exciting enough' (Hunsaker 2003). Another common theme was tension between the prison Chaplaincy and the faith-based unit. Such tensions were described in previous chapters in relation to Tomoka C.I., Marion C.I., HMPs Swaleside, Highpoint North and Highpoint South (for a time) and nearly all IFI units. Strong, positive relationships between the faith-based unit and the Chaplaincy were rare. Where they were positive, this was usually due either to the personalities involved or to the high level of responsibility the Chaplain had for the faith-based unit.

(e) Use of paid staff, volunteers and ex-offenders

Faith-based units differ widely in terms of the extent to which the human resources used to deliver the programme are split between paid staff and volunteers who have no previous offending history and ex-offenders, who may or may not be volunteers.

(i) Paid staff

At one end of the spectrum is APAC, which had few paid staff in relation to its degree of responsibility for running the prison. Indeed, APAC had only three paid members of staff for 750 prisoners in different stages, including parole (Colson 2000). APAC chose instead to rely on trained, unpaid volunteers and trusted ex-offenders, some of whom received remuneration. At the other end of the spectrum is IFI, a highly staff-intensive operation involving relatively large numbers of paid staff. IFI-Texas cost an estimated one million dollars in start-up costs and requires $400,000 per year to sustain a seven-person IFI team.

This contrast between APAC and IFI is interesting. IFI initially sought to present itself as being 'modelled' on APAC but, on this issue, IFI was happy to reject the APAC ethos. This found no favour with APAC:

> We were doing our own thing and I didn't feel like we needed APAC for us. I mean, they were doing their thing and we were doing our thing. But the rub, if you will, was the fact that we hired staff, and they were very concerned that staff were not equipped, nor was that what APAC was about. That people should be *giving* of their time, rather than getting paid to do a job.
>
> (Cowley 2004, emphasis original)

As we saw in Chapter 1, Ottoboni (2000) thinks using paid staff thwarts the 'spirit of gratuity' which he believes inspires personal change. Cowley (2004) is dismissive: 'That, in my opinion, to be very respectful, is hogwash. There's nothing that says that a missionary has to go around barefoot for people to listen and understand what he has to say. I think they can buy shoes and still be very effective in delivering God's message to people'. Indeed Cowley goes so far as to attribute the effectiveness of IFI to its staff, pointing out that paid staff can still, to some extent, embody the 'spirit of gratuity' and 'permanent presence' (Ottoboni 2003: 111) required of APAC volunteers. 'InnerChange was effective because of the staff. And they were very giving, they were very caring, they were very spiritual. They didn't get paid nearly enough money, they were at the unit almost constantly. So it was still a very mission-driven work, even though they were paid' (Cowley 2004).

One reason for IFI's preference for paid staff over volunteers for certain roles, according to Cowley, is a fear that some volunteers may lack the personal discipline and professionalism that is demanded in a Western context:

> I can tell you, over here in the States, [that] volunteers, as much as we need them in our programmes and as much as they're needed in prisons, are loose cannons and they have to be shepherded, and the only people that can do that are staff who are fundamentally aware of what's going on inside those prisons and [who] have the relationships both with the correctional staff and the volunteers.... As much as we've enjoyed [volunteers] – and InnerChange has to have volunteers – it would in my opinion be impossible to maintain the level of programming that we did with [just] volunteers.
>
> (*ibid.*)

Somewhere in the middle of this spectrum is Horizon, which typically costs $110,000 in its first year and $76,000 – 80,000 a year thereafter, largely spent on paying two staff (Griffin 2000). Although Horizon is less staff-intensive than IFI, Griffin shares the view that it is mistaken to try to replicate APAC's volunteer-dependent, 'skeleton-staff' approach:

> We have found that even though the volunteers do excellent work and we love to work with them, they are still volunteers and when push comes to shove, if they are not really keen on doing reports they will not do their reports.... If you are paying a salary to someone to do the work you can normally find someone that will perform up to the standard that you demand.
>
> (2003)

Over-reliance upon volunteers can also leave the programme vulnerable to changes in volunteer's personal circumstances:

> If they become ill they are not easy to replace.... If you are going with a volunteer they may be doing excellent work but your chances of finding someone to replace them if they depart for any reason, family, financial, whatever problems, then you are dead in the water. There is not the same obligation. And you do not have the income stream established to replace them with paid staff, so I would rather start with paid staff and just maintain the programme from that standpoint.
>
> (*ibid.*)

(ii) Volunteers

Whilst faith-based units differ in their degree of dependence upon volunteers, all accept that volunteers play a crucial role. We have seen that one of the greatest incentives for prisoners to come onto faith-based units is contact with volunteers. Volunteers are crucial first because, at their best, they model unconditional acceptance. This theme runs through interviewee sources from APAC, Horizon, IFI, Kairos and Kainos. One of APAC's founders describes the role of volunteers as 'seed[ing] love within the prisons' (Veronese undated). Second, as we have seen, they inspire a commitment to promoting the next generation (generativity). Third, volunteers offer pro-social accountability. Fourth, in the case of the APAC godparent, their role is to 'build a relationship so valued that the prisoner will not want to reoffend (Lee 1995); thus stimulating 'normative compliance' (Bottoms 2001, 2002).

The cruciality of the role of volunteers has a number of implications. First, and most obviously, it is advantageous for faith-based units to be located near to centres of volunteer strength. Horizon refused to open without first conducting research into local volunteer strength and proceeded only on the basis that this strength would be sufficient. By contrast, Kairos-APAC was willing to open in establishments with little consultation of local volunteer strength. Second, it is advantageous to have continuity in volunteer relationships. Volunteers' arrival and subsequent withdrawal, for whatever reason, can lead to feelings of abandonment on the part of prisoners. Third, the successful unit needs to provide volunteers with training and support, especially when volunteers are relied upon for more complex issues such as abuse and addiction. Finally, the successful unit needs to oversee its volunteers: the same vulnerability that makes volunteers valuable as a rehabilitative agent also makes them a security risk.

(iii) Ex-offenders

Ex-offenders may confer special benefits upon faith-based units (e.g. credibility with prisoners), especially when given a leading role. However, it is advisable that the risks are acknowledged, with extra vigilance and care exercised. Regardless of whether the ex-offender had a previous history with the institution sponsoring the faith-based unit, there are usually issues relating to authority and trust between the ex-offender and the institution which may make employing an ex-offender in this context difficult. The use of ex-offenders in the role of Programme Manager proved problematic in several faith-based units. It helps if offenders and ex-offenders can be eased into the role over time, with responsibility given in proportion to trust earned and personal knowledge of the offender that has been gained over a period of years although, even here, the successful unit should seek close and continuing accountability.

(f) Use of Fourth Day programmes

Faith-based units vary in the emphasis placed upon Fourth Day programmes; from APAC (which regards it as essential) and Horizon (where the Kairos Weekend is central) through to 'Compass' and 'New Kainos', neither of which run a Fourth Day programme.

Most faith-based units surveyed in this book have used Fourth Day programmes such as Cursillo or Kairos. A number of lessons can be learned. First, it is advisable for faith-based units hoping to use Kairos to locate in prisons with an established history of Kairos (as with Tomoka C.I. and Marion C.I.). Davis C.F. in the US and HMPs The Verne, Swaleside, Highpoint South and Highpoint North in the UK were all located in fairly remote countryside and lacked both previous experience of Kairos and an established volunteer base to deliver Weekends. All struggled to establish Kairos effectively.

Second, it is worth recognizing that Kairos can and does operate outside the context of the faith-based unit. Kairos is a ministry to the incarcerated and their families in support of the prison Chaplaincy. It can be used equally by the Chaplaincy to provide support for a closed community, or it can provide the normal stand-alone programme that is open to the whole prison population.

Third, when Kairos operates on its own, as it does in approximately 200 prisons in the US as well as in Canada, South Africa and Australia, only men with 18 months or more to serve are allowed to participate in order for the impact of the Kairos Weekend (plus follow-up) to have a lasting effect. Between 1999 and 2002, a number of prisons expressed an interest in holding a Kairos Weekend (Kairos UK 2001; Kairos UK 2000a; Kairos UK 1999). Three of these (HMPs Preston, Rochester and Stocken) are either Category C (medium-security) or male local establishments, whilst a fourth, HMP Leyhill, is an open (minimum-security) prison. Only HMP Hull, a Category B establishment (medium to high security), approximated the type of conditions for which Kairos was designed. To improve its success, Kairos UK might be more discriminating in terms of security classification.

Fourth, if Kairos is used in support of a faith-based unit it may be advantageous to maintain distance between itself and the unit. Griffin allowed The Verne to use the name Kairos in the title of its unit provided something else was attached to distinguish it from the Kairos ministry, thus Kairos-APAC was born. This was not sufficient to distinguish Kairos from the unit, and greater distance would have been advisable. Distance enables Kairos to stress that it is voluntary, even though participation in Christian meetings within the unit itself may be mandatory. When several prisons in the US decided to introduce faith-based units in prisons that already had Kairos, they decided participation in the Kairos Weekend should *not* be mandatory. If Kairos-APAC and later Kainos had done the same, they would have been less vulnerable to the charge of placing prisoners under 'religious pressure'.

Distance is also advisable to the extent that the Kairos Weekend and the faith-based unit may have different goals and prisoners in mind. For example, the former is supposed to target 'negative leaders', which is often not the case with the unit. Distance may also be helpful where there are tensions between the unit and the Chaplaincy. Kairos operates at the behest of the Chaplaincy and is thus in an entirely different position to the unit, which may operate entirely independently. Prison Chaplains in the UK did not always understand this. In Kairos-APAC, for example, there was no expectation that its prisoners should be involved in Chapel life. Worse, some Kairos-APAC prisoners gave the impression that they saw themselves as an 'alternative' Church group within the prison. This created problems between Kairos, Kairos-APAC and the Chaplaincy. Kairos, which serves the Chaplaincy, might not have been tarred with this brush had it maintained greater distance from the unit.

Generally speaking the relationship between the Kairos Weekend and the unit seems to have worked better in the US than the UK. This is largely because some of the units (e.g. Horizon) are based in prisons with substantial Kairos histories. This is plainly desirable, and the UK prisons never had this benefit. But even in the US there is a tension between the Weekend and the unit. Some men may be appropriate for the Weekend but not for the unit and *vice versa*. This may be unavoidable. For example, the requirement that prisoners should have at least 18 months to serve to take part in a normal, 'stand-alone' Kairos Weekend may not be appropriate for men on a unit in a minimum or medium-security prison.

Fifth, it is crucial to recognize that standard Kairos practice places more emphasis on the follow-up programme and less emphasis on the Kairos Weekend. In England and Wales, the attention was the other way round. The Kairos Weekend was used as a 'curtain-raiser' to the programme, and it seems that less thought was given to how to continue the Fourth Day experience. This was unfortunate because focusing solely on the Kairos Weekend rather than the follow-up programme 'always portends trouble' (Griffin 1996b). Hebbern (2003) suggested the Kairos 'prayer and share' groups were 'a bit of a romantic idea' (cf. Chapter 2).

Organizing small group reunions may be easier in maximum-security prisons, where the alternative to participation is remaining locked up, but is harder in lower-security prisons (such as The Verne), where prisoners have a higher degree of freedom (*ibid.*). Marion C.I., a medium-security establishment, provides formal support to the objective of building strong Christian communities in prison, including those outside the faith-based unit. Significantly, Marion's approach ensures that Christians on Horizon Interfaith interact with the wider Kairos and Christian community in the prison. This aids recruitment and prevents the unit from being seen as a rival 'church', which was a problem for some Chaplains where Kainos operated.

Sixth, where Kairos is used in support of a unit it is advisable that prisoners connect with the same prisoners and volunteers they encountered during their Kairos Weekend. This is because 'you have to have continuity in the relationships, people they already know and trust' (Respondent F 2003). This is standard practice on Horizon. Kainos originally resisted suggestions to keep prisoners in 'family groups', preferring to assign prisoners according to nationality or at random.

Finally, it is advisable that Trustees and prison Governors responsible for a faith-based unit with Kairos should understand what Kairos does. That may mean spending a Weekend experiencing what volunteers and prisoners experience. Some Governors in England and Wales felt that staying away from Kairos Weekends was essential to preserve their independence. The price for this was that some Trustees and Governors lacked sufficient knowledge to respond to claims that Kairos was 'proselytizing' prisoners or to defend what turned out to be a positive development in their prisons.[23]

(g) Measuring outcomes

Earlier chapters have shown the confidence with which faith-based units have predicted success, especially in the area of reconvictions. Research conducted thus far suggests that much of this confidence is misplaced. Kairos-APAC promised 'dramatic' effects upon reconvictions but Kairos-APAC and Kainos produced no statistically significant difference in reconviction rates (see Chapter 10). Supporters then tried to 'move the goalposts' by complaining the Prison Service placed too much emphasis on reconvictions but the goalposts had already been fixed. IFI's claims to have had a major impact on reconvictions have also been questioned (see Chapter 10). APAC has difficulty in acknowledging its apparent effect upon recidivism. Ottoboni (2003: 79) claims Johnson's three-year reconviction study bears out APAC's claim that reconviction is 'below 5 per cent', but this is incorrect. Johnson (2002) in fact reports a reconviction rate of 16 per cent and, as we saw in Chapter 10, due to problems with the data this figure may well be higher. This is perhaps typical of the manner in which rhetoric tends to outstrip reality in this area, especially when expected outcomes are not actual outcomes.[24]

Part of the reason faith-based organizations place undue emphasis upon reconvictions is because of a perception that 'that was what the state [of Iowa or Texas] wanted. The state would not have done InnerChange had it not been connected with recidivism' (Cowley 2004). This is understandable, although it is unfortunate if reconviction rates are emphasized at the expense of other indices, especially those where success might be hypothesized with greater justification. Improvements in the prison environment, prisoner well-being, and family relationships as well as promoting volunteer work are not irrelevant, especially if these turn out to be, at least in the short-term, the primary ways in which such programmes have positive effects. Caliber Associates' evaluation of Horizon measured its support for individual prisoners, their families and communities and the extent to which it represents 'best practice' for providing services to prisoners and their families (Caliber 2003). It is advisable for faith-based units to identify *actual* outcomes, as opposed to expected outcomes, and to ask whether these actual outcomes justify the effort and expense involved.

(h) True faith

Are there are any limits on the religions that can take part in a multifaith unit or form the basis of a single-faith-based unit? According to Horizon Multifaith's current policy, there is no limit. Does this mean that any group claiming to meet Horizon Multifaith's minimal requirements for participation qualify for inclusion? Could a group of Satanists with a developed curriculum and a group of volunteers willing to expound Satanist teaching be admitted? In terms of how Horizon Multifaith is currently structured, there seems to be no reason why not. This points to a flaw because, in the example given, a religion such as the 'Church of Satan', which appears to encourage vengeance, does not appear to be well-suited to promoting pro-social behaviour.[25]

The problem arises because Horizon Multifaith aspires on the one hand to be multifaith, but on the other, to be a community. This creates a tension when the teachings and the traditional practice of the faith group seeking inclusion undermine community. Horizon Multifaith will have to address two basic questions: what constitutes 'faith', and what criteria must a potential 'faith' satisfy if it is not to violate the unit's integrity? The question of what role different religions can play in different areas of public life, including correctional services, is beyond the scope of this book. However, it is important to consider the question in terms of equal opportunities. One way forward might be to acknowledge that admission to the Multifaith unit must require something *additional* to the ability to put together a programme, volunteers and willing prisoners. If that is so, then it makes sense that this additional requirement should somehow be related to the goals of the unit as a community.

Horizon Multifaith might thus set boundaries to the sort of religious groups that might be admitted to the unit whilst at the same time complying with both the letter and the spirit of equal opportunities legislation. Naturally, if Horizon Multifaith required Satanists, Scientologists and Spiritists to demonstrate the communitarian credentials of their beliefs, the same must equally apply to Christians, Jews, Muslims and Native Americans. Horizon Multifaith is still in the process of working this through (Key 2004). However, it states that all faiths currently involved meet the purposes of the unit (positive character development, strengthening family relationships, respect for others and community building) and that other faiths wishing to be a part of the programme would be required to meet them as well (*ibid.*).

(i) Multiple incentives

The eight broad categories of perceived incentives for joining faith-based units noted in relation to APAC (Chapter 1) also recur in relation to Kainos (Chapters 4–6). These are: (1) escape from the prevailing prison culture; (2) a 'softened' prison environment; (3) a more active regime; (4) progression through sentence; (5) a faith-based environment; (6) 'living in community'; (7) 'family' values; and (8) growth in maturity. (This does not, of course, exclude variations in the relative strength of the different factors). This picture is also consistent with the general descriptive account of Horizon Communities and IFI, although it would be interesting to test this, and the relative weight of these categories in different faith-based units, more closely.

(j) Older prisoners

Older prisoners tend to appreciate faith-based units. The psychosocial part of the Kainos evaluation (Chapter 9) found a majority of prisoners (55 per cent) were over 30 years of age. This was confirmed by the sample for Chapters 4–6, most of whom were over 30. This is broadly consistent with the older age profile of the Kainos Reconviction Sample in Chapter 10 (which excludes Swaleside), where 57 per cent were aged 30 or more at time of release (compared with 46 per cent for the Comparison sample released from similar prisons). It is probable that some relationship exists between the higher average age of Kainos participants and the basis of their selection, namely the desire to change. It is a well-attested criminological finding that prisoners tend to 'grow out' of crime and acquire the motivation to desist from crime with age (Farrington 1996).

Older prisoners also tend to have had greater experience of prison life. Prisoners who have spent longer in prison may be better placed to welcome the benefits of faith-based units, consistent with Ottoboni's (2003: 101) claim that the prisoner must experience 'the bitterness of prison' in order to appreciate the progressive aspects of the APAC regime. The Kainos evaluation found the Kainos Reconviction Sample had spent longer in prison than the non-Kainos Comparison sample.[26] Ottoboni also suggests that APAC may have greatest success with longer-term prisoners: 'There have been some cases in APAC when over two years were necessary for the *recuperando* to...change his way of thinking.... [N]ot being in a hurry is a virtue' (*ibid.*: 84). This is consistent with Kairos's preference for longer-term prisoners and hence maximum-security prisons. Although Kainos tended to be established in lower-category prisons, the psychosocial study of Kainos (Chapter 9) found Kainos prisoners tended to serve medium to long-term sentences.[27]

5. Global expansion

Faith-based units are expanding rapidly around the world. The following sets out some of the more notable examples, in chronological order.

(a) Crossings, New Mexico, United States

This began with 16 male prisoners in December 1998 at the Southern New Mexico Correctional Facility (SNMCF), a medium-security facility west of Las Cruces, New Mexico. The purpose of the programme is 'to expose the inmate to the Christian way of life' (Crossings Operations Manual 2003) and is 'Christ-centred and biblically based' (www.corrections.state.nm.us/programmes/volunteer.html; accessed 5 April 2005). Units range in size from 16 to 62 beds. Crossings graduates transferred from SNMCF to another institution (the Lea County Correctional Facility) whose Warden was apparently so impressed by the attitudes of Crossings graduates that Crossings was asked to begin a 65-bed programme there as soon as possible. This invitation was quickly followed by Wardens of the New Mexico Women's Correctional Facility, a 'low/medium'-security prison (offering a 10-bed unit); Guadalupe County Correctional Facility, a medium-security prison (with a 65-bed unit) and Roswell Correctional Centre (a 28-bed unit). In 2001, following a change in the security classification of SNMCF from medium to maximum security, Crossings were invited to the Paul Oliver Unit in Las Cruces, a 'low/ medium' custody facility (with a 55-man dormitory), whilst in 2003 Crossings began a 55-bed unit at the Central New Mexico Correctional Facility (CNMCF). Crossings' method of dealing with this rapid growth was to concentrate on building a model unit at SNMCF and to bring other units into compliance with that, rather than to control the actual expansion (Zornes 2004).

The programme has three six-month stages. Crossings' selection criteria require that prisoners have sufficient time to complete at least one phase. Its priority placement system includes favouring those transferring from other Crossings units, those who have sufficient time to complete the full 18-month programme and those who have attended a Kairos Weekend. Prisoners in each unit are grouped into 'families' of four to eight members. Prisoners stay in these groupings for six months at a time (Crossings Operations Manual 2003). In 2003, the New Mexico Corrections Department awarded Crossings 'Official Programme Status'. This empowers the unit to recommend a 30-day reduction in sentence (called a 'Lump Sum Award' or 'LSA') for completion of each of the three stages of the programme, to a maximum of 90 days. This was a turning point in terms of perceived incentives: 'We had difficulty filling beds until the 30-day LSA became available. Now we have a waiting list' (Zornes 2004). Crossings' total expenditure over the past six years has been a mere $13,000. Crossings receives monthly support from local churches for travel and certain other expenses; one local church meets photocopying needs whilst a Californian church sends materials. Given the number of prisons where Crossings operates, this is remarkable. Crossings is a potential model for small prisons that cannot afford full-time staff and contrasts with the expensive, staff-intensive approach modelled by IFI.

(b) Compass, England

In 2002, Kainos withdrew from HMP Highpoint South (see section 2 above), and the opportunity to run a faith-based unit in that establishment passed to Prison Fellowship England and Wales. This is quite significant. Whereas IFI and Horizon showed how faith-based units could be implemented by different organizations within the same country, 'Compass' showed how faith-based units could be implemented differently not just within the same Prison Service but within the same prison.

The impulse to invite Prison Fellowship came once again from within the Prison Service. The Senior Officer responsible for the then

Kainos Community at Highpoint South wrote a letter to the Governor, countersigned by other wing officers, asking if a faith-based community could be maintained. The Governor consulted the Chaplain, who invited Prison Fellowship to table a 'Christian values-based programme' in the prison in December 2001. The Executive Director of Prison Fellowship England and Wales, Peter Walker, had visited the APAC-inspired unit in Quito, Ecuador and IFI-Texas in 1999 and was keen to implement a similar programme in England and Wales (Walker 1999). The project began in May 2002 using existing Kainos personnel. Its stated aim is 'to enable participants in the Compass project to examine, understand, test and apply a Christian values-based lifestyle whilst part of the in-prison community and after release.'[28]

In setting up a faith-based unit in Highpoint South, Prison Fellowship made a number of strategic decisions. First, although Prison Fellowship was originally offered a 60-bed unit, the agency felt this was too large and opted instead for a 15-bed section. This targeting of resources was consistent with Prison Fellowship's decision not to take on the former Kainos Community at HMP Highpoint North, although this had also been offered. Second, the programme was adapted to fit the transient nature of the prison population. A 22-week programme was devised, recognizing that the average stay on the unit was only six months. Third, Prison Fellowship ensured that the Chaplaincy was fully involved and that the programme was perceived as part of Chaplaincy work in the prison. Fourth, unlike names such as Kairos-APAC and 'Kainos', Prison Fellowship chose the name 'Compass' because it was 'visual' and had meaning for prisoners. Fifth, the non-confrontational strap line 'Choosing the way for life' placed the emphasis on prisoner choice. Sixth, in stating that the aim of Compass is 'to enable participants...to examine, understand, test and apply a Christian values-based lifestyle' Prison Fellowship clearly identifies the faith-specific nature of the unit.

On the basis of literature circulated to the Prison Service and to prisoners, 'Compass' desires to establish 'a safe community' and to foster change through a variety of 'social learning, role modelling and programmatic elements' (Walker 2003a). There are also similarities at programme level, such as the use of a popular series about the Ten Commandments to lead discussion about ethics and a slightly-expanded version of Sycamore Tree. 'Compass' has a clear Christian identity, again on the basis of literature distributed. The programme is presented as part of Chaplaincy work in the prison (Walker 2003b) and basic introductions to the Christian faith are provided by several programmes: 'Start'; the 'Y' course (essentially a 'pre-Alpha' course), and the 'Alpha' course itself (which is widely used in prisons). 'Compass' prisoners are required to take part in 'Start' and 'Alpha' as part of the compact.

Prison Fellowship England and Wales is part of Prison Fellowship International, based in the United States, which runs IFI. However, 'Compass' is a different programme to IFI – it is much shorter and accordingly the 'phases' are less distinct (Walker 2003a).[29] Despite this, there is a natural affinity between Compass and IFI. Prison Fellowship England and Wales reviewed APAC and IFI before assembling 'Compass', incorporating aspects of IFI's structure (e.g. the use of programme 'phases') and content (e.g. the list of 'InnerChange values'[30]).

(c) He Korowai Whakapono ('A Cloak of Faith'), New Zealand

This faith-based unit opened in October 2004 at Rimutaka Prison, a low-security prison near Wellington with a 60-bed unit (www.pfnz.org.nz; accessed 5 April 2005). This partnership between the New Zealand Public Prisons Service and Prison Fellowship New Zealand (PFNZ) was the product of seven years' negotiation with the Public Prisons Service (Workman 2004).

The unit is expressly Christian-based, describing itself as 'a Christ-centred community' offering an 18-month 'Christian development programme' (PFNZ undated). The programme is in four stages: induction and orientation; 'spiritual transformation'; 'restoration'; and 'reintegration'. It contains Christian teaching, 'a prayer-centred daily routine and a combination of faith development programmes and regular worship involving a variety of external church groups and Christian volunteers' (*ibid.*). A Cursillo weekend also takes place three-quarters of the way through the programme.[31] The initiative presents itself as 'a biblically-based programme with an overt emphasis on spiritual growth and moral development' (PFNZ news release 2004). After four months, PFNZ staff 'realized that the biblical teaching programme was too intense' (Workman 2004), a move that recalls the change to IFI programming described in Chapter 8. The New Zealand setting tempers the IFI approach, allowing the unit to draw on local influences such as local restorative justice programmes and practices. Perhaps not surprisingly, the unit focuses on 'peace making, conflict resolution and the restoration of relationships' (*ibid.*). The unit is located close to a large urban centre (in fact, a capital city) allowing it to draw on a Christian community with a robust prison ministry and a sufficient pool of experienced prison volunteers. This is an excellent strategy adopted by surprisingly few faith-based units.

It seems that He Korowai Whakapono is evolving into something closer to APAC. Workman (2005) claims that: 'there is much more emphasis on informal discussion using local volunteers as 'passive mentors' who visit and engage in informal discussion with inmates on their spiritual growth....The [New Zealand] model is essentially about using church congregations to speak into the lives of prisoners, rather than the formal 'Bible College' model developed in IFI'. There is also heavy emphasis on family (*whanau*) reintegration and reconciliation, which again recalls APAC.

Prisoners are divided into four 15-person groups called 'Living Unit Groups', each group acting as 'a surrogate family' (PFNZ undated). These meet five times a week to provide affirmation, encouragement and resolve community issues. Prisoners remain part of the offender employment programme, spending 90 per cent of unlock time in work-related or constructive activity. In an echo of APAC's desire that there should be no 'contamination' of the rehabilitative environment (Chapter 1), all staff working at the unit (including all prison staff) 'must be able to fully participate in a faith-based community, and actively support and uphold Christian values and principles' (*ibid.*).

PFNZ also provides a church-based, non-residential Christian resettlement programme called 'Operation Jericho' which aims to provide 'intensive and ongoing pre- and post- release support' (*ibid.*). The programme begins six to eight months prior to release. Case managers train and oversee volunteer mentors drawn from local church groups, mainly in the Wellington area. The resettlement programme is only available for prisoners planning to live in the Wellington region, although PFNZ is seeking to extend to areas that have a high proportion of released prisoners, many of whom are Maori.

(d) Prisma, Germany

In Germany, Prison Fellowship run an APAC-inspired 'Prisma' faith-based prison programme for juveniles which opened in November 2003 (Prisma 2003; www.prisma-jugendhilfe.de). The target group is 14–18 year olds with two-year custodial sentences. The 12 to 18 month programme will include Sycamore Tree and Restorative Justice programmes. Remedial education, athletics and modelling pro-social family life are said to be important elements.

(e) Other programmes

In Australia, *Lives in Transition* (similar to Compass) began in September 2002 at Barwon prison, Victoria, with 12 prisoners. Run by Prison Fellowship Australia, the programme claims to be modelled on IFI.

Finally, Prison Fellowship Latvia opened a faith-based unit called MYRIAM in a women's prison in Riga in January 2003.

Perhaps the biggest innovation, at the time of writing, is the opening, in January 2004, of Lawtey C.I. in Florida by Governor Jeb Bush. This was unveiled, with much fanfare, as a 'Faith and Character Institution', making it the first totally faith-based prison in the West, catering for all faiths.

6. A signpost for correctional services

Religion is an intensely personal experience and the manner and extent to which it forms the basis of programmes in prisons must always be handled with extreme care. There are a number of risks: vulnerable prisoners may be exploited (deliberately or otherwise) and lack of sufficient informed consent may violate prisoners' conscience and freedom of religion. This can lead to accusations of 'brainwashing' and favouritism. Equality of opportunity can be violated. The personal nature of faith-based programmes also means they risk unearthing sensitive issues that staff and volunteers are not best qualified to deal with. Non-uniformed unit staff and outside volunteers risk being seen by uniformed staff and management as well-meaning but potentially dangerous amateurs. Volunteers and ex-offenders used as part of such programmes are potential security risks. There may be a high risk of tension with the prison Chaplaincy. Programmes can also be vulnerable to individual personalities involved in running them and their relations with key people in the rest of the prison.

Faith-based units need to continue to learn from best practice in both 'secular' and religious fields, adapt to local needs and opportunities, involve appropriate volunteers to the fullest extent possible, be clear in their identity and not compromise on their distinctiveness. It would be natural for units to explore further how they can implement the ideals of restorative justice in prison and show alternative, evolving ways to prepare prisoners for release and resettlement.

The Kainos evaluation concluded that, overall, Kainos 'may act as a signpost to the Prison Service in terms of promoting standards of decency, humanity and order in prisons' (Burnside *et. al.* 2001: 131). Much the same can be said of the other faith-based units considered in this book. But such units need to retain their faith-based identity. The following remark from a former Kainos governor applies to faith-based units as a whole:

> Ignore the spiritual aim, and Kainos can become a self-perpetuating, narrow, target-snatching, defensive and institutionalized corral.

Some might say that this should fit it nicely for today's prison world. But pay attention to it, challenge it, inject good staff, align its legitimate targets with those of the prison and the community, work hard at getting prisoners to do their own work and realize their spiritual worth, and you have a unique residential community which works as one for others including victims and those who are damaged by crime.

(Respondent J 2003)

At their best, faith-based units can be 'the home from which prisoners took on prison life and in which they established and took responsibility for love and forgiveness' (*ibid.*). They can help to foster a sense of maturity and responsibility and encourage prisoners to take more responsibility for themselves, their families and their communities, as well as greater responsibility with staff. Instead of apathy, stagnation and a fear of deterioration, they offer a place for reflection and the possibility of inner development, in terms of character, creativity, morality and spirituality. They consider what prisoners' strengths are, as well as their weaknesses. They are a chance to reorder personal values and to reconstruct a new identity. They can resymbolize the meaning of imprisonment.

We have also seen that they can be places of safety and 'real relating' in the often frightening and artificial world of prison. They offer humanity in the face of a dehumanizing prison environment, reinforcing pro-social attitudes and behaviours traditionally regarded as weaknesses in prisons. Beyond this, they can be a kind of 'counter-culture', challenging and subverting the prison 'honour code' whereby the strong subdue the weak. Intimidation can be replaced with vulnerability; hostility with friendship; suspicion with trust and isolation with community. They provide an approximation to living as 'family', often for those lacking any such experience. They provide more opportunities for interaction with people on the outside. They help to create 'permeable institutions', where society can assume visible responsibility for prisoners. They provide opportunities for benefiting others, building social capital within and without the prison walls. They increase the capacity of both churches and prisons to show compassion, humanity and mercy. Above all, faith-based units have not merely individual but organizational implications. They have the potential to reform the nature of the traditional prison environment; individual change and institutional change are complementary.

Finally, by making prisons more human and punishment more humane, faith-based units promote ethicality and legitimacy. They provide grounds for believing that prisons are places where punishment is just. Given the increasing pressures upon imprisonment at the start of the twenty-first century, this is significant. Faith-based units can be of great value – to keep faith in prisons.

Notes

1 Lords *Hansard*, 5 November 2001, col. 119.
2 *Op. cit.*, col. 122.
3 Press reaction at the time of the decision noted complaints from Muslim groups about the special position given to Christian denominations in prison. In the week that the news broke, the Commission on British Muslims and Islamaphobia said in a newsletter that: 'Muslim prisoners are not receiving equal access to pastoral care compared to prisoners from Christian backgrounds' (Johnston 2001a). This had been addressed in the evaluation, which noted that the Imam had open access to prisoners on three of the four Kainos units. Only in one prison was access restricted due to a clash between the Imam and the Kainos team. In this case Muslim prisoners had access to the Imam equivalent to prisoners elsewhere in the prison.
4 Jonathan Aitken is a former Conservative Minister of State, who was imprisoned for perjury and publicly converted to Christianity following his criminal trial.
5 Alan Duncan MP. House of Commons *Hansard*, 1 November 2001 (part 7); col. 1008.
6 Lords *Hansard*, 5 November 2001, col. 103.
7 *op cit.*, col. 116.
8 *op cit.*, col. 119.
9 *op cit.*, col. 122.
10 House of Commons *Hansard*, 9 Nov. 2001, col. 538.
11 *Ibid*.
12 The negative findings of the Prison Service's cognitive skills programmes such as Reasoning and Rehabilitation and Enhanced Thinking Skills (Ford 2003a, 2003b) might suggest an openness on the part of the Prison Service to approaches that are not based purely on cognitive skills but have a different mechanism, such as normative compliance (see Chapter 1). Faith-based units, it may be hypothesized, are in a potentially good position to stimulate normative compliance, not least because they tend to offer programming of a moral nature and contact with pro-social, non-uniformed staff and volunteers. Graham and Bowling (1995) have indicated the need for a moral dimension to be added to the development of cognitive skills.
13 See e.g. the headline of the *Baptist Times*: '*Shock as faith-based prison experiment is closed down*' which characterized Kainos as 'a network of Britain's most effective prison rehabilitation units' (Hogarth 2001: 1).
14 Lords *Hansard* 5 November 2001, col. 100.
15 Mark Hoban MP, House of Commons *Hansard*, 9 November 2001, pt. 17, col. 538.

16   This PSO supported the Regimes Standard that: 'Every establishment provides a constructive regime which addresses offending behaviour, improves educational and work skills and promotes law-abiding behaviour in custody and after release' (*ibid*.: 3).

17   This is to acknowledge that 'programmes work (have successful 'outcomes') only in so far as they introduce the appropriate ideas and opportunities ('mechanisms') to groups in the appropriate social and cultural conditions ('contexts')' (Pawson and Tilley 1997: 61).

18   At that time, Kainos described itself in its Vision Statement as 'an ecumenical Christian organization' (Kainos Community 2001) which offered the explicitly Christian Kairos Weekend and some of its follow-up programmes as a core part of the Community.

19   'Our aim is to create a learning atmosphere by helping prisoners to live lives that are socially positive where people feel safe to look at themselves' (Kainos Community Programme, revised January 2003, 1).

20   The evaluation found Kainos had no significant effect on Kainos prisoners' perceptions of safety from being injured, bullied or threatened, although this may have been due to a 'ceiling effect' (see Chapter 9).

21   It is clear that IFI has a different emphasis than Horizon. IFI emphasizes scriptural identification and interpretation of sin and salvation. Horizon is content to model Christ's love and acceptance without interpretation, even to those of other faiths. Yet both aspire to be Christian communities.

22   IFI's mission statement (see Chapter 8) marks it out as having a much more self-consciously 'Biblical' emphasis than was the case with Kairos-APAC or is the case with Horizon or New Kainos.

23   Hebbern (2003) claims: 'In my experience despite all the other kind of issues that we have problems with, it was the Kairos Weekend which was always the thing. No matter who you spoke to they always came out with the fact that this is a right-wing American evangelical thing. Which it never was of course, it was never any of those things, but you never ever got away from that'. [Interviewer:] *'Yet the Kairos Weekend was the one feature from the Report that was the most positive finding'.* [Interviewee]: 'Of course it was'.

24   As Pawson and Tilley (1997: 114) remind us: 'Outcomes only follow when particular mechanisms have been triggered in particular contexts'.

25   The encouragement of vengeance appears as one of 'Nine Satanic Statements' ('[No.] V Satan represents vengeance, instead of turning the other cheek!'; http://satanism3.0catch.com/info.html, accessed 4 April 2005).

26   By the time of release, the reconviction sample had spent an average of 26 months in prison since sentence, compared with 14 months for the non-Kainos comparison sample (Burnside *et al.* 2001: 125).

27   Nearly two-thirds were serving four years or more. Fourteen per cent had five years or more left to serve.

28   The programme is said to provide prisoners with an opportunity to consider their values and their offending behaviour, to take responsibility for their actions, and to develop constructive pro-social skills. Informed consent is gained through an induction period and compact. Prisoners have the

opportunity to leave the programme during an initial three-week orientation period. Programme components include courses addressing citizenship, money matters, employment and housing.

29 Its approach to resettlement, whilst certainly laudable, is inevitably less ambitious. Compass provides life skills and preparation for release elements within the curriculum and offers Compass participants countrywide follow-up through the network of Prison Fellowship groups.

30 Walker (2003a) lists these as: Transformation, Integrity and Truth, Restoration, Responsibility, Community building (fellowship), Affirmation and Productivity. Like IFI, 'Compass' uses the language of 'spiritual transformation' and 'inner change': 'It is the belief of the Compass project that...transformation is a cognitive, emotional and spiritual process, and that this inner change will affect outward actions' (*ibid*.).

31 In contrast to Kairos-APAC which ran the Kairos Weekend at the start of the programme.

Appendices

Appendix A

Logistic Regression results for the reanalysis of data from Johnson *et al.* (1997, Table 4) (see Chapter 10)

The data are for 401 released prisoners from New York State prisons. 201 have experienced a Prison Fellowship programme (99 low participation, 80 medium and 22 high). The comparison group were individually matched, and are therefore allocated in the same way in Johnson *et al.* Table 4, although clearly they have not participated in the PF programme (99 matched with low, 79 with medium,[1] 22 with high; *n* = 200).

All variables are categorical, and are coded as follows:

Variable	Coding	Comments
Arrest within a year	Not arrested/Arrested	Dependent variable
Main group	PF/Non-PF *	Independent variable; analysis 1
Participation	Low */Medium/High	Independent variable; analysis 1
Risk (of recidivism)	Low */Medium/High	Independent variable; analysis 1 and analysis 2
Subgroup	PF Low/PF Medium/ PF High/Non-PF *	Independent variable; analysis 2

Categories marked * are taken as the base for that variable in the logistic analysis. Other categories are compared with the base category (both collectively and individually) in the tables below. There are two analyses, which may be seen as alternatives. In the second, the two variables 'main group' and 'participation' are replaced by the single variable 'main group' where the whole of the non-PF comparison group is taken as one category.

Analysis 1: The joint effect of main group, participation and recidivism risk on likelihood of arrest.

Table A1   Logistic Regression Equation ($n = 401$)

Variable/category	B	S.E.	Wald statistic	d.f.	Sig.	Exp(B)
Participation			0.496	2	0.780	
Participation (medium)	0.204	0.290	0.496	1	0.481	1.227
Participation (high)	0.090	0.475	0.036	1	0.850	1.094
Main group (PF)	−0.032	0.273	0.014	1	0.905	0.968
Risk of recidivism			129.960	2	0.000	
Risk of recid (medium)	0.849	0.450	3.567	1	0.059	2.338
Risk of recid (high)	3.748	0.441	72.271	1	0.000	42.430
Constant	−2.600	0.439	35.012	1	0.000	0.074

Additional analyses were undertaken as follows. (1) A forward stepwise logistic regression with the same set of variables, which confirmed that only the risk variable was significant; (2) further logistic regressions including interaction terms, which showed that no interaction between the independent variables had a significant effect, and that only the risk variable was significant.

Analysis 2: The joint effect of subgroup and recidivism risk on likelihood of arrest

Table A2 Logistic Regression Equation ($n = 401$)

Variable/category	B	S.E.	Wald statistic	d.f.	Sig.	Exp(B)
Subgroup			2.837	3	0.417	
Subgroup (PF low partic)	−0.092	0.336	0.075	1	0.784	0.912
Subgroup (PF medium partic)	0.247	0.353	0.489	1	0.484	1.280
Subgroup (PF high partic)	−1.065	0.772	1.903	1	0.168	0.345
Risk of recidivism			128.915	2	0.000	
Risk of recid (medium)	0.819	0.451	3.298	1	0.069	2.268
Risk of recid (high)	3.701	0.440	70.674	1	0.000	40.483
Constant	−2.477	0.412	36.096	1	0.000	0.084

As with analysis 1, additional regressions were run. (1) A forward stepwise logistic regression with the same set of variables, which confirmed that only the risk variable was significant; (2) further logistic regressions including an interaction term, which showed that the interaction between the independent variables had no significant effect. Again, only the risk variable was significant.

These analyses therefore show no evidence for an effect of Prison Fellowship participation on recidivism, as measured by rearrest.

Note

1   One matching case was missing from Johnson *et al.* 1997, Table 4.

Appendix B

The Comparison sample as a 'standard' (see Chapter 10)

The rationale for the Comparison sample (CS) is that it acts as a 'standard' against which the results for the Kainos reconviction sample can be assessed. One way to approach this task systematically is to 'recalibrate' a risk score for two year reconvictions using the OGRS (Offender Group Reconviction Scale) predictor variables that were provided as the core of the CS data. The objective is to produce a calculation method for expected rates of two year reconviction that is specific to *released prisoners having served sentences of six months or more.* OGRS scores, which are routinely used by the Home Office and Prison Service, cannot be used as they stand since both OGRS1 and OGRS2 are known to over-predict reconvictions for prisoners who have served longer-term sentences (see Rose 2001).

The observed reconviction rates of the Kainos sample can then be compared with expectation.

Following the methods described in Copas and Marshall (1998) the 'recalibration' was undertaken and a 'two year reconviction risk score' (TYRRS) was produced. A brief account is given below and further details are dealt with in a paper prepared for the Home Office RDS (Rose 2001). The TYRRS is thus a prediction of risk, analogous to an OGRS score, based on a large sample (the CS); however, unlike OGRS it is not intended to be of general utility outside the confines of this study.

As a further refinement, the TYRRS was been developed in two forms:

- TYRRS1 is a prediction of the two year reconviction risk for released prisoners based on the comparison sample as a whole, and takes no account of prison establishment.

- TYRRS2 also takes account of whether the offender was released from The Verne, Highpoint North or Highpoint South.

There are no major differences between the two versions of the score, although TYRRS2 is utilized for sections of the results where distinctions are made between establishments.

Deriving 'two year reconviction risk scores' (TYRRS) using logistic regression

1 Using the comparison sample data, a logistic regression was undertaken with 'reconviction within two years' as the dependent variable and the OGRS predictor variables as independent variables. In order to improve prediction, 'months in prison' was added as an independent variable. 'Offence type' was categorized and weighted as in Copas and Marshall (1998). In the logistic regression equation, most of the variables were highly significant, following the general pattern of the various OGRS analyses (for further details see Rose 2001).

2 The two equations determining TYRRS1 were derived from this analysis, as follows (c.f. Copas and Marshall 1998: 161)

COMPUTE Y21 = COPAS * 4.801 + BURGLARY * 0.1584 –
AGEFRST2 * 0.0362 + OFFENCXX * 0.0422 – AGESEN2 * 0.0190 –
MONTHS * 0.0127 – PRECUS21 * 0.0452 + (GENDER –1) * 0.0149 –
BREACHES * 0.0395 – 2.1447.
COMPUTE TYRRS1 = (1 /(1 + EXP(-Y21)))+ 0.0003209.

The variables used in the equations are explained in more detail in Table B1, below.

3 For the TYRRS2 analysis, dummy variables representing release from The Verne, Highpoint North and Highpoint South were added to the logistic regression analysis. This resulted in slight improvements to the fit for the comparison sample data representing releases from these three institutions, as Table B2 shows.

4 It should also be noted that in the Kainos reconviction sample, the offenders are not necessarily *released* from the prison in which they were exposed to the Kainos programme, since many are transferred elsewhere before being discharged from the prison system. For the TYRRS2 analysis, we have simply taken Comparison sample prisoners who were released from one of the three named prisons as the only feasible control for the effect of being an inmate at those establishments.

Table B1 Variables contributing to the OYRRS prediction score

• COPAS	'Copas rate' - calculation based on the rate of court appearances over the whole criminal history.
• OFFENCXX	Offence category (nine groups) weighted as for OGRS1 computations.
• AGEFRST2	Age at first conviction.
• BURGLARY	Any burglary convictions?
• AGESEN2	Age at sentence.
• MONTHS	Months spent in prison after sentence.
• PRECUS21	No. of custodial sentences when age less than 21.
• GENDER	Male/Female.
• BREACHES	Any history of breaches (of court orders etc.)?

Table B2 Comparison sample: two-year reconviction rates, and predictions using TYRRS1 and TYRRS2 scores

Prison released from	No. cases	Actual reconviction rates	TYRRS1 scores: predicted reconviction rates	TYRRS2 scores: predicted reconviction rates
The Verne	249	45.8%	46.3%	45.8%
Highpoint South (male)	517	51.5%	48.4%	51.5%
Highpoint North (female)	50	26.0%	31.3%	26.0%
All other establishments	13,016	42.3%	42.4%	42.3%
Comparison sample: all cases	13,832	42.7%	42.7%	42.7%

Bibliography

Aitken, J. (2001) 'Does the Prison Service Want People to Stop Reoffending?' *Daily Telegraph*, 1 November, 26.

Aldred, I. (2004) pers. comm., 10 July.

Allport, G.W. and Ross, J.M. (1967) 'Personal Religious Orientation and Prejudice', *Journal of Personality and Social Psychology*, 5: 432–43.

Allport, G.W. (1959) 'Religion and Prejudice', *Crane Review*, 2: 1–10.

Allport, G.W. (1950) *The Individual and His Religion*. New York: Macmillan.

Anderson, M. (1991a) 'Brazil Facility Operates on Basis of Inmate Trust', *Corrections Today*, December, 96–103.

Anderson, M. (1991b) 'Beyond these walls', in D. Van Patten (ed.) *The Dysmas Project*, 20–30 unpublished.

Anonymous (1990) 'The Unguarded Prison', *International Jubilee Journal*, 1 (1): 2–4.

APAC (Undated circa 1994) 'Sistema APAC: Com 20 Anos de Evolucío' ('APAC System: 20 years of evolution'). Internal document in Brazilian Portuguese, São José dos Campos, Brazil: APAC.

APAC (1993a) 'Vantagnes do Sistema APAC Sobre o Sistema covencional ('Advantages of the APAC System over the Conventional System'). Internal document in Brazilian Portuguese, São José dos Campos, Brazil: APAC.

APAC (1993b) 'Secretary of the Penitentiary Administration Supports the Work of APAC' ('Secretário da Administração Penitenciária Apoia o Trabalho do Presídio da Apac'). *APAC Magazine (APAC em Revista)*, Year V, N 23 (May/July). São José dos Campos, 7: APAC.

APAC (1993c) 'Secretary of Public Security praises APAC Prison', *APAC Magazine (APAC em Revista)*, Year V, N 23 (May/July). São José dos Campos, 7: APAC.

APAC (1993d) 'Jornal Paulista Denuncia o Caos dos Presídios' ('São Paulo Newspaper Denounces the Chaos of Prisons'), *APAC em Revista* (*APAC Magazine*), São José dos Campos-Sp: Brazil, COBRAPAC, Year V, N 23 (May/ July), 14.

Bamber, D. (1999) 'Christian Help Group Faces Prisons Probe', *The Sunday Telegraph*, 25th April, 7.

Baptist Times (1997) 'More Prisons May Turn to Christian Volunteers', 16 January: 2.

Batson, C.D. and Schoenrade, P.A. (1991a) 'Measuring Religion As Quest. 1: Validity Concerns', *Journal For the Scientific Study of Religion*, 30 (4): 416–29.

Batson, C.D. and Schoenrade, P.A. (1991b) 'Measuring Religion As Quest. 2: Reliability Concerns', *Journal For the Scientific Study of Religion*, 30 (4): 430–47.

Beck, A.T., Brown, G., Steer, R.A. and Weissman, A. (1991) 'Factor Analysis of the Dysfunctional Attitudes Scale in a clinical population', *Psychological Assessment*, 3: 478–83.

Beckford, J.A. and Gilliat, S. (1998) *Religion in Prison: Equal Rites in a Multi-faith Society.* Cambridge: Cambridge University Press.

Beech, A., Fisher, D., Beckett, R. and Scott-Fordham, A. (1998) 'An Evaluation of the Prison Sex Offender Treatment Programme', *Home Office Research Findings* 79. London: Home Office.

Beer, P. (1997) *Collected Poems.* Carcanet Press.

Benda, B.B. (2002) 'Religion and Violent Offenders in Boot Camp: A Structural Equation Model', *Journal of Research in Crime and Delinquency*, 39 (1): 91–121.

Benda, B.B. (1995) 'The Effect of Religion On Adolescent Delinquency Revisited', *Journal of Research in Crime and Delinquency*, 32 (4): 446–66.

Board of Visitors (B.V.) HMP The Verne (2002) *Annual Report*, January/December 2001. Dorset: HMP The Verne.

Bonthrone, P.J. (2000) 'Prisoners Get a Taste of God Through Tea and Cakes', *The Times*, 8th September.

Bottoms, A.E. (2002) 'Morality, crime, compliance and public policy', in A.E. Bottoms and M. Tonry (eds) *Ideology, Crime and Criminal Justice: A Symposium in Honour of Sir Leon Radzinowicz.* Cullompton: Willan Publishing, 20–51.

Bottoms, A.E. (2001) 'Compliance and Community Penalties', in A.E. Bottoms, L.R. Gelsthorpe and S. Rex (eds) *Community Penalties: Change and Challenges.* Cullompton: Willan Publishing.

Bottoms, A.E. and Rex, S. (1998) 'Pro-social modelling and legitimacy', in S. Rex and A. Matravers (eds) *Pro-Social Modelling and Legitimacy: The Clarke Hall Day Conference.* Cambridge: University of Cambridge Institute of Criminology, 11–27.

Bottoms, A.E., Sparks, R. and Hay, W. (1996) *Prisons and the Problem of Order.* Oxford: Clarendon Press.

Bottoms, A.E., Knapp, M. and Fenyo, A. (1995) *Intensive Community Supervision for Young Offenders: Outcomes, Process and Cost.* Cambridge: Institute of Criminology.

365

Brandt, H. (IFI) (1998) 'Transformation: The InnerChange Freedom Initiative', cited in PFI (2002) 'Promoting APAC Faith-based Prisons', 2.

Bright Griffin, M. (2004) pers. comm., 12th February, 22nd April and 17th and 18th November.

Bright Griffin, M. (2003a) pers. comm. (undated).

Bright Griffin, M. (2003b) Recorded interview.

Bulmer, M. (1986) *Social Research and Social Policy*. London: Allen and Unwin.

Burnside, J. (2005) 'Criminal Justice', in M. Schluter and J. Ashcroft (eds) *Jubilee Manifesto*. Leicester: Inter Varsity Press, 234–254.

Burnside, J.P. and Baker, N. (eds). (2004) *Relational Justice: Repairing the Breach*. Winchester: Waterside Press.

Burnside, J.P. (2003) *The Signs of Sin: Seriousness of offence in Biblical Law*. Sheffield: Sheffield Academic Press.

Burnside, J.P., Adler, J., Loucks, N. and Rose, G. (2001) *Kainos Community in Prisons: Report of an Evaluation*. www.homeoffice.gov.uk/vol. 5/adhocpubs1. html.

Burnside, J. and Lee, P. (1997) 'Where Love is Not a Xuxury', *New Life*, 13: 36–54.

Burrell, I. (2000a) 'Head of Religious Prisons Charity Convicted of Stealing Funds', *Independent*, 25th February.

Burrell, I. (2000b) 'Director "Stole from Christian Jail Charity Funds"', 22nd February.

Burrell, I. (1999a) 'Prison Charity Boss Fired over Finance Allegations', *Independent*, 16th March.

Burrell, I. (1999b) 'Prison Charity Run by Conman', *Independent*, 8th January.

Burrell, I. (1999c) 'Evangelical Fraudster Charged with Showing Prisoners the Light', *Independent*, 8 January: 3.

Bush, G.W. (1997) Speech to Fourth Annual Criminal Justice Ministry Conference, Houston, February 7–8th. *Informs* Newsletter 4 (2).

Byrne, J. (2004) pers. comm., 22nd December.

Byrne, J. (2003) Recorded interview.

Caldwell, J. (2000) 'Forgiveness: A Layman's Journey in Ministry', *Sewanee Theological Review*, 43 (2): 172–83.

Caliber Associates (2004a) *Compassion Capital Fund Evaluation of the Kairos Horizon Communities in Prison Programme: Final Report*. Fairfax, VA: Caliber Associates.

Caliber Associates (2004b) *Navigating a New Horizon: Promising Pathways to Prisoner Reintegration*. Department of Health and Human Services USA: Caliber Associates.

Caliber Associates (2003) *Prisoner Re-entry, Religion and Research*. Department of Health and Human Services USA: Caliber Associates.

Campbell, D.T. and Stanley, J.C. (1963) *Experimental and Quasi-experimental Designs for Research*. Chicago: Rand McNally.

Carandiru (2003) Directed by Hector Babenco, Running time 2 hrs 28 mins, certificate 15.

Carter, K. (2001) 'Kainos Prison Wings Set to Close', *Christian Herald*, 10th November: 1.

Carter, M., Kay, W.K. and Francis, L.J. (1996) 'Personality and Attitude Toward Christianity among Committed Adult Christians', *Personality and Individual Differences*, 20 (2): 265–66.

Chapman, J. (2003) Recorded interview.

Choices UK (undated) *[Outline of] Choices Prison Ministry UK*. Unpublished.

Christianity Today (2001) 'Charity Hopes for New Beginning in Fight to Save Christian Prison Wings', www.christianitytoday.com, 17 December 2001.

Clear, T., Stout, B., Dammer, H., Kelly, L., Hardyman, P. and Shapiro, C. (1992) *Prisoners, Prison and Religion: Final Report*. New Jersey: School of Criminal Justice, Rutgers University.

Cohen, N. (1996a) 'St. Michael Sends his Apostles into the Prisons', *Observer*, 15th December: 13.

Cohen, N. (1996b) 'Cheap Deliverance for the Jailhouse Flock', *Observer*, 22nd December: 18.

Cole, G. (2005) 'Christianity as a relational religion', in M. Schluter and J. Ashcroft (eds) *Jubilee Manifesto*. Leicester: InterVarsity Press.

Colledge, M., Collier, P. and Brand, S. (1999) *Programmes for Offenders: Guidance for Evaluators*. Crime Reduction Programme – Guidance Note 2. London: Home Office.

Colson, C.W. (2000) 'Foreword', in M. Ottoboni (ed.) *Kill the Criminal, Save the Person: The APAC Methodology*. Washington DC: Prison Fellowship International, 1–3.

Colson, C.W. (2003a) Address to Prison Fellowship International Convocation, Toronto, 7th August.

Colson, C.W. (2003b) 'The Risk of Doing Good', *Breakpoint Online*, www.breakpoint.org, 14 February: 1–2.

Cook, T.D. and Campbell, D. (1979) *Quasi-Experimentation: Design and analysis issues for field settings*, Chicago: Rand McNally.

Copas, J.B. and Marshall, P. (1998) 'The Offending Group Reconviction Scale: a Statistical Reconviction Score for Use by Probation Officers', *Applied Statistics*, 47 (1).

Copas, J.B., Marshall, P. and Tarling, R. (1996) *Predicting Reoffending for Discretionary Conditional Release*. Home Office Research Study No 150. London: Home Office.

Cornett, E. (1996) pers. comm., 9th October, to Mary Alice and Reuben Garza.

Cowley, J. (2004) Recorded interview.

Creighton, A. (1993) *The APAC Prison*. Unpublished paper prepared for Winston Churchill Memorial Trust.

Creighton, A. (2001) In: Prison Fellowship International (2001) *Starting an APAC-Based Prison*, unpublished manual. Available through Prison Fellowship International (PFI), Washington DC to any interested Prison Fellowship National Ministry on the basis of a personal visit and presentation of the material by PFI Regional Service Team members.

Creighton, A. and Rennie. (1995) *APAC (Brazil) Prison Regime: Feasibility in the SPS*, unpublished paper submitted to Scottish Prison Service.

Crossings Operations Manual (2003) Unpublished, 8th October.

Curran, K.L. (2002) *Finding God Behind Bars: An Exploratory Study of the Relevance of Prison Conversions to Criminology.* Doctoral dissertation submitted to the Faculty of Law, University of Cambridge.

Dallas Morning News (2003) 'Inmates Seem to Respond to Faith-based Programme', 8th February.

Day, J.D. and Laufer, W.S. (1983) *Crime, Values and Religion.* Norwood, NJ: Ablex.

Dautrich, P. (2004) pers. comm., 27th December.

Dautrich, P. (2003) Recorded interview.

De Oliveira, A. (1993) pers. comm., 26th May, to Mario Ottoboni.

Deconchy, J.P. (1987) 'Methods in Psychology of Religion – Current Trends', *Archives De Sciences Sociales Des Religions*, 32 (63): 31–83.

Donahue, M.J. (1985) 'Intrinsic and Extrinsic Religiousness – Review and Meta-Analysis', *Journal of Personality and Social Psychology*, 48 (2): 400–19.

Dorset Echo (2000) 'Ex-Charity Boss Denies Swindle', 22nd February: 3.

Dorset Evening Echo (1996) 'Inmates to Run Wing at Verne Prison', 8th October.

Dye, S. (2004) pers. comm., 20th December.

Dye, S. (2003) Recorded interview.

Earley, M. (2003) Prison Fellowship News Release. 12th February: 1–4, *Prison Fellowship Newsroom:* www.demossnewspond.com

Eaton, M. (1993) *Women After Prison.* Buckingham: Open University Press.

Exline, J.J. (2002) 'Stumbling Blocks on the Religious Road: Fractured Relationships, Nagging Vices and the Inner Struggle to Believe', *Psychological Inquiry*, 13 (3): 182–89.

Exline, J.J., Yali, A.M. and Sanderson, W.C. (2000) 'Guilt, Discord and Alienation: The Role of Religious Strain in Depression and Suicidality', *Journal of Clinical Psychology*, 56 (12): 1481–96.

Fabelo, T., Eisenberg, M. and Trusty, B. (2002) *Overview of the InnerChange Freedom Initiative: The Faith-Based Prison Programme within the TDCJ.* Austin, Texas: Texas Criminal Justice Policy Council.

Fabelo, T., Trusty, B. and Eisenberg, M. (2003) *Initial Process and Outcome Evaluation of the InnerChange Freedom Initiative: The Faith-Based Prison Programme in TDCJ.* Austin, Texas: Texas Criminal Justice Policy Council.

Farrington, D. (1996) *Understanding and Preventing Youth Crime.* York: Joseph Rowntree Foundation.

Faulkner, D. (2002) 'Turning Prisons Inside-out', *Relational Justice Bulletin*, 16: 1–3, www.relationshipsfoundation.org, accessed 30th March 2005.

Fernandes, M. (1993) Transcript of talk given on first APAC *Journada* for prisoners' wives and partners.

Florida Department of Corrections (2000) *Comparing Tomoka C.I.'s Faith-Based Dorm (Kairos Horizons) (sic) with Non-Participants.* Tallahassee, FL: Florida Department of Corrections Bureau of Research and Data Analysis.

Ford, R. (2003a) 'Prisoners Fail to Curb their Inner Man', *The Times*, 18th November.

Ford, R. (2003b) 'Psychology Courses Fail to Reform Criminals', *The Times*, 31st December.

Ford, R. (2001) 'Jails to Cater for New Face of Faith', *The Times*, 18th December.

Francis, L.J. (1992) 'Is Psychoticism Really a Dimension of Personality Fundamental to Religiosity?', *Personality and Individual Differences*, 13 (6): 645–52.

Francis, L.J. (1993a) 'Personality and Religion Among College Students in the UK', *Personality and Individual Differences*, 14 (4): 619–22.

Francis, L.J. (1993b) 'Reliability and Validity of a Short Scale of Attitude Towards Christianity Among Adults', *Psychological Reports*, 72 (2): 615–18.

Francis, L.J. and Bolger, J. (1997) 'Personality and Psychological Well-being in Later Life', *Irish Journal of Psychology*, 18 (4): 444–47.

Francis, L.J. and Bourke, R. (2003) 'Personality and Religion: Applying Cattell's Model among Secondary School Pupils', *Current Psychology*, 22 (2): 125–37.

Francis, L.J. and Pearson, P.R. (1993) 'The Personality-Characteristics of Student Churchgoers', *Personality and Individual Differences*, 15 (4): 373–80.

Francis, L.J. and Wilcox, C. (1996) 'Prayer, Church Attendance and Personality Revisited: A Study Among 16- to 19-yr-old girls', *Psychological Reports*, 79 (3): 1265–66.

Francis, L.J., Lewis, J.M., Philipchalk, R., Brown, L.B. and Lester, D. (1995) 'The Internal Consistency Reliability and Construct-Validity of the Francis Scale of Attitude Toward Christianity (Adult) Among Undergraduate Students in the UK, USA, Australia and Canada', *Personality and Individual Differences*, 19 (6): 949–53.

Frenz, A.W. and Carey, M.P. (1989) 'Relationship Between Religiousness and Trait Anxiety – Fact or Artifact', *Psychological Reports*, 65 (3): 827–34.

Frude, N., Honess, T. and Maguire, M. (1998) *Crime Pics II Manual*, 2nd edn. Cardiff: Michael and Associates.

Ganzevoort, R.R. (1998a) 'Religious Coping Reconsidered, Part One: An Integrated Approach', *Journal of Psychology and Theology*, 26 (3): 260–75.

Ganzevoort, R.R. (1998b) 'Religious Coping Reconsidered, Part Two: A Narrative Reformulation', *Journal of Psychology and Theology*, 26 (3): 276–86.

Garland, D. (2001) *The Culture of Control*. Oxford: Oxford University Press, 171–182.

Genia, V. (1996) 'I, E, Quest and Fundamentalism As Predictors of Psychological and Spiritual Well-Being', *Journal For the Scientific Study of Religion*, 35 (1): 56–64.

Genia, V. (1993) 'A Psychometric Evaluation of the Allport-Ross-I/E Scales in a Religiously Heterogeneous Sample', *Journal For the Scientific Study of Religion*, 32 (3): 286–90.

Goldblatt, P. and Lewis, C. (eds.) (1998) *Reducing Offending: An Assessment of Research Evidence on Ways of Dealing with Offending Behaviour*, Home Office Research Study No 187. London: Home Office.

Goodstein, L. (2003) 'Group Sues Christian Programme at Iowa Prison', *New York Times*, 13th February.

Gorsuch, R.L. and Venable, G.D. (1983) 'Development of an Age-Universal I-E Scale', *Journal For the Scientific Study of Religion*, 22 (2): 181–87.

Gorsuch, R.L. and McPherson, S.E. (1989) 'Intrinsic-Extrinsic Measurement, I/E-Revised and Single-Item Scales', *Journal For the Scientific Study of Religion*, 28 (3): 348–354.

Gorsuch, R.L. (1988) 'Psychology of Religion', *Annual Review of Psychology*, 39: 201–21.

Graham, J. and Bowling, B. (1995) *Young People and Crime*, Home Office Research Study 145. London: HMSO.

Grey, S. (1997) 'Throwing the Prisoners to the Christians', *Sunday Times*, 30th March.

Griffin, I. (2004) pers. comm., 11th February and 24th November.

Griffin, I. (2003) Recorded interview.

Griffin, I. (2000) pers. comm. Notes from unrecorded interview.

Griffin, I. (1999a) *Memo: Kairos International Oversight of Faith-Based Communities.*

Griffin, I. (1999b) unpublished letter to the *Independent*, 9th January.

Griffin, I. (1998) pers. comm., 5th May, to Penelope Lee.

Griffin, I. (1997) pers. comm., 24th October, to Penelope Lee.

Griffin, I. (1996a) 'Kairos in England', *Kairos Newsletter* (November–December): 4.

Griffin, I. (1996b) pers. comm., 27th November and 16th December, to Penelope Lee.

Guerreiro, M. (1992) 'Massacre de Presos Divide População' ('Massacre of Prisoners Divides the People'), *O Estado de S. Paulo*, 11th October.

Guessous, F., Hooper, N. and Moorthy, U. (2001) *Religion in Prisons: 1999 and 2000 (England and Wales)*, Home Office Statistical Bulletin: www.homeoffice. gov.uk/rds/pdfs/hosb1501.pdf (accessed 30th March 2005).

Hackney, C.H. and Sanders, G.S. (2003) 'Religiosity and Mental Health: A Meta-Analysis of Recent Studies', *Journal For the Scientific Study of Religion*, 42 (1): 43–55.

Hall, T.W., Tisdale, T.C. and Brokaw, B.F. (1994) 'Assessment of Religious Dimensions in Christian Clients – a Review of Selected Instruments For Research and Clinical Use', *Journal of Psychology and Theology*, 22 (4), 395–421.

Hardy, J. (1996) 'Religious Sect to Take Over Prison Wing', *Sunday Telegraph*: 11.

Harrison, M.O., Koenig, H.G., Hays, J.C., Eme-Akwari, A.G. and Pargament, K.I. (2001) 'The Epidemiology of Religious Coping: A Review of Recent Literature', *International Review of Psychiatry*, 13 (2): 86–93.

Hebbern, G. (2003) Recorded interview.

Hebbern, G. (2001) 'Religion is good for prisoners and wardens', Letter to *Daily Telegraph*, 14th November.

Hebbern, G. (1999a) pers. comm., 15th June, to Ian Aldred.

Hebbern, G. (1999b) Unpublished talk given to ACF conference.

Hebbern, G. (1997) 'The Kairos-APAC Project', *Prison Service Journal*, 117: 42–3.

Hebbern, G. (1996) *The Verne APAC Project: Summary Document.*

Heffernan, E. (1972) *Making it in Prison.* New York: John Wiley and Sons.

HM Chief Inspector of Prisons (HMCIP) (1997) *Report on HM Prison The Verne.* London: Home Office.

Hester, M.P. and Paloutzian, R.F. (1998) 'The Status of Psychology of Religion: An Interview with Raymond F. Paloutzian', *Teaching of Psychology*, 25(4), 303–6.

Hills, P., Francis, L.J., Argyle, M. and Jackson, C.J. (2004) 'Primary Personality Trait Correlates of Religious Practice and Orientation', *Personality and Individual Differences*, 36 (1): 61–73.

HM Prison Service (2002) *Prison Service Order 4350: Effective Regime Interventions*, www.pso.hmprisonservice.gov.uk.

Hogarth, L. (2001) 'Shock as Christian-based Prison Experiment is Closed Down', *Baptist Times*, 8th November: 1.

Home Office (2001) *Making Punishments Work: Report of a Review of the Sentencing Framework for England and Wales.* London: Home Office.

Howse, C. (2001) 'Sacred mysteries', *Daily Telegraph*, 1st December: 27.

Hunsberger, B. (1991) 'Empirical Work in the Psychology of Religion', *Canadian Psychology-Psychologie Canadienne*, 32 (3): 497–507.

Hunsaker, J. (2003) Recorded interview.

Hunt, C. (2002) 'The Heart of the Problem', *IFI Newsletter* 3 (5): 1.

Hunter, I. (2001) 'Don't Mock It Till You Try It', *The Globe and Mail* (Toronto, Canada) 9th February.

Idler, E.L., Musick, M.A., Ellison, C.G., George, L.K., Krause, N., Ory, M.G., Pargament, K.I., Powell, L.H., Underwood, L.G. and Williams, D.R. (2003) 'Measuring Multiple Dimensions of Religion and Spirituality or Health Research – Conceptual Background and Findings from the 1998 General Social Survey', *Research On Aging*, 25 (4): 327–65.

Jackson, L.E. and Coursey, R.D. (1988) 'The Relationship of God Control and Internal Locus of Control to Intrinsic Religious Motivation, Coping and Purpose in Life', *Journal For the Scientific Study of Religion*, 27 (3): 399–410.

James, A. and Wells, A. (2003) 'Religion and Mental Health: Towards a Cognitive-Behavioural Framework', *British Journal of Health Psychology*, 8: 359–76.

John, J. (2001) *10+: A Group Study of the Ten Commandments.* London: Monarch.

John, J. (2000) *Ten: Living the Ten Commandments in the Twenty-First Century.* Eastbourne: Kingsway.

Johnson, B.R. with Larson, D.B. (2003) *The InnerChange Freedom Initiative: A Preliminary Evaluation of a Faith–Based Prison Programme.* University of Pennsylvania: Center for Research on Religion and Urban Civil Society.

Johnson, B.R., Tompkins, R.B. and Webb, D. (2002) *Objective Hope: Assessing the Effectiveness of Faith-Based Organizations: A Review of the Literature.* University of Pennsylvania: Center for Research on Religion and Urban Civil Society.

Johnson, B.R., Larson, D.B. and Pitts, T. (1997) 'Religious Programmes, Institutional Adjustment and Recidivism Among Former Inmates in Prison Fellowship Programmes', *Justice Quarterly*, 14: 145–66.

Johnston, P. (2002) 'Jail Reprieve for Christian wings', *Daily Telegraph*, 5th March.

Johnston, P. (2001a) 'Prison Service Shuts Down Christian Wings', *Daily Telegraph*, 1st November: 18.

Johnston, P. (2001b) 'Jail Staff Oppose Moves to Close Christian Wings', *Daily Telegraph*, 15th November.

Jones, K. (1998a) Article for the National Advisory Council of Boards and Visitors News-sheet, 6th May.

Jones, K. (1996a) 'Innovation on the Inside', *Kairos Newsletter*, November/December.

Jones, K. (1996b) 'Inmates to Take Over the Prison!', *Inside Time*, 23: 1.

Jornal da Tarde (1992) *'A Chacina – A Imprensa Não Teve Acesso ao Presídio e só Ouviu Relatos'* ('The Slaughter – The Press Did Not Have Access to the Prison, It Only Heard Accounts'), 5th October.

Joseph, S. and Lewis, C.A. (1997) 'The Francis Scale of Attitude Towards Christianity: Intrinsic or Extrinsic Religiosity?', *Psychological Reports*, 80 (2): 609–10.

Junior, M. (1982) pers. comm., 30th December, from Judge Manoel Lima to Mario Ottoboni.

Jupp, B. and Mulga, G. (1997) *Keeping the Faiths: The New Covenant Between Religious Belief and Secular Power.* London: Demos.

Kainos Community (2004) Memorandum, unpublished.

Kainos Community (2003) *Kainos Community Programme.* Unpublished.

Kainos Community (2002) *New programme*, Unpublished.

Kainos Community (2001) *Business Plan.* Unpublished.

Kainos Community (N. d.) *Information booklet.* Unpublished.

Kairos-APAC (1998) *The Brixton and Mountjoy Initiative.* Internal document. Unpublished.

Kairos-APAC (1996) *The Verne Kairos/APAC Project.* Publicity booklet.

Kairos Horizon Communities Newsletter (2004) 2 (1).

Kairos Horizon Communities Newsletter (2003) 1 (2).

Kairos UK (2001) 17th–18th July. Minutes of Kairos UK District Committee.

Kairos UK (2000a) Minutes of the Kairos UK District Committee, 25th January, 4th April, 26th July and 31 October.

Kairos UK, (2000b) District Observer's Report 12th–16th April. Report for HMP The Verne.

Kairos UK (1999) Minutes of Kairos UK District Committee, 19th April, 12th–13th July and 27 September.

Kairos UK (1998a) District Council Report, 12th October. Report for Kairos No. 1 at HMP Highpoint [North].

Kairos UK (1998b) Minutes of Kairos UK District Committee, 14th–15th July and 12 October.

Kairos UK (1997) Minutes of Kairos UK District Committee, 5th April and 1st July.

Katz, J. (1997) *Psychological Stability, Change and Mental Well-being in Stress-related Problems: The Exploration of Clinical and Non-clinical Populations.* Unpublished Ph.D., Cranfield.

Kendall, K. (2001) 'Time to Think Again about Cognitive Behavioural Programmes'. Presentation at the conference, *New Responses to Women Who Break the Law*, Regent's College, London, 12th June.

Kendall, K. (1993) *Programme Evaluation of Therapeutic Services at the Prison for Women.* Correctional Services of Canada.

Kershaw, A. (1999) 'God's Inmates', *Observer Magazine*, 3rd October: 26–34.

Kershaw, C. (1997) *'Reconvictions of Those Commencing Community Penalties in 1993, England and Wales'*, Home Office Statistical Bulletin 6/97. London: Home Office.

Kershaw, C., Goodman, J. and White, S. (1999) *'Reconvictions of Offenders Sentenced or Discharged from Prison in 1995, England and Wales'* Home Office Statistical Bulletin 19/99. London: Home Office.

Key, J. (2004) pers. comm., 12th November.

Key, J. (2003) Recorded interview.

King, J.E. and Crowther, M.R. (2004) 'The Measurement of Religiosity and Spirituality – Examples and Issues from Psychology', *Journal of Organizational Change Management*, 17 (1): 83–101.

Kleiman, M.A.R. (2003) *Faith-Based Fudging: How a Bush-promoted Christian Prison Programme Fakes Success by Massaging Data*, http://slate.msn.com/id/2086617/ (accessed 5 April 2005).

Kloos, B. and Moore, T. (2000) 'Introduction to Special Issue on Spirituality, Religion and Community Psychology', *Journal of Community Psychology*, 28 (2): 115–18.

Knox, D.B. (1988) *The Everlasting God.* Homebush: Lancer.

Koenig, H.G. (1995) 'Religion and Older Men in Prison', *International Journal of Geriatric Psychology*, 10: 219–30.

Kolker, C. (2000) 'Prison Hospices on Increase: Aid Dying Inmates, Cut Violence', *Schenectady Gazette*, 6th February 2000, H1–H2.

KPM Executive Committee (2004) *Policy Statement on Interdenominational Christian Ministry*, 16th March.

KPM Summer Conference, July–August (2003) Conference notes from KPM Summer Conference, Williamsburg, VA.

KPM Summer Conference, July–August (2003) Panel of Wardens and Chaplains, Kairos Summer Conference, 1st August. Williamsburg, VA.

KPM Board (2003) Minutes, 15th February.

KPM (1998a) *Kairos Organisational Manual: Release 1.1.* Winter Park, FL: KPM.

KPM (1998b) *Manual for Pre-Kairos and the Kairos Weekend.* Winter Park, FL: KPM.

KPM (1998c) *Kairos Monthly Report*, May.

KPM (1998d) *Kairos* National Board Meeting, 7th February.

KPM (1998e) *Kairos Newsletter*, July. Winter Park, FL: KPM.

KPM (1998f) 'Profile of Kairos', *Kairos Newsletter*, December: 1. Winter Park, FL: KPM.

KPM (1997) '*Kairos* Board Stresses Uniformity', *Kairos Newsletter*, March/April: 3. Winter Park, FL: KPM.

KPM (1996a) *Kairos Monthly Report*, September. Unpublished.

KPM (1996b) *Kairos Newsletter.* March/April: 2. Winter Park, FL: KPM.

KPM (1995a) *Kairos Continuing Ministry Manual.* Winter Park, FL: KPM.

KPM (1995b) 'The Prison Story', *Kairos Newsletter*, May/June: 1–2. Winter Park, FL: KPM.

KPM (1994a) 'Florida Holds First *Kairos* Outside', *Kairos Newsletter*, January/February: 1. Winter Park, FL: KPM.

KPM (1994b) 'Our Ecumenical Response', *Kairos Newsletter,* January/February: 3. Winter Park, FL: KPM.

Kunst, J.L. (1999) 'Understanding the Religious Ideation of Forensically Committed Patients', *Psychotherapy*, 36 (3): 287–97.

Kwilecki, S. (1988) 'A Scientific Approach to Religious Development – Proposals and a Case Illustration', *Journal for the Scientific Study of Religion*, 27 (3): 307–25.

Learmont Report (1995) *Review of Prison Service Security in England and Wales and the Escape from Parkhurst Prison on Tuesday 3rd January 1995*, Cm 3020. London: Home Office.

Lee, P. (2004) pers. comm., July.

Lee, P. (1999) pers. comm., 10th January, 30th March, 5th April and 24th May, from to Ike Griffin.

Lee, P. (1998) pers. comm., 11th and 24th March, 12th July, 29th August and 21st November, to Ike Griffin.

Lee, P. (1997) pers. comm., 23rd June and 29th August, to Ike Griffin.

Lee, P. (1996) pers. comm., 27th October, to Ike Griffin.

Lee, P. (1995) Transcript of soundtrack to film, *Love Is Not A Luxury*, Gateway Films: The Otter Production Company.

Lehane, T. (2003) Recorded interview.

Leong, F.T.L. and Zachar, P. (1990) 'An Evaluation of Allport's Religious Orientation Scale Across One Australian and Two United-States Samples', *Educational and Psychological Measurement*, 50 (2): 359–68.

Lewis, C. (2004) Unpublished memorandum for Kainos Community, 14th June.

Lewis, C.A. and Maltby, J. (1997) 'Reliability and Validity of the Francis Scale of Attitude Towards Christianity (adult) Among Northern Irish University Students', *Irish Journal of Psychology*, 18 (3): 349–54.

Lewis, C.A., Shevlin, M., Lloyd, N.S.V. and Adamson, G. (1998) 'The Francis Scale of Attitude Towards Christianity (Short Scale): Exploratory and Confirmatory Factor Analysis Among English Students', *Journal of Social Behavior and Personality*, 13 (1): 167–75.

Lewis, C.A., Shevlin, M., McGurkin, C. and Navr'atil, M. (2001) 'The Santa Clara Strength of Religious Faith Questionnaire: Confirmatory Factor Analysis', *Pastoral Psychology*, 249 (5): 379–84.

Liebling, A., Muir, G., Rose, G. and Bottoms, A.E. (1997) *An Evaluation of Incentives and Earned Privileges: Final Report to the Prison Service (Vol 1)*, Cambridge: Institute of Criminology.

Lloyd, C., Mair, G. and Hough, M. (1994) *Explaining Reconviction Rates: A Critical Analysis*, Home Office Research Study No 136. London: Home Office.

Loconte, J. (2001) *God, Government and the Good Samaritan: The Promise and Peril of the President's Faith-Based Agenda.* Heritage Foundation (www.breakpoint. org).

Longley, C. (2000) 'Anglicans Need New Spiritual Outlets', *The Daily Telegraph*, 23rd June: 29.

Longo, D.A. and Peterson, S.M. (2002) 'The Role of Spirituality in Psychosocial Rehabilitation', *Psychiatric Rehabilitation Journal*, 25 (4): 333–40.

Loucks, N. (2004) *Opportunities for Prisoners: A Review of the Literature.* Unpublished report. Edinburgh: Audit Scotland.

Loucks, N. (1998) *HMPI Cornton Vale: Research into Drugs and Alcohol, Violence and Bullying, Suicide and Self-Injury and Backgrounds of Abuse.* Scottish Prison Service Occasional Paper 1/98. Edinburgh: SPS.

Loucks, N. (1994) *Methods of Dealing with Perceived Misbehaviour in Prisons: A Comparative Study of Sweden, France and England.* Unpublished Ph.D. Dissertation, Institute of Criminology, University of Cambridge.

McAdams, D.P. and Logan, R.L. (2004) 'What is Generativity?', in E. de St. Aubin *et al.* (eds) *The Generative Society.* Washington, DC: American Psychological Association, 15–31.

McAdams, D.P. and de St. Aubin, E. (1998) *Generativity and Adult Development: How and Why We Care for the Next Generation.* Washington DC: American Psychological Association.

Maltby, J. (2002) 'The Age Universal I-E Scale-12 and Orientation Toward Religion: Confirmatory Factor Analysis', *Journal of Psychology*, 136 (5): 555–60.

Maltby, J. (1999a) 'The Internal Structure of a Derived, Revised and Amended Measure of the Religious Orientation Scale: The "Age-Universal" I-E Scale-12', *Social Behaviour and Personality*, 27 (4): 407–12.

Maltby, J. (1999b) 'Personality Dimensions of Religious Orientation', *Journal of Psychology*, 133 (6): 631–40.

Maltby, J. and Day, L. (2004) 'Should Never the Twain Meet? Integrating Models of Religious Personality and Religious Mental Health', *Personality and Individual Differences*, 36 (6): 1275–90.

Maltby, J. and Day, L. (2003) 'Religious Orientation, Religious Coping and Appraisals of Stress: Assessing Primary Appraisal Factors in the Relationship Between Religiosity and Psychological Well-being', *Personality and Individual Differences*, 34 (7): 1209–24.

Maltby, J. and Day, L. (2001) 'The Relationship Between Spirituality and Eysenck's Personality Dimensions: A Replication Among English Adults', *Journal of Genetic Psychology*, 162 (1): 119–22.

Maltby, J. and Lewis, C.A. (1997) 'The Reliability and Validity of a Short Scale of Attitude towards Christianity Among USA, English, Republic of Ireland and Northern Ireland adults', *Personality and Individual Differences*, 22 (5): 649–54.

Maltby, J. and Lewis, C.A. (1996) 'Measuring Intrinsic and Extrinsic Orientation Toward Religion: Amendments for Its Use Among Religious and Non-religious Samples', *Personality and Individual Differences*, 21 (6): 937–46.

Maltby, J., Talley, M., Cooper, C. and Leslie, J. C. (1995) 'Personality Effects in Personal and Public Orientations Toward Religion', *Personality and Individual Differences*, 19 (2): 157–63.

Marion Correctional Institution (2003a) *Agreement between MCI Horizon Interfaith and Dorm Resident.* Marion: MCI.

Marion Correctional Institution (2003b) *Institution Summary.* Publicity sheet.

Marshall, C.D. (2001) *Beyond Retribution: A New Testament Vision for Justice, Crime and Punishment.* Cambridge: Eerdmans.

Maruna, S. (2001) *Making Good: How Ex-convicts Reform and Rebuild Their Lives.* Washington DC: American Psychological Association.

Maruna, S. and LeBel, T.P. (2002) 'Revisiting ex-prisoner re-entry: a new buzzword in search of a narrative', in M. Tonry and S. Rex (eds) *Reform and Punishment: The Future of Sentencing.* Cullompton: Willan Publishing, 158–80.

Maruna, S., LeBel, T.P. and Lanier, C.S. (2004) 'Generativity behind bars: some "redemptive truth" about prison society', in E. de St. Aubin, D.P. McAdams and K. Tae-Chang (eds) *The Generative Society: Caring for Future Generations.* Washington DC: American Psychological Association, 131–51.

Mathewson, A. (1997) 'On Wings of Imagination'. *Baptist Times*, 14th November.

May, C. (1999) *Explaining Reconviction following a community sentence: the role of social factors.* Home Office Research Study No. 192. London: Home Office.

Mobley, A. and Terry, C. (2002) 'Dignity, resistance and re-entry: a convict perspective', in S. Maruna and R. Immarigeon (eds) *After Crime and Punishment: Ex-Convict Re-entry and Desistance from Crime.* Albany, NY: SUNY Press.

Money, C. (2004) pers. comm., 21st May.

Money, C. (2003) Interview.

Morris, R.J. and Hood, R.W. (1981) 'The Generalizability and Specificity of Intrinsic-Extrinsic Orientation', *Review of Religious Research*, 22 (3): 245–54.

Narey, M. (2001) 'Failed programme', Letter to the *Daily Telegraph*, 6th November: 23.

New Zealand Public Prisons Service (2002) Unpublished internal memorandum, 4th December.

O'Connor, D.B., Cobb, J.O. and Connor, R.C. (2003) 'Religiosity, Stress and Psychological Distress: No Evidence for an Association Among Undergraduate Students', *Personality and Individual Differences*, 34 (2): 211–17.

Ottoboni, J.M. C. B. (1998) *'Vida de Mário Ottoboni'* ('The Life of Mário Ottoboni'), São José dos Campos. Unpublished document in Brazilian Portuguese.

Ottoboni, M. (2003) *Transforming Criminals: An Introduction to the APAC Methodology.* Washington DC: Prison Fellowship International.

Ottoboni, M. (2000) *Kill the Criminal, Save the Person: The APAC Methodology.* Washington, DC: Prison Fellowship International.

Pargament, K.I. (2002) 'Is Religion Nothing But...? – Explaining Religion Versus Explaining Religion Away', *Psychological Inquiry*, 13 (3): 239–44.

Pargament, K.I., Koenig, H.G. and Perez, L.M. (2000) 'The Many Methods of Religious Coping: Development and Initial Validation of the RCOPE', *Journal of Clinical Psychology*, 56 (4): 519–43.

Pargament, K.I., Olsen, H., Reilly, B., Falgout, K., Ensing, D.S. and Vanhaitsma, K. (1992) 'God-Help-Me: 2, The Relationship of Religious Orientations to Religious Coping With Negative Life-Events', *Journal for the Scientific Study of Religion*, 31 (4), 504–13.

Pargament, K.I., Zinnbauer, B.J., Scott, A.B., Butter, E.M., Zerowin, J. and Stanik, P. (1998) 'Red Flags and Religions Coping: Identifying Some Religious Warning Signs Among People in Crisis', *Journal of Clinical Psychology*, 54 (1): 77–89.

Parker, L. (2003) pers. comm., 10th November.

Parry, A. and Doan, R.E. (1994) *Story Revisions: Narrative Therapy in the Postmodern World*. New York: Guilford.

Paternoster, R., Brame, R., Bachman, R. and Sherman, L.W. (1997) 'Do Fair Procedures Matter? The Effect of Procedural Justice on Spouse Assault', *Law and Society Review*, 31: 163–204.

Pawson, R. and Tilley, N. (1997) *Realistic Evaluation*. London: Sage.

Perettie, P.O. and McIntyre, F. (1984) 'Religious Dysfunctions of Incarceration', *Australian and New Zealand Journal of Criminology*, 17 (3): 177–80.

Pfankuch, T.B. (2002) 'Faith-based Prison Dorms, Programmes Raise Questions', *Florida Times-Union Metro*, 29th April; also at www.jacksonville.com/tu-online.

Phillips, M. (2005) pers. comm., 31st January.

Phillips, M. (2003) Recorded interview.

Pinho, M. (1998) pers. comm., 17th August, from Judge Manoel Ricardo Rebello to Mario Ottoboni.

Pinkham, P. (2003a) 'Lawtey to House Nation's First Faith-based Prison', *Florida Times-Union Metro*, 6th December; also at www.jacksonville.com/tu-online.

Pinkham, P. (2003b) 'Faith-based Prison Under Scrutiny', *Florida Times-Union Metro*, 13th January; also at www.jacksonville.com/tu-online.

Plante, T.G. and Boccaccini, M.T. (1997a) 'Reliability and Validity of the Santa Clara Strength of Religious Faith Questionnaire.' *Pastoral Psychology*, 45: 429–37.

Plante, T.G. and Boccaccini, M.T. (1997b) 'The Santa Clara Strength of Religious Faith Questionnaire', *Pastoral Psychology*, 45: 375–87.

Player, E. and Martin, C. (1996) 'The ADT Drug Treatment Programme at HMP Downview – A Preliminary Evaluation', *Home Office Research Findings 31*. London: Home Office.

Porteous Wood, K. (August 2000) 'Are Non-religious Prisoners Disadvantaged?', *Howard League Magazine*.

Prisma (2003) *Der Jugendhorf Seehaus: Ein Modellprojekt für Straffällige Jugendliche*. Leonberg: Prison Fellowship Germany.

Prison Fellowship England and Wales (2002) 'Compass: Choosing the Way for Life', *Prison Fellowship News* (October/February), 2.

Prison Fellowship England and Wales (1997) *Report of Proceedings on the APAC Conference Held at Church House, Westminster, 6th December 1996.* Chelmsford: Prison Fellowship England and Wales.

Prison Fellowship International (PFI) Convocation (2003) Unpublished data. Toronto, Canada, 6th–9th August.

Prison Fellowship International (PFI) (2002) 'Promoting APAC Faith-based prisons'.

Prison Fellowship News (2000) 'A Remarkable Inner Change', *Prison Fellowship News* (July–October), 1.

Prison Fellowship New Zealand (Undated) 'Faith-Based Unit – Policy and Procedures Manual'. Unpublished.

Prison Fellowship International (PFI) (David Van Patten *et al.*) (1991) *The Dysmas Project: A Report Prepared for the Eckerd Foundation by Prison Fellowship USA.* Washington: Prison Fellowship International.

Pryor, S. (2002) 'The Responsible Prisoner', *Relational Justice Bulletin*, 15: 1–3., www.relationshipsfoundation.org, accessed 30 March 2005.

Pryor, S. (2001) *The Responsible Prisoner: An Exploration of the Extent to which Imprisonment Removes Responsibility Unnecessarily and an Invitation to Change.* London: HM Inspectorate of Prisons.

Respondent A (2004) pers. comm., 30th March, former Assistant Chaplain-General.

Respondent B-E (2003) Interviews with Marion Correctional Institution prisoners.

Respondent F (2003) Interview with mother of Marion Correctional Institution prisoner.

Respondent G (2004) pers. comm., 12th April, former Governor.

Respondent H (2003) 'You Visited Me', Unpublished talk given by Marion Correctional Institution prisoner at Volunteers Appreciation Day, July.

Respondent I (2003) 'How Volunteers Have Affected my Life'. Unpublished talk given by Marion Correctional Institution prisoner at Volunteers Appreciation Day, July.

Respondent J (2003) pers. comm., former Governor, 31st July.

Rex, S., Lieb, R., Bottoms, A. and Wilson, L. (2003) *Accrediting Offender Programmes: A Process-based Evaluation of the Joint Prison/Probation Services Accreditation Panel.* Home Office Research Study 273. London: Home Office.

Robson, C. (1993) *Real World Research.* Oxford: Blackwell.

Roeger, D. (2004) pers. comm., 27th April.

Roeger, D. (2003a) *Opening Doors: Activities and Operation Information.* Ohio: Opening Doors.

Roeger, D. (2003b) 'Resolving Conflicts In Prison', *Relational Justice Bulletin*, 19: 4–5.

Rose, G. (2001) *Offenders Discharged from Prison, Reconviction Rates and OGRS Scores.* www.jiscmail.ac.uk/files/OI-USERS/doc (accessed May 2005).

Rosenberg, M. (1989) *Society and the Adolescent Self-Image*, Revised ed. Middletown, CT: Wesleyan University Press.

Ross, M. (2000) 'The Development of Kairos in Ireland', *Kairos Newsletter*, July, 10.

Rossman, E. (2003) Panel of Wardens and Chaplains, Kairos Summer Conference, 1st August.

Ruthven, D. (2000) 'Evaluating Kairos', *Prison Report*, 51: 25.

Sadgrove, M. and Wright, T. (1977) 'Jesus Christ the Only Saviour', in J. Stott (ed.) *Obeying Christ in a Changing World*. Glasgow: Fountain, 61–89.

Sampson, R.J. and Laub, J.H. (1993) *Crime in the Making: Pathways and Turning Points Through Life*. Cambridge, MA: Harvard University Press.

Sherman, A.C., Plante, T.G., Simonton, S., Adams, D.C., Harbison, C. and Burris, S.K. (2000) 'A Multidimensional Measure of Religious Involvement for Cancer Patients: The Duke Religious Index', *Supportive Care in Cancer*, 8 (2): 102–9.

Shipman, M. (1988) *The limitations of social research*. Harlow: Longman.

Shover, N. (1996) *Great Pretenders: Pursuits and Careers of Persistent Thieves*. Boulder, CO: Westview Press.

Siegel, K., Anderman, S.J. and Schrimshaw, E.W. (2001) 'Religion and Coping With Health-related Stress', *Psychology and Health*, 16 (6): 631–53.

Slater, W., Hall, T.W. and Edwards, K.J. (2001) 'Measuring Religion and Spirituality: Where Are We and Where Are We Going?', *Journal of Psychology and Theology*, 29 (1): 4–21.

Smartt, U. (2000) 'The Kairos-APAC Prison Ministry Project at HMP The Verne', *Prison Service Journal*, 129: 24–28.

Solomon, E. (1997) *Informs Newsletter: A [Texas] State-wide Criminal Justice Ministry Information Source*, 4 (2).

Solomon, E. and Edgar, K. (2003) *Having Their Say: The Work of Prisoner Councils*. London: Prison Reform Trust.

Sparks, J.R. and Bottoms, A.E. (1995) 'Legitimacy and Order in Prisons', *British Journal of Sociology*, 46: 45–62.

Spielberger, C.D., Gorsuch, R.L. and Lushene, R.E. (1970) *Manual for the State-Trait Anxiety Inventory*. Palo Alto, California: Consulting Psychologists Press.

Stern, B. (2004) 'Drummond Hunter Memorial Lecture 2004: International Perspectives on Criminal Justice', Howard League for Penal Reform, Scotland, 6th January.

Stow, B. (2002) *Outcomes and Process in Incentives and Earned Privileges: Does Justice Matter?* MST Thesis in Applied Criminology and Management. Cambridge: Insitute of Criminology, University of Cambridge.

Strizenec, M. (1997) 'On Assessment of Religiosity Using Questionnaires and Scales', *Ceskoslovenska Psychologie*, 41 (5): 410–14.

Strizenec, M. (1992) 'The Present Psychology of Religion', *Ceskoslovenska Psychologie*, 36 (1): 23–32.

Taylor, R. (2000) *A Seven-Year Reconviction Study of HMP Grendon Therapeutic Community*, Home Office Research Findings 115. London: Home Office.

Taylor, R. (1999) *Predicting Reconvictions for Sexual and Violent Offences Using the Revised Offender Group Reconviction Scale.* Home Office Research Findings No. 104. London: Home Office.

Thompson, J. (2004) pers. comm., 6th April.

Thompson, J. (2003) pers. comm., 11th and 12th November.

Thoresen, C.E. and Harris, A.H.S. (2002) 'Spirituality and Health: What's The Evidence and What's Needed?' *Annals of Behavioral Medicine*, 24 (1): 3–13.

Toch, H. and Adams, K. (2002) *Acting Out: Maladaptive Behaviour in Confinement.* APA Books.

Toral, C.J. (2000) *Towards Freedom.* Washington, DC: Prison Fellowship International.

Trimble, D.E. (1997) 'The Religious Orientation Scale: Review and Meta-analysis of Social Desirability Effects', *Educational and Psychological Measurement*, 57 (6): 970–86.

Trotter, C. (1996) 'The Impact of Different Supervision Practices in Community Corrections: Cause for Optimism', *Australian and New Zealand Journal of Criminology*, 29: 29–46.

Tyler, T.R. (1990) *Why People Obey the Law.* New Have: Yale University Press.

University of Pennsylvania (2003) *"Study: Faith-Based Rehabilitation Program Shows Promise"* (June 18, 2003). www.upenn.edu/researchatpenn/article.php?680@soc (accessed May 2005).

Van Ness, D. (2003) pers. comm., 7th November.

Van Ness, DW. and Strong, K.H. (2002) *Restoring Justice.* Cincinnati: Anderson.

Van Patten, D. *et al.* (1991) *The Dysmas Project.* Unpublished.

Varela, D. (1999) *Carandiru Station (Estação Carandiru).* Companhia das Letras.

Vennard, J. and Hedderman, C. (1998) 'Effective interventions with offenders', in P. Goldblatt and C. Lewis (eds) *Reducing Offending: An Assessment of Research Evidence on Ways of Dealing with Offending Behaviour.* Research Study 187. London: Home Office, 101–20.

Vernacular: The Newsletter of the Kairos-APAC Trust (1998a) Issue 3.

Vernacular: The Newsletter of the Kairos-APAC Trust (1998b) (Summer).

Vernacular: The Newsletter of the Kairos-APAC Trust (1997).

Veronese, H. (Undated, unpublished paper) *Roots of Crime, Paths to Rehabilitation.*

Wacquant, L. (2004) *The Prison System as Social Vacuum-cleaner of Market Society.* Plenary lecture, Prisons 2004 Conference, City University, London, June.

Walker, P. (2004) pers. comm., 10th December.

Walker, P. (2003a) pers. comm., 10th September.

Walker, P. (2003b) unpublished conference paper, August. Presented at Prison Fellowship International Convocation, Toronto.

Walker, P. (1999) *Key factors of the APAC Methodology.* Unpublished paper produced for Prison Fellowship England and Wales, October.

Watson, P.J., Morris, R.J., Foster, J.E. and Hood, R.W., Jr. (1986). 'Religiosity and social desirability', *Journal for the Scientific Study of Religion*, 25: 215–32.

Webster, R., Hedderman, C., Turnbull, P.J. and May, T. (2001) *Prison-based Employment Schemes*. Home Office Research Findings 151. London: Home Office.

Westermann, C. (1994) (tr. John J. Scullion) *Genesis 1–11: A Continental Commentary*. Minneapolis: Fortress Press.

Whatmore, P. B. (1987) 'Barlinnie special unit: An insider's view', in A.E. Bottoms and R. Light (eds) *Problems of Long-Term Imprisonment*. London: Gower.

White, M. and Epston, D. (1990) *Narrative Means to Therapeutic Ends*. New York: Norton.

Willey, E. (1998) 'From Convicts to Comrades', *The Tablet*. 30th May: 700.

Williams, G.P. (2003) Panel of Wardens and Chaplains, Kairos Summer Conference, 1 August.

Williams, R.N. and Faulconer, J.E. (1994) 'Religion and Mental-Health – A Hermeneutic Reconsideration', *Review of Religious Research*, 35 (4), 335–49.

Woodcock Report (1994) *The Escape from Whitemoor Prison on Friday 9th September 1994*, Cm 2741. London: Home Office.

Wong-McDonald, A. and Gorsuch, R. L. (2000) 'Surrender to God: An additional Coping Style?', *Journal of Psychology and Theology*, 28 (2): 149–61.

Woolf, L.J. and Tumim, S. (1991) *Prison Disturbances, April 1990: Report of an Inquiry*. Cm 1456. London: HMSO.

Workman, K. (2005) pers. comm., 3rd April.

Workman, K. (2004) 'Resolving Conflict and Restoring Relationships'. Unpublished paper presented to 'New frontiers in Restoring Justice' conference, Massey University, Albany, 2nd–5th December.

Wright, T. (2004) *Paul for Everyone: Romans Part 1*. London: SPCK.

Wright, T. (2001) *Luke for Everyone*. London: SPCK.

Wright, T. (1999) *The Myth of the Millennium*. Glasgow: Caledonian.

Wyner, R. (2003) *From the Inside: Dispatches from a Women's Prison*. London: Aurum Press.

Yin, R.K. (1994) *Case Study Research, 2nd edition*. London: Sage.

Zornes, T. (2004) pers. comm., 22nd December.

Index